Questions & Answers

Law of Torts

Questions & Answers Series

Series Editors: Rosalind Malcolm and Margaret Wilkie

The ideal revision aid to keep you afloat through your exams

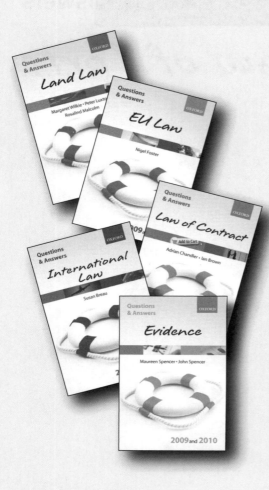

- **advice on exam technique**
- **summary of each topic**
- **bullet-pointed answer plans**
- **model answers**
- **diagrams and flowcharts**
- **further reading**

Questions & Answers

Law of Torts

FIFTH EDITION

David Oughton
Professor of Commercial Law, De Montfort University, Leicester

John Marston
Principal Lecturer, De Montfort University, Leicester

Barbara Harvey
Principal Lecturer, De Montfort University, Leicester

2009 and 2010

OXFORD
UNIVERSITY PRESS

OXFORD
UNIVERSITY PRESS

Great Clarendon Street, Oxford OX2 6DP

Oxford University Press is a department of the University of Oxford.
It furthers the University's objective of excellence in research, scholarship,
and education by publishing worldwide in

Oxford New York

Auckland Cape Town Dar es Salaam Hong Kong Karachi
Kuala Lumpur Madrid Melbourne Mexico City Nairobi
New Delhi Shanghai Taipei Toronto

With offices in

Argentina Austria Brazil Chile Czech Republic France Greece
Guatemala Hungary Italy Japan Poland Portugal Singapore
South Korea Switzerland Thailand Turkey Ukraine Vietnam

Oxford is a registered trade mark of Oxford University Press
in the UK and in certain other countries

Published in the United States
by Oxford University Press Inc., New York

© David Oughton, John Marston, and Barbara Harvey 2009

The moral rights of the author have been asserted

Crown copyright material is reproduced under Class Licence
Number C01P0000148 with the permission of OPSI
and the Queen's Printer for Scotland

Database right Oxford University Press (maker)

First published 1994
Second edition 1999
Third edition 2005
Fourth edition 2007
Fifth edition 2009

British Library Cataloguing in Publication Data

Data available

Library of Congress Cataloging in Publication Data

Data available

Typeset by Laserwords Private Ltd, Chennai, India
Printed in Great Britain
on acid-free paper by
Ashford Colour Press Limited, Gosport, Hampshire

ISBN 978–0–19–955958–9

1 3 5 7 9 10 8 6 4 2

Contents

The Q&A Series

Key features

The Q&A series provides full coverage of key subjects in a clear and logical way.

This book contains the following features:

- Questions
- Commentary
- Bullet-pointed answer plans
- Suggested answers
- Diagrams
- Further reading

 online resource centre
www.oxfordtextbooks.co.uk/orc/qanda/

Every book in the Q&A series is accompanied by an Online Resource Centre, hosted at the URL above, which is open-access and free to use.

The Online Resource Centre for this book contains revision and exam advice, a glossary of tort law terms, and links to websites useful for the study of tort law.

Preface

The degree of fear, apprehension, and circumspection felt by the authors prior to the publication of previous issues remains the same. One is always mindful of the response given to students who ask for the 'right answer' to a question on some aspect of law. As the common law is so rich and varied in its approach to legal issues, it is always the case that a novel set of facts can be approached from several different angles, so that in truth, it is almost impossible to say that there is a definitively correct final answer to a particular question. Nevertheless, we have attempted to give answers to questions of the type that students might expect to encounter in an examination on the Law of Torts, in the knowledge that there are others who might disagree with the approach that has been taken.

This edition has continued the change in format employed in the last edition in attempting to provide students with a range of wider reading that might be engaged in for the purposes of completing both hypothetical problem questions and essay questions as the case might be. Each question is also prefaced by a bullet-pointed list of the key issues students might expect to consider in answering the question. Some flow charts and diagrams are also included at various points.

As ever, the unwitting support of students at various Universities is gratefully acknowledged. Their questions, mistakes, and successes have all contributed to the content of this compilation of questions and answers by informing the authors of the areas of the Law of Torts that may give rise to some of the more difficult points of interpretation.

Developments in the law that have occurred since the last edition have been taken into account, as appropriate. Such changes are particularly noticeable in Chapter 6, which contains a new question dealing with some of the more complex issues in causation, and Chapter 13 which takes account of important changes in the law relating to economic torts. Developments relating to the protection of a person's privacy are also reflected at various points in this edition. The decision of the House of Lords in *Ashley v Chief Constable* which has established the principles governing self-defence and mistake in battery is applied and in defamation the cases which have applied the privilege first identified in the *Reynolds* case are woven into the answers.

Lastly, but far from least, David Oughton would like to say thank you to Sue, Gareth, and Karen for their love, support and encouragement throughout the process of preparing this edition. Barbara Harvey would again like to thank Jemima, Patrick, and David for all their support and encouragement. John Marston would like to thank Virginia, Katie, and Sophie for their continued love and support during the writing of the answers.

David Oughton
Barbara Harvey
John Marston
September 2008

Table of Cases

Table of Statutes

1

Introduction

1 The challenges of the Law of Torts

The Law of Torts is a subject you will have to take if you are pursuing a qualifying law degree, since it is one of the so-called 'core' subjects. However, superficially, it is a subject that most students think they have enjoyed. Unfortunately, appearances are deceptive. The Law of Torts might consist of some very interesting tales of human woe, ranging from snails in bottles of ginger beer, through dangerous under garments and ladies being accidentally locked in public toilets to domesticated (and some not quite so domesticated) animals causing a person the fright of her life. It also addresses issues as diverse as the liability of public bodies for failings in their operational activities; the right to personal integrity; human rights; whether a business can recover economic losses it has suffered as a result of the alleged negligence or deliberate action of another business concern; whether a person can prevent the activities of a neighbouring land-owner on his own land, on the basis that the activity constitutes an unreasonable inter-ference with his own way of life; whether there is a right to privacy and whether damage to one's reputation is actionable.

Like its common law sister, the Law of Contract, the Law of Torts is a system of legal rules designed to compensate a person (whether legal or individual) in respect of dam-age or loss caused by another person. However, unlike contractual liability, the tortious liability of a defendant is potentially unlimited. While a defendant in a contract action is generally limited in his liability to the other party to the contract, tortious duties (or at least the duty of care imposed by the tort of negligence) are owed by every one of us to anyone we can foresee would be likely to be affected by our actions. As a result of this, there is a massive potential for indeterminate liability—as it was once put by Cardozo CJ in the USA[1]—liability in an indeterminate amount, for an indeterminate time to an indeterminate class of people. In response to this haunting prospect for the insurance industry in particular, the courts have sought to impose a variety of pure policy-based restrictions on some of the boundaries of the Law of Torts. As it was once observed in the House of Lords, it is necessary to place restrictions on developments that allow a

---

[1] *Ultramares Corp* v *Touche* (1931) 174 NE 441.

claimant to allege negligence on the assumption that, Good Samaritans and Pharisees alike, we are all neighbours, and that someone solvent must be liable in damages.[2]

2 Examination preparation

Since the Law of Torts is likely to be a compulsory subject, it is assumed that you will face an unseen examination, in which you must prepare answers to about three or four questions in the space of about two to three hours. How you prepare your own revision work is a matter for you to decide on, since organizational preference is a matter of individual choice, but it is important to read as widely as possible. In general, you should gather together the materials you have accumulated in a logical order and learn both the principles of law and what you have picked up in tutorials etc. during the year on how to apply that law to the questions.

a. Before the examination

It is impossible to say how much time you will need to revise for the examination, because the requirements for each individual will differ. But it is worth remembering that while too little revision is fatal, too much is also dangerous since it is possible to reach a peak before the date of the examination. It is no use knowing everything perfectly two weeks before the examination, especially if you become stale thereafter. The key is to reach your peak on the day of the examination, which is all very well to say, but very difficult to put into practice.

A number of general points of common sense need to be made about the period prior to the date of your examination:

- Clarify the date, time and place of your examination for yourself. Do not rely on what others have told you.

- Be aware of the form of your examination—is it unseen, open-book, based on a 'seen' scenario. How long is the examination? How many questions have to be answered? Is there part of the examination that is compulsory? Is there more than one part to the examination and how many questions from each part have to be attempted?

- Reading past examination papers can be quite revealing. Some examiners may 'recycle' papers used in the past. However, be careful not to assume that a question that appears similar to one you have seen before (perhaps with different dates or characters) will be identical to the one you have before you. It is fairly common practice to make crucial factual changes that redirect the whole focus of the question.

- Listen to your tutors during the course of the year. Of course, you can only do this if you have attended classes during the year, but that goes without saying! Your tutors may have implicitly given guidance on the importance of a particular topic.

---

[2] See *CBS Songs Ltd* v *Amstrad Consumer Electronics plc* [1988] 2 All ER 484 at 497, *per* Lord Templeman.

- If your tutor has 'adjusted' the running order of materials dealt with in lectures/seminars/tutorials etc. in the period immediately before the date of the examination, you ought to be able to assume that the topics dealt with towards the end will be on the examination paper.

- If you have special needs of any kind, make sure that you claim any allowance to which you are legitimately entitled. Some students are entitled to use a word processor; may be given an extra time allowance or may be entitled to sit the examination in a private room.

b. The examination itself

The most important general note of guidance is not to panic. If you have revised well there will always be a sufficient number of questions on the paper for you to answer if you think in a cool, calm, and collected manner. Moreover, the easy part about taking an examination for which you have prepared well is getting to pass standard. It becomes progressively more difficult to go from a pass mark to lower second, upper second, or first-class standard.

You are now sitting in front of a collection of pens, chewing gum (valium??), a watch, an answer book, and an examination paper and the invigilator says you may commence. Remember do not panic.

Again a number of general points of guidance can be given:

- Check the examination rubric.

- Read the whole paper before you decide what to answer.

How long your examination will be may differ from institution to institution. In times past the examination might have been three hours in duration with instructions to candidates to answer four or five questions from a selection of eight or nine. However, in a world of modularity, generally the length of an examination has been reduced as has the number of questions you must answer. It should go without saying—make sure you know what is required of you before the date of the examination.

The questions you will encounter may be of two different types. Some will be hypothetical problem questions and some will be essay questions, usually based on quotations from either an academic text or from a judgment, sometimes followed by the unhelpful instruction, 'DISCUSS'.

You need to read the whole paper and decide which questions you wish to answer. Many institutions now give students reading time before the examination commences, but you will only have a limited time in which to answer these questions. It will usually pay dividends to sketch out a brief plan of each of your preferred choices. At this stage do not worry about the candidate next to you who has already filled two reams of paper. Content yourself that he/she is (a) writing irrelevant rubbish in a totally unplanned fashion and (b) will have to reconsider what he/she has written because he/she has no plan to work from and may have omitted important details.

The plan is time-consuming, but is worthwhile. The advantage of planning the questions you propose to answer is that what you write should be directly relevant and you will avoid the serious problem of writing irrelevant material about issues which do not form part of the answer to the question. Moreover, if you have time left at the end, you can check your answer against the plan you prepared earlier.

Time management is crucial. If you take 10 minutes to read the paper and plan your campaign, this leaves 42 minutes per question in a four-question examination. Remember to make corresponding adjustments for shorter examinations that require fewer questions to be answered. Do not be tempted to substantially overrun this time allocation. It is far better to hand in a script in which you have completed the required number of questions, albeit incompletely than to spend 90 minutes on question 1, and then rushed off the remaining questions in what time is left.

c. The questions you will encounter

The examination in the law of tort will consist of two types of question—hypothetical problems and essay questions.

A number of general points should be remembered:

- Use a conventional style consisting of paragraphs, a beginning, a middle, and an end.

- Try to avoid note-form and at all costs do not be tempted to write in 'Txt' language.

- Spelling and grammar are important. If you have any particular difficulties on this count, you should have taken action well before the date of the examination. Remember, universities provide a lot of general help for difficulties of this kind.

- The Law of Torts is a common law subject. As such, it is based on case law. It is crucial that you can cite authority to support the arguments you use in answering a question. The most important aspects of a case are the principle of law and, as appropriate, the facts of the case, related to the principle. Worry less about the name of the case and its date. Provided the examiner can recognize the principle you are seeking to apply, you will still get some credit.

(i) Essay questions

The key issue here is that if you do not understand precisely what the question asks you to do, do not answer it. Be honest with yourself when you ask what the question means. It is far too easy for a single word to be picked up from the quotation, taken in isolation, and misinterpreted. Not infrequently candidates take the opportunity to write everything they know on a topic regardless of its relevance. Candidates who do this invariably fail on the question on which that sort of approach is adopted. It is important to answer the question the examiner has set rather than the question you would have liked her to set!

In answering an essay question, you should produce a very brief introduction, identifying no more than the issues you propose to cover and any line of argument you propose to adopt. The main body of the essay will develop on those introductory issues and arguments and should relate them to the question which has been set and at all costs, you should use cases to support your argument. Finally, you need to conclude your essay by relating your arguments to the specific question set.

(ii) Hypothetical problem questions

Problem questions are often easier to answer than are essay questions since if you are prepared to look carefully, much of the answer is actually discoverable from the question itself. They are very similar to a crossword puzzle. There are clues telling you what you must or must not write about—these are usually in the rubric at the end of each question. For example, if you are told to advise Dick do not be tempted to advise Dora instead! Moreover, in many instances the facts of the problem will preclude a discussion of certain issues but highlight the importance of discussing other issues. For example, if you are told that a particular individual has done something negligently, there appears little point in discussing the issues of duty of care and breach of duty so that the question is likely to be on remedies, defences, remoteness, or causation.

When answering problem questions, it helps to state the relevant law in relation to particular issues and then apply that law to the relevant issue, making reference to the relevant facts of the problem. Do not be tempted to discuss legal principles which bear no relevance to the question. Here a plan of your intended answer is particularly useful. As you go along, it helps to relate each point you make to the question set. In practice, it is far better to state a legal principle and immediately apply it rather than to regurgitate all the law first and then apply it at the end of your answer. The importance of applying the law as you go along is that you can demonstrate to the examiner that you know what the law is, you understand it and that you can relate it to the problem. The last two stages are easily lost if you separate the law from its application. Moreover, the law first, application later, approach is distinctly 'examiner-unfriendly' because she/he has to flip back two pages to discover what was said about the law when it was stated to see if it has been accurately applied.

At all stages, you must support your argument with references to relevant case law or statutory authority. Do not be tempted to say, 'See Donoghue v Stevenson' since the examiner has 'seen' the case on many previous occasions. What you must do is to show that you understand the principle of law established by a case and why it is relevant to the question. In this process it may be necessary to relate the facts of the case, but more often than not, the facts of a case will not be relevant. Moreover, do not use an ability to tell stories about what happened in a particular case to disguise your knowledge of the law. From an examiner's point of view there is little more annoying than having to wade through pages of case facts, only to discover, at the end, that the candidate has little or no knowledge of the legal principle established by the case referred to.

Having stated the law and applied it, you may come to a definite conclusion, but you do not have to. The nature of problem questions is that they will be riddled with ambiguities. The important point is that you must be able to see all the various possibilities raised by the question, explain them, and show how they affect the particular facts of the problem. It is far better to present several possible arguments than to dogmatically insist that there is a right answer not permitting of any alternatives. Given that you may have several lines of argument, reaching a definitive conclusion may be difficult. But this does not matter. If you have presented the arguments for each of the alternative lines of thinking and you have applied your argument to the question in a logical fashion, that will suffice. Occasionally, you can be forgiven if you decide to sit on the fence. After all, if the right answer is so obvious, we would not need courts or lawyers and you would not be revising for this examination! As you will have appreciated by following a tort law course, there are endless problems of policy which make the subject very uncertain at times.

Showing that you appreciate what law is relevant is an important feature. You can do this by highlighting, in block capitals, the cases you use. But examiners should also read what comes between the case names, so that has to be accurate and relevant as well!

3 Coursework preparation

Unseen, and to a lesser extent, 'seen' examinations test your ability to remember relevant facts and principles of law and apply them to the situation identified by the examination question. But examinations should not be the only way in which your ability in the Law of Torts should be assessed. If this was the only method of assessment, students would be adept at giving a number of brief, handwritten summaries of solutions to a limited range of situations (usually selected for the academic difficulties they raise), in a ridiculously short period of time, without any detailed research in the light of the known facts. How many professional lawyers would give extempore advice to a client without having, first, researched the problem before giving that advice?

This is where coursework comes into its own. Most Law of Torts courses will contain an element of coursework that probably counts for about 40 or 50 per cent of the overall mark for the subject as a whole. On the percentage value, you should check the course documentation at an early stage in the year.

What a piece of coursework tests is your ability to research a topic and reflect upon the issues it raises. As such, starting your coursework the night before it is due to be handed in is not likely to yield wonderful results, as you will not have had the time to research the issues and reflect upon them. The fact that a coursework title is available well before the date for submission will allow you to discuss the problem with your peers. However, you should not allow this discussion to convert into collective plagiarism. All universities have rules on plagiarism and it is advisable to make yourself familiar with what you can and cannot do. Remember, if you do commit an act of plagiarism, you could be required to leave the university with no degree at all.

The following general points apply to coursework:

- High marks are achieved by depth of understanding, which can only be developed through extensive research. If you rely on just one secondary source e.g. Jones, *Textbook on Torts* or Lunney & Oliphant's *Tort Law, Text and Materials,* you probably have not done enough.

- Make use of primary sources and academic commentary other than basic student textbooks.

- Keep in mind, at all times, what question has been asked.

2

The role of the law of torts

Introduction

This chapter seeks to place the law of tort (or should it be the law of torts?) in context. This opening statement, perhaps, requires elaboration. It has to be recognized that one tort, in particular, has dominated the development of the common law of torts in the twentieth and twenty-first centuries, namely, the tort of negligence (considered in Chapters 4, 5 and 6) and its specific off-shoots relating to Employer's liability, (Chapter 7) Occupiers' liability, (Chapter 8) Liability for animals (Chapter 10) and Product liability (Chapter 9). Furthermore, much of the case law on General defences (Chapter 14) is specific to the tort of negligence, as is also the case with many of the rules on Remedies and limitation of actions (Chapter 15). The key feature of the tort of negligence is that it attributes responsibility on the basis of principles of personal fault that require individuals to adhere to a standard of reasonable care. A general feature of the tort of negligence is that, for the most part, it is concerned with actions that cause physical harm, although there is a growing body of case law that also attributes responsibility for acts (and some omissions) that cause foreseeable economic harm.

Despite the dominance of the tort of negligence, there are other torts, which seek to protect other interests. There is group of torts, loosely described in Chapter 3 as trespass to the person, which focus on personal integrity and may, to an extent, be relevant to the issue of individual privacy. Tort law also recognizes the interests and responsibilities of land owners, seeking to balance the right of a landowner to use his land as he wishes, against the right of neighbours to expect landowners to operate and maintain their land in a reasonable manner (Chapters 8 and 11). Other torts protect both personal and business reputations (Chapters 12 and 13). Thus, it is a tort to defame a person by seeking, intentionally, to lower that person's reputation in the mind of right-thinking persons generally. In relation to chattels and business interests, there is a range of diverse torts, broadly based on intentional conduct that protects the interests of a person who owns or is in possession against deliberate interference by others and torts that guard against conspiracy and inducement of another to commit a breach of contract.

What can be seen from this is that there is a wide range of torts, protecting a wide range of interests and those different torts may be based on principles of liability that differ from case to case. Accordingly, it may be more accurate to speak of a Law of Torts than a singular, common-principled, Law of Tort.

Question 1

'Contract and tort are like cheese and biscuits: different but complementary.'

(Holyoak 1983)

Discuss.

Commentary

This question examines the relationship between tort law and its common law partner, the law of contract. While the teaching of law conventionally pigeon-holes these major areas of study, it has to be appreciated that there are areas of overlap between the various core subjects. Of prime importance for the purposes of the relationship between the law of contract and the law of tort is the limited use of the tort of negligence as a means of dealing with the problem of economic loss. Some writers take the view that the juridical distinctions between the law of torts and other areas of common law civil liability have become so blurred that it might be better to speak of a law of obligations. However, there are features of the law of torts that serve to identify it as a set of ethical rules and principles of personal responsibility for one's actions that are primarily imposed by law.

Answer plan

- The major differences between contractual and tortious liability.
- The generalizations which are said to distinguish the two branches of the common law, including the difference between the expectation interest and the *status quo* interest, the difference between fault-based and strict liability and the view that contractual obligations are voluntarily assumed whereas tortious obligations are imposed by law.
- Whether there can be a concurrent liability in both contract and tort and whether contractual obligations override those which may be imposed by the law of tort.

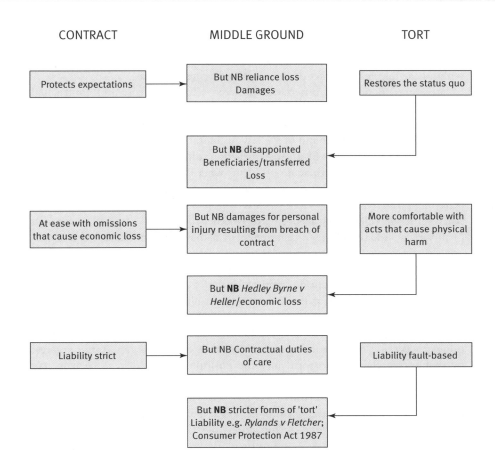

CONTRACT   MIDDLE GROUND   TORT

Protects expectations → But NB reliance loss Damages

Restores the status quo

But **NB** disappointed Beneficiaries/transferred Loss

At ease with omissions that cause economic loss → But NB damages for personal injury resulting from breach of contract

More comfortable with acts that cause physical harm

But **NB** *Hedley Byrne v Heller*/economic loss

Liability strict → But NB Contractual duties of care

Liability fault-based

But **NB** stricter forms of 'tort' Liability e.g. *Rylands v Fletcher*; Consumer Protection Act 1987

Suggested answer

At first sight, the essential characteristics of contractual and tortious obligations are very different. One view of contractual obligations is that they operate within a specific sphere of human activity, namely, the process of making market transactions: See Collins, *The Law of Contract*, 4th edn (Cambridge: Cambridge UP, 2003), p. 1. Alternative theories identify the essence of a contractual obligation as one that is promise or agreement-based: See Fried, *Contract as Promise* (Harvard UP, 1981). However, other writers prefer to define the core characteristic of a contractual obligation as founded in the notion of reliance. This theory places emphasis on the fact that a promise, seriously intended is capable of causing the promise to alter his position in the belief that the promise will be fulfilled and is enforceable because of the reliance engendered by it. It will be seen that this notion of reliance is also an important feature of a number of tortious obligations, and, it is in this arena that the closest similarities between the two types of obligation can be found. The idea that all contracts are literally agreement-based can be challenged on the basis that large numbers of contracts are made, particularly by consumers, without the relevant contract documentation having been read.

There are undoubtedly differences between liability in tort and contractual liability, but the differences may, at times, pale into near insignificance because of the interplay between these two branches of a broader law of obligations. The major differences can be found in the law of limitation of actions where different rules apply to the accrual of a cause of action, although, even in this area, the courts have been faced with acute problems where a limitation defence has been raised in a case where there is concurrent contractual and tortious liability: See *Midland Bank Trust Co v Hett, Stubbs & Kemp* [1979] Ch 384. Other areas where different rules apply according to whether the action is framed in contract or in tort include the issues of remoteness of damage; quantification of damages and the difference between non-feasance and misfeasance.

A number of generalizations are said to distinguish tortious and contractual liability. A primary distinction is said to be that the law of tort protects what a person already has, whereas the law of contract allows a person to become better off through the enforcement of promises: T. Weir, *A Casebook on Tort*, p. 2, 10th edn (London: Sweet & Maxwell, 2004). Another way of stating this distinction is to say that the law of contract protects the claimant's expectation interest by casting the claimant forward into the position he would have been in had the defendant performed his contractual promises (*Robinson v Harman* (1854) 1 Exch 850). In contrast, tort law is concerned with restoring the *status quo* by returning the claimant to the position he was in before the defendant committed his wrongful act (*Livingstone v Rawyards Coal Co* (1880) 5 App Cas 25). As with all generalizations, it is bound to break down from time to time. There are circumstances in which contractual remedies compensate *status quo* losses and in which tortious remedies protect a person's expectations. Tortious and contractual rules also have a deterrent effect. Tortious rules seek to deter others from engaging in socially unacceptable conduct. Contractual rules seek to deter breaches of contract, namely not doing that which has been promised. On this basis, the law of contract is more at ease with omissions to act, whereas the law of tort more easily concerns itself with positive acts of misconduct.

While the typical loss complained of by a claimant suing for breach of contract is the failure to make a gain which might otherwise have been made had the contract been performed, it should be appreciated that the loss of profit representing the claimant's expectation of gain also includes simple expenditure loss which, if included in the claimant's award of damages, will involve returning him to the position he was in before the contract was entered into. Moreover, in some instances, where the contract is of a highly speculative nature, such as the production of a film, the expectation loss suffered by the claimant may be incapable of calculation, in which case, a more appropriate measure of damages may be compensation in respect of the expense incurred by the claimant, thereby protecting the *status quo* interest alone (*Anglia TV Ltd v Reed* [1972] 1 QB 60).

The rule that the law of tort only returns the claimant to the position he was in before the defendant's wrong was committed is also one which is subject to exceptions. In particular, there are duties to exercise reasonable care which arise out of a contractual relationship, in which case it can be said that there is an expectation that such care will be exercised. An example of this kind of duty can be found in the field of occupiers' liability where the occupier is liable for acts and omissions that cause physical harm so as to make the claimant's position worse.

Moreover, there is a line of authority which establishes that a solicitor who negligently advises his client with the result that the intended beneficiary of a will fails to receive the bequest it was intended by the now deceased client that he should receive, may be liable, in the tort of negligence, for the failure to take reasonable care (*Ross v Caunters* [1980] Ch 297; *White v Jones* [1995] 2 AC 207). In these circumstances, the intended beneficiary has an expectation of gain (the intended bequest) which is not capable of protection by way of contractual rules, due to the restrictive effect of the doctrine of privity of contract, even after the enactment of the **Contracts (Rights of Third Parties) Act 1999**, since a person in the position of the intended beneficiary is not given any right by the *contract* between the solicitor and his client. Instead, it is the *will* that should have conferred the benefit, had it been correctly drafted. In these circumstances, the tort of negligence has been adapted to protect the intended beneficiary on the basis that it is reasonably foreseeable that such loss might be suffered by the claimant, that the relationship of proximity between the solicitor and the beneficiary is sufficiently close to justify the finding of liability and that the solicitor has voluntarily undertaken responsibility towards the beneficiary by undertaking to advise the client in such a manner as to ensure the effectiveness of the intended bequest (*Ross v Caunters* [1980] Ch 297; *White v Jones* [1995] 2 AC 207). The genesis of the reasoning on the issue of voluntary assumption of responsibility can be traced back to *Spring v Guardian Insurance plc* [1995] 2 AC 296 in which the writer of a reference was taken to have voluntarily assumed a responsibility towards the intended recipient of the reference. Equally, the recipient would have an expectation that the reference would be carefully prepared.

In relation to what is often regarded as the classic tort action, an action for damages for negligently inflicted personal injury, a substantial element of the claimant's action for damages will be in respect of expected future gains in the form of damages for lost earnings. Similarly, in an action for negligent misrepresentation, in which case damages are assessed according to tortious principles applicable to the tort of deceit (**Misrepresentation Act 1967, s. 2(1)** and *Royscot Trust v Rogerson* [1991] 2 QB 297) it is possible that a misrepresentee may have been induced to acquire a business from the defendant as a result of the latter's misrepresentation. In these circumstances, it is possible that the claimant will fail to make the profit he might have expected to make. Case law suggests that an award of damages may take account of the profit the claimant might have made if he had acquired a notional similar business in the area in which the business premises are located. However, the award must not place the claimant in the position he would have been in had the defendant's statement been accurate, since that would be tantamount to enforcing the defendant's 'promise': *East v Maurer* [1991] 2 All ER 773.

There have been cases in which a claimant has sought to recover damages for the loss of a chance, both in contract and in the tort of negligence. At one stage, a possible, but inaccurate distinction between those cases in which the claimant succeeded and those in which the claim failed was that a lost chance related to future gain and was therefore more amenable to an action for breach of contract. Thus in *Chaplin v Hicks* [1911] 2 KB 786 the claimant had been invited to enter a beauty competition by the defendant. The claimant was one of the fifty contestants voted the most beautiful by the readers of the newspaper running the competition, but she was denied the chance to attend an appointment that might have led to her progressing further in the competition. The Court of Appeal dismissed the argument that damages were incapable of assessment and as all of the final fifty contestants had about a one in four chance of being selected, the claimant was awarded 25 per cent of what she might have expected to gain had she been successful.

More recently, reasoning along these lines has been sought to be applied in medical negligence cases where a claimant has been denied the chance of future good health due to a failure to carry out a medical procedure that might have produced a more successful outcome than is in fact the case (see *Hotson v East Berkshire Area Health Authority* [1987] 2 All ER 909; *Gregg v Scott* [2005] 2 AC 176). However, the courts appear to have been reluctant to allow the claimant to succeed in most of these cases on the ground that the claimant must prove, on a balance of probability, that the defendant's act or omission was the cause of the claimant's condition. Thus in *Hotson*, since there was a 75 per cent chance that the claimant would have developed avascular necrosis, the condition in respect of which the claim was made and in *Gregg*, since there was only a 45 per cent chance that the claimant would have survived disease-free from the mis-diagnosis of a cancerous condition, the claimant in each case had failed to discharge the burden of proof.

It is important to appreciate that in both *Hotson* and *Gregg* the loss was deterministic, so that it was possible, albeit very difficult to prove what was the cause of that loss. In contrast, in *Chaplin* the loss was indeterministic, in that what the claimant might have gained was dependent on what others might have decided to do in a set of hypothetical circumstances. As such, it would be unreasonable to apply the normal rules on the incidence of the burden of proof in a civil action.

While the action in *Chaplin* sounded in contract, it does not follow that there cannot be tort cases in which the claimant's loss is also indeterministic. For example, where the professional negligence of a solicitor results in the claimant's action becoming time barred, the loss suffered by the claimant may be regarded as indeterministic, as the likelihood or otherwise of a successful action is based on hypothetical issues such as how would the witnesses have behaved in court or how would the advocacy teams of the parties have conducted themselves: see *Kitchen v RAF Association* [1958] 1 WLR 563. Similarly, in *Allied Maples Group Ltd v Simmons & Simmons* [1995] 1 WLR 1602 the defendants were negligent in advising the claimants, who were in the process of acquiring the shops of another chain of furniture retailers. Had the defendants advised appropriately, the claimants might have been able to secure protection from the liabilities of that group of companies. It was held that the claimants did not have to prove that they would have been successful in acquiring that protection, but merely that there was more than a speculative chance of success in this respect. Accordingly, the court could assess damages based upon what that chance was.

A second distinction between tort and contract is said to be that contractual duties are fixed by the parties to the contract, that is, they are voluntarily assumed, whereas tortious duties are fixed by law. To advance on this distinction it can be said that duties in tort are owed to persons generally so that a duty can be owed to a complete stranger, whereas contractual duties are owed specifically to the other party or parties to the relevant contract. However, in some contractual relationships the parties may not be directly known to each other, such as is the case with a typical hire purchase transaction in respect of a new car in which the car dealer fills out the paperwork but the contract is regarded, legally, as one between the customer and the finance company who make contact only by correspondence. While tortious duties are fixed by law, it should not be forgotten that some such duties arise out of a contractual relationship. This will often be the case where there is a contract for the provision of services under which there will be an implied term that the supplier will exercise reasonable care and skill in performing the contract (**Supply of Goods and Services Act 1982 s. 13**). However, this term is one that derives from the common law, and was originally justified on the basis that it represents the customer's reasonable expectation. Here, determining the extent of the supplier's duty to exercise reasonable care will require close attention to the specific undertakings which form the basis of the contract and it is important that any tortious duty found to exist should not undermine the express contractual undertakings of the parties: *Johnstone v Bloomsbury Health Authority* [1991] 2 All ER 293. Thus, although the tortious duty will remain as a static duty to exercise reasonable care and skill, there may be circumstances in which a contracting party has undertaken to achieve a higher level of performance than the basic tortious requirement: See, e.g. *Greaves & Co (Contractors) Ltd v Baynham, Meikle & Partners* [1975] 3 All ER 99.

Services contracts apart, the liability of an occupier to his visitors will also depend on any contractual relationship which exists between the parties (**Occupiers' Liability Act 1957, s. 2(1)**), so that regard must be had to the extent to which the occupier agrees to extend, limit or vary the duty normally owed to a lawful visitor under the general law of tort.

Under the rule in *Hedley Byrne & Co Ltd v Heller & Partners Ltd* [1964] AC 465 it was a requirement, on the particular facts of that case, that the defendant should have voluntarily assumed responsibility for the accuracy of a statement communicated to the claimant. Accordingly, since in *Hedley Byrne*, the defendant had disclaimed responsibility for the accuracy of a financial reference, it was considered by the House of Lords that the defendant would owe the claimant no duty of care. In time, the requirement of voluntary assumption of responsibility came to be replaced by a requirement of reasonable reliance as the key indicator of liability on the part of the maker of a statement, as the concept of voluntary assumption of responsibility was thought to be inconsistent with the view that tortious duties are imposed by law. Thus, in *Smith v Eric S Bush (a firm)* the defendants, a firm of surveyors carrying out a building society valuation, could still owe a duty of care to an impecunious consumer buyer of a house surveyed by them despite the fact that they disclaimed responsibility for the accuracy of the advice they gave. The basis of the decision was that regardless of the disclaimer, the advice given by the defendants was something which a person in the position of the claimants would reasonably rely upon. However, the requirement of voluntary assumption of responsibility has seen a revival, albeit explained in a somewhat different way to the way in which it appeared to be explained in *Hedley Byrne & Co v Heller & Partners Ltd*. In *Hedley Byrne* Lord Devlin considered the required relationship between the claimant and the defendant to be 'equivalent to contract' with the result that but for the absence of consideration there would have been a contractual relationship between the parties. In *Henderson v Merrett Syndicates Ltd* [1994] 3 All ER 506, it was considered that an insurance agent providing professional or quasi-professional services whose advice was relied upon by the claimant would owe a tortious duty of care to the claimant whether or not there existed between the parties a contractual relationship, provided the defendant had voluntarily assumed responsibility for the accuracy of the advice given. Moreover, it seems that this duty of care could be imposed despite the fact that the parties had chosen to structure their obligations through their contractual relationships. The difficulty this analysis presents, on the face of it, is that tortious duties are imposed by law rather than by way of any contractual arrangements. However, in *White v Jones* [1995] 1 All ER 691 a more detailed explanation of the nature of the voluntary assumption of responsibility test was given by Lords Goff and Browne-Wilkinson. In particular, in order to get round the criticism of the requirement in *Smith v Bush*, Lord Browne-Wilkinson explained that it was not the duty which was voluntarily assumed, since this must be imposed by law. Instead, in his Lordship's opinion, what has been voluntarily assumed is the relationship between the defendant and the claimant, from which relationship the duty can be inferred, especially in circumstances in which the claimant has reasonably relied upon the advice given by the defendant. The main problem with this particular analysis is that it is just as capable of applying to negligent acts, such as that of getting into a motor vehicle and driving it in a negligent fashion, which have been traditionally dealt with on the basis of an imposed duty not affected by considerations relating to the voluntariness of the defendant's conduct.

The developments unleashed in *Henderson v Merrett Syndicates Ltd* and *White v Jones* could be considered relevant only in the context of actions for negligently caused economic loss, but case law seems to suggest otherwise, especially in cases in which the defendant appears to have taken responsibility for a particular function. For example, an educational psychologist called in by a local authority to advise on a child may be taken to have 'assumed responsibility' sufficient to owe a duty of care: *Phelps v Hillingdon LBC* [2001] 2 AC 619. Similarly, a sports authority has been held to owe a duty of care in respect of the adequacy of the medical arrangements at fights for which it is responsible: *Watson v British Boxing Board Of Control* [2001] QB 1134; see also *Vowles v Evans* [2003] EWCA Civ 318 (referee of amateur rugby match). However, it has been held to be unrealistic to say that a bank had assumed responsibility to ensure compliance with a freezing order obtained by the claimants in respect of the VAT liability of two companies that held accounts with the bank, as a freezing order must be complied with as a matter of law and is best enforced by means of the law on contempt of court rather than a private law duty of care: *Customs & Excise Commissioners v Barclays Bank plc* [2006] UKHL 280.

A further distinction between contractual and tortious liability is said to be that contractual duties are strict whereas tortious duties are, generally, fault-based. However, there are numerous exceptions to this generalization. In particular, many contractual duties are fault-based, particularly those which are implied into contracts for the supply of services (Supply of Goods and Services Act 1982, s. 13). Moreover, the device of the collateral contract has been used in the past to impose liability on the maker of a misleading pre-contractual statement at a time when there was no liability in damages for negligent misrepresentation (*Esso Petroleum Ltd v Mardon* [1976] QB 801). In tort law the meaning of the term 'fault' is not easy to ascertain, but there are some torts that appear to impose strict liability. Examples include the liability of a keeper of an animal belonging to a dangerous species (Animals Act 1971, s. 2(1)), questionably, the rule in *Rylands v Fletcher* (1868) LR 3 HL 300, the provisions of the Consumer Protection Act 1987, Part I, the Nuclear Installations Act 1965 and the rules relating to the vicarious liability of an employer for the tortious acts of his employees. In relation to the last mentioned, it should be observed that while the employer may not be personally at fault, he is held liable for those torts committed by his employees in the course of their employment. Accordingly, there will usually have been a fault-based wrong committed by someone for whom the employer is held responsible. Furthermore, the way in which some so-called strict liability torts have been interpreted by the courts is such as to inject into them elements of fault. In particular, the interpretation of the non-natural use requirement of the rule in *Rylands v Fletcher* suggests that it is necessary to consider the general benefit to the community of the defendant's activity, the locality in which the accumulation took place and the reasonableness of the precautions taken by the defendant to guard against the risk of harm to others (*Mason v Levy Auto Parts of England* [1967] 2 QB 530; *Cambridge Water Co v Eastern Counties Leather plc* [1994] 2 WLR 53). These requirements sound suspiciously similar to those relevant to an enquiry into the issue of breach of duty of care in negligence or reasonable user in nuisance; both of which are substantially fault-based enquiries. The concept of defectiveness in the **Consumer Protection Act 1987, s. 3** has been defined in terms of legitimate consumer expectations, which can serve to impose a standard markedly stricter than the requirement that a defendant should exercise reasonable care: see *A v National Blood Authority* [2001] 3 All ER 289. However, the presence of a development risks defence in the **Consumer Protection Act 1987, s. 4(1)(e)** substantially reduces the impact of the Act, since it is a defence for a producer to show that the state of scientific and technological development at the time a product was put into circulation was not such as to allow a product defect to be discovered. Seemingly, this defence is unlikely to apply to anything other than design defects (*A v National Blood Authority* [2001] 3 All ER 289).

The best illustration of the complementary nature of contractual and tortious liability can be found in cases in which a person is concurrently liable in contract and in tort. Since tortious liability is regarded as parasitic (*Pacific Associates Inc v Baxter* [1990] QB 993), there is no sense in searching for liability in tort where the parties are in a contractual relationship (*Tai Hing Cotton Mill v Liu Chong Bank Ltd* [1986] 1 AC 801). It follows that liability in tort cannot be any greater than that expressly or impliedly created by the contract between the parties: but cf. *Holt v Payne Skillington (a firm)* [1996] PNLR 179; *contra*. Conversely, the mere fact that a contract exists between the parties and that they have chosen to structure their obligations by reference to that contract will not preclude the existence of a tortious duty of care where the contract remains silent on the matter which is in dispute (*Henderson v Merrett Syndicates Ltd* [1994] 3 All ER 506. Cf. *National Bank of Greece SA v Pinios SA* [1990] 1 AC 637). As Lord Goff noted, it may be that the facts of *Henderson*, considered above, are unusual, since in most cases where there is a chain of contractual relationships, the imposition of a tortious duty of care might be inconsistent with the contractual undertakings of the parties. Thus it has been observed that in the case of a building contract under which there are contractual arrangements between the building owner and the main contractor and arrangements between the main contractor and the various sub-contractors, it will not normally be the case that a sub-contractor will owe any tortious duty of care to the building owner, since the sub-contractor will not normally voluntarily undertake responsibility to the owner (*Barclays Bank plc v Fairclough Building Ltd* [1995] 1 All ER 289).

Furthermore, there may be circumstances in which the contractual undertakings of the parties are consistent with general tortious duties, especially those requiring the exercise of reasonable care. Thus, if an employer fails to provide a safe system of work by requiring an employee to be available for work for an average of 88 hours a week, the contractual term requiring attendance may amount to a limitation of liability in respect of negligently caused personal injury, so that the provisions of the **Unfair Contract Terms Act 1977, s. 2(1)** may be invoked (*Johnstone v Bloomsbury Health Authority* [1991] 2 All ER 293).

In conclusion, it is clear that there are differences between contractual and tortious liability, but the two branches of the common law of obligations work together towards the provision of workable remedies for the claimant. However, where tort and contract intermix, the generality of the tort system will normally give way to the more specific inter-party obligations undertaken by way of contract.

Question 2

Consider the defects, if any, in the fault system of accident compensation and the case for reform of the means of accident compensation.

Commentary

Question 2 seeks to consider a function served by tort law, although it has to be said that the objective of accident compensation is primarily achieved through State intervention and private insurance. Many of the criticisms of the role of the law of tort in this regard must be read in the light of the more detailed consideration of remedies for breach of tortious obligations in Chapter 12. Although tort law does play a minor role in the overall picture of accident compensation, it should be appreciated that it is only a very small part of a broader range of state-provided compensation schemes, albeit somewhat more generous to those who are successful.

Answer plan

- Criticisms of the tort system based on cost, delay, the lump sum method of compensation and general unpredictability of outcome.
- Alternatives to the tort system such as state insurance, no-fault accident compensation schemes and private insurance.

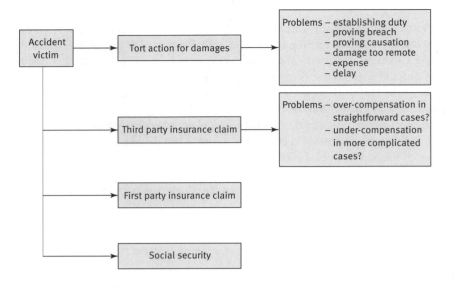

Suggested answer

In practice, much of the law of tort is concerned with compensating the victim of the defendant's accidental wrongdoing. Accordingly, at a general level, the function of a remedy in the law of tort is to relieve the claimant in respect of the loss or damage he has suffered rather than to punish the defendant. There is a range of means by which the compensation objective is sought to be achieved. These include a personal action for damages by the victim against a defendant he is able to prove to be at fault, but there are a number of deficiencies in this tort-based system. An alternative is private insurance, whether it be first-party insurance whereby the victim is insured against a specified type of accident or third-party insurance, whereby the accident causer is insured against harm that might be suffered by a third party. However, the victim of an accident faces a number of problems associated with dealing with insurance companies, where the defendant is insured or where the claimant seeks to recover under first-party insurance he may have taken out. Finally, the compensation objective may be achieved through State intervention in the form of social security payments. This is likely to be the most common source of accident compensation where a defendant, on whom to pin liability, cannot be found, as will be the case with most accidents at home. Although statistically, this is the most common means by which the compensation objective is achieved, it suffers from the drawback that state compensation schemes have to be paid for out of taxation, and taxing individuals is a politically sensitive process that can deter governments. Moreover, the payments received under State schemes are normally substantially lower than payments made in the form of an award of damages.

Generally, the tort system is concerned with *wrongs* in the sense that the defendant is required to compensate the claimant in respect of damage caused by some fault-based or culpable conduct on his (the defendant's) part. In this sense, tort liability rules are concerned with *loss shifting* in that they make the defendant responsible for the loss suffered by the claimant because he (the defendant) is in some way to blame for that loss.

The growth of the practice of insurance has introduced the notion of *loss distribution* under which the question is not who is to blame for an accident, but who can most easily bear the loss caused by a particular accident? For example, it was once observed by Lord Griffiths in *Smith v Eric S Bush (a firm)* [1989] 2 WLR 790 that:

There was once a time when it was considered imprudent even to mention the possible existence of insurance cover in a lawsuit. But those days are long past. The availability and cost of insurance must be a relevant factor when considering which of two parties should be required to bear the risk of a loss.

Where a potential cause of accidents is identified, such as the motor car or the work accident, insurance against the risk created may become compulsory or a regime of strict tort liability may be introduced by Parliament, e.g. the Road Traffic Act 1988, ss. 143–5 and the Employers' Liability (Compulsory Insurance) Act 1969. Moreover, in relation to motor vehicle accidents, there is also a safety net provided by the Motor Insurers' Bureau (MIB) which has an agreement with the Department for Transport that they will provide additional cover, funded by a pool derived from insurance premiums, in cases in which an accident is caused by an uninsured or untraced driver. The MIB will even be responsible in cases in which a driver has driven a car with the intention of causing injury (*Gardner v Moore* [1984] AC 548), but not where an accident takes place on private property, since the compulsory insurance scheme under the Road Traffic Act 1988 is inapplicable (*Charlton v Fisher* [2001] 3 WLR 1435). Strangely, although employers are also subject to a compulsory insurance scheme, there is no equivalent of the MIB agreement, which is regarded as a relevant factor by the courts in such cases (*Dunbar v A & B Painters Ltd* [1986] 2 Lloyd's Rep 38, 42–3 *per Balcombe LJ*).

Where an accident victim is able to satisfy the legal requirements necessary to make out a claim in tort, he stands to recover much more than will be available to a person who is unable to pursue a tort claim. The reason for this is that English law adopts a system of 'full compensation'. In personal injury cases, this means that tort compensation should be related to the actual earnings of the claimant. Moreover, the full compensation system pays damages in respect of both pecuniary loss (e.g. expense incurred) and non-pecuniary loss (e.g. pain and suffering). Conversely, the number of successful tort claimants is relatively small for a number of reasons. For example, in order to be able to recover, the claimant must be the victim of an 'accident', which may be the result of either the fault of the defendant or due to the commission of a wrong, in respect of which liability is strict. For these purposes, an 'accident' may include congenital disability and disease, where they are man-made, but there are a number of such conditions which may occur by accident but which are not attributable to the fault of an identified defendant. In such circumstances, for example, where disease occurs naturally, the tort system is likely to fail as a means of accident compensation by allowing a number of claimants to fall through the compensation net.

Other criticisms of the tort system as a means of accident compensation are those of cost, delay, unpredictability of outcome, the unbalanced way in which payments are made, and the problem of how compensation payments are used by the claimant after an award has been made.

So far as cost is concerned, it was established by the Pearson Report (Report of the Royal Commission on Compensation for Personal Injuries, Cmnd 7054, 1978) that the administrative cost of tort compensation was 85 per cent of the total amount paid out in 1977. In contrast, the equivalent cost of compensation under the social security system came to only 11 per cent. Moreover, since the outcome in a tort action is dependent on litigation commenced by the claimant, the litigant must be in a position, subject to the limited availability of legal aid, to be able to fund the process of litigation. An attempt to resolve this problem was to permit the development of 'no-win, no fee' schemes for some personal injury cases. Such arrangements would result in the legal adviser not being remunerated in the event that the action was unsuccessful. As a result of this, there is the possibility that a lawyer might negotiate a settlement with the defendant's insurer that produces compensation on the low side. Moreover, there is also some evidence to suggest that insurers may prefer to settle a claim rather than litigate in order to avoid the costs associated with the latter. The down side to 'no win no fee' arrangements is that, arguably, they may lead to the development of a 'compensation culture' which in turn could promote an insurance crisis. However, there is no immediate evidence that this is the case and the Better Regulation Task Force suggests that the number of personal injury claims has fallen: *Better Routes to Redress* (2004). Nevertheless, even if there is a popular myth to the effect that a compensation culture has developed, this in itself could lead potential defendants to adopt excessive safety precautions in order to protect the reckless and the foolhardy from obvious risks of danger. However, recent case law suggests that the judiciary is aware of that danger and has sought to assert the importance of personal responsibility for one's own actions: *Tomlinson v Congleton BC* [2004] 1 AC 46.

The cost of the tort system is intimately associated with the requirement of fault. Much expense is incurred in identifying who is at fault and therefore potentially responsible for the harm suffered by the claimant. Costs are incurred in assessing how much compensation should be paid, since there must be an investigation into the consequences of an accident, involving the preparation of expert reports etc. Moreover, because of the adversary system, these costs are duplicated since each party will have to call his own experts.

The tort system is also very slow in delivering compensation, again due in part to the adversary system. The more complicated the case, the greater will be the likelihood of delay. The Civil Justice Review (Cm 394, 1988) revealed that the average time from accident to trial in the case of a High court action was five years and in the case of a county court trial, three years. Moreover, defendants and their insurers had every incentive to throw obstacles in the path of a claimant in the hope that litigation will be suspended. The review of the Civil Justice system undertaken by Lord Woolf (Access to Justice, 1996) suggested radical reforms designed to speed up the whole system of dispensing civil justice. The Woolf proposals have now been introduced with the result that there is a fast-track procedure for personal injury actions involving a sum not more than £10,000. In addition, the jurisdiction of the county court small claims procedure has been extended to cover personal injury cases up to a value of £3,000. A trial must normally take place within 30 weeks of the date on which the writ was issued and trials are expected to last hours rather than days. In the case of complex claims, such as those for medical negligence (whether above or below the £10,000 threshold) and all claims valued at more than £10,000 there is a multi-track system subject to close judicial scrutiny for the purposes of time management. The notion of judicial case management is intended to cut out the possibility of proceedings being unduly lengthened by time-wasting tactics on the part of large corporate defendants and their insurers. A claimant may make an offer of settlement, similar to the previous system whereby a defendant could make a payment into court. Importantly, an unreasonable refusal by a defendant to accept the offer of settlement may work against him.

The unpredictability of the tort system is notorious. As Lord Scarman observed in *Lim Poh Choo v Camden & Islington AHA* [1980] AC 174, '(there is really one certainty: the future will prove the award to be either too high or too low)' Even where the claimant can show that he is owed a duty of care, he must also establish breach of that duty, factual causation and hope that the loss he has suffered is not too remote and that the court does not regard his losses as having been exaggerated: *Painting v University of Oxford* [2005] EWCA Civ 161. Even where the claimant is successful, the final award may be less than was anticipated at the outset, which must be offset against the cost of bringing the action in the first place. Because of this pressure, claimants will often settle out of court, resulting in under compensation in more complicated cases. At the same time, the administrative cost incurred by insurance companies in processing smaller claims may lead to an over-generous settlement, if this serves to reduce those administrative costs, thereby demonstrating the unbalanced way in which compensation may be paid.

The means of paying damages in the form of a lump sum has been criticized as it requires the court to guess at what the future might bring, at the time of trial. Damages assessed in this way may fail to take account of later events that exacerbate the claimant's loss. Courts can make an award of provisional damages where it is proved or admitted that there is a chance that the claimant will develop some disease or suffer serious deterioration in his physical or mental condition: Senior Courts Act 1981, s. 32A.

Given the uncertainties surrounding lump sum payments, it is not surprising that in the case of traumatic, long-term injuries, the accountancy-driven system of structured settlements has begun to prove popular (see Damages Act 1996, s. 5). Initially, a claimant could not be compelled to accept payment of damages by way of periodic payments (see Damages Act 1996, s. 2). However, since the Courts Act 2003, the Damages Act 1996, s. 2 has been amended so that, provided the continuity of payment under the order is reasonably secure, a structured settlement may be made, involving the substitution of an annuity-based pension in place of a lump sum payment. For these purposes continuity of payment is regarded as secure if there is a Financial Services Compensation Scheme in place under the Financial Services and Markets Act 2000, s. 213, or a government minister has provided a guarantee in respect of a designated body under the Damages Act 1996, s. 6, or where the defendant is a government department or health service body. The annuity, purchased by the defendant's insurers, can make provision for events which may affect the need for increased compensation at various stages in the continued life of the accident victim and avoids the problem of profligacy on the part of claimants following receipt of an award of lump sum damages.

The decision to allow courts to order a means of compensation other than that asked for by the claimant is, in itself, controversial. The periodic payment system also has, as its focus, the annual financial needs of the long-term accident victim. This different focus is argued to result in increased compensation in many cases that will have to be funded by the defendants' insurers. (See Lewis, 'The Politics and Economics of Tort Law' (2006) 69 MLR 418, 442.) The advantages of the structured settlement fall on both sides. Not only does the annuity system avoid payment of tax by accident victims (Taxes Act 1988, ss. 329A and 329B, added by the Finance Act 1995, s. 142) but it also results in substantial savings over the normal lump sum system so far as insurers are concerned. An immediate lump sum can be paid to the victim, however, to meet identified need, e.g. the adaptation of a house for the purposes of a quadriplegic accident victim. In contrast, probably the most serious criticism of the system of structured settlements is that a very small percentage of accident victims are deriving a substantial benefit at the expense of ordinary taxpayers, which effectively benefits such victims to an even greater extent than is already the case where an accident victim is successful in an action for damages. By way of contrast, there may be ordinary taxpayers who have subsidized the award to such a victim who are themselves injured, but unable to maintain an action for damages themselves because they have suffered a non-tortious injury (see *Hodgson v Trapp* [1988] 3 All ER 870 at 876 *per Lord Bridge*).

Alternatives to the fault-based tort system include private insurance by the victim and the tortfeasor; the greater use of rules of strict liability based on an assumption that the potential tortfeasor should be insured against the possible risk of damage to others; public insurance schemes such as the social security system and more wide-ranging public insurance schemes such as that employed in New Zealand by virtue of the **Accident Rehabilitation and Compensation Insurance Act 1992** which effectively eliminates the need to have recourse to the law of tort as system of accident compensation.

Some types of accident damage can be insured against by both the victim and the wrongdoer. In particular, life, permanent health, and personal accident policies are readily available to all potential accident victims. Moreover, some employers will take out occupational sick pay policies which go beyond State provision for short-term income replacement. At present, the likelihood that such policies will exist depends greatly on the social class into which the accident victim falls and the nature of his employment. Before private insurance can replace the tort system, there must be a distinct change in taxation policy so that all members of society are paid in such a way that they can afford to take out private insurance. There still remains the problem that the low paid will not have the resources to cover themselves adequately against all possible eventualities. The fact that private insurance policies exist does not, at present, make any difference to an award of tort damages since the courts do not wish to discourage thrift, so payments out of privately arranged insurance will not be deducted from an award of tort damages (*Bradburn v Great Western Railway* (1874) LR 10 Ex 1).

The present social security system provides for payment in respect of a number of injuries which may or may not result from the fault of an identified defendant and some of which are based on nothing more than the means of the claimant (e.g. income support and housing benefit). Payments, generally, are based on subsistence levels rather than the total loss suffered by the claimant and, as such, will be considerably less than an award of tort damages.

Roughly, benefits can be divided into those relating to non-industrial injuries and those relating to injury suffered at work. The former include statutory sick pay, which is replaced by incapacity benefit after 28 weeks of illness, provided there have been sufficient contributions to the national insurance scheme. Claimants not qualifying for the latter, however, may claim severe disablement allowance. In severe cases, where constant care is required, a claim for disability living allowance may be permitted. In respect of industrial injuries, disablement benefit may be awarded to an injured employee. The important consideration concerning these benefits is that, at present, they are deductible from an award of tort damages, but they are not based on the principle of full compensation since the amount payable is based on average earnings rather than on the actual earnings of the accident victim. On the other hand, as has been observed, the social security system is more efficient in terms of the cost of making payments to individuals and can be geared to the needs of the claimant as and when new financial difficulties might arise.

Dissatisfaction with the tort system of compensation has led to the introduction of a comprehensive no-fault scheme of compensation in New Zealand. This system replaces the victim's earnings at 80 per cent of his pre-accident earnings, subject to a maximum ceiling. In addition, a lump sum can be awarded in respect of permanent disablement, but payments for pain and suffering and loss of amenity are minimal. Moreover, the cost of the scheme must be related to the type of economy which exists in New Zealand, which is largely agricultural. It is arguable that the same system would not translate to a more industrialized economy in which there are substantial numbers of industrial injuries resulting from production processes. Moreover, there still remains the political problem that public schemes have to be paid for out of public funds, which tends to make them less popular with those who have the resources to make private arrangements.

Question 3

'Economic efficiency can never be an all-embracing explanation of the objective of the law of torts. . . Economic efficiency is simply one of the many (sometimes conflicting) objectives of tort law.'

(**Murphy**, *Street on Torts*)

In the light of this statement, discuss the extent to which efficiency and justice are objectives of the law of tort.

Commentary

This question deals with the law of tort as a deterrent to harm-causing activities. The previous question considered the compensation objective of the tort system. It was noted that the process of compensation is concerned with the loss suffered by the victim. However, the mere existence of potential liability on the part of a defendant also serves as a deterrent to others that might persuade them not to engage in conduct that might lead to civil liability for a breach of duty. In part, this raises the matter of the relationship between the law of tort and the criminal law, but also considers the increasing interest of economists in the use of tortious rules as a means of achieving efficient results. An answer should consider the various objectives of tort law, in particular whether the compensation objective is ever sacrificed at the hands of arguments based on economic efficiency, but other factors, such as justice, are also relevant in ascertaining the role of tort law.

Answer plan

- The primary objectives of economic analysis of legal rules.
- Efficiency versus justice as objectives of the law of tort.
- The distinction between loss shifting and loss distribution.
- The role of private first-party and third-party insurance.
- The different notions of justice across the whole range of tortious liability.

Suggested answer

The law of tort is primarily concerned with accidents which result in physical harm to the person or to property, although it may also protect the economic interests of the claimant in a limited number of cases. The law of tort may serve a number of different purposes. Liability rules may serve to deter wrongdoers from engaging in activities which harm others, whilst the law should also seek to provide a remedy for those who are harmed as a result of the defendant's wrongs.

On an economic analysis, the desire to deter a person from engaging in activities which cause harm to others is seen as a primary objective (see Calabresi, *The Cost of Accidents* (1970), Posner, *The Economic Analysis of Law*, 6th edn (Aspen: 2003). A legal rule is perceived to be efficient if it deters wrongdoing in a cost effective manner, but while the deterrent effect of a rule of the law of tort may be important, it should not be promoted to the extent that the plight of an injured person is forgotten. Somehow, in applying legal rules, the courts have to reach a suitable balance between efficiency and justice. If we have a rule that a claimant is entitled to sue a defendant for the losses caused by his wrong-doing the costs and benefits of such a rule need to be balanced. There are costs in having courts to hear tort cases; costs of employing lawyers; costs associated with the recovery of damages from a defendant once an award has been made; costs of taking out liability insurance to protect against being sued and there are costs arising out of the possibility that defendants may take unnecessary precautions to avoid being sued. In contrast with these costs the benefits of a liability rule are, first, that the public purse is relieved of the financial cost of treating the injured claimant, secondly, the disruption to the claimant's life is minimized by the receipt of the award and, thirdly, others may be deterred from engaging in similar conduct to that of the defendant.

The deterrent effect of legal rules can be overstated. In the first place, only a small number of torts are based on deliberate misconduct and, in particular, the tort of negligence gives rise to liability only in the event of carelessness. However, there are instances where tort law can be viewed as having a deterrent effect. For example, in some instances it may be possible to award exemplary damages (see *Cassell & Co v Broome* [1972] AC 1027).

The conflict between efficiency and justice can be seen most clearly in cases of negligence, especially when it comes to be determined whether the defendant's actions constitute an actionable breach of duty. The goal of efficiency is probably best served by the rule that an act is only negligent if reasonable precautions have not been taken by the defendant (*Latimer v AEC Ltd* [1953] AC 643), since it is clear that taking every possible precaution to guard against a minor risk of harm would be uneconomic. For example, it might be possible to reduce the number of road traffic accidents by requiring vehicle manufacturers to produce cars which could not travel any faster than 10 mph, but this would hardly be acceptable in terms of economic efficiency, nor would this solution be socially acceptable.

It should be appreciated that virtually every activity has some capacity for causing harm, but to take every possible precaution to guard against minimal risks would not make sense. Thus when the evidence shows that in a period of 30 years, only six cricket balls have been struck from the defendant's cricket ground to the outside, the excessive precaution of substantially raising the height of the perimeter fence is not necessary to guard against such a minimal risk of harm to others (*Bolton v Stone* [1951] AC 850). However, the rule that the magnitude of risk created by the defendant should be considered is based on the notion that a particularly vulnerable claimant should be treated more carefully than others by the wrongdoer (*Paris v Stepney BC* [1951] AC 367) thereby illustrating the importance of practical justice in special cases. Risk assessment is an increasingly common practice in almost all businesses and professions and if a particular risk is a distinct possibility, such as the risk of a passenger falling overboard from a cross-channel ferry, the defendant should at least take the precaution of training the captain and crew in how to effect a rescue: see *Davis v Stena Line* [2005] EWHC 420 (QB). However, to require a defendant to take precautions to guard against the crass stupidity of the claimant would be to go too far; see e.g. *Tomlinson v Congleton BC* [2004] 1 AC 46.

If the law imposes liability in damages for certain acts, this would appear to serve a deterrent purpose, since few people will wish to engage in conduct which they realize is likely to result in them having to pay another in respect of the harm which has been caused. There are occasions, however, on which there may be little the defendant can do to avoid causing harm to others. For example, since the test of liability is objectively based, the defendant who does his incompetent best may still be liable since he is judged by the standards of the reasonable man and not by reference to his own ability (*Nettleship v Weston* [1971] 2 QB 691). Moreover, in many cases the defendant's fault amounts to little more than inadvertence, so that the defendant may not have foreseen the danger he creates, but the law may state that he has not acted in the same way as a reasonable man would have acted and is therefore liable.

The view that tort rules serve a deterrent purpose is readily understandable where liability is based on the notion of loss shifting. Loss shifting as a method of compensation has its roots in the nineteenth-century notion that there should be no liability without proof of fault and that a person who is at fault should pay for the losses he has caused. Modern tort law is now dominated by the presence of an insurance market and there has been a move from loss shifting as a system of compensation to one based on the notion of loss distribution. The insurance market is such that major causes of accidents can be identified and those who engage in accident causing activities, such as employers, drivers, and manufacturers, may be required or encouraged to take out insurance to cover potential risks of loss. Moreover, in most cases, the insured accident causer can pass on the cost of insurance to the consumers of his product or his service, thereby spreading the costs associated with the accident risk more broadly. Since the accident causer must be or ought to be insured the problem is that it is not the wrongdoer who pays damages, but his insurer. The widespread availability of insurance also serves to undermine the argument that tort rules serve a deterrent purpose, since it is rarely the defendant, but his insurers who foot the bill where an award of damages is made. Insurers themselves might appear to be able deter tortious misconduct, but there is little evidence that they do. It is possible to raise premiums in the case of bad risks, but this is never likely to deter mere inadvertence.

Even in professional negligence cases where tort rules might conceivably have a deterrent effect, the inadvertence argument once more becomes relevant. It is also arguable that the threat of liability based on the notion of fault is likely to result in the adoption of over-defensive practices which might prove detrimental to the interests of the client or patient. A further consideration is that if tort rules do operate in a deterrent fashion, then steps may be taken by potential defendants to guard against being sued which may be out of proportion to what is considered reasonably necessary. The possibility that such disproportionate steps may be taken is often put forward as a reason for not imposing a duty of care. Thus if there is a danger that doctors may engage in 'defensive medicine' this may be a reason for declining to hold that a duty of care exists in particular circumstances. But the concept of defensive practices is not confined to cases of medical malpractice and may extend into other areas such as the exercise of statutory powers by a public authority charged with a responsibility for protecting others (see X *(minors) v Bedfordshire County Council* [1995] 3 WLR 152) or the police (see *Hill v Chief Constable of West Yorkshire* [1988] 2 All ER 238; *Brookes v Metropolitan Police Commissioner* [2005] 1 WLR 1495; *M v Metropolitan Police Commissioner* [2007] EWCA Civ 1361), the Crown Prosecution service (see *Elguzouli-Daf v Metropolitan Police Commissioner* [1995] 1 All ER 833) a coastguard service (see *Skinner v Secretary of State for Transport* (1995) *The Times*, 3 January) or a ship classification society (see *Marc Rich & Co v Bishop Rock Marine Co Ltd* [1995] 3 All ER 307). More recently, there is evidence that some senior members of the judiciary, at least, are prepared to be more flexible than they might have been in the past and place less emphasis on the possibility that the imposition of liability in negligence might result in defensive practices: see *Fairchild v Glenhaven Funeral Services Ltd* [2003] 1 AC 32, Lord Bingham; *Gregg v Scott* [2005] UKHL 2, Lord Nicholls (dissenting).

The deterrent effect of tort rules is closely related to the economic efficiency argument that if an activity imposes costs on others, those costs should be reflected in the true cost of the harm causing activity (see Calabresi, *The Cost of Accidents* (1970), p. 69). For example, on this theory the cost of a car not fitted with seatbelts, or one which is to be driven by a 17-year-old, would have to reflect the increased accident costs associated with the use of such a vehicle. The main difficulty with this theory is that it is often difficult to identify the true cause of an accident. For example, if a collision occurs at a road intersection, is the true cause of the accident the fact that the cars have been driven carelessly, the fact that the traffic lights are not working properly, the fact that the road surface is unduly worn, or the fact that the tyres on one of the vehicles are defective? In each case the answer reveals a different defendant.

The principal problem with rules based on efficiency is that what is an efficient solution is not necessarily a fair solution. For example, the person whom an economist might regard as being in the best position to avoid the risk of a particular loss might be the accident victim himself. This may typically be the case where the harm suffered by the claimant is harm against which he could have readily insured, since on an economic analysis he is the best insurer and therefore the better risk-bearer.

Fairness or justice is seen by lawyers as the main reason for the existence of tort rules. The notion of justice takes a number of different forms. For example, there is a rights-based justice under which the claimant is entitled to protection against unjustifiable interferences with his civil rights. Prime examples of such tortious rules are those which protect against battery, assault and false imprisonment. However, it would appear that there is no general tortious principle that promotes a right to respect for private life (see *Wainwright v Home Office* [2003] 3 WLR 1137), although there appears to be a right to prevent the wrongful disclosure of private information based on the European Convention on Human Rights, art. 8 (see *Campbell v MGN* [2004] 2 AC 457; *McKennitt v Ash* [2008] QB 73; *Murray v Express Newspapers* [2008] EWCA Civ 446).

A second notion of justice is based on a balance of competing interests such as those of neighbouring landowners, best represented by the rule in *Rylands v Fletcher* (1868) LR 3 HL and the tort of private nuisance. Both torts seek to achieve a fair balance between competing ownership rights; private nuisance, in particular, is said to be based on the notion of give and take. What is important is whether the defendant's use of his land is reasonable, having regard to matters such as the locality in which the nuisance is caused, the duration of the nuisance, whether the claimant's land use is unduly sensitive and, in so far as remedies are concerned, whether the defendant's activity is socially useful.

Perhaps the most important notion of justice in tort law is that of needs or compensation-based justice. Where a claimant is injured as a result of the defendant's tort, there is a primary need that the harm he has suffered should be adequately compensated. It is here that the tort of negligence plays a partial role, although there are other methods of compensation. It is generally accepted that victims of modern social conditions should not be left to bear all the costs. Thus in addition to liability rules under which most of the costs are borne by insurance, there are public compensation schemes to deal with matters such as invalidity payments, sickness benefit, and other forms of social security payment. The principal issue has become not who is to blame for a particular variety of harm, but who is in the best position to pay for the consequences of that harm? Instead of simply shifting losses from the claimant to the wrong-doing defendant, modern tort law and its accompaniments work on the basis of loss spreading. This notion is well reflected in modern tortious rules on vicarious liability and product liability under which it has been recognized that employers and producers are in a unique position to be able to spread the cost of accidents by charging higher prices for the products they produce or the services they provide or by other cost cutting measures within their own businesses, combined with the secure knowledge that relevant insurance will cover any award of damages which might be ordered.

Question 4

'The trouble with English tort law is that it fails to provide sufficient protection to each citizen's inalienable right to bodily integrity and freedom from interference.'
  Discuss.

Commentary

This question centres upon the limits of the torts of assault, battery, intimidation, and the rule in *Wilkinson v Downton*. It also considers the stringent 'property' test for the right to sue in private nuisance re-asserted by the House of Lords in *Hunter v Canary Wharf*. The case law, generally, shows that on those occasions a litigant has sought to use the law of torts to assert a right to privacy, the limits of the torts of assault, battery, nuisance, and the statutory protection afforded by the Protection from **Harassment Act 1997** have proved to have only limited success in providing relief. However, the **Human Rights Act 1998** may be relevant where the alleged invasion of privacy is perpetrated, especially in the context of the wrongful disclosure of private information.

Answer plan

- Harassment as a tort.
- Limits of the tort of private nuisance.
- Limits of the torts of assault, battery and false imprisonment.
- Scope of the **Protection from Harassment Act 1997**.
- Effect of the **Human Rights Act 1998**.

Suggested answer

Common law rules do not overtly recognize a specific right to privacy (see *Wainwright v Home Office* [2003] 3 WLR 1137; *Wong v Parkside NHS Trust* [2003] 3 All ER 932). However, aspects of several different torts do have the effect of protecting a person's privacy, provided the specific ingredients of that tort are satisfied. Moreover, one of the effects of the Human Rights Act 1998 is to make it easier for a claimant to sue in respect of the wrongful disclosure of private information.

At common law it appears that harassment is not a discrete tort (*Kaye v Robertson* [1991] FSR 62; *Patel v Patel* [1988] 2 FLR 179) nor does it fall within the scope of the intentional torts against the person.

The tort of private nuisance, in certain circumstances, may provide a solution. In *Hunter v Canary Wharf* [1997] 2 All ER 426 it was held that an act of harassment might amount to a private nuisance if there was an unreasonable interference with the claimant's proprietary interest in the land subject to the act of harassment, however that action would not protect a person with no protected proprietary interest. In any event, *Hunter* was not concerned with the tort of harassment, but with the proper scope of the tort of private nuisance. Since the decision in *Hunter* it has been suggested in *McKenna v British Aluminium Ltd* [2002] Env LR 30, that a person with no proprietary interest might have an arguable case under the Human Rights Act 1988 if there is an interference with family and private life.

The issue of whether there is a common law tort of harassment has since become academic due to the intervention of Parliament in the form of the Protection from Harassment Act 1997, considered below.

It is also clear that nuisance is not alone in restricting the number of citizens to whom protection from non-tangible interferences is afforded. To begin with, assault is said to depend upon the direct infliction of a reasonable apprehension of a battery (*Thomas v NUM* [1986] Ch 20). This means that if the defendant's wrongdoing consists of persistent abusive telephone calls then it would not be possible for the claimant to allege that he or she was reasonably fearful of the immediate infliction of a battery, as he or she must (*Cole v Turner* (1704) 6 Mod Rep 149). It was for this reason that, in *Thomas*, the claimant, who was on a coach and behind a police cordon, failed to make out reasonable fear of an impending battery. It is the absence of any prospect of violation of the claimant's physical integrity which dictates that assault fails to cover a clear interference.

Similarly, the tort known as the rule in *Wilkinson v Downton* [1897] 2 QB 57 insists that the defendant must have 'wilfully done an act calculated to cause harm to the claimant'. This fails to cover cases in which harm is indirectly inflicted where the defendant occasions the claimant harm through good intentions (albeit according to *Wilkinson* an objective view of the defendant's intention is taken). Thus, it has been held that no tort of intentional infliction of harm is committed where fellow office workers behave in a rude and unfriendly manner with the result that the claimant suffers physical and psychiatric illness as a result of that conduct, provided it was not calculated to cause the illness (see *Wong v Parkside Health NHS Trust* [2003] 3 All ER 932).

The difficulty with the wording of the principle in *Wilkinson* is that if the words are uttered affectionately, or as a joke, how can it be said that there is an intention to cause harm? The required state of mind on the part of the defendant was considered by the Court of Appeal and the House of Lords in *Wainwright v Home Office* [2003] 3 WLR 1137 affirming [2002] QB 1334. In that case, the claimants had been strip-searched before they were allowed to go on a prison visit. It was accepted that the prison officers had acted in good faith, albeit sloppily and in doing so, had caused humiliation. However, they had not intended to cause humiliation. In the Court of Appeal, Lord Woolf CJ appeared to accept as a principle, that the defendant must have acted in a manner that he knew was unjustified or, at least, not care whether or not he caused harm ([2002] QB 1334, 1350). In the House of Lords, Lord Hoffmann wished to reserve judgment on the question whether a genuine intention to cause distress was actionable ([2003] 3 WLR 1137, 1149). Accordingly, it was held that there is no common law tort protecting the privacy of an individual from a one-off event that causes distress or anxiety and it is necessary for there to be a course of conduct in order to invoke the Protection from Harassment Act 1997.

Thus far we have seen that interferences in the nature of harassing conduct fall outside the ambit of all the relevant (i.e. non-contact based) intentional torts against the person. Harassment has, however, received limited protection under statute. The Protection from Harassment Act 1997 provides for the civil law remedies of damages or an injunction for harassing conduct but only where that conduct has proven injurious effects (either in terms of health or in terms of resulting financial loss: s. 3(2)). Similarly, one-off incidents are not protected by the Act for 'harassment', for the purposes of the statute, demands that the conduct complained of should have occurred on at least two occasions (s. 7(3)).

Leaving aside non-tangible forms of harm, we must also consider the limits of the torts of false imprisonment and battery. In relation to the former, it has never been authoritatively settled whether the claimant needs to be conscious of the fact of their imprisonment in order to be able to sue. The authorities that are directly in point are divided on the matter (compare *Herring v Boyle* (1834) 1 Cr M & R

377 and *Meering v Graham-White Aviation* (1920) 122 LT 44) and there is only *obiter* authority from the House of Lords that such knowledge is not required (*Murray v MOD* [1988] 2 All ER 521). Technically, then, the matter is still open to resolution at common law. On this basis, it is legitimate to argue that English law does not at present cater adequately for the insane, unconscious, or immature claimant who is 'wrongly' imprisoned by another.

On the final point—the shortcoming in the law of battery—the matter is again one in which English law flounders in the absence of clear authority. It is this. Where A attempts to strike B but instead strikes C, it is, technically, unresolved whether A commits a battery against C. The problem centres on the fact that whilst it is clear that battery is an intentional tort (*Stephens v Myers* (1830) 4 C & P 349) it is by no means clear whether the intention must relate to the conduct (i.e. striking out) or the outcome (in our case, making violent contact with C). Although it is possible that the notion of transferred intent which exists in the criminal law may be adapted to fit the tortious counterpart of a criminal assault (i.e. a tortious battery), on present authorities, English law is uncertain in the extent to which it would protect C in the hypothetical example advanced.

The protection of a person's right to privacy has to be reconsidered in the light of the **Human Rights Act (HRA) 1998** which requires, where possible, that legislation must be interpreted in a way that is compatible with rights provided for in the **European Convention on Human Rights (HRA, s. 3)**. Furthermore, it is also provided that it is unlawful for a public authority to act in a manner that is incompatible with a Convention right (**HRA, s. 6**). One of the rights provided for in the Convention is a right to respect for private and family life (**ECHR, art. 8**). This might suggest that the restrictive approach to the issue of privacy adopted at common law might change, at least where the actions of public authorities are concerned. This raises the question of what constitutes a public authority. Clearly, actions on the part of the Home Office would fit this description, but the Convention also covers 'persons whose functions are functions of a public nature' (**HRA, s. 6(3)(b)**). This would include the actions of universities, schools and local authorities, but, arguably, might also include a tabloid newspaper, insofar as information provision can be regarded as a 'public function'.

In *Campbell v MGN Ltd* [2004] 2 WLR 1232 a newspaper published a story to the effect that Ms Campbell was a drug addict, seeking treatment through Narcotics Anonymous. The report was also accompanied by a photograph of Ms Campbell leaving a Narcotics Anonymous meeting. It was accepted that the facts relating to drug addiction and its treatment could be published, but it was contended that the publication of the photograph amounted to the commission of a tort. The House of Lords were unanimous that X will commit a tort if he unjustifiably discloses to Y information about Z (the claimant) that X knows or ought to know is private information. By a majority of 3 to 2, the House of Lords held that MGN Ltd had committed this tort, which has its roots in the equitable wrong of breach of confidence, but is not constrained by some of the limits applicable to the long-established equitable wrong (see *Theakston v MGN* [2002] EMLR 137).

The new tort requires the courts to perform an unusual balancing act in that it straddles two distinct human rights. On the one hand X, in the example above, has a right to freedom of expression (ECHR, art. 10), while Z has a right not to have private information about him unjustifiably disclosed to a third party (ECHR, art. 8), and it is the balance between these two articles that forms the content of the new tort: *McKennitt v Ash* [2007] 3 WLR 194 at [11] *per* Buxton LJ. Thus a court will be faced with difficult questions such as how private is the information and how important is it that this aspect of the claimant's privacy should be protected? On the other side it will be necessary to ask whether, in disclosing the information to Y, X was expressing himself. If this is the case, it must then be asked how important is it not to restrict X's right to do so?

In determining what is private information, Lord Nicholls and Baroness Hale considered that the test to apply is whether the claimant has a reasonable expectation that his or her privacy be protected. However, this is a difficult test to apply because of its circularity, and in other jurisdictions a test based on the reasonable person's reaction to publication has been used (see *Australian Broadcasting Corp v Lenah Game Meats* (2001) 208 CLR 199, [99] *per* Gleeson CJ). However, the 'reasonable person's reaction test' may be criticized on the ground that it may not work where the information relates to a disturbed adult or a very young child (see *T v BBC* [2007] EWHC 1683; *Murray v Express Newspapers plc* [2008] EWCA Civ 446).

An important consideration is whether or not the information is of a type that the claimant would want to control the dissemination of (*Campbell v MGN* [2004] 2 WLR 1232 at [51] *per* Lord Hoffmann). It would appear that information related to a person's sexuality or his or her health, information that has been stored secretly, such as that in a private diary, information supplied consequent to a confidential relationship and, perhaps, financial information will normally fall within this reasonable expectation test. However, some such information may have become so widely available that the claimant can no longer claim to have a reasonable expectation of controlling its dissemination (*Lord Browne of Madingley v Associated Newspapers Ltd* [2007] 3 WLR 289).

On the other side of the balance, it needs to be determined what constitutes freedom of expression. For these purposes, political speech in a democratic society is most deserving of protection. Other factors to consider include whether or not it is in the public interest to disclose the information. Some guidance on this matter may be found in the Press Complaints Commission's Code of Practice which indicates that the public interest includes (a) detecting or exposing crime or a serious demeanour, (b) protecting health and safety and (c) preventing the public from being misled by some statement or action of an individual or organization. In interpreting the first of these public interest factors, it would appear that the crime alleged to have been committed must be of a serious nature and will not include sexual misconduct which does not involve a significant breach of the criminal law (*Mosley v News Group Newspapers Ltd* [2008] EWHC 1777).

Moreover, it would appear that public figures, including famous football players and other types of celebrity may have to expect a greater degree of exposure as they have chosen to place themselves in the 'public eye' especially if the 'celebrity' has made untrue public denials relating to extra-marital affairs (see *A v B & C* [2003] QB 195). However, the decision in *Campbell* does indicate that public figures cannot always expect information of any type concerning their private lives to be publishable.

Further reading

Atiyah, P. S., and Stapleton J., 'Tort, Insurance and Ideology' (1995) 58 MLR 820.

Atiyah, P. S., *The Damages Lottery* (Oxford: Hart Publishing, 1997), ch. 8.

Burrows, A., 'Dividing the Law of Obligations', ch. 1 in *Understanding the Law of Obligations* (Oxford: Hart Publishing, 1998).

Bamforth, N., 'The Application of the Human Rights Act 1998 to Public Authorities and Private Bodies' (1999) CLJ 159.

Buxton, R., 'The Human Rights Act and Private Law' (2000) 116 LQR 48.

Cane, P., *The Anatomy of Tort Law* (Oxford: Hart Publishing, 1997), ch. 6, especially pp. 181–6 and 201–4.

Cane, P., *The Anatomy of Tort Law* (Oxford: Hart Publishing, 1997), ch. 7 'Anatomy, Functions and Effect'.

Cane, P., *Atiyah's Accidents: Compensation and the Law?* (Cambridge: Cambridge University Press, 2006), chs 16 and 19.

Cane, P., *Tort Law and Economic Interests* (Oxford: Clarendon Press, 1996), ch. 10, 'The Province and Aims of Tort Law'.

Holyoak, J., 'Contract and Tort after *Junior Books*' (1983) 99 LQR 591.

Lawson-Cruttenden, T., and Addison, N., Protection from Harassment Act 1997 (Oxford: OUP), ch. 3.

McBride, N., and Bagshaw, R., *Tort Law*, 3rd edn (Harlow: Pearson/Longman, 2008), ch. 15.

Moreham, N., 'Privacy in the Common Law: A Doctrinal and Theoretical Analysis' (2005) 121 LQR 628.

Morgan, J., 'Tort, Insurance and Incoherence' (2004) 67 MLR 384.

Smith, S., *Contract Theory* (Clarendon Law Series) (Oxford: OUP 2004), pp. 43–6, 72–4 and 96–7.

Whittaker, S., 'The application of the broad principle of Hedley-Byrne as between parties to a contract' (1997) 17 LS 169.

Williams, G., 'The Aims of the Law of Tort' (1951) CLP 137.

3

Trespass to the person

Introduction

Trespass to the person is one of the oldest torts and overlaps with the criminal law. Many of the wrongs which amount to a trespass to the person also amount to the commission of a crime, but be careful not to introduce Criminal Law concepts into answers on Tort. These torts are fault-based and require proof of intention; they are also actionable *per se*, that is, there is no need for the claimant to prove that damage has been suffered. Instead, it is sufficient that the defendant has infringed the claimant's interest in bodily integrity. However, the fact that there has been no damage may be relevant in determining the remedy. The interest primarily protected by the torts of battery, assault and false imprisonment is the right of the individual to respect for bodily integrity. As such these are 'civil liberties' torts and have lost a lot of their importance due to the rise of the tort of negligence in the field of accident compensation. The three questions which follow cover a range of issues arising out of all three of the torts amounting to trespass to the person, as well as considering the possibility of liability arising under the principle in the case of *Wilkinson v Downton* [1897] 2 QB 57, a principle the relevance of which has been diminished in recent cases.

Question 1

Harry, a young man of dishevelled appearance is passing the time of day with his friend Terry, both sharing a bottle of cheap sherry.

Gino, accompanied by his 15-year-old daughter, Bella, passes by on the other side of the street and makes loud derogatory comments on Harry's and Terry's appearance. Harry moves towards Gino, shouting obscenities and brandishing the bottle in a menacing manner, but is unable to cross the road due to the volume of traffic.

Gino returns ten minutes later, carrying a baseball bat. Gino takes a swing at Harry, but misses and strikes Terry instead, rendering him unconscious. Harry, fearing for his own safety, strikes Gino over the head with his bottle, which breaks, causing a splinter of glass to cut Bella, who runs home. David, a witness to these events, grabs Harry by the neck and restrains him by means of a stranglehold until PC Plod arrives. Terry, still unconscious, is taken to hospital where Dr John decides that emergency surgery is necessary, entailing a blood transfusion, to which Terry would have objected on religious grounds had he been conscious.

Bella is taken to hospital by her mother, Sophia. Dr John advises Sophia that it would be wise for Bella to have an antibiotic injection. Bella objects because she is vehemently opposed to all drugs that have been developed using animal testing, but Sophia tells Dr John to ignore her daughter's objections. Accordingly, Dr John arranges for the injection to be given.

Advise all the parties of their potential liabilities in trespass to the person.

Commentary

The principal issues raised by this question relate to the torts of assault and battery, and relevant defences. Battery and assault should be treated discretely e.g. all events that might be batteries should be dealt with and explained at the same time. This has the advantage of avoiding repetition. A problem of this nature demands a close analysis of each tort with specific emphasis to the point raised by the facts e.g. there is a distinction to be drawn between the derogatory comments and the threats. There is only limited scope for addressing false imprisonment so a brief reference to this will suffice – sufficient to reveal that you know the core elements and how it overlaps with battery. The rubric precludes discussion of negligence so there is no need to stray into that area. Logically, the defences fall to be discussed and applied only when the substance of the torts has been established.

Answer plan

- State the core elements of battery and assault.
- Distinguish battery from assault.
- Identify and discuss capacity to carry out the threat and imminence of the harm threatened.
- Discuss the core content of battery.
- Identify the notion of transferred intent.
- Consider the ingredients of self-defence.
- Consider the possibility of lawful arrest.
- Discuss the role of consent and necessity in relation to medical battery.

Suggested answer

Trespass to the person comprises three torts: assault, battery and false imprisonment. These torts involve intentional acts (but not omissions) and are actionable without proof of harm.

Harry's threatening attitude towards Gino and Gino's swinging of the baseball bat require consideration of assault, which is defined as an act which causes another person to apprehend the infliction of immediate, unlawful, force on his person (*Collins v Wilcock* [1984] 3 All ER 374). Gino's comments are unlikely to convey the threat of harm and when Harry utters obscenities in response to Gino's comments, it may be that the content of his words is insufficient to amount to a threat. Until recently, there was no clear legal authority that words alone could constitute an assault. Dicta went both ways (see *Meade's case* (1823) 1 Lew CC 184 (no assault); *R v Wilson* [1955] 1 WLR 493 (assault)). The House of Lords in *R v Ireland* [1997] 4 All ER 225 took the view that even a silent phone call could amount to an assault and suggested that words spoken amount to the doing of something. In that case the making of the call coupled with either words or silence was capable of amounting in law to an assault. Accordingly it is now clear that the use of words alone may be an assault taking into account all the surrounding circumstances. What is clear is that where there are words accompanied by a threatening act or gesture, as in the question, there can be an assault (*Read v Coker* (1853) 13 CB 850).

So, if Harry's words and actions are capable of amounting in law and in fact to an assault, there remains the issue that there cannot be an assault unless the threat is immediate and gives rise to a reasonable apprehension of the imminent infliction of a battery. Thus a threat, no matter how violent, cannot be an assault if the claimant does not reasonably fear for his own safety because, for example, he is sitting safely on board a moving bus (*Thomas v N.U.M. (South Wales Area)* [1986] Ch 20). In this case, the claimant was on a bus full of working miners during the miners' strike. Although the threats from striking pickets were violent and extremely threatening, there could be in law no reasonable apprehension of immediate battery due to the safety of the bus and the presence of a police escort. In the problem, the barrier posed by the volume of traffic on the road dividing Harry from Gino may suggest that there is no reason to believe that a battery was imminent.

Of course, when Gino returns with the baseball bat and takes a swing at Harry there may well be an assault as it would be reasonable for Harry to anticipate an immediate battery in the circumstances. In this circumstance the swing may also be an assault on Terry who receives the blow.

Battery is defined as 'the actual infliction of unlawful force on another person' (*Collins v Wilcock* [1984] 3 All ER 374), and requires a direct intentional contact. Thus in this problem the potential batteries are first, when Gino strikes Terry with the baseball bat (and, depending on whether Terry was aware of the impending impact, this could be an assault), secondly the use of the bottle, thirdly the arrest, and fourthly the interventions by the doctor. In all of these instances there are intentional direct acts resulting in contact, that go well beyond anything that could be regarded as acceptable in everyday life, thus rendering any detailed analysis of the possible meaning of 'hostility' (*Wilson v Pringle* [1986] **2 All ER 440**, *per* Croom-Johnston LJ and Lord Goff's view in *F v West Berkshire Health Authority* [1989] **2 All ER 545**) somewhat redundant.

Even if hostility is an element in battery (a view rejected by Lord Goff) the use of a baseball bat is clearly motivated by hostility. On the other hand it would be difficult to characterize the involvement of the doctor as hostile as expressly recognized by Lord Goff. The better view seems to be that all that is required is an intentional contact (not intentional harm) and that hostility is not a necessary element in battery.

It would seem, then, that the problem in the question is one of intention. Gino intends to hit Harry, but in fact strikes Terry. It is important to remember that for trespass, the intention should relate to the act rather than to the consequences of the act. But there still remains the undecided issue of whether English tort law recognizes the notion of transferred intent. This concept is recognized in English criminal law: *R v Latimer* (1886) 17 QBD 359 and in the civil law of the USA, but there is no direct authority for the purposes of tort law, save for the old decision in *Scott v Shepherd* (1773) 2 Bl R 892 (which considered the meaning of directness of harm for the purposes of the old pleadings on trespass or an action on the case) and dicta in the Northern Irish case, *Livingstone v Ministry of Defence* [1984] NI 356. But it seems logical that if Gino intends to strike Harry he should also be liable in damages for the infringement of Terry's personal security.

It is unlikely that Gino can successfully plead self-defence. This defence requires that the actions in self-defence should be proportionate to the threat. Although this will not be measured using fine measuring techniques, the use of an offensive weapon is probably out of proportion to the threat posed by a bottle in the hands of two abusive delinquents who were on the other side of a busy street. And, in any event the events occur some time after the event when the threat, if any, has disappeared. A modern example is *Cross v Kirby* (2000) *The Times,* 5 April where the defendant was attacked by the claimant (a baseball bat wielding anti-hunt protestor). After having been struck several blows he wrestled the bat from the claimant and struck him with it, fracturing his skull. The Court of Appeal held that the trial judge had weighed the conduct too finely and that the use of force was not disproportionate.

On the other hand, Harry's response to the threat posed by Gino may be justified in self-defence. In light of the threat posed by a person wielding a baseball bat, it is possible that the use of a bottle may be regarded as proportionate and he may be taken to have acted reasonably in all the circumstances. *Cross v Kirby* is also relevant here.

There remain the issues of consent and public policy, which are relevant to the fight between Gino and Harry. It has been said that in the case of an ordinary fight with fists, none of the participants will be permitted an action for damages on the ground that they all consent to their injuries but that if the claimant's conduct is trivial and the defendant's conduct is totally out of proportion the defences referred to will not be available. This was the gist of *Lane v Holloway* [1968] 1 QB 379 where the response of the defendant was grossly excessive compared to the conduct of the plaintiff. That case also rejected provocation as a defence; as here the perceived insult could not deprive Harry of his action in assault. Moreover, a person who sets out to attack another but who 'gets more than he bargained for', as seems to be the case with Gino, may also find his claim barred on grounds of public policy (*Murphy v Culhane* [1977] QB 94). The so-called 'illegality defence', or *ex turpi causa non oritur actio*, operates to prevent a successful action by an individual whose claim depends for its success on an unlawful act of the claimant of a very serious nature. As a matter of public policy the courts will not be seen to be supporting a claim in such circumstances (*Murphy v Culhane*; *Cross v Kirby* (2000) *The Times*, 5 April, CA). Lastly, despite the fact that, prior to the enactment of the Law Reform (Contributory Negligence) Act 1945, it was disputed whether the defence of contributory negligence applied to the tort of trespass, it was held in *Barnes v Nayer* that a claimant's contributory negligence can amount to fault for the purposes of the 1945 Act.

Applying a stranglehold is capable of amounting to a battery, and if it constitutes an 'unlawful imposition of constraint on another's freedom of movement from a particular place' (*Collins v Wilcock*) it may be a false imprisonment. The circumstances suggest that David does this by way of a citizen's arrest and a trespass is only actionable if unlawful. The Police and Criminal Evidence Act 1984 (PACE) excuses a private individual who makes an arrest when correctly exercising the powers in PACE, s. 24A. This provides that a person other than a police officer may arrest a person actually committing or reasonably suspected of committing an indictable offence. If an indictable offence has been committed then the citizen may arrest the person who committed it or who he reasonably believes committed it. A serious assault on an individual is an indictable offence and it is reasonably clear that an offence has been committed as David has witnessed the events. PACE, s. 24A also sets out further conditions which include that arrest is necessary to prevent injury to another or to prevent the suspect escaping, and that it is not practicable to wait for a police officer to make the arrest. Under PACE, s. 28, the person arrested must be told that he is under arrest and the reason for his arrest, either at the time, or as soon as practicable thereafter. If the arrest is made by a person who is not a constable, as here, the common law rule is that the arrested person does not have to be informed of the reason for his arrest if the circumstances make the reason obvious – in *Christie v Leachinsky* [1947] AC 573 the House of Lords suggested that this would be so if someone were caught red-handed. As *John Lewis & Co Ltd v Tims* [1952] AC 676 shows once the arrest is complete, the arrested person must be taken before a magistrate or to a police officer as soon as is reasonably possible; failure to do so will make the arrester liable in false imprisonment. All of these requirements seem to be satisfied with the result that David probably has not committed a tort. But, the conditions set out in s. 24 A are very strict and a citizen arrests at their peril.

Another power which would serve to excuse David is the power at common law to restrain someone to prevent an actual or reasonably apprehended imminent breach of the peace, or renewal of a breach of the peace. *R v Howell* [1981] 3 All ER 383 defined breach of the peace as involving violence and identified that there was a power of arrest. In addition, there is a right in a citizen to take reasonable steps to prevent an actual or imminent breach of the peace—as occurred in **Albert v Lavin** [1981] 3 All ER 878 where an off-duty police officer was held to be entitled to restrain someone who was a threat to the peace provided reasonable force was used and provided that the restraint was for no longer than necessary to prevent the threat to the peace. David seems to have used only reasonable force and for no longer than necessary to control the threat to the peace.

Dr John's surgical treatment of Terry is, *prima facie*, a battery within the definition given above, and the usual defence in relation to medical treatment—consent—is not an option since Terry is unconscious. Clearly, it would not be in the public interest for the treatment of patients incapable of consenting to be an actionable battery, so there must be some other justification. One might, for example, be able to construct some kind of argument based on implied consent, though the bounds of such consent might be hard to establish and the argument is bound to encounter problems when the patient would, in fact, have refused consent as in Terry's case. Alternatively, as was argued earlier, one could argue that the surgeon's action lacks the element of hostility identified by Croom-Johnson LJ as a crucial factor in *Wilson v Pringle*, though such an approach was rejected by Lord Goff in *F v West Berkshire Health Authority*. In that case the House of Lords explained the nature of the defence of necessity, which permits, in the case of an emergency concerning a temporarily incapacitated patient, such treatment as is necessary in order to save life, ensure improvement, or to prevent physical or mental deterioration, and no more (although that case concerned a patient who was permanently incapacitated). The scope of the intervention is to be tested according to the *Bolam* test used in considering the appropriate standard of care in medical cases. This approach is consistent with public policy, which recognizes a presumption in favour of the preservation of life. Since the operation on Terry is considered to be essential, the defence of necessity would seem to apply unless Dr John can be taken to have been aware of Terry's objection to receiving blood other than his own. On the facts, there is nothing to suggest that Dr John is aware of Terry's religious objections, in which case, his actions will probably be justified and excused.

The injury to Bella, though not intentional in the ordinary sense, may be a further battery if the same reasoning is applied as when Gino struck Terry, subject only to whether or not Harry is able to successfully plead that he was acting proportionately in self-defence. A further battery may occur when Dr John proceeds to administer an injection. Here, the defence of necessity is not appropriate as there are several potential sources of consent by which the act may be rendered lawful. First, there is parental consent by Sophia, Bella's mother. As Bella is 15 years old, and therefore a minor, her mother's consent is valid. Then there is Bella, herself. If Bella had been aged 16, she would be considered, in law, to have the capacity to give or withhold consent (**Family Law Reform Act 1969, s. 8(1)**). However, being aged only 15, this provision will provide no assistance; however, since *Gillick v West Norfolk & Wisbech Area Health Authority* [1986] AC 112, the courts have adopted a test based on the understanding of the child patient. Mrs Gillick sought judicial review of a policy that children under 16 could be given contraceptive advice without parental consent. The House of Lords said the issue was whether the minor had sufficient maturity and understanding of the treatment. Under this test, provided Bella was of sufficient maturity to understand what is involved in having an injection, she could consent for herself.

The situation in the problem, however, is complicated by the fact that Bella, far from agreeing, is withholding her consent. Dr John is faced with two opposing views, a consent (from the mother) and a refusal (from the patient, herself). In *Re R (a minor)* [1991] 4 All ER 177, a 15-year-old girl who suffered phases of disturbed behaviour had refused sedative treatment and wardship proceedings were commenced by a local authority. The Court of Appeal considered that a court has wider powers than a parent and can override a withholding of consent if this is in the patient's best interests, thereby seemingly undermining the *Gillick* principle of self-determination. It appeared from that case that there was some kind of balancing process to be undertaken, between the respective strengths of the child's refusal and the opposing consent. In *Re W (a minor) (medical treatment)* [1992] 4 All ER 627, Lord Donaldson reconsidered and rejected his analogy in *Re R* that those capable of giving consent could be regarded as 'keyholders', as this implied that the status of refusal was equal to that of consent. On reflection, he said that a better analogy was that of a 'flak jacket', since 'anyone who gives [a doctor] a flak jacket (i.e. consent) may take it back, but the doctor only needs one and so long as he continues to have one he has the legal right to proceed'. In the problem, provided Dr John has valid consent from Bella's mother he commits no battery on Bella.

Question 2

Eric had just won a darts game in the Dog & Duck public house. As he returned to his seat he was cheered on by his friends; Jockey, his opponent, slapped his shoulder in a hearty fashion to congratulate him on his victory. Eric was off balance at the time and tumbled over, injuring himself. Eric shouted at Jockey, 'You swine, you did that on purpose, I'll see you outside in two minutes.'

Fearing the worst, Sid, the owner of the Dog & Duck, grabbed Eric by the shirt collar and frog-marched him to his office. Eric resisted violently, aimed a punch at Sid, but missed.

Sid managed to calm Eric and persuaded him to remain in the office in order to avoid further trouble. Having left the office, Sid asked two burly friends, Peter and Phil, to ensure that Eric did not leave the ground floor room. Four hours later, Sid called the police. In the meantime, Eric slept off the effect of the alcohol and was unaware that Peter and Phil were there.

Consider whether or not any causes of action in trespass to the person are revealed by these facts.

Commentary

This question provides an opportunity to discuss elements of the three torts which cumulatively are described as trespass to the person together with a brief analysis of the defence of lawful justification. The rubric to the question deliberately steers you towards trespass and it would be wrong to deal with any other tort at length even though the first paragraph would seem to demand a treatment of negligence. Although the question tends to turn on its own facts there is scope for commenting on the principles underpinning the various versions of trespass to the person. The opening remarks in the answer may be used to conveniently summarize the common elements of the forms of trespass. By dealing with matters thematically much repetition can be avoided e.g. take all the possible instances of battery together, then all the instances of assault. Deal with the application of each tort or defence as you work your way systematically through the answer.

Answer plan

- Brief overview.
- Definition of battery.
- The requirement of intention.
- Definition of assault.
- Words alone as an assault.
- False imprisonment.
- Knowledge of the fact of imprisonment.
- Defences and the requirements for a lawful arrest.

Suggested answer

Trespass to the person is divided into three distinct torts (battery, assault, and false imprisonment) which have certain characteristics in common. The torts require acts rather than omissions ('not doing is no trespass': *Case of the Six Carpenters*

(1610) 8 Co Rep 146a), they are probably now capable of being committed only intentionally (see Lord Denning in *Letang v Cooper* [1965] 1 QB 232), by direct means and are complete without the need for proof of actual harm (actionable *per se*). The latter point makes the torts very effective as a means of controlling invasions of liberty (especially by those in authority).

What batteries are revealed by these facts?

Battery may be defined as the intentional application of direct force to the person which is undesired by the claimant. According to the House of Lords in *R v Ireland* [1997] 4 All ER 225 (*obiter* since the case concerned assault) a touching is still required. As Goff LJ showed in *Collins v Wilcock* [1984] 3 All ER 374 the simple touching of one person by another may be a battery and the extent of the force used is irrelevant to whether or not a battery is made out. In that case the simple holding of the arm of the defendant by the police officer was a battery which took the police officer outside the execution of her duty. But, battery now requires intention to touch, and, in the absence of intention, mere carelessness will not suffice: this is the view of the majority in *Letang v Cooper* in respect of the unintentional act of driving over the plaintiff's legs as she lay sunbathing. The historical development of trespass as demonstrated by cases such as *Stanley v Powell* [1891] 1 QB 86, *Fowler v Lanning* [1959] 1 All ER 290, and *Letang v Cooper* is that in an action in trespass the burden is on the claimant to demonstrate an intentional touching. Thus, for Eric to succeed in battery it would be necessary to demonstrate that Jockey and Sid intended the contact but need not show that he intended the harm which results. This was the approach to the point adopted by the Court of Appeal in *Wilson v Pringle* [1986] 2 All ER 440, the case where the schoolboy deliberately pulled the shoulder bag from his colleague causing the victim to fall to the ground and suffer injury. There is an argument derived from Diplock LJ in *Letang v Cooper* that it is possible to commit a battery carelessly, but the net result will be the same because the burden will be on the claimant to show carelessness and because the law requires proof of actual harm where carelessness is alleged. The point has most relevance in modern times for the application of the periods of limitation. These are shorter for negligence, nuisance, or breaches of duty (but extendable at the discretion of the court) than for other torts but the longer period cannot be extended. The House of Lords in *A v Hoare* [2008] UKHL 6 has now confirmed that an action in battery may be classed as a breach of duty so as to fall within the shorter but extendable period of limitation. This decision departed from the earlier decision of the House of Lords in another case of intentional sex abuse, *Stubbings v Webb* [1993] 1 All ER 322, which had led to unfairness and difficulty in practice.

On the face of it, slapping on the shoulder is a battery: there has been an intentional touching without the consent of the claimant. The law was clearly stated in *Collins v Wilcock* that the merest touching would suffice because the law could not be expected to distinguish between varying degrees of force. Goff LJ then made the point that this general principle was designed to protect the value that the law placed in the liberty of the subject and the inviolability of the human body. He then indicated that the broad principle was a starting point and there was a general exception to it to cover all touchings which were generally acceptable as part and parcel of everyday life. He gave examples of this type of contact, e.g. tapping someone on their shoulder to gain their attention. This approach was also adopted by Lord Goff in *F v West Berkshire Health Authority* [1989] 2 All ER 545, and he deprecated the attempt by Croom-Johnson LJ in *Wilson v Pringle* to introduce the concept of a hostile touching. The lack of content to 'hostile' and the circularity of Croom-Johnson's attempt (he described the touching in *Collins v Wilcock* as unlawful and therefore hostile and therefore a battery) mean that hostile intention is probably not a requirement for a battery. Lord Goff suggested, *obiter*, that such things as a prank that gets out of hand, an over-friendly slap on the back, or an operation where the surgeon mistakenly thinks that there is consent when there is none, could not be categorized as hostile but could still be held to be unlawful. So here it would have to be decided whether or not the contact went beyond general touching acceptable in everyday life.

Whether the grabbing of Eric by Sid and the frog-marching amounts to a battery will be tested by reference to the approach in *Collins v Wilcock*. It is likely that the type of touching goes beyond what is generally acceptable in everyday life, as indeed was the detention for questioning in that case. If this is so, Eric may have a defence, see later.

What assaults are revealed?

An assault may be defined as an act which causes another to apprehend the infliction of immediate, unlawful force on his person (see Goff LJ in *Collins v Wilcock*). Often it will accompany a battery but the two are not conjoined. For example, if I strike a sleeping person then there is no assault but there is a battery. If I threaten another but am prevented from carrying out the threat then provided the threat gives rise to a reasonable apprehension of the impending infliction of a battery, an assault will be complete. Thus, in the course of resisting violently, Eric aims a punch at Sid, but misses. The fact that there is no contact means that there cannot be a battery, but there is the possibility of an assault since a violent punch is likely to cause Sid to fear, quite reasonably, for his own safety.

Eric shouts abuse at Jockey and threatens to see him outside in two minutes. The words alone may be no more than mere abuse but may amount to an assault provided that they would arouse in a reasonable person the apprehension of the immediate infliction of a battery and do so. The contradictory *dicta* (no assault, see *Meade's case* (1823) 1 Lew CC 184; assault: *R v Wilson* [1955] 1 WLR 493) are rendered redundant in the light of the decision of the House of Lords in *R v Ireland* that a silent telephone call (as well as one where words are used) may be an assault where it creates the necessary element of apprehension in the mind of the claimant. In any case, Jockey would have to show that the words used and the general behaviour of Eric disclose an immediate threat. He does indicate that he wishes to speak with Jockey in two minutes' time but the whole of the behaviour has to be examined in the light of its impact on the claimant and a reasonable person. Thus, it is clear that the language used by the threatener will have to be examined to determine whether his words contain an immediate threat of violence or whether the words used negate the threatening nature of the rest of the defendant's language: *Turbervell v Savadge* (1669) 1 Mod Rep 3 where the defendant was held in essence to have said, 'I will not attack you now.'

Moreover, before anything can be done to carry out the threat, Sid intervenes to prevent any escalation. A threat, no matter how violent, cannot be an assault if the claimant does not fear for his own safety or if the person threatening is unable to carry out the threat and this is known to the claimant: *Thomas v N.U.M. (South Wales Area)* [1986] Ch 20. Accordingly, if Eric is safely in Sid's office there seems little for Jockey to fear.

Are there any false imprisonments?

In taking hold of Eric and frog-marching him into his office Sid may commit not only a battery but also a false imprisonment, and by detaining Eric in the office, he may also be committing false imprisonment. This is defined as the unlawful and total restraint of the person so that the person restrained is not at liberty to go where he pleases: *Meering v Grahame-White Aviation* (1919) 122 LT 44. In order to amount to a false imprisonment, the restraint must be total: *Bird v Jones* (1845) 7 QB 742 where the fact that the plaintiff could proceed by an alternative, albeit more lengthy, route meant that he had not been subject to a tort and was not justified in using force to make his way past an obstruction. This raises the issue whether there is any alternative and safe means of leaving the office such as an open window through which Eric can escape. The House of Lords in *R v Bournewood Community and Mental Health NHS Trust ex parte L* [1998] 1 All ER 634 has confirmed that there must be circumstances amounting to a factual detention of the claimant, although there were significant differences between the majority and minority on the facts of that case which concerned a voluntary mental health in-patient who would have been restrained had he attempted to leave a hospital and who was subject to ongoing supervision. This was not held to be false imprisonment.

On the facts, Eric does not know that if he tries to leave the office, he will be prevented from doing so by Peter and Phil. It must be considered whether a claimant must be aware of the fact of restraint in order for the tort to be committed. The House of Lords in *Murray v Minister of Defence* [1988] 1 WLR 692 resolved the conflict between two earlier cases and decided this point in favour of the view that the claimant need not know of the fact of restraint. The House of Lords described the decision in *Herring v Boyle* (1834) 149 ER 1126 as extraordinary; this was the case where the mother twice went to school to collect her son but the headmaster refused to allow her to do so because the fees had not been paid. The son was not aware of what was going on and the equivalent of the Court of Appeal held that in the absence of knowledge there was no false imprisonment. The House of Lords preferred the approach of Atkin LJ in *Meering v Grahame-White* (even though the decision was *per incuriam* since the Court of Appeal omitted to consider the binding decision in *Herring's* case). This case concerned the detention of the plaintiff in an office pending the arrival of the police. Security guards had been placed there after he had gone into the room to wait and he was unaware that he would have been detained had he tried to leave. Lord Atkin concluded that this amounted to false imprisonment in the same way as someone could be falsely imprisoned when asleep, or drunk or insane, or only an infant. The other members of the Court of Appeal were not consistent with their view of the facts as to when the detention commenced.

The House of Lords concluded that there were good policy reasons why the tort should continue to protect the claimant even though they were unaware of the fact of detention. This analysis suggests that the basic elements of false imprisonment are made out, but the other important element is that the arrest must be unlawful.

What defences are available to Eric?

Under the **Police and Criminal Evidence Act 1984** (as amended) two defences are available. The first is under **s. 24A(1)**: any person may arrest without a warrant anyone who is or whom he has reasonable grounds to suspect to be committing an indictable offence. The second is under **s. 24A(2)**: anyone can arrest without a warrant a person where an indictable offence has been committed and that person has reason to believe the person arrested has committed that offence. The first offers more protection to the citizen since it may be based on reasonable grounds. The second offers a very limited protection to the claimant and it depends upon an indictable offence having been committed. The power of arrest is also subject to further conditions such as the need to prevent injury. It would seem that realistically, no indictable offence within the Act has been or is reasonably suspected of being committed. In any event, first, what Sid does falls short of arrest since it fails to comply with the requirements of **s. 28** as regards the required statement on arrest, and, secondly, what he does is based on persuasion rather than the element of coercion inherent in an arrest. Further, in the case of arrest by a citizen the arrested person must be taken before a magistrate or given over to a police officer as soon as is reasonably possible: *John Lewis & Co Ltd v Tims* [1952] AC 676. The delay would render any arrest unlawful and remove the justification for the detention.

The only other power available to Eric would be the power under the common law to deal with actual or reasonably apprehended breaches of the peace: see *Albert v Lavin* [1981] 3 All ER 878. If Eric's behaviour gives rise to a threat to the peace then the consequent detention may be lawful provided it is not for an unreasonable period. Breach of the peace involves violence or the threat of violence (*R v Howell* [1981] 3 All ER 383) and in response to this the citizen is entitled to do what is reasonable to deal with it, e.g. to detain the person, as happened in *Albert v Lavin*. But, what is done must be reasonable and the delay of four hours may well take the action beyond what is reasonable and turn a justified detention into a false imprisonment.

Question 3

During a party at Yasser's house, Barney, a house guest and known prankster, jumped from the doorway in a darkened corridor, with a sheet over his head just as Wilma, another guest, was passing but he did not make physical contact with her. Wilma fainted with shock and banged her head causing bruising. Barney carried her into a room and left her there to recover. Yasser saw Barney leave the room and, fearing that someone might tamper with his valuable stamp collection in that room, he locked the door.

One hour later, Barney went to see if Wilma had recovered, but found the door locked. Barney asked Yasser for the key, having explained what had happened. Yasser said he was too busy, but that he would open the door later on.

Thirty minutes later Yasser and Barney went to the room and found Wilma asleep. Barney shook her. Wilma awoke, and believing she was being attacked, struck violently at Barney with a poker from the fireplace. Barney suffered a fractured skull.

Consider the potential liability of the parties in trespass to the person and the principle in *Wilkinson v Downton*.

Commentary

This question centres on the constituent elements of the intentional torts relating to trespass to the person: assault; battery; and false imprisonment. The question does call for some comment on the principles underpinning the various torts. But the question also requires an explanation of the principle in *Wilkinson v Downton*. When dealing with this principle the answer should show how it has undergone a major examination by the Court of Appeal in *Wong v Parkside Health NHS Trust* and more importantly by the House of Lords in *Wainwright v Home Office* which has placed the tort firmly within the family of intentional infliction of harm, although not a trespass. Deal with each tort distinctly e.g. all the possible batteries should be examined together. The question does make a highlight of the defence of self-defence and this will require a competent knowledge of the decision of the House of Lords in *Ashley v Chief Constable* [2008] UKHL 25 which has established the principles governing self-defence and mistake of facts.

Answer plan

- Brief description of the relevant torts.
- The content of assault.
- *Wilkinson v Downton*.
- The content of battery.
- The requisite intent.
- False imprisonment and awareness of the fact of detention.
- Omissions.
- Defence of necessity.
- Self-defence.

Suggested answer

Trespass to the person is divided into three distinct torts (battery, assault, and false imprisonment) which have certain characteristics in common. The torts require acts rather than omissions ('not doing is no trespass': *Case of the Six Carpenters* (1610) 8 Co Rep 146a), they are probably now capable of being committed only intentionally (see Lord Denning in *Letang v Cooper* [1965] 1 QB 232), by direct means and are complete without the need for proof of actual harm (actionable *per se*). The latter point makes the torts very effective as a means of controlling invasions of liberty (especially by those in authority). The principle in *Wilkinson v Downton* [1897] 2 QB 57 as currently explained by the House of Lords in *Wainwright v Home Office* requires an intention to cause harm but differs from trespass in that the harm will arise indirectly.

Will an action lie in assault in respect of the prank where Barney jumps out? Assault has been defined as an act that causes another to apprehend the infliction of immediate, unlawful force on his person (*Collins v Wilcock*) so the question here is whether or not Wilma was placed in such a fear. If she was then she may succeed in assault. Although Barney may well say that he did not intend any harm; in line with the view on battery intention in harm is not relevant. Barney may also say that he was hostile, it was a joke. But, again in line with battery (see later) hostility is not an element and the action should be judged objectively.

It may also be possible to establish that in respect of Barney's prank an action may lie under the rule in *Wilkinson v Downton* even though more harm resulted than was intended. Thus, in *Janvier Sweeney* [1919] 2 KB 316, some harm had been intended but greater harm resulted. In *Wainwright v Home Office* [2003] 4 All ER 969, the House of Lords has now held that liability under this rule is dependent upon an actual intention to cause harm and it may well be the case that Barney was merely engaging in well intentioned horseplay so as to contribute to the party atmosphere. The problem with the law at the time of *Wilkinson v Downton* was that psychiatric injury was not recoverable under the law of negligence. The court therefore had to adopt the convoluted terminology of conduct 'calculated to cause harm' to ensure that recovery was permissible. These problems were no longer the case at the time of *Janvier v Sweeney*, but that was a case where some harm through terror was intended. The principle remains useful in so far as indirect intended harm is concerned, and a case such as *Wilkinson v Downton* itself might be decided the same way, although the negligence route would be as useful. To recover under the principle it would have to be shown that Barney had actually intended to cause harm to Wilma even though this might have occurred indirectly. But here the problem may be whether or not the faint would be sufficient harm for these purposes. The House of Lords in *Wainwright* confirmed that anything less than actual physical damage or psychiatric damage was unlikely to be recoverable under the principle in *Wilkinson v Downton* and neither Lord Hoffmann nor Lord Scott were keen to see the tort extended.

Battery is the intentional application of direct force to the person which is undesired by the claimant. According to the House of Lords in *R v Ireland* a touching is still required and the House deprecated the attempt in the Court of Appeal in that case to class as a battery a psychiatric injury caused by a series of silent telephone calls. As Goff LJ showed in *Collins v Wilcock*, the simple, intentional touching of one person by another may be a battery and the extent of the force used is irrelevant to whether or not a battery is made out. The general principle is that for the defendant's conduct to amount to battery, it must have been a direct and intentional act of touching (*Letang v Cooper*, approved in *Wilson v Pringle* [1986] 2 All ER 440, CA). Professor Rogers has expressed the view that the net result of these cases has been the disappearance of actions for unintentional trespass (Rogers, W. V. H., *Winfield and Jolowicz on Tort* (London: Sweet & Maxwell, 2006), p. 121). As there was no initial physical contact with Wilma no battery has been committed by Barney at that stage.

On the other hand, there was some physical contact between them when Barney picked her up and, later, when he shook her, and Wilma may have an action for battery in respect of these touching no matter how slight unless a defence applies. In *Cole v Turner* (1704) 6 Mod 149, Holt CJ said that 'the least touching of another in anger is a battery'. The Court of Appeal in *Wilson v Pringle*, held that for an action in battery to succeed, the 'touching must be proved to be hostile touching'. The requirement of hostility, and more particularly its meaning, has generated controversy. This view is inconsistent with the earlier comments of Goff LJ in *Collins v Wilcock* [1984] 3 All ER 374 and the later comments of Lord Goff in *F v West Berkshire Health Authority* [1989] 2 All ER 545). These were that there was a general principle that all touchings no matter how slight were capable of amounting to battery but that this was subject to the general defences and to the general exception in respect of all touching acceptable as part and parcel of every day life. The view of Lord Goff is preferable given the *lack* of clarity as to what is meant by hostility and that the only explanation of this in *Wilson v Pringle* was largely circuitous. Lord Goff questioned whether there is any requirement that the physical contact must be hostile and he stated that a prank that gets out of hand, or an over-friendly slap on the back could amount to battery even though they are not hostile acts. Similarly, a person who pushes another into a swimming pool by way of a joke would also be liable for battery (*Williams v Humphrey* (1975) *The Times*, 20 February). On this basis, Barney could be liable unless he is able to show that picking Wilma up as a consequence of the prank was 'generally acceptable in the ordinary conduct of daily life'. Similarly, when Barney shook Wilma, the gentleness of the shake is not the key point. This is whether the shake could be described as contact generally acceptable in everyday life. In *Mepstead v DPP* the gentle holding of the arm of a motorist to calm him down when a fixed penalty notice had been given was not sufficient to amount to a battery and it remained generally acceptable as part of ordinary life.

Of course, when Wilma lashes out violently at Barney and causes substantial harm to him there is, on the face of it, a battery. The real issue there is the availability of self-defence, which will be discussed later.

False imprisonment has been defined as the unlawful imposition of constraint on another's freedom of movement from a particular place so that he is not at liberty to go where he pleases (*Collins v Wilcock*; *Meering v Grahame-White Aviation Co Ltd* (1920) 122 LT 44). The House of Lords in *R v Bournewood Community and Mental Health NHS Trust ex parte L* [1998] 1 All ER 634 has confirmed that there must be circumstances amounting to a factual detention of the claimant, although there were significant differences between the majority and minority on the facts of that case which concerned a voluntary mental health in-patient who would have been restrained had he attempted to leave a hospital. This was held not to be false imprisonment. Any restriction, in the absence of consent, on a person's right to leave a place will amount to false imprisonment. The restraint must be complete so that if there is a reasonable means of egress there is no imprisonment (*Bird v Jones* (1845) 7 QB 742).

It is a vexed question whether the tort requires an intention to imprison or simply an intention to do the act which causes the imprisonment in fact. Thus turning a key in a lock without checking if anyone is inside a room may or may not be an intentional imprisonment. The better view would be that the tort requires knowledge that someone is being imprisoned. When Yasser locks the door he appears to be unaware of Wilma's presence in the room and so false imprisonment is not committed at that time.

However, upon being informed of the situation by Barney, does his refusal to unlock the door amount to the false imprisonment of Wilma? Her liberty is restrained within an area delimited by Yasser.

But all trespasses involve acts not omissions and Yasser does nothing. The question of when something is an act and when it is an omission may be clouded, e.g. in *Fagan v Metropolitan Police Commissioner* where the defendant drove his car on to a police officer's foot (without the driver being aware of this) put the car into neutral, applied the handbrake, got out of the car and was then told by a police officer that the car was on his foot. He was charged with assaulting a constable in the execution of his duty. He was convicted because the court formed the view that the whole process amounted to an act and knowledge that the car was on the police officer's foot was present at the latter stage even though not at the start. There was a vigorous dissent when the judge said that the defendant had done nothing when told that the car was on the foot, and doing nothing is not trespass. The point may also be seen in *Herd v Weardale*, where, on the facts, there was no false imprisonment of a miner who for 30 minutes was refused permission to enter a lift and reach the surface during the course of his shift. He was eventually allowed to use the lift but the House of Lords held that he had not been falsely imprisoned because he had agreed to go down the pit for the duration of his shift. The House of Lords did not consider what would have been the position had there been a contractual obligation to allow him to use the lift and whether or not the breach of that duty would have been sufficient to amount to a positive act of trespass.

There is no requirement that Wilma should be aware of her detention so that if she in fact slept through it, an action will nevertheless lie. In *Meering v Graham-White Aviation Co Ltd*, Atkin LJ stated that the plaintiff's ignorance of his false imprisonment was irrelevant, so a person could be falsely imprisoned while unconscious or insane or otherwise unaware of his position. The problem with *Meering's* case was that it failed to take into account the binding authority of *Herring v Boyle* which had concluded the opposite. Either view is sustainable as a matter of principle, and the principle in *Herring* not only forms the basis of the Restatement of Torts in the United States but also was accepted by the Court of Appeal in Northern Ireland in *Murray v Ministry of Defence*. The House of Lords in that case then reversed the Court of Appeal's decision and preferred the view that the tort was designed to protect the liberty of the citizen and as such required that it should be complete without proof that the claimant was aware of the fact of detention. Thus, Wilma's unconsciousness does not prevent an action being made out. As was pointed out in *Murray v Ministry of Defence* [1988] 2 All ER 521, a claimant who is ignorant that she has been falsely imprisoned may receive only nominal damages since no harm would have been suffered.

Are any defences available to the parties? Undoubtedly the touching of Wilma by Barney when he picked her up amounts on the face of it to a battery, but was it justifiable? The only defence that seems to be relevant is that of necessity. This was explored in *F v West Berkshire Health Authority* and it was held in the case of the mentally deficient adult that the principle of necessity could operate to justify sterilization even though neither she nor anyone else was able to give or withhold consent to this treatment. The guiding principle was what was in the best interests of the patient judged according to the principle in *Bolam v Friern*

Hospital. On this basis the behaviour of Barney may be justified but it was held in *Rigby v Chief Constable of Northamptonshire* [1985] 2 All ER 985 (a case on trespass to land) that the defence of necessity cannot be relied on where the necessity derives from the tortious behaviour of the defendant. In that case the necessity to use violence to enter land did not stem from any negligence on the part of the defendant. If the original action of Barney was a tort then necessity may not be available as a defence.

As regards self-defence and Wilma, there are two distinct issues. Is self-defence available where there is a mistake as to the facts? What degree of force is available to the victim? In *Ashley v Chief Constable of Sussex Police* [2008] UKHL 25 the House of Lords addressed the first question. A police officer was part of a group of armed officers executing an arrest of the claimant's brother. The police officer mistakenly thought that he was under threat of attack and fired his weapon, killing the brother. There was a preliminary issue as to whether or not the case should be allowed to go for trial and, if so, what was the test which governed the use of violence in such circumstances. The House of Lords confirmed the decision of the Court of Appeal that the necessity must be judged on the facts as the defendant honestly believed them to be, but if he made a mistake of fact then it would have to be shown to be a reasonable mistake. Here the circumstances might suggest that it was reasonable to suppose that there was an attack in progress and there is no suggestion this was not an honest belief.

As regards the degree of force used, the law demands that this should be reasonable and proportionate to the perceived threat but the courts are keen to ensure that this is not weighed too finely. For example, in *Cross v Kirby* (2000) *The Times,* 5 April, the Court of Appeal held that a defendant who had been struck several times by a baseball bat wielding assailant had not reacted disproportionately by using the bat to strike the claimant, breaking his skull.

Further reading

Bailey-Harris, R., 'Pregnancy, Autonomy and Refusal of Medical Treatment' (1998) 114 LQR 550.

Bridge, C., 'Religious Beliefs and Teenage Refusal of Medical Treatment' (1999) 62 MLR 585.

De Cruz, P., 'Adolescent Autonomy, Detention for Medical Treatment and Re C' (1999) 62 MLR 595.

Johnson, A., 'Putting the cart before the horse? Privacy and the Wainwrights' (2004) 63 CLJ 15.

Seabourne, G., 'The Role of the Tort of Battery in Medical Law' (1994) 24 Anglo-Am LR 265.

Tan, F. K., 'A Misconceived Issue in the Tort of False Imprisonment' (1981) 44 MLR 166.

4

Negligence I: duty of care

Introduction

Modern tort law is dominated by the tort of negligence. The principal requirements of the tort are that the defendant should owe the claimant a duty of care, that there should be a breach of that duty and that breach of duty should cause actionable damage to the claimant which is not too remote.

The duty issue is primarily based on the notion of reasonable foresight of harm to the claimant. This involves foresight of harm occurring at all, and that this particular claimant should fall within the class of persons who could foreseeably be affected—a factor most usually referred to as proximity, describing the legal relationship between defendant and claimant. A further factor has evolved, namely that it should be 'fair just and reasonable' for a duty to be owed by the defendant to the claimant. This last factor allows a full range of policy considerations to be taken into account, not the least of which is the effect on the public at large were a duty to be found to exist.

As negligence as a tort has, over time, expanded beyond its original objective in compensating negligently inflicted personal injury and property damage, certain policy factors have become particularly relevant. In particular, where negligence is used by people seeking compensation in relation to economic losses, the courts have developed policy driven control devices to ensure that the tort does not run out of control into areas it was never intended to enter. Similarly, in cases of negligently inflicted psychiatric injury the courts have developed control mechanisms aimed at limiting the potentially vast numbers of claims from friends and relatives of a victim physically injured by the defendant's negligence.

(1) General principles

Question 1

'[T]he only necessary function performed by the duty of care concept in the present law is to deal with those cases where liability is denied not because of a lack of foreseeability, but for reasons of legal policy . . .'

(*Winfield & Jolowicz on Tort*)

Discuss.

Commentary

This question calls for a consideration whether reasonable foresight alone is a satisfactory test for determining when a duty of care is owed or whether, and, if so, in what circumstances, policy issues also play a part.

Answer plan

- The basis on which ***Donoghue v Stevenson*** was decided.
- The relationship between the elements of reasonable foresight of harm, proximity of relationship, policy and justice.
- The meaning of policy and the range of factors which may influence a decision on the duty issue for reasons of policy.
- How policy considerations affect different types of negligence action in different ways.

Suggested answer

This question is concerned with the requirements for the establishment of a duty of care in the tort of negligence. In particular, it requires discussion of the extent to which the criteria for the existence of a duty situation have changed since the time prior to *Donoghue v Stevenson* [1932] AC 562 when duty situations were identified by reference to the relationship between the parties and were limited in number (e.g. occupier/visitor, doctor/patient, employer/employee). Since that time, the tort of negligence has undergone substantial periods of change and in many situations the role of policy has become crucial in identifying when a duty of care is owed.

Donoghue v Stevenson established the principle that a defendant owes a claimant a duty of care if there is a relationship of neighbourhood in the sense that the claimant can be reasonably foreseen as likely to be affected by the defendant's act (or, in limited circumstances, omission). What this test does is to identify the person to whom a duty of care may be owed, but it says little about when or in what circumstances the duty is owed. A test based solely on reasonable foresight is not fully satisfactory in that it omits essentials and takes into account non-essential issues (*Yuen Kun Yeu v Attorney-General for Hong Kong* [1988] AC 175). Instead, the modern approach requires an incremental development of the duty issue by reference to or by analogy with established categories of recognized duty situation, as proposed by Brennan J in the High Court of Australia in *Sutherland Shire Council v Heyman* (1985) 60 ALR 1. Although in Australia, where this test was first set out, there appears to have been some degree of departure from the incremental approach, at least regarding the position of builders (see *Bryan v Moloney* (1995) 128 ALR 163).

The main considerations in a duty enquiry, following *Yuen Kun Yeu and Caparo plc v Dickman* [1990] 2 AC 605 are reasonable foresight of harm, proximity of relationship, and whether it is fair, just and reasonable to hold that the defendant owes the claimant a duty of care. Crucially, what is considered by the court to be fair, just and reasonable will be much influenced by questions of policy, especially any effect that a finding of liability in an individual case may have on the development of the law and on the wider public interest. Moreover, in appropriate cases, particularly those which fall within the general scope of the rule in *Hedley Byrne & Co Ltd v Heller & Partners Ltd* [1964] AC 465 concerning economic loss caused as a result of the provision of negligent advice, it has become apparent that an additional consideration is whether the defendant has voluntarily undertaken a responsibility towards the claimant for the accuracy of the advice given (see *Spring v Guardian Assurance plc* [1994] 3 All ER 129; *Henderson v Merrett Syndicates Ltd* [1994] 3 All ER 506; *White v Jones* [1995] 1 All ER 691).

These criteria form part of a composite test based on the necessary relationship between the parties (*Yuen Kun Yeu*, above) and it must be appreciated that they all interrelate. For example, what is foreseeable depends on issues of policy, justice, and proximity. But what is a proximate relationship depends on the other criteria and so on. For this reason, Lord Wilberforce in *Anns v Merton LBC* [1978] AC 728 has been shown to be wrong in separating the issues of foresight of harm and policy in his two-stage test.

The question refers to the fact that a relationship of proximity alone is not conclusive. For example, *Donoghue v Stevenson* shows that there is a sufficient relationship of proximity between a manufacturer and a consumer in respect of physical harm caused by a negligently produced article. But the existence of such a relationship is inconclusive if the consumer suffers economic loss (*Muirhead v Industrial Tank Specialties* [1986] QB 507; *Murphy v Brentwood DC* [1991] 1 AC 378). This is because the length of the chain of distribution is so long that it would be unreasonable to hold the defendant liable when the claimant has a more direct claim against his retail supplier.

In truth, as the question suggests, the real issue is one of policy, namely, is it right that the law should impose a duty of care in the particular circumstances of the case? The main policy issues are, first, the floodgates argument; is this a field that would be better legislated by Parliament; thirdly, has Parliament already legislated; fourthly, what practical effects might the imposition of a duty of care have; and finally, should the claimant do something other than sue the defendant? There may also be human rights issues to be taken into account.

The floodgates argument asks the question: would the establishment of a duty situation raise the spectre of a large number of, possibly, unwarranted claims? This was probably at issue in *Alcock v Chief Constable of South Yorkshire Police* [1992] 1 AC 310 and characterizes the development through case law of the legal principles in relation to psychiatric harm negligently inflicted on 'secondary' victims, i.e. those who were not themselves at risk of physical injury. In respect of this kind of harm there has been a past fear of the 'gold-digging claimant' (though arguably this should be met by the requirement that a medically identifiable psychiatric illness has been suffered). In the case of secondary claimants in negligently inflicted psychiatric injury, the potential numbers of claims arising out of any incident are limited by the so-called control mechanisms set out in *Alcock*, which allow any person with a close tie of love and affection with the victim of the defendant's negligence to sue, provided they were present at the scene of the accident or came upon its immediate aftermath. This serves to eliminate more remote claimants such as those who read of an accident in a newspaper, or are told of it by friends. But arguably, this goes too far by preventing any person not at the scene of the accident from recovering at all, which could cause injustice in exceptional cases. These cases would have been met by the more flexible reasonable foresight test applied by Lords Bridge and Scarman in *McLoughlin v O'Brian* [1983] AC 410. (See also the proposals of the Law Commission, *Liability for Psychiatric Illness* (Law Com 249, 1998) which recommends that the requirement of spatial and temporal proximity should be dispensed with provided a close relationship with the victim can be established.)

Apparently, the same issues do not arise in psychiatric damage cases where the claimant is a 'primary' victim in the sense that he is objectively placed at risk of physical injury by the defendant's negligence (*Page v Smith* [1995] 2 All ER 736; *White v Chief Constable of South Yorkshire Police* [1999] 1 All ER 1) as opposed to the situation in *Alcock* and *McLoughlin* in which the defendant's negligence exposed a 'secondary' victim such as a close relative of the claimant to the risk of injury. Generally, the number of 'primary' victims would be relatively small, though it is not impossible to envisage negligently triggered disasters in which the casualty list might be substantial. This reasoning reflects the second aspect of 'floodgates': namely that the principle is concerned not only with the potential size of the class of claimants, but also with the possibility of ascertaining with certainty the limits of that class. It is not considered fair or reasonable for a defendant to be burdened with liability in negligence to individuals who cannot be accurately, and reasonably promptly, identified.

The floodgates issue is also pertinent in many economic loss claims, especially where negligent advice is concerned, since words spread more rapidly and widely than actions. Any number of people may hear and act on advice originally given by the defendant. Accordingly, in such cases, it is important to consider why the advice was prepared and communicated and who can reasonably be expected to rely on it. Thus in *Caparo v Dickman*, advice prepared by an auditor could conceivably have been acted on by anyone who read the public document in which it was contained. But the advice was only intended for consumption by the company to which the report was directed. It was not intended that potential investors should take account of the contents of the document, even though many such people might choose to consult it. In contrast, the advice prepared in *Morgan Crucible v Hill Samuel Bank* [1991] 1 All ER 142 was specifically directed at inducing the claimant to make an investment, with the result that he was owed a duty of care by the advice giver.

The issues of prospective or actual Parliamentary intervention are often related to matters of consumer protection, which may impinge on the general issue of freedom of contract. Here the court may be disinclined to restrict that freedom by imposing a tortious duty of care. Moreover, if Parliament has already acted, the courts may be disinclined to impose a common law duty which goes further. This seems to have been a motivating factor in *Murphy v Brentwood DC* where the *Defective Premises Act 1972* was thought to be the appropriate route, despite the fact that it was so narrow in scope as to be almost useless!

There is the question whether the claimant should proceed in some way other than via the tort of negligence. Often the claimant may sue for a breach of contract or may be expected to insure himself against the risk of loss created by the defendant. This may be the case where economic loss is caused by a defective product. Also in cases of negligence by builders, there may be a clear expectation that the building owner should be covered by insurance in respect of risks created by a sub-contractor (*Norwich City Council v Harvey* [1989] 1 All ER 1180). In some instances, the claimant himself may be expected to guard against the risk of harm rather than the defendant. For example, it would be unreasonable to impose a duty of care on the Civil Aviation Authority to ensure that the owner of an aeroplane has properly maintained the aircraft, since the proper role of the CAA is to protect the public rather than to protect individuals from their own failures (*Philcox v Civil Aviation Authority* (1995) *The Times*, 8 June).

A related matter to consider is whether an alternative remedy already exists, in which case it might not be appropriate to impose a duty of care. For example, particularly in the case of alleged negligence on the part of a public body or official, there may be an existing remedy in the form of judicial review (*Rowling v Takaro Properties Ltd* [1988] 1 All ER 163) or there may be some other source of compensation such as claim against the Criminal Injuries Compensation Scheme (*Hill v Chief Constable of West Yorkshire Police* [1989] AC 53). Similar considerations also apply where there exists an action for breach of contract, even in circumstances where the contractual defendant may not be the same person as the claimant could have sued in tort (*Banque Financière de la Cité v Westgate Insurance Ltd* [1988] 2 Lloyd's Rep 513).

Policy is also overtly relevant when the courts consider the practical effect of a decision to impose a duty of care. For example, decisions such as *Hill v Chief Constable of West Yorkshire Police* [1989] AC 53 and *Marc Rich v Bishop Rock Marine Co Ltd* [1995] 3 All ER 307 reflect the House of Lords' concern that the risk of civil liability might cause organizations whose general task was to work for the collective welfare of the public to introduce defensive practices which, in the long run, might slow down the investigation process (in the case of the police) or to require unduly burdensome safety requirements to be met (as in the case of marine surveyors). It might even deter, for example, local authorities from undertaking certain safety inspections altogether. The detrimental effect of all this on the public interest is sufficient, it is argued, to outweigh the apparent injustice of denying a small number of injured individuals their remedy, though it is sometimes difficult to see why the possibility that a defendant might engage in defensive practices should justify a decision to the effect that no duty of care is owed. For example, in *Spring v Guardian Assurance plc* [1994] 3 All ER 129, Lord Woolf appeared to have some difficulty in accepting the argument in the context of an action for negligence arising out of the activity of giving an employment reference.

This idea of the public interest as an overriding policy consideration developed across a wide range of activities during the 1990s, including child protection agencies (*X (minors) v Bedfordshire County Council* [1995] 3 WLR 152), the Crown Prosecution Service (*Elguzouli-Daf v Metropolitan Police Commissioner* [1995] 1 All ER 833), coastguards (*OLL Ltd v Secretary of State for Transport* [1997] 3 All ER 897) and the fire brigade (*Capital and Counties plc v Hampshire County Council* [1997] 2 All ER 865), sometimes being described merely as a policy issue and a factor to be taken into account, and sometimes as an 'immunity' effectively barring any possibility of a claim. An extreme example of the immunity operated in relation to advocates in respect of the conduct of litigation. If an advocate were to owe a duty of care, it was said, this might result in endless numbers of cases being retried at the instance of dissatisfied litigants (*Rondel v Worsley* [1969] 1 AC 191). Similarly, if an advocate's advice culminated in a settlement which required the approval of the court, without the immunity, the judge might have been forced to explain what he had said or done (*Kelley v Corston* [1997] 4 All ER 466). The prospect of the Human Rights Act 1998 coming into force in 2000 prompted a number of actions challenging the legality of such immunities in negligence and may well have been influential in the most recent approach, which requires a balancing of all the policy issues relevant to any individual case. In particular, the blanket immunity enjoyed by advocates was abolished by the House of Lords in *Arthur J. S. Hall & Co (a firm) v Simons* [2000] 3 All ER 673—the arguments that had previously been thought overwhelming were now seen, by reference to experience from other jurisdictions and by comparison with other professionals to whom they might equally apply, to be overcautious and unnecessary.

A somewhat different aspect of public policy influenced the outcome in *Greatorex v Greatorex* [2000] 4 All ER 769, in which a father whose motorist son had been injured by his own negligence suffered psychiatric illness consequent on attending the accident. Part of the justification for denying liability was a public interest in protecting the integrity of family life, which would, the judge reasoned, be put at risk were the distress of such an accident to be exacerbated by litigation. Direct physical injury inflicted by one family member on another is actionable, but mental suffering, he concluded, must be accepted as part of ordinary family experience unless inflicted by a third party.

In summary, policy considerations feature strongly in determining whether a duty of care is owed and the simple fact of a particular type of relationship is not conclusive. This is because regard must be had to the kind of harm suffered and the way it was caused. The use of a criterion of reasonable foresight of harm on its own, in some cases, might create the danger of indeterminate liability. Thus, while it has been said that physical injury is almost always foreseeable (*Alcock v Chief Constable of South Yorkshire* [1992] 1 AC 310 *per* Lord Ackner), it has also been observed that the relevant considerations such as foreseeability and proximity are merely convenient labels (*Caparo plc v Dickman* [1990] 2 AC 605 *per* Lord Oliver) and that what is foreseeable harm may, at times, be a matter prone to manipulation. While the courts may be disinclined to take on the role of legislators, they do have to take steps to keep the tort of negligence within reasonable bounds and it is the use of policy considerations which allows them to do this.

(2) Psychiatric harm

Question 2

Don, the driver of a stock car, negligently fails to maintain his vehicle. In the course of a race, which is being televised, Don's brakes fail and his car crashes into a crowd of spectators. The car narrowly misses Albert but strikes and kills Bob. Bob's daughter, Claire, is very badly injured, but survives and is taken to hospital.

Albert, a person of unusually nervous disposition, develops an anxiety neurosis.

Freda, a friend of Bob, is present at the scene of the accident. At first, she attempts to help, but realizing that Bob is dead and that Claire is being dealt with by professionals, Freda rushes back to tell Bob's wife, Glenda, what has happened. Some time later, Glenda, who is also Claire's stepmother of six months' standing, drives to the hospital and asks to see Bob and Claire. Glenda is shown Bob's body, and sees Claire on a hospital trolley, awaiting treatment, crying in pain, and in a badly disfigured state.

Harriet, Bob's mother, sees a live television broadcast of the events, recognizes her son in the crowd and realizes that Don's car has crashed into the area where her son is standing.

Freda, Glenda, and Harriet are all horrified by what has happened. Both Freda and Glenda suffer from reactive depression. Harriet helps care for Glenda and Claire following the accident and becomes a recluse because of her inability to come to terms with the psychological suffering of Glenda and the physical injuries suffered by Claire.

Advise Albert, Freda, Glenda, and Harriet.

Commentary

This question involves a discussion of the principles relating to negligently inflicted psychiatric harm. It is essential to explain the distinction between primary and secondary claimants, and its effect on the likely success of a claim. It is also important to explain in detail and apply the various control mechanisms in *Alcock* and subsequent cases.

Answer plan

- Has the claimant suffered legally recognizable psychiatric harm?
- Is the claimant a primary or a secondary claimant?
- Is the relationship between the various secondary claimants and the victims of the defendant's negligent act sufficiently close?
- Is the claimant proximate in terms of time and space to the scene of the accident?
- How was the psychiatric damage caused?
- What duty, if any, is owed to a rescuer?

Suggested answer

Since candidates are informed that Don is negligent in maintaining his vehicle, there is no need to consider the issues of duty and breach of duty in respect of the harm to Bob and Claire. Assuming the death of Bob and the injuries to Claire are caused by Don's negligence and that harm is not too remote, Don will be liable in damages to both Claire and Glenda, the latter representing the estate of the deceased and being a dependant, thereby being able to recover damages under the Law Reform (Miscellaneous Provisions) Act 1934 and the Fatal Accidents Act 1976, respectively.

When considering the issue of psychiatric damage, it is important to be able to identify the types of harm which may form the basis of an action for negligence. Not every form of mental suffering will be sufficient to establish a duty situation. It is a requirement of English law that the claimant should have suffered an identifiable psychiatric illness. It is now well established that mere grief, sorrow or upset are normal human emotions in respect of which no duty of care is owed (*McLoughlin v O'Brian* [1983] 1 AC 410; *Attia v British Gas* [1988] QB 304; *Reilly v Merseyside Regional Health Authority* (1995) 6 Med LR 246). The mere fact that a person actually involved in a road traffic accident feels 'shocked and shaken up' will not give rise to a duty in negligence (*Nicholls v Rushton* (1992) *The Times*, 19 June). Moreover, it is expected that people should possess sufficient fortitude or 'phlegm' to be able to overcome the normal distress at witnessing an accident (*Bourhill v Young* [1943] AC 92). On this basis, the fact that Freda, Glenda, and Harriet are 'horrified' will not suffice. By contrast, the reactive depression suffered by Freda and Glenda, as a recognizable psychiatric illness, will be sufficient, as will Albert's anxiety neurosis (*Chadwick v British Transport Commission* [1967] 2 All ER 945). Harriet's personality change and inability to cope with everyday life would seem to indicate a qualifying condition, but her claim will fail because the condition was caused not by shock, a sudden assault on the senses, but by the long term effects of caring for the other victims (*Alcock v Chief Constable of South Yorkshire Police* [1992] 1 AC 310).

For each claimant, the next question to be asked is whether they are to be regarded as a primary or secondary claimant. Primary claimants are those described by Lord Oliver in *Alcock* as being 'involved, mediately or immediately, as a participant', and by Lord Lloyd in *Page v Smith* [1996] AC 155 as being within the class of persons who, without the benefit of hindsight, might foreseeably have suffered physical injury. In *Page*, the driver of a car involved in a minor collision was physically unhurt but nonetheless suffered a recurrence of ME (myalgic encephalomyelitis), a condition he had suffered from intermittently over many years, but from which he was in remission at the time of the accident. The test applied in the House of Lords was to ask whether it was foreseeable to the defendant that her conduct would expose the claimant to a risk of personal injury, whether physical or psychiatric. If the answer to that question was in the affirmative, it was irrelevant that the claimant did not suffer physical injury or that the claimant's actual injury was due to his 'egg-shell personality', since the defendant was required to take the claimant as he found him. However, where the claimant has an 'egg-shell skull' personality, the quantum of damages he receives may be reduced to take account of the fact that the claimant might have suffered the illness complained of despite the defendant's negligent act (*Page v Smith (No. 2)* [1996] 1 WLR 855). Lord Lloyd indicated that in cases such as these there is no floodgates risk, and therefore no need for the control mechanisms used in the case of secondary claimants to limit the number of claims.

If Albert, having been 'narrowly missed', can show that he falls within a class who could foreseeably have been physically injured his claim will succeed, despite the fact that he is a person of unusually nervous disposition. Alternatively, he may seek to rely on those cases in which the claimant fears for his own safety as a result of what the defendant has done, and in consequence suffers psychiatric harm (*Dulieu v White* [1901] 2 KB 609). Although this sounds as though it offers an additional line of argument, recent cases have shown that a very restrictive approach is taken to the question whether the claimant's fear, even where it is accepted as genuine, is to be regarded, in law, as reasonable (*McFarlane v EE Caledonia Ltd* [1994] 2 All ER 1; *Hegarty v EE Caledonia Ltd* [1997] 2 Lloyd's Rep 259). If Albert cannot show that he is a primary claimant, he must satisfy the requirements for a secondary claimant, as with Glenda, Freda, and Harriet.

Secondary claimants are those whose psychiatric harm stems from their reaction to physical harm caused to someone else by the defendant's negligence. Clearly, for every physically injured primary victim there may be a great number of potential claims from relatives, friends, and witnesses of the event, all saying that they have been affected by the defendant's negligence. It is concern about this possible proliferation of claims, the floodgates issue, that has driven the courts' restrictive approach to the existence of a duty of care in such cases. This approach manifests itself in the so-called 'control mechanisms', a series of tests set out by the House of Lords in *Alcock*, following the Hillsborough tragedy. These tests represent a modification of the three *Caparo* requirements for the existence of a duty of care in negligence, namely foreseeability, proximity and fairness, justice and reasonableness, not replacing them, but recasting them in a form more readily applicable to psychiatric injury cases.

Although there are variations in their Lordships' speeches, some general consensus has emerged and has been applied in subsequent cases. First, as regards the class of persons who may claim it would seem that the test is that of a 'close tie of love and affection' with the primary victim. This might be presumed in the case of parents/children, spouses, and (perhaps) engaged couples, though evidence might be brought to rebut the presumption. For all others, a relationship qualitatively similar to those listed must be proved. It was held that the closeness of the relationship was what made it foreseeable that the claimant would suffer psychiatric damage, while those with a lesser tie may generally be foreseen as possessing sufficient 'phlegm and fortitude' to cope with the incident (*Bourhill v Young* [1943] AC 92). Secondly, the claimant must be proximate in time and space to the incident (i.e. actually be there), though their Lordships approved the extension in *McLoughlin* to a claimant who comes upon the 'immediate aftermath'. In that case, a mother arrived at hospital, some two hours after a road traffic accident involving her husband and children, and was faced with one dead child and the rest of her family injured and not yet cleaned up or treated. The impact of the scenes to which she was exposed, and within such a short timescale, was held to be equivalent to having been present at the accident. The last factor is the manner in which the claimant learned of the incident, which must cause actual shock, a 'sudden assault on the senses', and learning of events through a third party will not be enough.

Turning back to the claimants, Albert, if his claim as a primary claimant is rejected, will not be able to establish the requisite close tie of love and affection with the victims, which places him in the class of 'bystander'. Under *Alcock*, it appeared that a bystander might be able to claim if something sufficiently gruesome happened sufficiently close to him, the scenario suggested in *McLoughlin* was of a situation in which a petrol tanker crashed into a school in session and exploded in flames. In such a situation, it was thought, it was foreseeable that even a bystander might suffer psychiatric damage. This line of reasoning was rejected in *McFarlane v EE Caledonia* [1994] 2 All ER 1, a case arising out of the Piper Alpha disaster, both on grounds of practicality (how does one measure gruesomeness?), and of principle—to accept it would be to base liability solely on a test of reasonable foreseeability. Although critics have challenged the latter assertion, this approach to bystanders has been endorsed by the House of Lords in *White v Chief Constable of South Yorkshire Police* [1999] 1 All ER 1. As a secondary claimant his claim is doomed to fail.

Although Freda was present at the scene of the accident, there is no suggestion that she was close enough to be a primary claimant. As a secondary claimant, she must first establish that she has a close tie of love and affection with the victims. Merely being a friend of Bob will not be enough, unless she can prove that their friendship was equivalent to a close familial tie. If she can do so, she will certainly satisfy the other requirements having been proximate in time and space to the shocking event and having experienced it with her own unaided senses. If she cannot establish the requisite tie, then she is a bystander. Under *Alcock*, a person who performed the role of rescuer was seen, for policy reasons, as an exception to the bystander class in much the same way as rescuers enjoy a special position in relation to the rules of negligence in all other cases (*Chadwick v British Transport Commission* [1967] 1 WLR 912). The problem, however, with acts of rescue leading to psychiatric injury is that it is very difficult for courts to identify exactly what an individual must do in order to claim the special status, bearing in mind the essentially restrictive approach that is taken to secondary claimants generally. For example, in *McFarlane* the claimant had assisted with survivors by handing out blankets, which was not held to be sufficient to make him a 'rescuer'. The problem for the law became acute in *White v Chief Constable of South Yorkshire Police* [1999] 1 All ER 1, where the rescuers in question were police officers working with the dead and injured at Hillsborough. A majority of the Court of Appeal had held that the activities of certain of the officers sufficed to warrant the label of rescuer and hence the special treatment. This analysis was rejected by the majority in the House of Lords, on the basis that a class incapable of being defined in law cannot be sustained, and that justice would be better served by applying the ordinary rules in all cases, with the result that any claimant lacking a close tie with the victims must either be objectively at risk of physical injury or reasonably believe themselves to be so (i.e. be a primary claimant). This decision is fatal to any claim by Freda based solely on rescuing activities since, although the defence of *volenti* continues to be nullified in the case of rescuers in respect of their voluntarily leaving a safe place in order to assist (as in *Chadwick*), on the facts given there is no suggestion of any ongoing risk to people at the scene.

Glenda, as Bob's wife will be presumed to have a close tie of love and affection, and as a stepmother of six months' standing may have begun to develop the required bond with Claire. She was not at the scene of the accident when it happened, and being told of the incident by Freda will not be sufficient to establish the existence of a duty of care (*Hambrook v Stokes Bros* [1925] 1 KB 141).

Although she was not at the scene of the accident, Glenda's experience at the hospital may suffice provided it may be categorized as the immediate aftermath. She arrives 'some time later', and it is not clear what length of delay may still qualify as immediate—a time lapse of eight hours in *Alcock* and one of five hours in *Chester v Waverley Municipal Council* (1939) 62 CLR 1 was considered too great, while two hours was accepted in *McLoughlin*. As well as immediacy, the word 'aftermath' must be considered since in *McLoughlin* it was the state of the victims and the impact on the claimant's mind that was important. In *Alcock*, it was considered relevant that the relatives had turned up at a mortuary in order to identify the bodies of their loved ones. While Lord Ackner was prepared to regard this as part of the 'aftermath' of the accident, it was not part of the *immediate* aftermath, but Lord Jauncey opined that the experience of going to identify a body is not the same as attendance at the aftermath of an accident for the purpose of providing comfort and care to a person who may still be alive (see also Handford, 'Compensation for Psychiatric Injury: The Limits of Liability' (1995) 2 *Psychiatry, Psychology and Law* 37). Provided Glenda arrives at the hospital very soon after the incident at the race track, and does so with a view to providing comfort and care, it would appear that she should be able to recover damages in respect of the reactive depression she suffers. On the facts, it seems to be the case that Glenda is already aware that Bob is dead, but she is able to provide her stepdaughter, Claire, with care and compassion.

Harriet is probably ineligible due to her psychiatric illness being gradual and not caused by shock. Her claim also faces another difficulty. Although, as Bob's mother, there will be a presumption of love and affection, Harriet is not present at the scene of the accident, but she observes the events on a live television broadcast. In *Alcock* it was emphasized that it is also necessary to look at the means by which the shock is caused. In that case, it was considered relevant that the police were aware that the football match was being televised (thus eliminating any argument that broadcast by a third party was a *novus actus interveniens*), but they were also aware of a code of ethics which forbade the showing of pictures of suffering by identifiable individuals, and entitled to rely on it. There was also doubt as to whether scenes viewed on a television screen could ever be 'equiparated with the viewer being within sight or hearing of the event . . . or as giving rise to shock, in the sense of a sudden assault on the nervous system' (*Alcock*, *per* Lord Keith). This would seem to suggest that Harriet would not have a claim.

Question 3

Adam arranges to meet his girlfriend, Sally, at the Roxy cinema. As he is walking to the cinema he is daydreaming and steps into the road. He is struck and seriously injured by a car driven negligently and at grossly excessive speed by Ranjit, a 16-year-old, who has taken a car without the owner's consent and who is showing off to Manjit, his nine-year-old sister who is a passenger in the car.

Sally visits Adam in hospital as soon as she hears of the accident, six hours after the incident. Sally is extremely upset and depressed after observing Adam's facial injuries.

Manjit is crushed against the dashboard of the car and is seriously injured. Manjit was not wearing a seatbelt at the time of the accident.

Advise Ranjit of his potential tortious liability.

Commentary

This question raises the principal issues of recovery by a secondary claimant for psychiatric damage, contributory negligence and the public policy defence of *ex turpi causa non oritur actio*. It is complicated by the age of the participants. The answer should consider the application of the control mechanisms applicable to secondary claimants. There has been some activity in the fields dealt with by the problem, e.g. there has been a Law Commission report relating to liability for negligently caused psychiatric damage and a consultation paper on the principle *ex turpi causa*.

Answer plan

- What standard of care can be expected of a 16-year-old driver?
- What is contributory negligence and what rules attach to this defence?
- What are the restrictive rules on recovery of damages for psychiatric harm?
- Is Diana's involvement in the joy-riding incident sufficient to disentitle her to an award of damages under the principle *ex turpi causa non oritur actio?*
- How does the defence of contributory negligence apply to her?

Suggested answer

It is likely that the Motor Insurers' Bureau under its agreement with the Department of Transport, in respect of uninsured drivers, will stand in the shoes of the uninsured Ranjit. It is well established that one road user owes a duty of care to anyone who also uses the road—this includes pedestrians such as Adam. In order to succeed, Adam will have to show that Ranjit was in breach of that duty. The test is to ask what a reasonable man would do or would not do in the circumstances: *Blyth v Birmingham Waterworks Co* (1856) 11 Ex 781. The standard to apply is that of the reasonably competent qualified driver: *Nettleship v Weston* [1971] 2 QB 691 and the fact that he is somewhat young and inexperienced will make no difference, though common sense dictates that this standard could not realistically be applied to a much younger child.

Ranjit was negligent and as regards Adam there is the issue of contributory negligence.

Under the Law Reform (Contributory Negligence) Act 1945 contributory negligence ceased to be a complete defence and became a partial defence. It applies where a person has suffered damage partly as the result of his own fault and partly as a result of the fault of another person. The Act permits the court to reduce the damages to the extent the court thinks just and reasonable having regard to the claimant's share in the responsibility. The Act applies where the claimant has failed to take reasonable care for his own safety, thereby contributing to the damage suffered or the extent of the damage suffered, but there is no need for the claimant to owe the defendant a duty of care because the Act operates as a shield and not as a sword.

Contributory negligence requires fault on the part of both Adam and Ranjit. Adam's fault requires consideration of two issues. First, is whether or not Adam has failed to take reasonable care for his own safety: *Jones v Livox Quarries* [1952] 2 QB 608. Day-dreaming in the middle of the road, for whatever reason, seems to suggest that he has not.

The second issue is that of causation as to the harm suffered. It must be asked whether, but for the day-dreaming, Adam would have been injured. In *Jones v Livox Quarries*, the plaintiff was injured in a collision when he was riding on the back bumper of a slow-moving quarry vehicle. Lord Denning made the point that had he been injured by a shot fired by a negligent sportsman the Act would have had no application because his fault would have had nothing to do with the injury and the means by which it occurred. Again, there seems little doubt since a person who was not day-dreaming would have stayed on the pavement; it would have been otherwise had Ranjit driven the car on to the pavement.

The third issue in contributory negligence cases is the matter of apportionment of damages. There is considerable scope for the courts to reach an equitable solution with a flexible approach looking at issues of causation of damage and blameworthiness. If the blameworthiness of Adam is small, as seems to be the case, even if he is in the road, a low reduction of, say 10–20 per cent may be likely under the Law Reform (Contributory Negligence) Act 1945, s. 1(1). Alternatively, if Adam's fault is great one might analyse the incident in terms of joint causation, as in *Fitzgerald v Lane* [1988] 2 All ER 961 in which a negligent pedestrian was struck and injured by two negligent motorists. This could be significant in relation to Sally's claim (see below).

Sally is upset and suffers depression at the sight of Adam's injuries. This raises the issue of psychiatric damage. The law has evolved slowly in this area from a position where 'nervous shock' in negligence was not recoverable, e.g. *Victorian Railway Commissioners v Coultas* (1888) 13 App Cas 222 to the present day where it is recognized but hedged about with control mechanisms. The law distinguishes between a primary claimant (someone who is involved in an incident and who could foreseeably have been injured or who reasonably fears for their own safety) and secondary claimants (someone who witnesses the event or comes upon the immediate aftermath of it). As Lord Lloyd said in *Page v Smith* [1995] 2 All ER 736, in regard to secondary claimants, the law insists on control mechanisms 'in order as a matter of policy to limit the number of potential claimants'.

First, it must be established that the depression Sally suffers is a medically recognizable psychiatric illness. This has been a consistent theme of all the decisions in this area such as *McLoughlin v O'Brian* [1983] AC 410 and *Alcock v Chief Constable of South Yorkshire Police* [1991] 4 All ER 907. Sally does satisfy this criterion if there is clinical depression, but the mere fact that she is upset will not suffice.

The result from *McLoughlin v O'Brian* and *Alcock* is that the control mechanisms amount to three elements: (1) the claimant must fall into the relevant class of persons whose claims should be recognized; (2) the claimant must have proximity in time and space to the accident; and (3) the court must have regard to the means by which the shock has been caused.

A person may sue provided that they have a close tie of love and affection with the injured victim of the defendant's negligence. This may be presumed to exist, e.g. in cases of spouses, children and parents, or (perhaps) as between engaged couples, though in all other cases would have to be proved.

In relation to the requirement of proximity in time and space, *McLoughlin v O'Brian* extended the law by permitting recovery where the claimant saw not the accident or event itself but the immediate aftermath of the event. Since Sally was not at the scene of the accident, but only visits Adam in hospital the following morning, it must be decided if she is present at the *immediate* aftermath. In *McLoughlin v O'Brian* a period of two hours was short enough to come within the aftermath principle, but in *Chester v Waverley Corp* (1939) 62 CLR 1, a six-hour delay before the victim's body was found was considered too long. So also in *Alcock*, visits by relatives of the victims of the Hillsborough tragedy to a mortuary some eight to nine hours after the initial accident, for the purposes of identifying bodies was considered to be too long a period to fall within the definition of the 'immediate aftermath'. One factor may well be the state of the victim and the purpose of the visit. In *McLoughlin v O'Brian* the victims were still in a very distressed state and had not yet been fully treated or cleaned up after the accident. The reference in the question to 'the following morning' suggests a very long time, during which Adam has probably been cleaned up and installed in a hospital bed, so Sally has probably come too late to fall within the rule. The essence of recovery for psychiatric injury in this type of case is shock and in the absence of something equivalent to a sudden assault on the senses recovery will not usually be possible.

A further obstacle to Sally's claim could be posed by the decision in *Greatorex v Greatorex*, in which it was held that a defendant will not be liable for psychiatric injury arising from their own negligently self-inflicted injury. In part, the justification for this was said to be that a legal responsibility to take care of oneself to avoid psychiatric harm to others would unduly curtail the right to self-determination. The impact of this principle on Sally's case would seem to hinge on the extent of Adam's own contribution to his injuries.

Since Manjit is a passenger in the car, she is owed a duty of care in the same way as any other road user. Since this is a road traffic accident, the defence of *volenti*, even if its ingredients were satisfied, is ruled out statutorily where the vehicle must be compulsorily insured against third party risks: **Road Traffic Act 1988, s. 149(3)**.

Manjit's involvement in the joy-riding incident may be sufficient to invoke the public policy defence of *ex turpi causa non oritur actio* (although strictly it is a bar to an action proceeding rather than a defence). Two approaches to this have been evident. The first involves an idea that injury occurring through immoral or criminal conduct should not be the basis of recovery because this would offence the public conscience. The other is that if it is found that a duty of care is owed then the criminal behaviour might mean that it is impossible for the court to fix a standard of care. In *Pitts v Hunt* [1990] 3 All ER 344, the defendant had actively encouraged the defendant to drive in an extremely dangerous manner and the principle was applied but the members of the Court of Appeal did not agree on which of the two bases the principle applied. On the facts of the problem, there is no suggestion that Manjit has actively encouraged Ranjit. The test applied in *Pitts v Hunt* is whether Manjit's involvement is such as to prevent the court from being able to identify an appropriate standard of care.

The precise scope of the *ex turpi causa* defence is difficult to ascertain. One view is that the defence amounts to a more or less automatic bar on the recovery of damages where the claimant is involved in a joint criminal enterprise with the defendant (*Ashton v Turner* [1981] QB 137), but this does seem rather draconian. Alternatively, the less severe test in *Pitts v Hunt* requires the court to consider whether it is possible to determine what standard of care should be owed by the defendant to the claimant, with the result that if the claimant's injuries arise directly, as opposed to incidentally, out of the illegal act, damages should be denied. A third possible approach was that the principle would be applied if the behaviour offended the public conscience, but this rather vague test was rejected by the House of Lords in *Tinsley v Milligan* [1993] 3 All ER 65 in which emphasis was placed upon the public policy base of the defence and the extent of the court's discretion. According to *Tinsley*, it is necessary to weigh the adverse consequences of giving a remedy against the consequences of refusing that remedy.

More recently in *Vellino v Chief Constable of Greater Manchester* [2002] 3 All ER 78, the claimant had attempted to evade arrest by jumping from a second-floor window but he was severely injured. He claimed that the police officers had acted negligently. In the Court of Appeal the majority found that escape from custody was a sufficiently serious criminal offence to permit the principle to be applied. Therefore the police did not owe an arrested person a duty to take care that he was not injured in a foreseeable attempt to escape police custody. Sir Murray Stuart-Smith said that:

'The operation of the principle arises where the claimant's claim is founded upon his own criminal or immoral act. The facts which give rise to the claim must be inextricably linked with the criminal activity. It is not sufficient if the criminal activity merely gives occasion for tortious conduct of the defendant . . . this has to be sufficiently serious to merit the application of the principle.'

In the circumstances, it seems likely the fact that Manjit is only nine years old may be significant, since she may be considered too young to appreciate the risks involved, and that the *ex turpi causa* defence will not operate against her.

A second issue is whether Manjit is contributorily negligent in getting into the car with an unlicensed, uninsured, and probably incompetent driver. Manjit's age, once again, will be relevant, as the courts are disinclined to hold that a person so young could have foreseen the risk of harm: *Yachuk v Oliver Blais* [1949] AC 386. In *Gough v Thorne* [1966] 1 WLR 1387, Lord Denning suggested that very young children would not be guilty of contributory negligence and that as they got older whether they would be guilty was a question of degree. More recently, in *N (A Child) v Newham LBC* [2007] CLY 2931, a 7-year-old schoolboy who was injured when he punched the glass panel in a classroom door was held 60 per cent to blame. This was because N knew right from wrong, that it was wrong to punch, and that when punched glass was likely to break and injure him. On this reasoning, perhaps Manjit is old enough for the defence to apply since the need to wear seatbelts is well known, even to very young children.

While Manjit has not caused the accident by her conduct, she has materially increased the risk of injury by not wearing a seat-belt. A formula for compensation stated in *Froom v Butcher* [1976] QB 286 suggests a 25 per cent reduction if no injury would have been suffered had the seat-belt been worn, a 15 per cent reduction if the injury would have been less severe had the seat-belt been worn and no reduction at all if the same injury would have been suffered whether or not a seat-belt was worn. Being thrown out of her seat suggests at least a 15 per cent if not a 25 per cent reduction in damages, but this is subject to the issue of Manjit's age.

(3) Economic loss

Question 4

Badman Batty, construction contractors, are engaged by Crumbridgeshire County Council to resurface a 10-mile stretch of the Crumbridge ring road. Badman Batty hires a surface stripping machine in order to facilitate the work.

Bob, a surveyor, employed by the County Council, but on loan to Badman Batty decides he is capable of using the surface stripping machine but sets the controls in such a way that too deep a cut is made. As a result of this, the machine severs a water main with the result that the road and a nearby power generator are flooded. The following parties claim damages for negligence:

(a) Peter, a businessman, was driving on the ring road at the time of the incident and claims he has been prevented from attending a meeting at which he had high hopes of securing a £500,000 contract with another business;

(b) Power-Green Ltd, the owners of the generator engulfed in water from the severed main claim in respect of the cost of repairing their damaged generator and the profit they would have made had the generator been operative during the five days it takes to effect repairs;

(c) Plasticraft Ltd, the owners of a factory on an industrial estate supplied with electricity generated by Power-Green's incapacitated generator, complain that their operations were interrupted for five days. They point to the fact that they had to dispose of a batch of plastic plates, valued at £10,000, as the plastic congealed as a result of the power interruption. The cost of cleaning congealed plastic from their machines is assessed at £2,500. Plasticraft Ltd also claim damages for loss of business profit on operations they could have carried on during the remainder of the five-day interruption to their power supply.

Advise Badman Batty of their potential liability in tort.

Commentary

This question is concerned with economic loss caused by a negligent act. Generally, the courts have been reluctant to allow an action in this area and have imposed severe restrictions at the duty stage of the inquiry. However, the economic loss may or may not have been caused by a person who is an employee of the defendants and thus raises the issue of the vicarious liability of an employer.

Answer plan

- Who is an employee and who is an independent contractor for the purposes of the doctrine of vicarious liability?
- Is the employee's act done in the course of his employment: *Rose v Plenty; Lister v Hesley Hall*?
- When is economic loss caused by a negligent act recoverable and what is the relevance of the 'floodgates' argument: *Spartan Steel & Alloys Ltd v Martin*?

Suggested answer

'Bob's actions result in physical damage to the water main. Generally, the rule in *Donoghue v Stevenson* makes it clear that in respect of physical harm, a defendant owes a duty of care to those he can reasonably foresee as likely to be affected by his actions. By using the surface stripping machine to cut too deeply, it seems that Bob has acted in a manner in which the reasonable surveyor would not have acted, thereby establishing a breach of duty, giving rise to liability in negligence so long as the damage suffered by others is not too remote. Bob is normally employed by the County Council, but has been 'lent' to Badman Batty, presumably to oversee this particular job. It needs to be ascertained who is Bob's employer for the purposes of rules on vicarious liability. It might be thought that the terms of any contract between Crumbridgeshire County Council and Badman Batty would determine this issue, but that was held not to be the case in *Mersey Docks & Harbour Board v Coggins & Griffith (Liverpool) Ltd* [1947] AC 1 in which it was held that the burden of proof rests on the permanent employer to show that the employee is employed by the 'borrowing employer'. In *Viasystems (Tyneside) Ltd v Thermal Transfer (Northern) Ltd* [2006] QB 510 and *Hawley v Luminar Leisure Ltd* [2006] EWCA Civ 18 it was held that the appropriate test to apply is the control test, that is, it needs to be ascertained which of the two employers was best positioned to prevent the tort from being committed. The answer to this starts from an initial presumption that the lending employer still remains responsible, (*Hawley*) but that the presumption can be displaced if the employee was so much under the control of the borrowing employer that he can prevent the employee from committing the tort (*Viasystems* at [16]). Applying these tests, both the 'borrowing' and 'lending' employers of a negligent fitter were equally liable for the tort in *Viasystems*. Assuming sufficient control has passed to Badman Batty, they may be regarded as the responsible employer, which might be a reasonable conclusion to arrive at if Crumbridgeshire County Council has no obvious means of preventing any tort from being committed.

Bob acts on behalf of Badman Batty, but it is necessary to decide if he is an employee or an independent contractor. If he is the former, Badman Batty may be vicariously liable for Bob's negligence, if he acts in the course of his employment.

Although this rule departs from the fault principle, it is justified on the basis that employers rather than employees are best positioned to bear the loss through insurance (see *British Telecommunications plc v James Thomson & Son (Engineers) Ltd* [1999] 1 WLR 9.

The classic test for determining who is an employee has been traditionally based on the concept of control. Thus an employee is a person engaged to obey his employer's orders from time to time, whereas an independent contractor is employed to do work but has a discretion as to the mode and time of doing the relevant work: *Honeywill v Stein & Larkin* [1934] 1 KB 191. The difficulty with the control test is that there are now many professional employees whose skill is such that the employer may have little knowledge of how the work is done. This may present a problem so far as Bob is concerned, since the skill of the job of a surveyor may be such that Badman Batty have no detailed knowledge of the type of work he does. Nevertheless, the control test can be helpful in many circumstances, although the courts are likely to take into account other factors such as the method of paying the employee, who provides the tools and equipment required to complete the job, whether or not there is a power of dismissal and the extent to which the 'employee' has put a personal investment into the enterprise.

Other distinctions between employees and independent contractors are that employees are engaged under a contract of service whereas an independent contractor is employed under a contract for services. In the former the employer can stipulate not just what has to be done but also the manner in which it is to be done: *Collins v Hertfordshire County Council* [1947] KB 598. Moreover in a contract of service, the employer has a power to select his employees, a power to pay wages, and a power to dismiss or suspend. In the case of a contract for services, the contractor is in business on his own account (*Lee Tin Sang v Chung Chi-Keung* [1991] 2 WLR 1173) and may be able to delegate the task to others (*MacFarlane v Glasgow City Council* (2001) IRLR 7). Whether Bob is an employee will depend on the detailed wording of his contract with Badman Batty, which is not revealed in the question. But if Bob's work is done as an integral part of Badman Batty's business it would appear that he is likely to be regarded as an employee: *Stevenson, Jordan & Harrison Ltd v MacDonald* (1952) TLR 101.

Assuming Bob is an employee, Badman Batty, as employers, may be vicariously liable for Bob's torts committed in the course of employment. Although Bob's tortious acts are likely to constitute the common law tort of negligence, the employer's liability is not extinguished even if the tort committed is a statutory tort such as that of harassment (see *Banks v Ablex Ltd* [2005] EWCA Civ 173; *Majrowski v Guy's & St Thomas's NHS Trust* [2007] 1 AC 224). As a surveyor, he is unlikely to be employed to operate a surface stripping machine. On the other hand he may have been employed to supervise and give orders to those who do. It would appear that if an employee does an act he is not employed to perform, he may still be held to have acted within the general scope of his employment provided what he does is a method, albeit unauthorized, of performing his ordinary duties: *London County Council v Cattermoles (Garages) Ltd* [1953] 1 WLR 997. If an employee borrows his employer's property and misuses it in a way that harms the claimants he may still be regarded as acting in the course of employment (see *Weir v Chief Constable of Merseyside Police* [2003] EWCA Civ 111).

On the other hand, if Bob is taken to have done an act he was never employed to perform, he might not be acting in the course of his employment: *Iqbal v London Transport Executive* (1973) 16 KIR 329. In contrast, there is authority which suggests that acts of employees which benefit the employer's business are acts done in the course of employment even where the act has been prohibited: *Rose v Plenty* [1976] 1 WLR 141. Here there is no evidence that Bob has been prohibited from operating the machine and it does appear that he is trying to further his employer's business.

Bob's act results in damage to the road and to a water main. In the unlikely event that this was done deliberately, this might constitute the criminal offence of causing criminal damage. This raises the question whether an overtly criminal act can be done in the course of employment. Generally, if the act is done with a view to furthering the employer's interests, it may still be regarded as an act done in the course of employment: *Poland v Parr* [1927] 1 KB 236; *Vasey v Surrey Free Inns* [1996] PIQR P373. Generally, the approach now adopted is that provided the act is sufficiently closely connected with the work the employee is employed to do, it will be fair and just to hold the employer responsible for the act: *Lister v Hesley Hall Ltd* [2002] 1 AC 215. In essence, the key question is whether the tort that has been committed constitutes a risk that is inextricably linked to the type of business carried on by the employer. This would all seem to point towards an act by Bob that was done in the course of his employment.

As Peter is unable to secure a lucrative contract he might have hoped to make, he appears to have suffered pure economic loss which is not directly related to the severance of the water main. This raises a serious 'floodgates' problem. In *Ultramares Corp v Touche* (1931) 174 NE 441 it was stated that the law should not guard against liability in an indeterminate amount to an indeterminate class for an indeterminate time. The particular problem with Peter is that any number of other motorists could be affected in the same way, so that there may be an indeterminate class of potential claimants. Because of this the court is likely to conclude that no duty of care is owed to the likes of Peter. To reinforce this view the Court of Appeal in *Spartan Steel & Alloys Ltd v Martin & Co (Contractors) Ltd* [1973] 1 QB 27 has established a 'bright line' rule in respect of pure economic loss caused by the defendant's negligence. While a defendant will be liable for negligently caused physical harm and for economic loss directly consequent on that physical harm, there is no liability for pure economic loss which flows indirectly from a negligent act. The loss of the £500,000 contract must be regarded as falling within this principle and is therefore loss in respect of which no duty of care is owed.

In any event, the loss suffered by Peter is speculative, so that all he has lost is the chance to secure a lucrative contract. In *Hotson v East Berkshire Health Authority* [1987] 2 All ER 909 it was held that a claimant must prove, on a balance of probability, that the defendant was the cause of the harm complained of. According to the House of Lords, where there was a 75 per cent chance that the harm would have occurred regardless of the defendant's misdiagnosis the claimant had failed to satisfy the burden of proof. However, in other types of case a different approach was taken. For example in *Allied Maples Group Ltd v Simmons & Simmons* [1995] 1 WLR 1602 it was held that if the claimant can prove that he had a real or substantial chance of making a gain rather than merely a speculative chance, that chance can be evaluated as part of the quantum of damages (see also *Dixon v Clement Jones* [2004] EWCA Civ 1005). In *Gregg v Scott* [2005] UKHL 2 by a bare majority, the House of Lords considered that in cases of clinical omission a defendant should not be liable for a mere possibility that the claimant's chance of recovery has been harmed. But, consistent with the policy considerations taken into account in *Fairchild v Glenhaven Funeral Services Ltd* [2002] UKHL 22, if the defendant is guilty of an act that increases the risk of serious illness (mesothelioma caused by exposure to asbestos dust), the defendant should be held responsible for that increased risk in proportion to the amount of time the claimant was employed by the defendant. The effect of *Gregg* is to apply different rules to clinical negligence cases, so that the medical profession is treated more kindly than others whose acts cause physical or financial harm.

Since the loss suffered by Peter is economic loss, he will have to show that there was a substantial, rather than merely speculative chance that he would have been successful in securing the contract lost because of his late arrival at the meeting. However, this is likely to be very difficult to prove.

Power-Green Ltd has suffered physical damage to their generator. On the assumption that Bob's negligence is something for which Badman Batty are vicariously liable, it is likely that this loss will be regarded as recoverable. The loss of profit arising from the direct damage to the generator also seems to fall within the *Spartan Steel v Martin* principle above. It is economic loss which flows directly from physical damage to property owned by Power-Green Ltd and on this basis should be recoverable.

Plasticraft Ltd also suffer physical harm as a result of Bob's negligence in that the plastic plates in process at the time of the interruption to the power supply have to be disposed of. Moreover the cost of cleaning congealed plastic from their machine will also fall within the general description of physical harm, similar to the additional labour costs incurred in *Muirhead v Industrial Tank Specialties Ltd* [1985] 3 All ER 705 when the defendants negligence caused the failure of a water filtration system used by the claimant for storing live lobsters. Moreover, any economic loss directly consequent on this physical damage, such as the resale value of the plates in process at the time of the interruption to the electricity supply will be recoverable: *Spartan Steel & Alloys Ltd v Martin (Contractors) Ltd* [1973] 1 QB 27. However, the loss of general business profits resulting from the inability to continue operations during the total period of interruption to the electricity supply is irrecoverable on the basis that it amounts to indirect economic loss: *Spartan Steel & Alloys Ltd v Martin (Contractors) Ltd*. The rule is arbitrary, but does make the limits of the law clear and was said by Lord Denning MR to be based on the policy ground that were such an action to be permitted, there would be no end of claims. Moreover, as the decision in *Murphy v Brentwood DC* [1991] 1 AC 398 shows that, to extend the law of tort so as to make a person liable for the defective quality of his work would be to introduce a transmissible warranty of quality, which is generally only provided by the law of contract: see *Williams v Natural Life Health Foods* [1998] 2 All ER 577.

Question 5

Constructors Ltd supplied and installed a compression system in a factory owned by Bodgit Ltd. A pipe attached to the compressor was damaged by an employee of Constructors Ltd, but the defect was not immediately noticeable as the piping was contained in a protective sleeve. Around seven years later Bodgit Ltd sold their factory and stock-in-trade to O'Bottle. At the time of sale, O'Bottle inspected the compressor and noticed cracking in a pipe leading from the equipment, but due to a failure to take care, the cause of the cracking was not identified.

Eleven years after installation of the compression system, there was an explosion caused by the rupture of the pipe in which cracking had been discovered at the time Bodgit Ltd sold their factory. The explosion totally destroyed the compressor and seriously damaged the rest of the factory. The cost of repairing the factory is assessed at £2 million, but the market value of a similar factory is considered to be £1.75 million.

At the time of the explosion, the compressor was being used to process a toxic gas, which escaped and severely burned Alice's face. Alice was a production line worker in O'Bottle's factory. Due to inexcusable delay on the part of her solicitors, Doohey, Cheetham & Howe, a writ is not issued until more than three years after the date of the explosion, by which time the normal limitation period for personal injury actions has expired.

Advise Alice and O'Bottle of any remedies they may have in tort.

Commentary

This question is concerned with the liability of an installer for his defective workmanship, where this results in both economic loss and physical harm. The issue of limitation of actions also requires consideration, since the damage suffered by the claimant is only discovered some considerable time after the date on which it was, initially, caused.

Answer plan

- Whether the installation amounts to a defective product under the *Consumer Protection Act 1987*.
- Whether an installer can be a producer for the purposes of the rule in *Donoghue v Stevenson*.
- Whether the damage is actionable under the rule in *Donoghue v Stevenson*.
- How damages in respect of harm to property are assessed.
- How the provisions of the **Limitation Act 1980** affect the product liability action, the negligence action in respect of the events leading up to the explosion and whether the court has a discretion to allow the personal injury action to commence out of time.

Suggested answer

Initially, any defect in the compression system would have been actionable by Bodgit Ltd against Constructors Ltd in accordance with the terms of the contract they made. Failing the presence of any express term, there would have been an implied term to the effect that the goods supplied were of satisfactory quality and fit for any purpose made known by the customer to the supplier at the time of contracting. However, the business and stock-in-trade has been sold by Bodgit Ltd to O'Bottle, whose action can only lie in tort, either in an action for common law negligence or, possibly, under the Consumer Protection Act (CPA) 1987.

Under the CPA 1987, s. 2(1), the producer of a defective product is strictly liable for physical harm to the person or to property other than the defective product itself: CPA 1987, s. 5(2). For the purposes of the Act, a producer does not generally include a mere supplier, unless the user has asked for identification of the producer and the supplier is unable to comply with the request within a reasonable time: CPA 1987, s. 2(3). This would seem to suggest that Constructors Ltd are not producers for the purposes of the 1987 Act. Moreover, the only physical harm to the person and property other than the product itself occurs 11 years after the defective product was first put into circulation. Under the Limitation Act 1980, s. 11A(3), no action in respect of a defective product may be brought after the expiry of 10 years from the date on which the product was put into circulation. It follows that any action under the CPA will be time barred.

A manufacturer owes a common law duty of care in respect of physical harm to the ultimate user of his product if it reaches the consumer in the form in which it left him and with no reasonable possibility of intermediate examination: *Donoghue v Stevenson* [1932] AC 562. For the purposes of the rule, any person who puts a defective product into circulation is a manufacturer and this includes not just suppliers, but also installers of equipment: *Brown v Cotterill* (1934) 51 TLR 21 which would cover Constructors Ltd.

The principal difficulty facing O'Bottle in an action for negligence in respect of an alleged defective product is that he will have to show that he has suffered actionable damage. At one stage, it was accepted that if a structure or product was defective so as to create an imminent danger to health, a duty of care might be owed: *Anns v Merton London Borough Council* [1978] AC 728. But it has been held subsequently, that where a building or product is merely defective, as opposed to being dangerous, the ultimate user suffers only economic loss: *Murphy v Brentwood District Council* [1991] 1 AC 378; *D & F Estates Ltd v Church Commissioners for England* [1989] AC 177 (but contrast the position in other parts of the common law world after the decision of the Privy Council in *Invercargill City Council v Hamlin* [1996] 1 All ER 756). The decision in *Murphy*, in particular, makes it clear that economic loss suffered as a result of the mere qualitative defectiveness of a product does not disclose a duty situation. The reasons for this are largely policy based. First, the claimant may have an alternative action in contract or may have a legitimate claim against his insurers. In any case, it has also been held that to extend the law of tort in such a way that it imposes liability for a transmissible warranty of quality would be to usurp the role of the law of contract and that there is no need for the law of tort to fulfil this role: *Williams v Natural Life Health Foods* [1998] 2 All ER 577. In general, English law has set itself against the recovery of pure economic loss through an action for negligence, unless there is evidence of reliance on a negligent misstatement or there is a uniquely close relationship of proximity between the parties. Neither of these exceptions would seem to apply in this case. Since the piping attached to the compressor is defective without, initially, having caused damage elsewhere, relevant damage for the purposes of a negligence action is only suffered when the explosion occurs.

Eleven years after installation of the compression system, there is an explosion which damages the factory and the compressor owned by O'Bottle and injures Alice. If the compressor and the defective pipe are treated as a composite single product, the problem of economic loss considered above will arise, and O'Bottle will be unable to pursue Constructors Ltd in an action for negligence. However, it may be possible for the court to regard the pipe and the compressor as separate parts of a complex structure, in which case the damage to the compressor may be regarded as distinct property damage caused by the defective pipe. This complex structure theory was first advanced in *D & F Estates Ltd v Church Commissioners for England* [1989] AC 177 as a possible explanation of the decision in *Anns v Merton London Borough Council* [1978]. However, the theory has proved unworkable, and it is unlikely to be of any assistance to O'Bottle.

The damage to the factory is actionable on proof of a failure to take reasonable care on the part of Constructors Ltd and subject to the operation of rules on contributory negligence and limitation of actions. The defect in the pipe is stated to have been caused by the actions of one of Constructors' employees. Assuming this amounts to negligence, O'Bottle will be able to recover the loss he has suffered through the damage to his factory. The basic principle which lies behind an award of damages is that of *restitutio in integrum*, that is the claimant must be put back into the position he was in before the damage was caused. How damages are assessed may present a problem, since there are two possible rules of assessment. The claimant may be able to recover the diminution in market value of the building or he may be able to claim the cost of repairing the damage. Which measure applies is dependent on the claimant's intended use. Generally, if the claimant uses his land as an economic asset, the appropriate measure of damages will be based on the diminution in its capital value: *Taylor v Hepworths Ltd* [1977] 1 WLR 1262. However, if the land is required for commercial occupation, as appears to be the case here, the cost of repair or reinstatement is appropriate: *Harbutt's Plasticine Ltd v Wayne Tank & Pump Co Ltd* [1970] 1 QB 447.

Any award of damages which may be made will probably be reduced in accordance with the provisions of the **Law Reform (Contributory Negligence) Act 1945** to take into account O'Bottle's contributory negligence in not identifying the cause of the cracking in the pipe attached to the compressor. Contributory negligence consists of a failure, by the claimant, to take reasonable care for his own safety: *Jones v Livox Quarries Ltd* [1952] 2 QB 608. In determining whether the claimant is guilty of contributory negligence it is also necessary to determine the extent to which the claimant's failure to take care is a cause of the damage he has suffered: *Jones v Livox Quarries Ltd*. In this particular instance, O'Bottle's failure to take care may be more than just causative of the increased damage, but may be, in part, a cause of the accident which results in that damage. In such cases, the courts have been prepared to make substantial reductions in the claimant's damages on the basis that his blameworthiness in relation to the harm suffered is substantial. For example, in *Stapeley v Gypsum Mines Ltd* [1953] the claimant's damages were reduced by 80 per cent where he disobeyed safety instructions with the result that the roof of a mine collapsed on him.

Whether O'Bottle's action is defeated by lapse of time depends on the date when damage is said to have been caused since time, for the purposes of a tort action runs for six years from that date: **Limitation Act 1980, s. 2.** Since economic loss appears not to be actionable, no damage can be said to have been caused until the date of the explosion: *Nitrigin Eireann Teoranta v Inco Alloys Ltd* [1992] 1 All ER 854. This means that if a writ is issued within six years of the date of the explosion, the action will be in time. Moreover, it appears not to make any difference that O'Bottle ought to have discovered the cause of the cracking. This is relevant only to the issue of contributory negligence which applies in relation to the measure of damages awarded rather than in relation to the issue of accrual of a cause of action: *Nitrigin Eireann Teoranta v Inco Alloys Ltd* [1992].

Alice is employed by O'Bottle and is injured as a result of the defectiveness of equipment he has acquired via Bodgit Ltd from Constructors Ltd. Her action for damages for personal injuries would lie against Constructors Ltd for their negligence or against O'Bottle under the **Employers Liability (Defective Equipment) Act 1969**. If she were to proceed on the latter basis, O'Bottle would be deemed liable for her injuries provided the defect in the equipment is attributable wholly or in part to the fault of a third party: **Employers Liability (Defective Equipment) Act 1969, s. 1(1)**. Thus, it is still necessary to establish fault on the part of the producer or installer of the equipment.

In the case of personal injury actions, the relevant limitation period runs for three years from the date of accrual of the cause of action or for three years from the date when the claimant became aware of her injuries or could reasonably have done so: **Limitation Act 1980, s. 11(4)**. For these purposes, knowledge does not mean that the claimant must know with absolute certainty that she has been injured (*Halford v Brookes* [1991] 3 All ER 559; *Collins v Tesco plc* [2003] EWCA Civ 1308), but if one is involved in an explosion, it is reasonably certain that one should realize this might be due to the fault of the person who controls the thing which explodes. Alice must also be aware that the injury is attributable to the fault of the defendant (**Limitation Act 1980, s. 14(1)(b)**) and be aware of the identity of the defendant (**Limitation Act 1980, s. 14(1)(c)**). Both of these requirements would appear to have been satisfied. Moreover, the claimant's belief that she had a claim is relevant, even if that belief is unfounded (see *Gravgaard v Aldridge & Brownlee (a firm)* [2004] EWCA Civ 1529). However, in any event, it seems likely that the two alternative limitation periods will produce an identical starting date for the running of time, namely, the date of the explosion in 1990. The question states that the normal three-year period has expired, but in personal injury cases, the court has a discretion to allow an action for damages to be commenced out of time where it is equitable to do so: **Limitation Act 1980, s. 33**. A number of guidelines relevant to the exercise of this discretion are given in s. 33(3). These include the degree of prejudice to the claimant and the defendant should the discretion be exercised or not, the length of and reasons for the delay, the cogency of the evidence in the light of the delay and the promptness, and reasonableness of the claimant's action after becoming aware of the cause of action. On the facts, the length of the delay does not appear to be too great, since, on the assumption that Alice's cause of action accrues at the time of the explosion, the writ has been issued out of time. A lot will depend on the length of the delay. The question states that the action is commenced more than three years after the explosion. If the delay is only a matter of days or weeks rather than years, the court may exercise its discretion in Alice's favour (see *Hartley v Birmingham City District Council* [1992] 2 All ER 213—one day late). This is particularly important since the later the writ is issued, the greater will be the prejudice to the defendant in having to face a stale claim which might be difficult to defend (*Donovan v Gwentoys Ltd* [1990] 1 All ER 1018).

The prejudice issue is one which works both ways, since if the court exercises its discretion to allow the action to proceed out of time, there is inevitable prejudice to the defendant since he will be denied a 'windfall' limitation defence (see *Buckler v Finnegan* [2004] EWCA Civ 920). But there is also prejudice to the claimant where he is told that he may not proceed with his action because he is out of time. Factors which may be relevant here are the length of the delay (*KR v Bryn Alyn Community (Holdings) Ltd* [2003] EWCA Civ 85), whether it is proportionate to allow the claim to proceed (*McGhie v British Telecommunications plc* [2005] EWCA Civ 920), the strength or weakness of the claimant's case, the size of any possible award of damages and whether the claimant has an alternative defendant to sue. This last issue is particularly relevant to Alice since she may have an action for professional negligence against her legal adviser, in which case it may be argued that the court should decline to exercise its discretion under s. 33. But requiring the claimant to sue her solicitor can prejudice her if the professional negligence case is not cast iron: *Conry v Simpson* [1983] 3 All ER 369. It is also relevant that requiring the claimant to sue her legal adviser will result in additional litigation and this is a relevant factor since s. 33 requires the court to have regard to all relevant circumstances: *Ramsden v Lee* [1992] 2 All ER 204. Moreover, if the claimant is required to sue her solicitor, regard should be had to the fact that she is being forced to give up an action against a tortfeasor who may know little of the weaker aspects of his case, to bringing an action against a person who knows all the finer details of that case by virtue of having represented the claimant: *Hartley v Birmingham City District Council* [1992] 2 All ER 213. All of this may suggest that the court might be inclined to exercise their discretion in order to allow Alice to sue out of time, so that she does not have to pursue her solicitors, Doohey, Cheetham & Howe.

Question 6

Punter, a partly qualified accountant, has recently been left a substantial sum of money by his late aunt, which he now wishes to invest. He is told by Spiv, a stockbroker client of his employers, that Flybinight plc is currently enjoying considerable success and that since the company's shares are underpriced Punter should buy now. He offers to undertake the purchase for Punter when given the go-ahead by him. Punter meets Hackett, an old friend of his, for a drink in a pub. Hackett has recently been appointed under-manager at Eastminster Bank and Punter asks him about the wisdom of buying the shares. Hackett says that although he does not have much experience in financial advising as yet, he is interested in business matters and always reads the relevant papers. He says that *Whizz Weekly*, one of the more respected financial papers, predicts that Flybinight is undervalued since the company seems poised to declare record profits. Hackett therefore concludes that on the basis of this report and his general overview of business affairs, Punter should go ahead and buy.

Following the advice he received, Punter invests heavily in the company. After two months the company is put into liquidation by its creditors and Punter loses his investment.

Advise Punter as to whether he has any legal redress to recover his losses against Spiv, Hackett, and *Whizz Weekly*.

Commentary

Generally, the tort of negligence is more attuned to dealing with actions that result in physical harm to the person or to property. However, in limited circumstances it may also be used to deal with financial losses, particularly those caused by negligently prepared or communicated statements. Generally, physical harm tends to 'lie where it falls' so that the range of possible claimants will be limited. Words or advice present different problems since words can be heard and acted on by a much wider range of individuals.

This question requires consideration of the rules governing economic loss caused by negligent statements. In particular an examination of the principles governing the imposition of a duty of care is required.

Answer plan

- Why is the advice both prepared and communicated: *Caparo plc v Dickman*?
- Is advice given on a social occasion actionable: *Choudhry v Prabhakar*?
- Have any of the advisors voluntarily assumed a responsibility to Punter for the advice they give: *Henderson v Merrett Syndicates*?
- Is there a distinction between those who merely transmit information and those who produce it?

Suggested answer

Liability for economic loss caused by negligent misstatement is not determined by the *Donoghue v Stevenson* [1932] AC 562 neighbour principle alone, but in accordance with more restrictive tests which govern the imposition of a duty of care for such statements. This is because the potential liability of the representor is far wider than that where the issue involves a negligent act since a statement can affect a large indeterminate class of claimants. Claims for negligent misstatement can often involve potentially huge sums of money because unlike physical harm, where events tend to rest where they fall, advice can be relied upon by any number of people who come into contact with it. In formulating the rules governing liability, the courts have long been mindful of the so-called 'floodgates' argument which is encapsulated by Cardozo CJ's warning delivered in *Ultramares Corporation v Touche* (1931) 174 NE 441, of opening 'liability in an indeterminate amount for an indeterminate time to an indeterminate class'.

Whether Spiv owes Punter a duty of care in respect of his advice to purchase the shares will depend on one of three different tests identified in *Customs & Excise Commissioners v Barclays Bank plc* [2006] 3 WLR 1. It has been held that it is necessary to ask whether the defendant has voluntarily assumed responsibility for what he said and did. Alternatively, other cases require satisfaction of the three-fold test of reasonable foresight of loss; whether the relationship between the parties is sufficiently proximate and whether it is fair, just, and reasonable to impose liability (see *Caparo Industries v Dickman* [1990] 2 AC 549). Thirdly, there is the incremental test (*Sutherland Shire Council v Heyman* (1985) 157 CLR 424, 481 *per* Brennan J) that indicates that new duty situations should be developed only incrementally and by analogy with existing cases, rather than by massive leaps into new areas.

These alternative tests assist in identifying whether the relationship between the parties can be described as a 'special relationship' for the purposes of the rule in *Hedley Byrne & Co v Heller & Partners Ltd* [1964] AC 465. For these purposes the relationship between representor and representee must be such that the latter reasonably relies on the advice given by the former and that the representor is, or ought to be aware of this. Furthermore, in advice cases where the defendant gives information to X on behalf of Y, it needs to be asked whether the defendant has assumed responsibility to X or whether he was merely discharging his responsibility towards Y (*Williams v Natural Life Health Foods Ltd* [1998] 2 All ER 577). The assumption of responsibility test has been noted to be particularly useful in determining whether a defendant owes a duty of care in respect of advice given by him to the claimant (see *Customs & Excise Commissioners v Barclays Bank plc* [2006] 3 WLR 1, para. [35] *per* Lord Hoffmann). Thus it is helpful to ask whether the defendant has assumed responsibility for advice given to the claimant that he knows will be relied upon (*Hedley Byrne & Co v Heller & Partners Ltd* [1964] AC 465). Likewise, it is relevant to consider whether the defendant has assumed responsibility for advice given for one purpose, when the claimant relies on that advice for another, different purpose (*Caparo Industries v Dickman* [1990] 2 AC 605). In determining whether there is a voluntary assumption of responsibility, it is important to apply the test objectively and it is not to be answered by reference to what the defendant thought or intended (*Henderson v Merrett Syndicates Ltd* [1994] 2 AC 145). Thus, as was observed by Lord Griffiths in *Smith v Eric S Bush* [1990] 1 AC 831, 862, the phrase 'assumption of responsibility' can only have any real meaning if it is understood as referring to the circumstances in which the law will deem the defendant to have assumed responsibility to the claimant (see also *White v Jones* [1995] 2 AC 207).

Generally, the decision in *Caparo Industries v Dickman* [1990] makes four factors relevant to the question whether a duty of care is owed, namely:

(a) Was the representor fully aware of the nature of the transaction which the claimant had in contemplation?

(b) Did the representor know that the information would be communicated to the claimant, either directly or indirectly?

(c) Did the representor know that it was very likely that the claimant would rely on the information when deciding whether or not to engage in the transaction in question?

(d) Was the purpose for which the claimant relied on the information one that is connected with interests which it is proper to expect the representor to protect?

In applying the rules laid down in *Hedley Byrne* (as interpreted by the House of Lords in *Caparo v Dickman and Customs & Excise Commissioners v Barclays Bank plc*) to Spiv, it is suggested that a 'special relationship' may be found to exist given that Spiv, as a stockbroker, must know that his advice would be relied upon for investment purposes. That advice was communicated directly to Punter and he is advised to 'buy now' and there is direct contact between Spiv and Punter. As a professional, Spiv obviously has skill and it is reasonable and proper to expect Spiv to have due regard to the interests of those who receive his advice and information. The meaning of 'special skill' has been held to include special knowledge (*Henderson v Merrett Syndicates Ltd* [1995] 2 AC 145, *per* Lord Goff). Further, as a stockbroker, Spiv may be held to be in a fiduciary relationship with Punter. In *White v Jones* [1995] 2 AC 207, which concerned an action by two intended beneficiaries against a solicitor who negligently failed to amend a will before the testator's death, Lord Browne-Wilkinson extended the *Hedley Byrne* principle by holding that there is no requirement on the claimant to prove foreseeable reliance where a fiduciary duty is owed to him or her by the defendant. His Lordship observed that in the case of a fiduciary, it was sufficient that the defendant was aware that the claimant's financial welfare was dependent upon the exercise of proper care by him and as such, a 'special relationship' arises. The decision clearly broadens the ambit of *Hedley Byrne* given that on its facts, there was no reliance on the solicitor's skill by the claimants but rather it was the deceased testator who had placed reliance on him. This dilution of the reliance requirement is also discernible in *Henderson v Merrett Syndicates Ltd* and *Spring v Guardian Assurance plc* [1995] 2 AC 296. The essential issue identified in all three of these recent House of Lords cases was the question of finding a sufficient degree of proximity so as to accord with the second limb of the tripartite test promulgated in *Caparo*. It is suggested that such proximity can be said to exist between Spiv and Punter because, in the language of Lord Atkin in *Donoghue v Stevenson* [1932] AC 562, Punter was clearly 'closely and directed affected' by Spiv's negligent advice.

With respect to Hackett, the circumstances in which the advice is given and the nature of the relationship between him and Punter are material. It was stated by Lord Reid in *Hedley Byrne* that when opinions are expressed on social occasions, they are often made without the care that would normally be accorded if asked for professionally. Hackett's status at the bank as under-manager is also significant given that his degree of expertise must be open to question. In *Choudhry v Prabhakar* [1988] 3 All ER 718 the defendant, who was a friend of the claimant, offered to help her find and purchase a car. Although not a mechanic, he told her that he had a good knowledge of cars. The claimant specifically requested that he help her find a car which had not been crashed. The defendant found a low-mileage vehicle which he knew had had its bonnet repaired or replaced. It was unroadworthy, a fact not discovered before the sale because of the defendant's advice not to have the car inspected by a professional mechanic. The Court of Appeal held the defendant liable on the ground that this was not a purely social relationship given the claimant's reliance upon the defendant's skill and his knowledge of that reliance. However, it is pertinent to note that the decision was based on a concession by counsel that there was a duty situation. Thus the decision was arrived at, purely on the basis that there had been a breach of duty by the defendant. In the light of later authority, the same facts might pose greater difficulties in establishing the existence of a duty of care, bearing in mind that the imposition of a duty in such circumstances might make 'social regulations [*sic*] and responsibilities between friends unnecessarily hazardous' (ibid. at 275, *per* May LJ).

Since Hackett had informed Punter that he lacked relevant experience and did not profess to be an expert, coupled with the fact that the advice appears to be tendered on a social occasion, the court is unlikely to impose a duty of care in these circumstances. Further, in *Royal Bank Trust (Trinidad) v Pampellonne* [1987] 1 Lloyd's Rep 218, the Privy Council drew a line between those who merely transmit information and those who produce it. A duty of care would only arise with respect to the latter. On this view, Hackett's advice would seem to fall into the former category. However, more recently the distinction between advice and information has been limited to the issue of determining the scope of the duty of care, so that the mere provision of information may now fall within the *Hedley Byrne* principle (see *South Australia Asset Management Corporation v York Montague Ltd* [1997] AC 191). Nevertheless, taking all the circumstances into account, it is unlikely that the court would consider it just, fair or reasonable to impose a duty of care on Hackett.

The imposition of a duty of care on *Whizz Weekly* is also unlikely. In *Hedley Byrne* the House of Lords recognized the danger of formulating rules which could result in the maker of a careless **statement** being liable to a wide, indeterminate class of claimants. For this reason, Lord Bridge in *Caparo* stressed the necessity of 'proximity' between the claimant and defendant and warned against the dangers of holding a defendant liable 'to all and sundry' for any purpose for which they may choose to rely on it. The statement that the shares of Flybinight are 'undervalued' does not amount to an unequivocal recommendation that the company's shares should be bought. Moreover, there does not appear to have been any direct or indirect contact between *Whizz Weekly* and the claimant such as to give rise to an inference that there has been a voluntary assumption of responsibility for the advice contained in the paper (*Williams v Natural Life Health Foods* [1998] 2 All ER 577).

(4) Omissions

Question 7

David, a painter and decorator, lived across the road from a block of flats in which Hayley lived. He saw her trying to paint her window frames and offered to do the job for her at the weekend saying that it would be no trouble and that if he ever needed a return favour he would know where to come.

On the Saturday when David did the job, Hayley spent the afternoon sunbathing in her garden which lay to the rear of her ground-floor flat. In view of the nice weather and in order to let the premises 'air' he left the front door open.

While David was painting the kitchen window, Tommy Leaf, a local petty criminal crept in and stole many valuable antiques from Hayley's apartment. In addition he took the opportunity of being inside the main door to the block of flats to break into and burgle Pam's third-floor apartment as he knew her to be away on holiday in Greece.

Tommy Leaf has not been caught.

Advise David, Hayley and Pam as to their respective rights and duties.

Commentary

This question requires consideration of the general rule that tortious liability is not ordinarily imposed for the failure to act to prevent harm (nonfeasance), in the absence of any voluntary assumption of responsibility on the part of the defendant.

Answer plan

- The nature of David's undertaking to Hayley.
- The limited circumstances in which occupiers of property may be placed under a duty to take reasonable precautions against the wrongdoing of third parties to determine whether Hayley owes a duty of care to Pam.

Suggested answer

The essential issue which arises from the given facts revolves around the failure of David and Hayley the occupier of the flat, to prevent the infliction of damage by the act of a third party. The general rule is that there is no duty at common law to prevent persons harming others by their deliberate wrongdoing, however foreseeable such harm may be in the absence of steps being taken to prevent it. This proposition arises from the notion that ordinarily liability is not imposed for pure omissions. In *Smith v Littlewoods Organisation Ltd* [1987] AC 241, the defendants bought a disused cinema which they left unoccupied for a period of time pending its demolition. During that period vandals broke into the empty premises and lit a fire which spread to neighbouring properties causing serious damage. Littlewoods were unaware of the general reputation for vandalism which the particular locality possessed. The owners of those damaged properties sued the supermarket chain. It was held by the House of Lords in rejecting the claim, that the duty of care did not extend to a duty to take 'exceptional' care. Of primary concern to their Lordships was the issue that if a duty of care were to be imposed on occupiers of property in such circumstances, it could not be discharged short of placing an intolerable burden on the occupiers to mount 24-hour guards on empty premises.

In examining David's duty to Hayley, it is of crucial importance to determine the nature of the undertaking he makes to her since an affirmative duty to prevent harm may arise depending on what was said and understood by both parties. It is clear that if there is a contractual relationship between them, liability for the theft of the antiques may be borne by him. In *Stansbie v Troman* [1948] 2 KB 48, a decorator was instructed by the householder to lock the door if he went out. He went out leaving the door on the latch whereby a thief entered the house and stole jewellery. The decorator was held liable for the loss. The decision has been explained on the basis of an implied term of the contract that in decorating the house the decorator would exercise reasonable care in respect of its contents (*P Perl (Exporters) Ltd v Camden London Borough Council* [1984] QB 342, *per* Oliver and Goff LJJ). Further, in *Home Office v Dorset Yacht Co Ltd* [1970] AC 1004, a group of young offenders who were under the supervision and control of three officers, escaped while the officers were asleep in breach of their instructions not to leave the youths unsupervised. The youths boarded a nearby yacht and caused it to collide with a yacht owned by the claimant. The Home Office was held vicariously liable for the negligence of the officers. The House of Lords held that a duty of care arose out of the special relationship between the youths and their custodians since the youths were under the control of the officers and 'control' imports responsibility. Lord Diplock stressed that liability should be restricted to the harm caused in the course of the escape to those in close physical proximity.

Applying these authorities to the facts of the problem, it seems unlikely that David will be considered to owe a duty of care to Hayley. Carrying out the job on the loose understanding that if he 'ever needed a return favour he would know where to come' does not of itself suggest a contract between them from which a term can be implied to keep the door locked. Also, since Hayley is in her garden (so still on the property) he does not appear to have the requisite 'control' of the premises under which he may bear responsibility for Tommy Leaf's entrance into the flat. He is not therefore under a legal obligation to control the activities of the thief.

Pam is in an analogous position to the neighbouring property owners in *Smith v Littlewoods Organisation Ltd*. In considering the situation where a thief gains access to property through the failure of an adjacent neighbour to keep his property lockfast, Lord Goff opined that liability cannot be imposed on the neighbour for the burglary since every occupier must take such steps as he thinks fit for the protection of his own property. His Lordship stated that when considering what precautions should be taken, an occupier should take into account the fact that from time to time his neighbours may leave their properties unlocked. Such a proposition follows from the rule that there is no general duty to prevent third parties causing damage to others. As Lord Keith observed in *Yuen Kun Yeu v Attorney-General of Hong Kong* [1988] AC 175, there is no liability in negligence on one who sees another about to walk over a cliff with his head in the air, and fails to shout a warning. Lord Goff went on to explain that exceptionally liability for the activities of others may arise in two situations. First, where a landowner has knowledge, or means of knowledge, that trespassers have created a risk of fire on his property, and then fails to abate the risk of that fire from damaging neighbouring property. It is clear that the given facts do not fall within this exception. Secondly, where a landowner creates, or allows to be created, an unusual source of danger on his land and it is reasonably foreseeable that a third party may interfere with it thereby causing damage to another (*Haynes v Harwood* [1935] 1 KB 146). Lord Goff stressed that liability under this principle should only be imposed where a defendant has negligently caused or permitted a source of danger and it is foreseeable that a third party may 'spark it off'. Hayley's failure to ensure that her decorator keeps the apartment block locked is not of itself likely to result in theft to a resident, and therefore cannot be described as creating a source of danger which was foreseeably 'sparked off' by Tommy Leaf.

The decision of the Court of Appeal in *P Perl (Exporters) Ltd v Camden London Borough Council*, is also of particular significance to Pam's legal position. Briefly, the facts were that a local authority which owned a block of flats failed to secure a basement flat which was unoccupied. Burglars entered this flat and knocked an 18-inch hole through the party wall and burgled the claimant's property. It was held that the relationship of neighbouring property owners was not of itself sufficient to impose on one owner the duty to guard the other against the foreseeable risk of burglary through unsecured property. The court pointed out that to impose such a duty would place an unreasonable burden on ordinary householders and an unreasonable curb on the ordinary enjoyment of their property.

In *Smith v Littlewoods* Lord Goff was of the view that *Perl* was correctly decided and pointed out that the law has to accommodate 'the untidy complexity of life' and therefore there are situations where considerations of practical justice will pre-empt the imposition of a duty of care. This approach was more recently followed in *Topp v London Country Bus Ltd* [1993] 1 WLR 976, where the defendant had left a minibus unattended outside a pub at a bus stop for some nine hours with its door unlocked and with its key still in the ignition. A thief stole the bus and knocked over and killed the claimant's wife. The thief was never detected and the claimant sued the defendants as owners of the bus. Both May J at first instance and the Court of Appeal found that there was a relationship of proximity between the defendants and the deceased. However, applying the language of *Caparo Industries plc v Dickman* [1990] 2 AC 605, it was held that it would not be 'fair, just and reasonable' to recognize a duty of care on the facts since any affirmative duty to prevent deliberate wrongdoing by third parties, if recognized by English law, is likely to be strictly limited. Accordingly, it is submitted that Pam is not owed a duty of care by Hayley to prevent the thief, Tommy Leaf, gaining access to the building by her failure to ensure that her decorator kept the building lockfast during the repainting. Given that this factual situation does not fall within the exceptional circumstances outlined by Lord Goff, it would not be just and reasonable to subject Hayley to such a duty. As such, the facts fall squarely within the principle formulated by Lord Sumner in *Weld-Blundell v Stephens* [1920] AC 956, that in general, 'even though A is at fault, he is not responsible for injury to C which B, a stranger to him, deliberately chose to do'.

Further reading

Cane, P., *Tort Law and Economic Interests*, 2nd edn (Oxford: Clarendon Press, 1996).

Gilliker, P., 'Revisiting Pure Economic Loss' (2005) *Legal Studies* 49.

Hepple, B., 'The Search for Coherence' (1997) 50 *Current Legal Problems* 69.

Murphy, J., 'Expectation Losses, Negligent Omissions and the Tortious Duty of Care' (1996) CLJ 43.

Stapleton, J., 'Duty of Care and Economic Loss: A Wider Agenda' (1991) 107 LQR 249.

Stapleton, J., 'Duty of Care: Peripheral Parties and Alternative Opportunities for Deterrence' (1995) 111 LQR 301.

Whittaker, S., 'The Application of the Broad Principle of Hedley Byrne as between Parties to a Contract' (1997) *Legal Studies* 169.

Witting, C., 'Justifying Liability to Third Parties for Negligent Misstatements' (2000) 20 OJLS 615.

Witting, C., 'Distinguishing between Property Damage and Economic Loss in Negligence: A Personality Thesis' (2001) *Legal Studies* 481.

5

Negligence II: breach of duty

Introduction

Breach of duty involves an objective consideration of what a reasonable person in the same position as the defendant would have done. Thus it is necessary to ask if the defendant has reached the standards set by a reasonable person, or the 'man on the Clapham omnibus'. Expressed in this way, the test sounds perfectly straightforward and designed to achieve certainty (and therefore justice) in the law since it appears to eliminate any consideration of the personal characteristics of individual defendants. In reality, of course, other factors may be taken into account, and the law is prepared in some circumstances to accept a lower standard, for example, from children and may expect a higher standard from, for example, a skilled professional. Policy issues are again relevant, especially in relation to medical negligence where judgments as to the applicable standard must not have a detrimental effect on the development of new techniques and procedures.

Once a suitable description of the appropriate standard has been identified, in any problem, there remains the question, 'What steps would such a person be required to take?' This will involve an analysis of the factors that might raise or lower the level of precautions needed. Such factors include: an assessment of the degree of risk, by reference to the likelihood of harm occurring together with the potential severity of the harm, should it occur; the social utility of the defendant's activity; and the practicability of any precautions that might be needed. It should be remembered that in negligence one is expected to act reasonably *in all the circumstances*, and that an answer that fails to go through the full reasoning process is incomplete.

As always, examiners are looking for evidence of a thorough knowledge of the relevant legal principles, and students must be especially careful to avoid reading the question as a story and responding with a common sense, rather than a legal, answer.

Question 1

'In general the relevant circumstances [occasioning variations in the standard of care] will be the physical conditions in which the act takes place . . . and should exclude those factors which describe the actor rather than the act'.

(Kidner)

To what extent is this, and should it be, the case?

Commentary

This question requires consideration of the factors which, in English law, are relevant to the process of determining whether the defendant is in breach of a duty of care in a negligence action. In particular, it is inviting the student to question the suggestion that individual characteristics of the defendant are always to be disregarded, and to consider the justice of any such variation.

Answer plan

- Special characteristics of the tortfeasor (the 'actor' in the quote).
- The circumstances in which the alleged negligence took place.
- The question also requires an intelligent critique of whether factors which are germane to the actor should ever be relevant to the setting of a standard of care which purports to be objective in nature.

Suggested answer

For the most part, it is true to assert that the idiosyncrasies of the tortfeasor are irrelevant to ascertaining the requisite standard of care in a negligence action. This is because, according to received wisdom, the standard of care is an objective one (*Blyth v Birmingham Waterworks* (1856) 11 Ex 781 *per* Alderson B), and as such, a question of law to be determined by the courts (*Nettleship v Weston* [1971] 2 QB 691). Even so, as will be explained, there are factors which relate to the defendant as *a member of a particular class* of persons which can equally affect the level of care that must be shown in order to avoid liability in negligence. It is not, however, all classes of person that seem to attract 'special treatment' under the law. This fact no doubt forms the basis of the generalization comprising the essay title. But it remains, nonetheless, a generalization. As such, it is necessarily destined to be least helpful where specificity and precision are most needed.

A sophisticated analysis of the law relating to the standard of care might seek to argue that the (seeming) inconsistency in the decided case law stems from the several, sometimes conflicting, objectives which the law of tort strives to achieve.

Thus, briefly to supply an example (which will be further considered below), the desire to ensure that a 'worthy' claimant receives compensation might conflict, for example, with the aim of the tort system to do justice. Accordingly, in *Nettleship v Weston* [1971] 2 QB 691, the price of compensating the injured party was holding a learner driver liable for failure to meet the driving standard one would expect of a qualified driver. This, on one conception of justice, might seem unreasonable and mightily unfair on the learner driver, but equally it would seem unduly hard on a victim to deprive them of compensation simply because their injuries happened to be caused by a learner. For present purposes, appropriate scrutiny of the hypothesis put forward in the title entails a two-step approach. First, it is necessary to assess whether the standard of care is indeed more responsive to changes in the physical conditions in which the act takes place than the particular characteristics of the defendant. Secondly, it is necessary to explain why the law should take this approach.

To begin with, it is clear that the standard of care is fixed with the circumstances in which the accident takes place very much in mind. No more stark example of this may be supplied than the case of *Watt v Hertfordshire CC* [1954] 2 All ER 368. There, because of an accident, a woman found herself trapped under a lorry. In a hurry to release her, a truck ill-suited to transporting a heavy jack was used for just that purpose. In braking suddenly, the jack was propelled forwards and it injured the claimant, one of the firemen, on his way to releasing the trapped woman. In finding the defendants not negligent, Denning LJ stated that:

> 'If this accident had occurred in a commercial enterprise without any emergency, there can be no doubt that the servant would succeed. But the commercial end to make profit is very different from the human end to save life or limb. The saving of life or limb justifies considerable risk.'

It is also clear that other circumstantial factors may affect the level of care demanded of the defendant, such as the relative cost of precautionary measures (*Latimer v AEC Ltd* [1953] AC 653); the likelihood of harm occurring (*Bolton v Stone* [1951] AC 850); the severity of harm should it occur (*Paris v Stepney Borough Council* [1951] AC 367); and the social utility of the defendant's conduct (*Daborn v Bath Tramways* [1946] 2 All ER 333). In short, in respect of the first limb of Kidner's proposition, it would be incorrect to assert that the scenario in which the accident occurs is unimportant. But that is, in truth, only part of the matter. There are equally as many factors which relate to the characteristics of the defendant (albeit as a member of an identifiable class) that affect the level of care expected at law.

The first factor which the courts take into account in ascertaining the appropriate standard of care is the youth of the defendant. In *McHale v Watson* (1965) 111 CLR 384, for example, a decision of the High Court of Australia, the fact of the defendant's age (he was a 12-year-old boy) was held relevant to the standard of care issue. This approach has more recently been adopted in England by the Court of Appeal in *Mullin v Richards* [1998] 1 All ER 920, reflecting a similar attitude to the level of care to be looked for from children in relation to the defence of contributory negligence. It had been held at Court of Appeal level that age is a relevant criterion when the court assesses the degree of care that that child can be expected to take for his or her own safety (*Gough v Thorne* [1966] 3 All ER 398). Clearly, therefore, English law does take account of youth in setting the standard of care.

A second factor which the courts may take into account is the degree of skill or professionalism that can be expected of the particular defendant. Thus, in *Philips v William Whiteley Ltd* [1938] 1 All ER 566, for example, it was held that a jeweller performing an ear-piercing was not expected to adhere to the same standards of hygiene as a surgeon performing a comparable 'operation'. But the point must be stressed that the standard of care expected of the jeweller in that case is the standard to which *all* ear-piercing jewellers must aspire. The standard was set by reference to the jeweller, not as an individual, but as a member of a particular class. It is clear that there will not be variations of the standard of care within a class. Thus, a junior and overworked houseman is expected to demonstrate the same standard of care as a more experienced doctor occupying the same post (*Wilsher v Essex AHA* [1987] QB 730). To allow a lower standard would be to:

> 'subordinate the legitimate expectation of the patient that he will receive from each person concerned with his care a degree of skill appropriate to the task that [the doctor] undertakes to an understandable wish to minimize the psychological and financial pressures on hard pressed young doctors.'

A final factor that describes the actor more than the act, and which is again relevant to setting the standard of care, is the fact that the defendant was, at the time of the accident, engaged in a sporting pursuit. Here the standard of care will be lowered to take account of the fact that the sporting arena is one which naturally gives rise to the need to take spur-of-the-moment decisions (*Wooldridge v Sumner* [1963] 2 QB 43). But even here, outright recklessness on the part of a sportsperson will not be tolerated (*Condon v Basi* [1985] 2 All ER 453; *Caldwell v Maguire and Fitzgerald* [2001] All ER (D) 363 (Jun)).

So, it may be seen that English law takes account of many factors in setting the relevant standard of care. Some such factors do relate to the characteristics of the defendant, perhaps more than Kidner's suggestion that this is not generally the case would imply. However, those factors which describe the actor, and which are relevant in this context, do so *only* so far as they take account of the defendant as a member of a defined class of persons. But this does not derogate from the importance of asking whether such factors ought to be relevant in the first place. Simply to identify that certain characteristics of the defendant are taken into account by the courts is not also to justify them.

It can certainly be argued that no variations in the standard of care should properly be founded on the idiosyncrasies of the defendant. To do so would be to drive a sledgehammer through the principle that the standard of care is an objective one, intended to promote certainty both as to when a defendant will be held negligent and as to the level of safety a claimant may legitimately expect. The same objection—i.e. the loss of objectivity—arises when the standard is set with a class of persons in mind as it is ultimately the judiciary who are final arbiters of when class status is made out. This is important since the standard of care may only be adjusted if such class status (and where its boundaries lie) is recognized. Such determinations may be policy-driven so that in order that an insurance company ultimately bears the loss rather than an individual citizen, the standard can be artificially kept high by refusing to recognize class status. Thus, learner drivers, an ostensibly distinct class of road users, are simply bracketed with qualified drivers and the fact of compulsory insurance means that such a driver can be held liable in negligence to ensure that anyone injured by the mishap will receive compensation (*Nettleship v Weston* [1971] 2 QB 691). Equally, policy might be said to underpin the approach taken in *Wilsher* where Mustill J was clearly of the view that patients must be able to have confidence in the quality of their health care regardless of the absence of seniority in the doctor in attendance. Arguably flexibility promotes justice, whilst rigid objectivity promotes certainty. Certainty is something which may be valuable in relation to any set of legal rules, but at what price it should be bought is matter for debate. Ultimately, taking characteristics of the defendant into account militates against the principle that the standard of care is an objective one. This can promote justice. But if the courts' approach to the matter of identifying a class of persons that deserve individual treatment lacks consistency, as seems to be the case in English law, then, it may be argued, neither justice nor certainty are achieved and, particularly in relation to some areas of potential liability, the law may have the appearance of being both inconsistent and flawed.

Question 2

Consider the issues of standard of care and breach of duty in negligence raised by the following facts:

Clarence, who was walking along the street, was hit by a milk bottle which fell from one of the upper windows of the local primary school. The local education authority claims that there were no children in the school at the time because lessons had ended 45 minutes earlier and all the children had gone home. Clarence wishes to sue the local education authority in negligence.

Omolade was cut when, on hearing an explosion in the street outside, Liz, her manicurist, momentarily took her eyes off Omolade's hand. At the time, Liz simply gave her a sticking plaster for the cut, but since then the cut has turned septic causing Omolade considerable pain. Omolade seeks your advice as regards suing Liz in negligence.

Pierre was injured when he was rescued by the air-sea rescue team after the weather capsized his boat. The rescue team used only a rope, instead of the padded harness usually employed by rescue teams, to hoist him into a helicopter. Pierre received several cracked ribs in the process. He seeks your advice in relation to a potential negligence action against his rescuers.

Commentary

This question raises three different, but related, kinds of problems associated with breach of duty in the tort of negligence. It calls for a detailed consideration of the factors defining the appropriate standard, and of the elements of the balancing process a defendant must engage in so as to meet foreseeable risks with reasonable precautions.

Answer plan

- Proof of fault and the role of the doctrine of *res ipsa loquitur*.
- The relevant standard in the light of characteristics particular to the defendant.
- Variations in standard in the light of the particular circumstances in which the event took place.

Suggested answer

Since Clarence was oblivious to the milk bottles above him, and because there is no obvious explanation as to why the milk bottles should have fallen, Clarence faces a problem of proving negligence on the part of the local education authority. However, as the accident is of a kind that does not normally occur in everyday life, Clarence may invoke the doctrine of *res ipsa loquitur* (let the thing speak for itself). Although it is sometimes said that this raises a rebuttable presumption of negligence on the part of the defendant it has more recently been said to be no more than an inference of negligence drawn from the facts. More specifically, in order to invoke this doctrine, Clarence must, on the authority of Erle CJ in *Scott v London and St Katherine Docks Co* (1865) 33 H & C 596, show three things. He must show first that the accident was of a kind that does not normally occur in the absence of a want of care. Secondly, he must show that the defendant had exclusive control over the thing which has occasioned him harm and he must show, finally, that the defendant has no plausible alternative (innocent) explanation of what caused the accident to occur.

In respect of the first of these, there is ample authority to suggest that falling objects are within the class of things that do not normally occur without negligence (*Byrne v Boadle* (1863) 2 H & C 722, barrels of flour from a warehouse; *Scott v London and St Katherine Docks Co*, bags of sugar from a hoist).

In respect of the second limb, it is clear that bottles fell from the premises of the defendants and were thus under their exclusive control since the school had closed some 45 minutes earlier and the bottles, like the underwear in *Grant v Australian Knitting Mills* [1936] AC 85, could not have been interfered with by an intermediary. In relation to the third hurdle, the local education authority, on the facts that we are given, does not appear able to disprove negligence. Nor does it appear able to supply evidence of a plausible alternative explanation of how the bottles fell (which is all it need do to rebut the inference of negligence raised by the *res ipsa loquitur* doctrine: *Ng Chun Pui v Lee Chuen Tat* [1988] RTR 298).

With respect to Omolade's injury, several potential instances of negligence need to be considered. First, whether Liz's momentary inattention due to the explosion could be characterized as negligence; secondly, whether her subsequent treatment of the cut could amount to negligent conduct; and, thirdly, whether it could be established that any lack of hygiene in relation to her manicuring tools was negligent.

As regards the infliction of the cut, the starting point is to note that the law of negligence distinguishes between (actionable) negligence and (non-actionable) errors. The law does not demand that a defendant, on pain of suit for negligence, should act to the maximum attainable standard of which human beings are capable. Instead, it requires only that the defendant should have behaved in a manner consistent with the actions of a reasonable person (*Blyth v Birmingham Waterworks Co* (1856) 11 Exch 781; *Glasgow Corporation v Muir* [1943] AC 448), i.e. doing what a reasonable person would have done or omitting to do what a reasonable person would not have done. Moreover, the standard demanded will vary according to circumstances and the type of activity undertaken, thus in *Blyth v Birmingham* it would be the standard of the reasonable operator of waterworks and pipes, and in *Glasgow Corporation v Muir* it would be the standard of the reasonable manager of a café who should be neither too fearful of something happening nor over confident that accidents will not happen. The standard will vary according to the calling of the defendant: it would be expected that a doctor's conduct would be tested against the standard of a reasonably competent medical practitioner rather than the reasonable person. In our case, it is arguably material that Liz's slip stemmed from the 'heat of the moment' in which the explosion took place. In *Marshall v Osmond* [1983] QB 1034, it was held that errors of judgement in the heat of the moment should be regarded as errors that the reasonable man might make and that they should, therefore, not be actionable.

In relation to the second point—the mere (and insufficient) application of a sticking plaster to Omolade's injury—there can be little doubt that Liz owed a duty to Omolade on the basis of her assumption of responsibility towards Omolade (*White v Jones* [1995] 1 All ER 691). In this case, then, it is relevant to ask whether her 'treatment' of Liz was negligent. Here, it is to be noted that the standard demanded of Liz will not, on the authority of *Philips v William Whitely* [1938] 1 All ER 566, be the same as that demanded of a doctor, had a doctor been summoned to treat Omolade. In the *Philips* case, which is clearly analogous, a jeweller was held not to be liable in respect of an infection in the plaintiff's ears caused by the jeweller's ear-piercing. The court in that case held that the standard of care in respect of hygiene etc. was that of a jeweller doing such work, not that of a doctor. In our case, then, Liz will be required to meet the standard of care of the reasonable manicurist not that of the reasonable doctor. Arguably, she has met this standard in supplying her client with a sticking plaster.

In light of the fact that Omolade's cut has turned septic, she may seek to argue that Liz has been negligent in failing to keep her manicuring tools in a suitably hygienic state. Since there are many possible ways in which a cut may become infected, the doctrine of *res ipsa loquitur* (let the thing speak for itself) will not assist Omolade and she would need evidence on the actual cleanliness of Liz's tools. Whatever the outcome of this enquiry, the standard Liz has reached will be judged according to what is reasonable in all the circumstances. Relevant information could be gained from the hygiene practices customary amongst competent manicurists, though this will not be legally definitive and so the standard will also be measured by a balancing of reasonably practicable precautions against risk. So, the likelihood of breaking the skin during a manicure may be judged from the frequency with which it occurs (*Bolton v Stone* [1951] AC 850—the fact that very few cricket balls had escaped over a period of decades was evidence of low statistical probability); and the potential severity of any infection should also be taken into account as a factor increasing overall risk (*Paris v Stepney BC* [1951] AC 367—more protection was needed against potential injury to an employee with only one eye).

The standard of care demanded by the law of negligence of the (presumably professional) rescue team is that of any such persons possessed of the skills required to do that job, namely 'the standard of an ordinary skilled man exercising and professing to have that special skill' (*Bolam v Friern Hospital* [1957] 1 WLR 582, 586). The fact that we know of another air-sea rescue team that uses different, safer equipment begs the question whether the team were negligent in merely using a rope. The answer to this lies in two stages. First, and by analogy with the law's approach to medical practitioners, it could be argued that so long as a significant body of professional opinion, gleaned from other rescue teams, backs the use of a rope alone that, *prima facie*, will exculpate the team in our case. As Lord Scarman put it in *Maynard v West Midlands RHA* [1984] 1 WLR 634: '[A] judge's preference for one body of distinguished professional opinion to another also professionally distinguished is not sufficient to establish negligence'. However, the policy reasoning in favour of greater flexibility for medical practitioners (so that advances in medical science are not stifled by fear of litigation) rather lacks conviction when applied to air-sea rescue. Should it apply, however, if the decision to use a rope alone could be shown to be so unreasonable a choice that no reasonable rescue team could have made it, an action for negligence might still lie (see *Bolitho v City and Hackney Health Authority* [1997] 4 All ER 771). As regards the reasonableness of using a cheap rope rather than an expensive harness, the court would be entitled to consider whether the cost of preventing an injury outweighed the risk of the injury (both in terms of the magnitude and likelihood of that injury occurring: *Bolton v Stone* [1951] AC 850; *Latimer v AEC Ltd* [1953] AC 643).

Even if all other rescue teams would not use merely a rope it remains to be asked whether the rescue team may nonetheless escape liability on other grounds. The rescue team might argue that, had they had more time they could have procured a harness to use in the operation but, since it was a life and death situation they were forced to act swiftly with whatever (non-ideal) tools they had to hand. Such an argument would clearly be premised on the analogous case of *Watt v Hertfordshire CC* [1954] 1 All ER 835 where the emergency services used an inappropriate lorry to transport a jack desperately needed to rescue a casualty. A fireman was injured when steadying the jack on the lorry. The employer was held not liable. But there have been cases where emergency vehicles going to an emergency have been driven carelessly causing harm and liability has been found, e.g. *Ward v London County Council* [1938] 2 All ER 341. Equally the risk to the claimant in not doing anything to rescue him was apparent and this may have outweighed the risk in using the rope.

Further reading

Witting, C., 'Res ipsa loquitur: some last words?' (2001) LQR 117, 392.

6

Negligence III: causation and remoteness of damage

Introduction

The defendant who has failed to reach the standard of the reasonable man is not necessarily liable for harm suffered by the claimant since his breach of duty must also have caused that harm, both factually and legally. Since the burden of proving all elements in the negligence process falls on the claimant, there is every chance of failure at some stage.

Factual causation is established in most cases initially, but not exclusively, by reference to the 'but for' test, which asks whether it is true to say that the harm would not have occurred to the claimant 'but for' the defendant's negligence. In most circumstances this works admirably as a first filter for eliminating those defendants whose negligent acts were not the cause of the claimant's loss or damage. In many cases, of course, a defendant's negligence is only the first step in a chain of events. Some of the claimant's own acts, and of those of third parties who become involved, are so connected with the negligence that they may be regarded, in law, as the responsibility of the defendant. Other events that impact on the claimant's loss or damage may be wholly independent and therefore are said to break the chain of causation. Problem questions on this area call for a systematic and carefully reasoned analysis of all the relevant factors, and a student needs to be especially careful when dealing with questions in which there are competing causes, whether concurrent or consecutive.

Even damage that has been factually caused by the defendant may be regarded as legally too remote if it is of a kind that could not reasonably have been foreseen. Another deceptively simple test since judges, as the determinants of reasonable foreseeability, will necessarily be influenced by their own views, and what may seem to one judge as an obvious consequence may be regarded by another as quite improbable. A finding that the damage in question was too remote may also reflect a policy-based decision that the claimant *ought* not to be compensated.

Question 1

Adeel is crossing a pedestrian crossing when he is struck by a car driven by Beatrice. Adeel is knocked to the ground and staggers to his feet, but is concussed and blinded by blood from a head wound. He is then hit by a car driven by Cassandra, who was texting on her mobile at the time, and knocked to the ground again, unconscious. Beatrice and Cassandra have both been breath-tested by the police, and Beatrice has been found to be significantly affected by alcohol.

Adeel is found to have serious injuries which will make it impossible for him to work again, but his doctors are not able to say which car caused those injuries. Adeel's laptop computer was also damaged, causing information to be destroyed which led to loss of business for his employers, FatCat Ltd.

Advise Adeel and FatCat Ltd whether they have any remedy against Beatrice and/or Cassandra.

Commentary

The question is about the tort of negligence. For a full answer, issues of duty and breach must be looked at but will, in the main, readily be answered. The main issues to be considered concern factual and legal causation, and the problems raised when the damage is associated with two rapidly consecutive events.

Answer plan

- Beatrice and Cassandra are joint tortfeasors.
- Does the law of negligence require particular damage to be ascribed to particular defendants?
- Does the criminal act of a third party amount to a *novus actus interveniens*?
- Does a motorist owe a duty of care to persons not present at the scene of an accident, particularly if they only suffer economic loss?

Suggested answer

Assuming Adeel's injuries have been caused by the traffic collision, it is necessary to consider the liability of Cassandra and Beatrice. There will be no dispute about the duty of care which Beatrice and Cassandra, as motorists, owe to Adeel, another road user (*Nettleship v Weston* [1971] 2 QB 691). If either driver is convicted of a criminal offence relating to her driving, or her fitness to drive, the conviction will be admissible evidence against her in any relevant civil proceedings brought by Adeel (Civil Evidence Act 1968, s. 11). A heavy burden of proof will lie upon Beatrice if she contends that the criminal court made a mistake (*Stupple v Royal Insurance Co Ltd* [1971] 1 QB 50).

There is little to choose between Beatrice and Cassandra so far as their breach of duty is concerned. Nevertheless, it is possible that Cassandra may argue that she was not to blame (or not solely to blame) for the second collision with Adeel because he stumbled unpredictably into her path. This would involve focusing the whole of the allegation of negligence against Beatrice on the basis that Adeel was still suffering from the effects of the first collision at the time. However, it is more likely that Beatrice and Cassandra will both be regarded as causes of the harm suffered by Adeel and that the issue of contribution between joint tortfeasors will arise. Such argument is permissible under the Civil Liability (Contribution) Act 1978, s. 1 (*Pride of Derby and Derbyshire Angling Association Ltd v British Celanese Ltd* [1952] 1 All ER 1326; *Fitzgerald v Lane* [1989] AC 238).

So far as the Civil Liability (Contribution) Act 1978 is concerned, it will make no difference whether Beatrice acted deliberately and Cassandra only negligently, since they will both be regarded as joint tortfeasors. Both may be required to make a contribution under the terms of the Act, and it will not be a defence for the merely negligent to argue that the degree of fault of the other tortfeasor was greater. Thus it has been held that the defence of *ex turpi causa non oritur actio* will not apply as between joint tortfeasors (*K v P (J third party)* [1993] 1 All ER 521). However, the greater degree of fault of one joint tortfeasor will clearly be a relevant consideration in determining what share of responsibility should be allocated to each defendant.

If Beatrice tries to put all the blame for Adeel's injuries on to Cassandra, she faces two problems. First, the medical evidence does not support such an allegation since we are told that Adeel's doctors cannot say which car was the cause of his serious impairment. Secondly, she cannot reasonably expect to escape being brought in as a joint tortfeasor, even if it could be shown that Cassandra's car caused the greater amount of the injuries to Adeel.

This is a case in which it is known that Beatrice caused at least some of the injuries suffered by Adeel and the only question to be resolved is whether Cassandra added to those injuries or not. Since the second collision has rendered Adeel unconscious when, previously, he was in a concussed state, this would suggest that the added damage would be attributable to Cassandra under the 'but for' test (*Barnett v Kensington & Chelsea Hospital Management Committee* [1969] 1 QB 428). This case is not to be likened to *Baker v Willoughby* [1967] AC 467, where there was a pre-existing disability caused by one tortfeasor and a subsequent worsening of that disability by another tortfeasor, there being no connection between the two tortfeasors or between the two incidents giving rise to the successive disabilities. Moreover, in *Baker* there were also important policy considerations since the later injury was caused by a criminal who shot the claimant in the leg, causing that leg to be amputated. This later act was held not to affect the claimant's existing claim for damages against the first defendant for injuries caused to the same leg in a road traffic accident. Ignoring the 'but for' test, the first defendant (the negligent driver) was held liable for the loss resulting from the original accident but the additional damage caused by the criminal being discounted. Had the claimant sought to bring an action in respect of the later injuries caused by the criminal, it was considered that the pre-existing injuries to the leg would have to be taken into account, thereby reducing the claimant's quantum of damages. However, since the criminal would not have been insured in respect of the damage he had caused there was probably little likelihood of the criminal being able to pay the damages even if the claimant had chosen to sue him.

As an alternative to the *Baker v Willoughby* approach, it was held in *Jobling v Associated Dairies Ltd* [1982] AC 794 that a court should take account of the vicissitudes of life, such as in that case the subsequent development of the disease myelopathy, thereby reducing the claimant's projected working lifespan and hence his overall claim for damages against the defendant in respect of a negligently caused work injury. However, it may be argued that the second road accident in the problem is not a 'vicissitude of life' but a separate tortious act, which is a cause of the harm suffered by Adeel rather akin to that in *Baker*. In any case, in both *Baker* and *Jobling* the supervening event – whether tortious or natural – occurred well after the original negligence, whereas here the events come in very close proximity.

The present case should also be distinguished from the situation which arises when the claimant *must* have been injured by one of two defendants, but it cannot be determined which of the two is responsible. This type of scenario has come under recent scrutiny in the context of mesothelioma caused by exposure to asbestos, where the damage must have been caused by one of a series of negligent defendants (*Fairchild v Glenhaven Funeral Services Ltd* [2002] 1 WLR 1052). Ordinarily, a claim would fail wherever the claimant was unable to satisfy the 'but for' test and prove that a specific defendant had caused the injury. In *Fairchild*, however, the House of Lords, in recognition of the injustice that would result were the test to be applied too rigidly, identified such circumstances as calling for an alternative approach. This was a scenario better dealt with by an application of the approach in *McGhee v NCB* [1973] 1 WLR 1, namely that if the defendant had negligently exposed the claimant to a material risk of injury and the injury actually suffered fell within the foreseeable range, causation is made out.

The question arises whether FatCat Ltd can successfully sue Beatrice or Cassandra for the loss of business that was due to the destruction of data on Adeel's computer. Such a claim would face two possible problems. First, a negligent motorist may not owe a duty of care to the employers of a pedestrian who is injured as a result of the motorist's negligent driving, since, arguably, they would not meet the *Caparo* requirements of foreseeability, proximity and fair just and reasonableness. Secondly, the employers have suffered pure economic loss, at least against Beatrice and Cassandra since the loss of their property is not connected with any damage to FatCat's property caused by the two defendants. The House of Lords has held that, in cases where damage might have been caused by one tortfeasor or by natural causes, the tortfeasor cannot be held responsible unless it can be shown that the tortfeasor's negligence is, on the balance of probabilities, the most likely cause of the damage (*Wilsher v Essex AHA* [1988] AC 1074). When there is doubt as to whether a particular defendant caused certain damage to the claimant, or whether it was caused by a *novus actus interveniens*, English law seems to dictate that there is no substitute for proof, except in certain very narrow circumstances when public policy and notions of justice might promote a modified approach.

Question 2

Graham, a professional cricketer, had been driving along the motorway when he noticed that a lorry, owned and operated by Speedy Ltd, had stopped in the middle lane ahead of him, having run out of fuel. Graham slowed but was struck by a car driven by Tom, which had crossed the central reservation from the other side of the motorway. Tom's attention had been drawn to the stationary lorry on Graham's side of the road and he had crashed through the central reservation.

Graham's leg was badly injured in the collision and, while he was awaiting medical treatment at the roadside, Nick, a thief, stole his wallet and made off with it.

At the hospital Graham was treated for his injuries by Dr Botch who, tired after working 20 hours with few breaks, failed to take proper notes of his medical history. The drug she mistakenly prescribed because of this failure caused a severe allergic reaction. As a result, Graham was left with permanent damage to the sight in one eye, and the emergency resuscitation procedure delayed treatment for his leg injuries.

It soon became clear that Graham would never play cricket again and that he would lose earnings of £60,000 per year for the next two years.

Advise Speedy Ltd, Tom, and the doctor as to their respective potential liabilities in tort.

 ## Commentary

Once again, the issues relating to duty of care and to breach are quite clear-cut, but the question of liability and on whom it should fall will require a detailed consideration of both factual and legal causation.

 ## Answer plan

- What is the cause of the crash? Is there a *novus actus interveniens*?
- In what circumstances is negligent medical treatment a *novus actus*?
- How far is the extent of damage suffered a relevant consideration? Is there an egg-shell skull claimant?

Suggested answer

The first problem facing Graham is that of identifying whom to sue in respect of the injuries sustained in the car crash. There is *prima facie* evidence of negligence on the part both of Speedy Ltd (in their failure to ensure that the lorry was fit for motorway driving) and of Tom (who failed to drive with sufficient attention). This, however, does not resolve the difficult causation question of who, for the purposes of the tort of negligence, may be held responsible for the several losses that have been suffered by Graham. For the purposes of clarity of analysis, it is best to treat each head of loss separately.

In respect of the initial injuries occasioned by the crash between Tom and Graham, it is clear that the usual determinant of causation—the 'but for' test propounded in *Barnett v Chelsea and Kensington HMC* [1969] 1 QB 468—is of limited use, as this applies only to situations in which there is clearly only one factor that has caused the claimant's loss, though it may result in the elimination of a competing cause. In the present situation there are the two possible causes alluded to. The relevant law in this context is that contained in *Rouse v Squires* [1973] QB 889. There, Cairns LJ said that:

'If a driver so negligently manages his vehicle as to cause it to obstruct the highway and constitute a danger to other road users, including those who are driving too fast, or not keeping a proper look-out, but not those who deliberately or recklessly drive into the obstruction, then the first driver's negligence may be held to have contributed to the causation of an accident of which the immediate cause was the negligent driving of the vehicle which because of the presence of the obstruction collides with it or with some other vehicle or some other person.'

In applying that speech to the present facts it is apparent that if Tom's driving was merely negligent, then both he and Speedy would be liable for the injuries suffered by Graham. If, however, Tom's driving was reckless—and the fact that he was apparently oblivious to what was happening in own carriageway suggests this— then Tom's act will constitute a *novus actus interveniens* rendering him solely liable for the injuries suffered by Graham (*Wright v Lodge* [1994] 4 All ER 299).

Since there is no evidence to suggest any contributory negligence on Graham's part it can be stated with some measure of confidence that (at least) Tom (if not Tom and Speedy jointly) may be held liable for the full extent of those losses flowing from the original accident. The key question thus becomes: which of the losses may be treated, in law, as having been caused by the original accident? As regards the loss of Graham's wallet, as an act by a third party it will break the chain of causation unless it could be said to be a natural and probable consequence of the negligence (*Knightley v Johns* [1982] 1 All ER 851). It is likely that the courts would take the view that the intervention of an opportunistic thief was too unforeseeable an event to be regarded as flowing from the initial accident. Accordingly, it would mark a break in the chain of causation and hence be something for which neither Tom nor Speedy could be held liable.

In respect of the allergic reaction to medical treatment, this could, by virtue of a chain of causation, be attributed to the negligent driver(s) in that it would not have occurred but for the negligent collision. Clearly, the medical treatment will be raised as a *novus actus* so the question is, in what circumstances will medical treatment break a chain of causation. *Knightley* is authority that negligent acts are more likely than mere errors of judgment to constitute a *novus actus*, and on the facts given it would appear that Dr Botch was negligent. However, negligence mirrors the position in criminal law so that the courts are most unwilling to allow even negligent medical treatment to absolve a negligent defendant (*Hogan v Bentinck West Hartley Collieries (Owners) Ltd* [1949] 1 All ER 588), even if the medical intervention is such as would give rise to liability in negligence on the part of the doctor (*Webb v Barclays Bank plc* [2001] All ER (D) 202).

A further question arises in respect of any impact the delay has had on Tom's leg injuries. Even if the medical negligence is capable, in law, of constituting a *novus actus*, it must still be established that it has caused his long-term disability, in the sense of shifting his prospects from one who would (statistically, at least) have recovered, into someone who will not. In other words, it would need to be shown that Dr Botch's negligence has deprived him of a better than 50 per cent chance of recovery (*Hotson v East Berkshire AHA* [1987] 3 WLR 232). If this cannot be shown, liability will remain with the negligent driver(s).

So far as remoteness of damage is concerned, Tom's leg injuries fall within the *Wagon Mound* test of 'damage of a kind that was foreseeable'. As for the loss of sight, this, although arguably unforeseeable as a result of the original crash, occurred due to Tom's idiosyncratic reaction to the drug he was mis-prescribed, and therefore falls within the 'egg-shell skull rule'. This principle, which states that defendants must take their victims as they find them, was questioned following the decision in *Wagon Mound (No. 1),* but it was subsequently confirmed by the House of Lords in *Smith v Leech Brain & Co Ltd* [1961] 3 All ER 1159 that the new approach to remoteness had no impact on the principle. So Tom's loss of sight is not too remote.

Overall, it is best not to assume that Graham's loss of a professional cricketing career is attributable to any unitary cause and the likelihood is, given the complex facts, that Graham would sue them all as joint defendants. This would be advisable since it would help to ensure the recovery of compensation by way of damages. Assuming that a remedy could be awarded, damages would not be calculated on the usual multiplier basis because of the short-term nature of sports careers. We are told that Graham only had a very limited number of years to go and this would figure in the assessment of damages.

Question 3

Will, a student, invited a couple of mates from university, Qing and Emma, to stay at his family's farmhouse during the vacation. One day, keen to impress his friends, Will proposed taking shotguns up into the fields to see what they could shoot. Neither Qing nor Emma had ever handled a shotgun before, but Will announced that there were enough guns to go round and that he would show them what to do. When Will opened the gun cabinet he noticed that his shotgun licence had expired several months previously, but as he did not want to look silly in front of his friends he gave each a gun and some cartridges from the store. Although they had been intending to shoot in a field across the road from the farmhouse, the sight of a road sign proved too much temptation for them and all three fired at it at once. Pat, the village postwoman who had just cycled into range, was struck in the eye by a single pellet, while Will suffered a number of injuries from pellets ricocheting off the sign. Both casualties were rushed to hospital, where the shotgun pellets were removed but there was nothing to indicate from whose gun any of the pellets had been fired.

Consider the potential liability of the parties in negligence. You may assume that issues relating to duty of care and breach have already been resolved.

Commentary

The question is about the tort of negligence, and focuses on the issue of causation – in particular the courts' approach when there are competing causes, only one of which can actually be responsible for the damage. It will be necessary to consider the standard test for causation, as well as the circumstances in which, for policy reasons, this might be adapted. A good answer will also examine the rationale expressed in cases that have departed from the orthodox approach, and question its application to certain facts in this problem.

Answer plan

- Standard 'but for' approach to causation.
- Applicability of joint tortfeasors.
- Development through case law of a modified approach.
- Application to facts.
- Defences?

Suggested answer

This is a complex situation, in which the two claimants are Pat, the injured postwoman, and Will, who is also a potential defendant along with his two friends, Qing and Emma. In the interests of clarity, each claimant will be considered separately. Although many of the principles will apply to both, one's instinctive reaction is that their claims are not equally valid (at least in moral terms) and it will be necessary to explore the ways in which the law can respond to perceived notions of justice.

Since the issues of duty and breach are said in the question to have been resolved, the starting point is with causation. Taking Pat as the first claimant, the orthodox approach would be to apply the 'but for' test (*Barnett v Chelsea & Kensington Hospital Management Committee* [1968] 1 All ER 1068, in which a doctor's negligence in failing to see a patient was eliminated as a factual cause because the victim was already beyond saving prior to the time of the negligence), and ask whether, but for the negligence of the defendant(s) she would not have been injured. Clearly, if the defendants were to be considered as a single unit this would be true, but the law calls for a claimant to prove their case against defendants as individuals. In the right circumstances, it may be possible to establish that more than one defendant contributed to the overall damage without being able to attribute each separate element (as in *Fitzgerald v Lane* [1989] AC 328, where a careless pedestrian suffered multiple injuries from being struck by two negligently driven vehicles). On the facts in the problem, however, Pat has been injured by a single pellet so only one of the defendants is responsible, and the burden of proof lies on Pat to show, on the balance of probabilities, which one. This will be an insuperable problem, since statistically the likelihood of any one of the defendants having been the guilty party is, in the absence of any further evidence (*Wilsher v Essex AHA* [1988] AC 1074) one in three, or 33 per cent. The facts state that there is nothing to distinguish between any of the individual pellets so the orthodox approach will not assist Pat.

In certain circumstances, the House of Lords has adopted, in order to meet what it has seen as the justice of the case, a modified approach to the test for causation. The majority of these cases involve the workplace, and employees who have suffered injury or illness through exposure to a single substance, but in circumstances where they cannot prove as a fact (a) in some of the cases that it was the negligent (as opposed to another, innocent) exposure by their employer that caused the harm; or (b) in other cases that it was a specific employer out of a number of equally negligent candidates who bore the responsibility. So, in *Wardlaw v Bonnington Castings* [1956] 1 All ER 615 and *McGhee v NCB* [1972] 3 All ER 1008, the claimants suffered, respectively, from pneumoconiosis and dermatitis from exposure to dust. In *Wardlaw's* case, the claimant worked in an environment in which negligent mica dust was mingled with dust that could not reasonably have been avoided and which was therefore classed as 'innocent'. McGhee worked in a hot sweaty environment where brick dust became (unavoidably) stuck to his body, but the negligent failure of his employer to provide showers prolonged the contact since he was obliged to travel home in the same condition. Neither claimant was in a position to prove scientifically that it was the 'guilty' or negligent dust that had caused the damage, as opposed to the innocent.

In *Wardlaw*, the House of Lords concluded that it was sufficient for the claimant in circumstances such as these to prove on the balance of probabilities that the negligent dust had 'materially contributed to the disease' (*per* Lord Reid). A similar approach was applied in *McGhee*, and although it was noted that while it could be shown pieces of brick dust had contributed to McGhee's condition (by contrast with *Wardlaw's* case in which every particle of dust could be shown to have played its part in causing the disease), Lord Reid observed that, 'From a broad and practical viewpoint I can see no substantial difference between saying that what the respondents did materially increased the risk of injury to the appellant and saying that what the respondents did made a material contribution to his injury.'

While it is true that this distinction between contribution to the *damage* and contribution the *risk* of damage may be of little significance in cases in which an accumulation of some substance (through prolonged exposure to it) lies at the root of the damage, it becomes crucial when the form of damage suffered stems from a single exposure amongst many different exposures experienced by the claimant, as was the case in *Fairchild v Glenhaven Funeral Services Ltd* [2003] 1 AC 32. These appeals concerned sufferers from mesothelioma, a cancer caused by exposure to asbestos but, so far as is best understood at this time, which may be triggered by inhalation of a single fibre, rather than by an accumulation of asbestos. Logically, therefore, any individual who had been negligently exposed to asbestos during periods of work for different employers could never prove scientifically that any individual employer had caused the disease, nor could he prove that any individual had materially contributed to it. This was a situation in which the law is left with a stark choice between two potential injustices: apply a strict test for causation – proof of causation of the *damage* or, at least, of material contribution to it – and the rights of the gravely injured employees must go unprotected; or apply a modified approach – material contribution to the *risk* of damage – and a defendant may be obliged to shoulder liability without factually having been responsible. The House of Lords was unanimous in adopting the modified approach. Building, amongst other things, upon the reasoning in *McGhee* that to allow the current shortcomings of medical science to thwart the claims of injured employees would be to empty the employer's duty of any legal content. Lord Hoffmann, in *Fairchild*, observed, 'the purpose of the causal requirement rules is to produce a just result by delimiting the scope of liability in a way which relates to the reasons why liability for the conduct in question exists in the first place' and that the law must reflect the fact that, 'the just solution to different kinds of case may require different causal requirement rules'.

Lord Bingham, in *Fairchild*, considered cases from a range of jurisdiction, each involving negligent shootings (*Litzinger v Kintzler* Cass civ 2e, 5 June 1957, D 1957 Jur 493; *Summers v Tice* (1948) 199 P 2d 1; *Oliver v Miles* (1926) 50 ALR 357; *Cook v Lewis* [1951] SCR 830) and which involved findings of joint and several liability on the part of each defendant who had fired. In each case, this outcome had been held preferable to the prospect of leaving a negligently injured claimant uncompensated. Turning back to the problem, this line of reasoning could undoubtedly assist Pat, since it would relieve her of the burden of proving causation on the 'but for' test. Each of the three defendants has, by discharging their gun, materially contributed to the risk of Pat's injury so causation is made out. Remoteness of damage is readily established, and there are no applicable defences.

No doubt Will would be pleased to adopt the same argument regarding causation. Although he has suffered a number of injuries, there is still nothing to indicate from whose gun the pellets were fired, and it is even possible they all came from his own weapon. His position (being also one of the defendants in the case) is, on the face of it, somewhat analogous to that of one of the mesothelioma victims in *Barker v Corus* [2006] UKHL 20, who had also been exposed to asbestos during a period of self-employment. The House of Lords, in *Barker*, reconsidered the justice of holding each defendant jointly and severally liable and adopted a new approach, quantifying the liability of each according to his contribution to the overall exposure. This approach was, arguably, unsatisfactory as being just to neither party and any prospective effect of the ruling was nullified by Parliament, at least in asbestos cases, by the passing of the **Compensation Act 2006**.

So, it would appear that Will can establish causation. On the other hand, what might seem to be very clearly the justice of the case in respect of the negligently injured Pat feels instinctively far less acceptable in respect of Will, who was the instigator of the whole incident. A court wishing to avoid compensating Will would have two options open to it: (a) revisit the test for causation in his case; or (b) use other principles to deny him a remedy. Option (a) would be a problem, because it risks bringing the *Fairchild* principle into disrepute, both by undermining its relative certainty and by giving the appearance that rules may be made and broken at whim so as to allow courts to administer rough justice. However, other principles may well offer a 'just' solution. It could be argued either that the principle of *volenti* applies, since Will was in a position to understand the nature of the risk involved in this joint enterprise and yet went ahead, thereby voluntarily assuming the very risk that materialized. Alternatively, it could be argued that the principle *ex turpi causa non oritur actio* (also known as the illegality defence) would act as a bar to an action (*Ashton v Turner* [1980] 3 All ER 870; *Pitts v Hunt* [1990] 3 All ER 344). On one analysis, this requires that the activity engaged in by the claimant at the time of the negligent injury was not only unlawful but so wrong as to make it morally unacceptable for the court to assist him in seeking compensation. Arguably, the mere expiry of his shotgun licence would not on its own be enough to trigger the defence, but proceeding to encourage and participate in the discharge of shotguns on the highway, especially in light of Pat's injury, might well suffice. Will is therefore unlikely to succeed in his claim.

Further reading

Burrows, A., 'Uncertainty about uncertainty: damages for loss of a chance' [2008] JPIL 31.

Cox, N., 'Civil Liability for Foul Play in Sport' (2003) 54 NILQ 351.

Khoury, L., 'Causation and risk in the highest courts of Canada, England and France' (2008) 124 LQR 103.

McGregor, H., 'Loss of chance: where has it come from and where is it going?' (2008) 24(1) PN 2.

Stapleton, J., 'Cause in Fact and the Scope of Liability for Consequences' (2003) 119 LQR 388.

7

Employers' liability

Introduction

There is a personal, non-delegable duty of care owed by an employer to his employees. This is fault-based and can be discharged by the exercise of reasonable care. Where the duty applies, it is to take reasonable care to provide a competent staff, a safe place of work and a safe system of work. Moreover, since the duty is non-delegable, it is no defence for the employer to claim that he expected another person to ensure that the duty was complied with. This is an aspect of the general law of negligence and is not dealt with in this chapter.

A further basis for the liability of an employer is that he may be in breach of a statutory duty giving rise to a civil cause of action in damages. It is frequently the case that industrial safety legislation creates penalties for a failure to keep a safe place of work. Notably the **Health & Safety at Work etc. Act 1974** specifically excludes a civil liability for a breach of the duties within the Act itself (whilst permitting a civil action in respect of the Regulations unless the Regulations specifically preclude this). In respect of other statutes it must also be decided whether the statutory provision also confers an action in tort. Generally it is said that the test to apply involves ascertaining the intention of Parliament, but this may not always be easy since what Parliament intended may not be immediately apparent. Having established that a cause of action exists, it then has to be determined whether the duty is owed to the claimant, whether it has been broken and whether the breach is the cause of the harm complained of by the claimant. In other words that the process normally encountered in negligence cases applies equally here.

Where an employee commits a tort in connection with his work so that another person (a fellow employee or a stranger) suffers actionable damage, the employer may be held vicariously liable. Since there is no fault on the part of the employer, this is a variety of strict liability and is justified on the basis that the employer is in a unique position to be able to spread the cost of accidents by way of insurance and must bear any additional costs as an aspect of the liabilities of the enterprise. The key issues here are whether the person who commits the tort is an employee or servant and whether the tort is committed in the course of employment.

Question 1

The (fictional) Safety at Work (Miscellaneous Provisions) Regulations 1994 state:

(i) Employers shall ensure, so far as is reasonably practicable, that all abrasive wheels are safe to use.

(ii) It shall be the responsibility of both employer and employee to ensure that safety harnesses are worn when work is carried out more than six metres from ground level.

(iii) Where inflammable materials are stored in the workplace, it shall be the responsibility of the employer to ensure that for the protection of employees and the community at large all fire appliances are adequately maintained.

The regulations state that breach of the provisions is a criminal offence punishable by the payment of a fine. No provision is made for civil law remedies.

Eric and Roland are employed to clean the windows in a factory operated by Plasticraft Ltd. Neither is wearing a safety harness. Roland is working five metres from ground level and Eric is working seven metres from ground level. Eric slips and falls on to Roland. Both are injured. The noise causes Norman to look away while he is sharpening a chisel on an abrasive wheel. Norman's finger is badly injured when it touches with the rotating wheel. Evidence shows that a device could have been fitted to the wheel which would cause it to stop as soon as a chisel ceases to make contact. Plasticraft Ltd claim not to have the resources to be able to fit such a device. During the incident, Norman drops a burning cigarette, which ignites some rags on the floor. Because fire extinguishers have not been properly maintained, the fire spreads and damages a car owned by Percy, a visitor to the factory.

Advise Plasticraft Ltd of their tortious liability for breach of the Regulations.

Commentary

The question assumes the application of settled general principles governing the common law tort of breach of statutory duty, and does not require or call for any detailed knowledge of specialist legislation, although cases on such legislation may illuminate the answer if relevant. The question is best addressed by describing the nature of the tort and the general principles underpinning it. It calls for knowledge of a wide range of cases and these should be described as accurately as possible with clear statements as to both the legal and the factual outcomes. These principles can then be applied to the facts of the problem.

Answer plan

- The general nature of the tort.
- Consider whether the statutory provision confers an action in tort.
- Explain what approaches help to give the answer.
- Assuming such an action does exist, consider whether the standard of liability is strict or fault-based.

- Consider whether there is a breach of the duty imposed by the statute.
- If there is consider whether this was, if proved, the cause of the harm complained of.

Suggested answer

Two principal issues arise when it comes to be decided whether the breach of a statutory regulation gives rise to an action for damages. First, it must be asked whether the regulation confers an action in tort and the second question is whether there is an actionable tort.

Whether or not a statutory provision creates a civil cause of action (known as an action for breach of statutory duty *simpliciter* by Lord Browne-Wilkinson in *X (minors) v Bedfordshire County Council* [1995] 3 WLR 152) turns on an interpretation of the intention of Parliament (*Hague v Deputy Governor of Parkhurst Prison* [1991] 3 All ER 733), although Lord Denning thought (in *ex parte Island Records*) that you might as well toss a coin to decide the point. There is a primary assumption that where a statute creates an obligation and provides for its enforcement in a particular manner, it does not confer a civil cause of action unless it is intended to protect an identified class of persons (*Lonrho Ltd v Shell Petroleum Ltd* [1981] 2 All ER 456).

The regulations in this question impose a fine in the event of breach, which might result in a decision to the effect that this is the only intended consequence of breach, as was the case in *Atkinson v Newcastle Waterworks Co* (1877) 2 Ex D 441 where the statutory scheme was regarded as representing a broad agreement that the water company would provide a service but that its obligations would be limited to those it owed to the public at large rather than particular individuals injured in breach of its statutory obligations. Indeed, if the statutory provision does provide an adequate remedy, there is a presumption that there will be no civil action for damages (*Wentworth v Wiltshire County Council* [1993] 2 WLR 175). However, the emphasis here is upon the adequacy of the statutory remedy. Thus there may be cases in which a remedy is provided which a civil court may not regard as adequate recompense for an injured claimant. For example, in *Read v Croydon Corporation* [1938] 4 All ER 631 a penalty was provided for by the Waterworks Clauses Act 1847, but this did not affect the decision to confer a civil right of action for failure to provide a wholesome water supply, although, in this case there was also evidence of negligence on the part of the defendants (see also *Reffell v Surrey County Council* [1964] 1 All ER 743).

Even if the presumption against a civil cause of action were not to apply, it would also have to be established by the various potential claimants that they formed part of an identifiable class of persons Parliament intended to protect. For these purposes, it is generally assumed that employees are a sufficiently identifiable class to warrant protection (*Groves v Lord Wimborne* [1898] 2 QB 402).

Moreover, a visitor to premises which are not safe because of a breach of fire safety regulations may also be treated as falling within an identifiable class of persons (*Solomons v Gertzenstein Ltd* [1954] 2 QB 243). Conversely, a statutory provision which purports to protect the whole community, such as highway users (*Phillips v Britannia Laundry Ltd* [1923] 2 KB 832) or the water consuming public (*Atkinson v Newcastle Waterworks Co*) is considered not to confer an action in tort. Generally, the rule based on the class protected has not proved helpful since it may be invoked or ruled out depending on what the court, on a particular occasion, regards as a class of people protected by the statutory provision (see *Richardson v Pitt-Stanley* [1995] ICR 303). These rules might be taken to indicate that regulations (i) and (ii) which are intended for the benefit of employees will confer an action in tort, but that regulation (iii) may be construed so as not to give rise to an action in tort. It is worth emphasizing that fire safety regulations are likely to be aimed at the protection of individuals rather than their property. This would seem to suggest that Percy may have no cause of action under the 1994 Regulations in respect of the damage to his car.

Norman is likely to bring an action for damages based on the breach of regulation (i) which requires employers to ensure, so far as is practicable, that all abrasive wheels are safe to use. The duty clearly rests on the employer, but it must be asked whether the reference to reasonable practicability imposes a fault-based or a strict standard of liability. The use of the phrase 'so far as practicable' might suggest a standard of reasonable care on the part of the employer, although the phrase has been held to impose a stricter standard (*Edwards v National Coal Board* [1949] 1 All ER 743). In *Larner v British Steel plc* [1993] 4 All ER 102 the Court of Appeal held that for the purposes of the **Factories Act 1961, s. 29(1)**, which uses similar language, it was for the employee to prove that the workplace was unsafe and that this lack of safety was the cause of his injury, but that it was for the employer to prove that reasonably practicable precautions could not have been taken to guard against the harm caused (see also *Nimmo v Alexander Cowan & Sons Ltd* [1968] AC 107). Moreover, it is for the defendant to plead and prove that it was not reasonably practicable to keep the workplace safe, which will involve an assessment of the degree of risk and the time and cost involved in averting the risk (*Mains v Uniroyal Engelbert Tyres Ltd* (1995) *The Times*, 29 September).

The question states that a safety device could have been fitted, but that Plasticraft Ltd could not afford to install such a device. On the assumption that the cost of fitting the safety device is not exorbitantly expensive, this may seem to suggest that reasonably practicable precautions have not been taken by Plasticraft Ltd and that they may be liable for the injury suffered by Norman.

Paragraph (ii) of the Regulations places a joint responsibility on the employer and his employees to ensure that safety harnesses are used when work is carried out at a height greater than six metres from ground level. The wording of regulation (ii) is so specific that it seems unlikely that anyone working at a height lower than

6 metres will be owed a duty (*Chipchase v British Titan Products Ltd* [1956] 1 QB 545). On this basis, regulation (ii) will provide no remedy in favour of Roland since he is working only five metres from ground level. Conversely, Eric was working at the specified height when he fell, with the result that it must be considered whether Plasticraft's alleged breach of the duty is the cause of the harm suffered by Eric. Matters are complicated by the fact that Eric is also in breach of the duty which rests on him to ensure that a safety harness is used. Which breach is the cause of the harm complained of will often turn on whether there were further precautions which could have been taken by the employer to ensure compliance with the safety regulation. Thus in *Ginty v Belmont Building Supplies Ltd* [1959] 1 All ER 414, the employer could not have done more than he had to explain to employees the importance of using crawling boards when working on an unsafe roof. Accordingly, the employee's deliberate breach of the instructions given to him was regarded as the cause of the harm complained of. In contrast, in *Boyle v Kodak Ltd* [1969] 2 All ER 439, the employer had failed to give adequate instructions on how to use a ladder, with the result that his breach of duty was regarded as the cause of the injury. The question does not state what precautions have been taken by Plasticraft Ltd, but if there is more they could have done, this would seem to suggest that their failure to ensure that a safety harness is used by Eric is the cause of the injury.

Question 2

Sanjay is a petrol tanker driver for British Diesel Fuels Ltd (BDF); he is an employee employed under a contract of service.

Sanjay has been told not to offer lifts to anyone. In breach of this instruction, he takes his 17-year-old son, Nilesh, on a delivery round. They take a brief detour so that Sanjay can collect some winnings from a betting shop. Sanjay negligently fails to apply the brake to his tanker while he goes into the betting shop. While he is away, he asks Nilesh to look after the vehicle. The tanker rolls forward and strikes a petrol pump owned by Petrol Dispensers Ltd, causing a fire in which Nilesh is badly burned.

Subsequently, when Sanjay is collecting his new tanker from the depot he spots Alphonse, another employee of BDF, who had been responsible for a particularly cruel joke on Sanjay. Still enraged by this earlier incident Sanjay remonstrates with Alphonse and when no apology is forthcoming he struck him on the nose causing very serious injury for which he has now been prosecuted.

Advise British Diesel Fuels Ltd of their potential for vicarious liability for these incidents.

Commentary

Vicarious liability lends itself conveniently to a problem type of question but it is not unusual to find a discursive essay question about the policy, purpose and function of vicarious liability. When dealing with a problem based question recall that the general principles should be stated with as much accuracy as is possible, and the cases applying them described factually so as to reveal how the principles were applied, i.e. the legal outcome. But, it should be noted carefully that cases in this area tend to be very fact sensitive, and it is best to avoid naïve statements which elevate issues of fact into matters of law.

The question's focus is on vicarious liability and there is little scope for analysis of the personal or primary liability of the employer. But, the inclusion of a brief comment about these will allow you to make clear distinctions between the two forms of tortious liability. Likewise the principle relies on the existence of a tort committed by an employee — usually this will be self-evident and it will rarely be necessary to do anything other than briefly identify the relevant tort. If establishing a tort requires extensive treatment then this will be obvious from the question: here the torts are self-evident and do not require more than a brief assertion.

Vicarious liability is simply a legal device to achieve a fair result between two innocent parties but it has recently been the subject of considerable analysis by the House of Lords in *Lister v Hesley Hall* and *Dubai Aluminium v Salaam* **[2003] 2 AC 366**, and by the Privy Council in several Caribbean cases, and these cases should be referred to whenever appropriate with the caveat that the earlier cases may well have been decided differently had the test in that case been applied. Typically, the question asks you to deal with torts which have been committed carelessly where it is relatively easy to use the *Salmond* test as it has been used over several generations of lawyers. But, again typically, the question also asks you to address torts of intention which have been the subject of radical recent judicial intervention and redesign of the appropriate test for vicarious liability.

Finally, as drafted, this problem does not call for a discussion of whether or not Sanjay is an employee or an independent contractor. That question may better be termed an employment rather than a tort question although it is not unusual to find a problem calling for a discussion of the control, integration and commercial risk tests.

Answer plan

- Describe the principle of vicarious liability and the underlying policy.
- Identify briefly the torts Sanjay may have committed.
- Explain the test(s) for concluding whether Sanjay has acted in the course of his employment.
- Apply these tests to the facts and use illustrative cases.

Suggested answer

Vicarious liability applies to torts committed by a servant (an employee) in the course of their employment by the master. It does not usually apply in other employment or social relationships unless statute provides otherwise. In certain limited circumstances an employer may be made liable for the torts of an independent contractor but these are usually regarded as non-delegable duties placed on the employer in particular circumstances. Vicarious liability may be contrasted with personal or primary liability of the employer, e.g. as to a safe system of work. This liability is fault based in contrast to the strictness of liability in respect of vicarious liability.

As was pointed out by Lord Millett in *Lister v Hesley Hall*, vicarious liability is a 'species of strict liability' which 'is not premised on any culpable act or omission on the part of the employer'. The notion is a loss-distribution device that reflects judicial ideas as to social or economic policy. It is thought broadly to reflect the enterprise risk model, which states that fairness requires that a person who employs others in pursuit of economic gain should be made liable for losses incurred during the course of the enterprise. It is perhaps because of these policy considerations that the law has developed in a rather ad hoc fashion.

One matter which is certain is that there must be an employee, and we are told that Alphonse is an employee.

The second preliminary point is that vicarious liability involves making the employer liable for the torts of another. This notion of responsibility for an employee's torts was asserted by the House of Lords in *Staveley Iron and Chemical Co v Jones* [1956] AC 627. It is possible to identify two torts. First, Sanjay's failure to apply correctly the brake to his vehicle arguably amounts to negligence: a driver owes a duty of care to other road users and in not applying his brakes, Sanjay falls below the standard expected of a reasonable driver. Secondly, Sanjay's deliberate blow is a battery and also a criminal offence.

Thirdly, the existence of vicarious liability does not relieve the employee of personal liability and each of them remains as tortfeasors who may well be joined in the action. There are obvious advantages to the victims to be able to obtain judgment against the employer who will, usually, have insurance cover for such eventualities. It is also worthwhile recalling that there is an employer's indemnity which permits employers to recover their outlay from the employee: *Lister v Romford Ice & Cold Storage Co* [1957] AC 555. This is not usually invoked.

The question at the heart of the problem is whether or not the torts which occurred were committed by an employee acting in course of their employment. There is no problem where the action is authorized expressly or by implication but vicarious liability goes wider than this and, according to the test in *Salmond and Heuston on Torts*, 21st edn (London: Sweet & Maxwell, 1996) encompasses liability for acts the employer has not authorized 'provided that they are so connected with acts which he has authorized that they may be regarded as modes—although improper modes—of doing them'. The test involves imposing liability for the way in which an employee does an authorized act.

This test was useful for torts involving carelessness but was not so convenient for torts involving intention, particularly where there was an element of personal greed or self-interest that was not closely linked to the interests of the employer, e.g. theft or battery in some circumstances. The law did not impose a requirement that the conduct had to be in the interests of the employer. This was established as early as *Lloyd v Grace Smith* [1912] AC 716 and *Morris v Martin* [1965] 2 All ER 725 although the potential width of the principles in those cases was only recently recognized by the House of Lords. This major reform of the law occurred in *Lister v Hesley Hall* [2002] 1 AC 215 where the House of Lords in a sex abuse case accepted that policy demanded that the test should not be whether there was a tort that was an unauthorized mode of doing an authorized act, but whether there was a close connection between the tort and the employment. Accordingly there was no reason in that case where the sex abuse could not be a matter to which vicarious liability would apply; application of the unauthorized mode test would have lead to the opposite conclusion.

Generally, an employer will be vicariously liable if an employee carelessly performs a function he is employed to carry out: *Century Insurance Ltd v Northern Ireland Road Transport Board* [1942] AC 509 (lighting a cigarette whilst unloading a petrol tanker), but will not be liable if the employee is engaged on a 'frolic of his own' *Joel v Morrison* (1834) 6 C & P 501 or does an act he was never employed to do. The breadth of these statements masks the difficulty found in applying them in practice.

Apart from the problem of prohibited acts, Sanjay has detoured to a betting shop at the time the accident occurs. In *Joel v Morrison* (a detour case) it was said that there could be no vicarious liability for a driver 'on a frolic of his own' but this formulation really does not provide any guidance. It has been held that an employee who takes a meal break no longer acts in the course of his employment if he is the cause of an accident while on the break: *Crook v Derbyshire Stone* [1956] 1 WLR 432 and *Hilton v Thomas Burton (Rhodes) Ltd*. But it was held otherwise in *Harvey v O'Dell* where a builder took a five-mile detour to buy tools and get lunch. In *Whatman v Pearson*, an employee was prohibited from going home for lunch or to leave his horse and cart unattended. He did both and the horse bolted, causing some property damage. The employers were held vicariously liable because the employee was employed to look after the horse and cart wherever it was at the time. The issue may resolve into a question of degree. Sanjay has detoured briefly and is still in charge of his vehicle and he may therefore still be acting in the course of his employment.

Secondly, the failure to apply the handbrake was a careless way of performing his usual driving tasks. This is almost self-evident and BDF will be liable vicariously to Petrol Dispensers Ltd. The second point is that the courts will ask whether or not the giving of a lift to Nilesh in breach of the express prohibition will take Sanjay outside the scope of his employment. The mere fact that there has been an express prohibition does not necessarily mean that the forbidden act is not done in the course of employment. For example, in *Limpus v General Omnibus Co* (1862) 1 H&C 526, the defendant's bus driver was forbidden to race competitors to bus stops. When an accident occurred the defendant was held liable despite the driver having been racing. In *Twine v Bean's Express* (1946) 62 TLR 458, a prohibition on giving lifts to others was held to exclude the possibility of vicarious liability where a hitch-hiker was injured in a collision caused by the employee's negligence. However, in *Rose v Plenty* [1976] 1 WLR 141, regard was had to the purpose for which the prohibited act was done. It followed that an express prohibition against giving lifts to others had no effect where a milkman had asked the plaintiff to help him on his milk round. The prohibited act had been done for the purposes of the employer.

These two cases are very difficult if not impossible to reconcile. *Rose v Plenty* is a more sympathetic approach and is consistent with the approach in *Lister v Hesley Hall* which gave tacit approval to the conclusion reached in *Rose v Plenty*. This case, which related to intentional torts, is discussed later. The issue resolves into one difficult factual question: was the prohibition concerned with the mode of doing a job he was employed to do, or did it relate to the scope of what he was required to do, i.e. the sphere of his employment? The conclusion must be that the carelessness of Sanjay did not serve to take him outside the scope of his employment but was an improper mode of doing an authorized act and accordingly BDF will be liable vicariously to Nilesh.

More difficulties arise in connection with the attack on Alphonse. The issues raised are close to those identified in *Lister v Hesley Hall*: What is the appropriate test for determining whether or not an employer will be responsible for the deliberate torts of their employee? In *Lister's* case the defendants ran a school for boys with behavioural difficulties. A warden employed by them systematically sexually abused boys and was convicted of serious offences. The claimants said that the defendant was vicariously liable for the abuse. The House of Lords overturned an earlier Court of Appeal decision and held that when determining whether an employer was vicariously liable in such circumstances it was necessary to concentrate on the relative closeness of the connection between the nature of the employment and the particular wrongdoing. The defendants had undertaken to care for boys and the warden had been employed for this purpose. There was therefore a very close connection between his employment and the abuse because it had been committed at the defendant's premises when he was supposed to be caring for the boys whilst carrying out his duties. The House of Lords said that the tort did not have to be committed for the benefit of the employer.

Some earlier decisions supported the imposition of vicarious liability for intentional torts—indeed in two of the most difficult cases (*Lloyd v Grace Smith* [1912] AC 716 and *Morris v Martin* [1965] 2 All ER 725) the House of Lords had accepted that there could be vicarious liability where the criminal acts had been committed without any furtherance to the employer's business interests. The earlier cases on personal violence against customers may well have to be reconsidered in the light of what was said in *Lister v Hesley Hall*, but the following examples show the difficult grey areas. In *Fennelly v Connex South Eastern Ltd* there was a dispute between a ticket inspector and a traveller which began at a time when the ticket inspector was entitled to challenge the traveller but where a battery occurred some time later. Similarly, in *Mattis v Pollock*, an exceptionally serious battery was committed by a nightclub bouncer. The Court of Appeal applied the *Lister* principles and found sufficient connection between this and the employment even though the attack had taken place some time after the original dispute and when the bouncer had returned home to collect a weapon. The Court of Appeal held that it would be fair, just, and reasonable to impose vicarious liability, even though he had been motivated by revenge and had attacked the claimant a long time after an incident at the club the same night. *Dyer v Munday* [1895] 1 QBD 742 (where the employer was held vicariously liable for a criminal assault committed by his employee while attempting to repossess his employer's property) may be contrasted with *Warren v Henlys Ltd* [1948] 2 All ER 935 (where a petrol pump attendant assaulted a customer as a result of a dispute over payment). The latter case was explained in *Lister v Hesley Hall* as turning on the point that the employer was not liable because it was no part of the duties of the pump attendant to keep order.

These principles were applied in *Brown v Robinson* [2004] UKPC 56 where the Privy Council adopted the *Lister* approach that the key question was the closeness of the connection between the job description and the tortious behaviour, and to ask if the connection was so close that it would be just and reasonable to hold the employer liable. In this case, the shooting by a security guard of a person trying to gain entry to a football match fell within this and was a tort motivated by revenge or retaliation. But, in *Attorney-General British Virgin Islands v Hartwell* [2004] 1 WLR 1273 the use of a police pistol by a police officer was entirely unconnected with his role as a police officer and was motivated only by way of jealous revenge.

Accordingly in this case since there was no close connection between what Sanjay had done and the terms of his employment duties, there would be no basis under the *Lister* approach to require the imposition of vicarious liability for the battery.

Further reading

Buckley, R. A., 'Liability in Tort for Breach of Statutory Duty' (1984) 100 LQR 204.

Gilliker, P., 'Rough Justice in an Unjust World' (2002) 65 MLR 269.

Gilliker, P., 'The Ongoing March of Vicarious Liability' [2006] CLJ 489.

Levinson, J., 'Vicarious Liability for Intentional Torts' [2005] JPI 304.

McBride N. J., 'Vicarious Liability in England and Australia' (2003) 62 CLJ 255.

McKendrick, E., 'Vicarious Liability and Independent Contractors—A Re-examination' (1980) 53 MLR 770.

Newark, F. H., 'Twine v Bean's Express Ltd' (1954) 17 MLR 102.

Stanton, K. M., 'New Forms of the Tort of Breach of Statutory Duty' (2004) 120 LQR 324.

Stanton, K. M., *Breach of Statutory Duty in Tort (Modern Legal Studies)* (London: Sweet & Maxwell 1986).

Stanton, K. M. et al., *Statutory Torts* (London: Sweet & Maxwell 2003).

Weekes, R., 'Vicarious Liability for Violent Employees' (2004) 63 CLJ 53.

Williams, G. L., 'Vicarious Liability: Tort of the Master or of the Servant' (1956) 72 LQR 522.

Williams, G. L., 'The Effect of Penal Legislation in the Law of Tort' (1960) 23 MLR 233.

Occupiers' liability

Introduction

Although the **Occupiers' Liability Acts of 1957** and **1984** are based on the previous common law rules which they replaced, they are a self-contained code for imposing a duty of reasonable care on an occupier in favour of either a visitor or a non-visitor. Trespassers are the commonest form of non-visitor but that category will mask the potentially very wide range of potential unlawful entrants, from the burglar to the wandering child. The duty, where one exists, is based on reasonable care under all the circumstances and questions of breach will tend to attract similar issues as breach of the ordinary common law duty in negligence. Issues of causation and remoteness are as likely to occur in connection with the liability of an occupier as with any other action in negligence. Commonly, an occupier will attempt to warn of a particular danger or to exclude liability for any potential liability. In respect of the latter, but not the former, the provisions of the **Unfair Contract Terms Act 1977** may become relevant.

Question 1

Multimillion plc owns a building and contracts with Shambles Ltd to demolish it. Shambles Ltd is responsible for the security of the site and it leaves it unattended on Sundays when work is not in progress. The site is protected by a perimeter fence topped with razor wire.

During working hours, Sven, an electrician from another company, has been called to the site to repair a defective generator. He is told by a security guard that he must report to the site office in order to be provided with protective headgear to guard against the risks present on a demolition site, especially the possibility of debris falling from overhead operations which are in progress.

Sven sees the defective generator and decides to make a preliminary inspection before reporting to the site office. As he approaches the generator, Sven stumbles over a drainage pipe left on the ground and as he limps to the site office he is struck by a brick which fell off a wall.

As a result of these incidents Sven suffers head and leg injuries. Some time after the event, Shambles Ltd put up a notice near the site office which states clearly that visitors should keep their eyes on the ground to avoid tripping over articles left temporarily on the site.

On Sunday, Fabio, aged 20, decides to enter the site to take scrap metal to exchange for cash. He climbs over the tall fence but falls off because the top strand of wire is loose, and breaks an arm. As he tries to recover a handful of brass fittings he slips into a deep trench and is injured.

Advise Multimillion plc and Shambles Ltd as to their potential liability under the Occupiers' Liability Acts 1957 and 1984.

Commentary

This question raises the narrow issue of occupiers' liability under the legislation and does not require an account of potential liability under other possible causes of action such as negligence or breach of statutory duty. The **1957 Act** refers to 'visitors' and it is advisable to employ this term in the answer even though occasionally even the judges refer to 'lawful visitors' as if to suggest that there may be 'unlawful visitors'. The **1984 Act** refers to 'non-visitors'. Trespassers are the most frequently encountered category of non-visitor and that term may be used provided the point is made clear at the outset that this is for convenience. In an examination, unless the statute is provided, there will be a temptation to use a short version of each of the sections since 100 per cent recollection and reproduction verbatim is unlikely. Concentrate on encapsulating accurately within your version of each section the important aspects, e.g. in **s. 2(4)(a)** the warning must be sufficient to enable the visitor to be *reasonably safe*, not to be *safe*. Answers should contain reference to those recent cases which address broad issues of principle.

Answer plan

- Identify who is the occupier, and there may be more than one.
- Identify what duty is owed and to whom.
- Consider when an occupier is able to discharge (perform) their duty by using an independent contractor.
- In order to effectively discharge the common duty of care, identify what a warning must do.
- Consider who is a non-visitor and the nature of the duty owed to a non-visitor.
- State in what circumstances that duty is broken.

Suggested answer

Both Acts deal with harm arising from dangers due to the state of the premises rather than activities on the premises. Such occupancy duties are to be distinguished from activity duties, this was recently restated by the Court of Appeal in

Fairchild v Glenhaven Funeral Services Ltd [2002] 1 WLR 1052, although *dicta* in *Tomlinson v Congleton* [2003] 3 All ER 1022 have been read as suggesting that the Act will deal with both occupational and activity duties. Under the Act an employer of a sub-contractor will not be liable in respect of damage arising from the work practices adopted by the contractor unless they affect the state of the premises, but such liability may arise at common law, see a case such as *Makepeace v Evans* [2000] BLR 287 where such a duty arose. In *Gwilliam v West Hertfordshire Hospital NHS Trust* [2003] QB 443, the majority of the Court of Appeal made it clear that the activity duty at common law effectively mirrored that in respect of state of the premises duty under the Act. The minority did not draw the clear distinction suggested above.

Both the 1957 and the 1984 Act require that there has to be a danger arising from 'the state of the premises', a phrase examined in depth in *Tomlinson v Congleton* and which signifies something unusual and dangerous for that type of premises. In *Tomlinson* the House of Lords, by a 4:1 majority, held that there was no such risk because the lake was much the same as any other lake, i.e. shallow at the margin with muddy water and uneven depth; but in *Rhind v Astbury Water Park* [2004] EWCA Civ 756 the presence of a large fibreglass object embedded in the lake floor created a danger due to the state of the premises. Here it is arguable whether the risks in the problem arise from the state of the premises and are within the range of the Acts. For example, the building site could well be regarded as the same as any other building site and as containing no additional risks but the fence had a loose strand of wire which suggests that it is defective. The remainder of the answer will proceed on the basis that in each case there is a danger due to the state of the premises.

Another issue common to the injured parties is whether or not a duty of care is owed and by whom. To decide this preliminary point it has to be established who the occupier is, since the duty flows, if at all, from occupation. The duties under the 1957 and the 1984 Acts are based not on ownership but on occupation of premises. Under the 1957 Act a duty is automatically owed by an occupier to visitors, but under the 1984 Act the duty may be owed to non-visitors only provided certain pre-conditions are satisfied—it is not an automatic duty. In *Wheat v Lacon & Co* [1966] AC 552, construing the Occupiers' Liability Act 1957, s. 1(2)(a), occupation was held to relate to control. 'Occupier' was not defined for the purposes of either Act and applying the common law it was held that to be an occupier the person must have sufficient degree of control to put them under a duty of care to visitors (or non-visitors under the 1984 Act). Furthermore, it was held in *Wheat v Lacon & Co* that it is possible for there to be more than one occupier of premises. For example, in *Collier v Anglian Water* (1983) *The Times*, 26 March, a local authority was occupier of a sea-wall and so too were the water company. But, the control exercised by each was different and the water company controlled the physical integrity of the sea-wall and was the responsible occupier when the uneven surface caused the plaintiff to trip. It would have been otherwise had she slipped on a banana skin left lying around in breach of duty by the local authority whose control extended to cleaning the surface. Here it is likely that both Multimillion plc and Shambles Ltd will be occupiers and that each will owe a duty dependent upon their degree of control and its nature.

Once it is decided that both parties may be occupiers then under the 1957 Act a duty of care will be owed towards visitors. This is the common duty of care (which simply means that it is owed to anyone who would have been classed as a licensee or invitee at common law). Is Sven a visitor? He has been told that he must report to the site office but he does not do so. This breach of the condition on which entry was granted may effectively render him a trespasser and therefore a non-visitor and thus outside the scope of the 1957 Act. This point will be addressed later. On the assumption that he is a visitor, Sven is owed the common duty of care, under s. 2(1). Under s. 2(2), the common duty of care is one to take such care as is necessary to see that the visitor is reasonably safe in using the premises for the purposes for which he is invited by the occupier to be there.

The issue is whether or not Multimillion plc has discharged its duty of care towards Sven, the visitor. The 1957 Act, s. 2(4)(b) provides that an occupier is not to be treated as answerable for damage caused by any work of construction, maintenance or repair by an independent contractor if, in the circumstances of the case, it was reasonable to entrust the work to an independent contractor and that such steps as are reasonable have been taken to ascertain that the contractor was competent and the work was properly done. In *Ferguson v Welsh* [1987] 3 All ER 777, it was held using a purposive approach to statutory interpretation that demolition fell within the scope of s. 2(4)(b). Here it would be reasonable to entrust demolition to an expert and Multimillion plc would have to show that they had exercised reasonable care in the selection of the independent contractor. If the work done by the contractor is technical, which the occupier cannot be expected to check, it may be sufficient that the occupier has ascertained that the contractor is competent before employing him, for example in *Haseldine v Daw & Sons Ltd* [1941] 2 KB 343 where the independent contractor was an expert lift company. But in *AMF International Ltd v Magnet Bowling Ltd* [1968] 2 All ER 789, it was suggested that the more complex the project then the more complex had to be the supervision, in that case it was a major building project. Accordingly it is suggested that Multimillion have discharged, i.e. performed, their duty of care since it would not be reasonable to employ another contractor, such as an architect, to supervise the work.

Since Shambles Ltd carry out demolition work for which they are responsible and they are in charge of the security of the site, it is to be assumed that they have control of the premises and are occupiers for the purposes of both the 1957 and 1984 Acts: *AMF International Ltd v Magnet Bowling Ltd*, and *Collier v Anglian Water*.

The duty under the 1957 Act, s. 2(2) is to take reasonable steps under the circumstances to ensure that the visitor is reasonably safe for the purposes for which he is invited or permitted to be there, not absolutely safe. Reasonable care only need be taken having regard to all the circumstances including the nature of the premises and skill and knowledge of the claimant.

More specifically, warning of a risk can discharge the duty owed by an occupier, but the warning must be such as would enable the visitor to be reasonably safe: s. 2(4)(a). It might be argued that the warning given to Sven concerning the risks present on a building site serves to discharge the duty owed by Shambles Ltd to Sven. However, in relation to the risk of tripping over a pipe, the warning is non-specific. If Sven had gone to the site office, he would have been provided with a hat, which might have protected him from falling rubble, but it would have little effect in relation to the risk of harm resulting from tripping over a pipe. By contrast in *Roles v Nathan* the chimney sweeps were clearly told that entering a particular alcove with the sweep-hole in the flue open and with the fire lit would place them in peril. They proceeded despite this warning and died as a result. It was held that the warning was sufficient under the circumstances to allow them to be safe – they knew what to avoid.

Moreover, it has been held that there is no need to warn in respect of obvious dangers, such as the presence of slippery algae on a sea-wall in *Staples v West Dorset DC* (1995) 93 LGR 536 or the steep cliff in *Cotton v Derbyshire Dales* (1994) *The Times*, 20 June. It might be argued that the presence of a pipe on the ground on a building site is such an obvious possibility that no warning needs to be given, although it has been observed, in another context, that pedestrians in the street cannot be expected to walk around all day with their eyes to the ground (*Haley v London Electricity Board* [1965] AC 778). Sven might argue that the subsequent erection of a notice warning of the danger which has resulted in his injury is some admission of liability; however, there is authority to suggest that this is not the case, provided the danger is one which was obvious at the time of the accident (*Staples v West Dorset DC*).

Not all visitors are the same, e.g. children or visually handicapped persons may have different needs. In the case of experts, the occupier can expect a skilled person to guard against risks ordinarily incident to the job he does: s. 2(3)(b) as explained in *Roles v Nathan* [1963] 2 All ER 908: the sweeps were expert and the risk of entering the sweep-hole was one which was incidental to the calling. The pipe and the brick might be regarded as a general risk rather than one specific to the calling of an electrician.

In any event, what has to be shown is a failure to take reasonable care. It would have to be shown that leaving the pipe in that position amounted to carelessness in breach of the duty under the Act.

Suppose that Sven is a trespasser? This would place him in the same position as Fabio, i.e. a non-visitor outside the scope of the 1957 Act.

The 1984 Act, s. 1(3) lays down three criteria to be satisfied before a duty of care will be owed by an occupier to a non-visitor. First Shambles Ltd must be aware of the danger or have reasonable grounds for believing that it exists:

s. 1(3)(a). Here the danger due to the state of the premises has already been identified (see *Tomlinson v Congleton Borough Council* [2003] 3 All ER 1022 and
Rhind v Astbury Water Park [2004] EWCA Civ 756). In Tomlinson of course the
House of Lords by a 4:1 majority made it perfectly clear that there was in that
case no risk due to the state of the premises and that the claimant had chosen to
execute an activity in itself dangerous. In Sven's case an occupier would be aware
of the dangers inherent in a building site such as the falling brick and the pipe.
In *Rhind* as a matter of fact viewed objectively the occupier could not have been
expected to be aware of the danger hidden in the bottom of the murky lake.

Secondly, Shambles Ltd must have known or must have had reasonable grounds
to believe that the particular non-visitor is in or may come into, the vicinity of the
danger: 1984 Act, s. 1(3)(b). They know that Sven is on site and must be aware that
he is or may come into the vicinity of the danger. On the other hand, there would
have to be evidence that a trespasser such as Fabio would have been anticipated at
that time. In *Higgs v Foster* [2004] EWCA Civ 843 it was not anticipated that a
trespassing police officer would enter a bus depot and come into the vicinity of an
uncovered inspection chamber into which he fell. The provision of a fence should
not normally be taken as an acceptance that trespassers are likely (see *White v St
Alban's*) and there would have to be sufficient evidence that there had been previous trespasses or attempts.

The third requirement is that Shambles Ltd must be aware that the risk is one
against which they could reasonably be expected to offer the particular non-visitor
some protection: s. 1(3)(c). This may require consideration of the practicality of
taking greater precautions and the range of matters considered in *Tomlinson v Congleton Borough Council* where the House of Lords extensively reviewed the law
under s. 1(3). It was made clear that the range of matters would include the utility
of the defendant's behaviour and the nature of the claimant's behaviour. In that case
the House regarded high spirited recreational activity, diving into lakes, as being
normal but as carrying dangers against which it would not be reasonable for the
occupier to have to take precautions when balanced with the impact of such precautions on other non-dangerous behaviour, e.g. families playing in the sand beside the
lake. The majority in the House of Lords agreed that had the claimant been a visitor
then the content of the duty would not have included a requirement to prevent entry
to the water or to warn of dangers (because the dangers were obvious). Thus, if no
such duty were required as regards visitors then no such steps could be required as
regards non-visitors under the 1984 Act since that Act was intended to provide a
lesser degree of protection.

Thus, it may be that in the case of the trespassers intent on theft it would not be
reasonable to offer any protection but that in respect of the 'innocent' trespasser
it might be reasonable to expect some protection.

Assuming there is a duty of care, breach of that duty must also be established.
For these purposes, the 1984 Act, s. 1(4) provides that Shambles Ltd must take
reasonable care to ensure that the non-visitors do not suffer personal injury or

death due to the danger arising out of the state of the premises. Thus, it will be necessary to consider factors such as the magnitude of risk, precautions necessary to guard against that risk and the cost of taking such precautions, the objective to be attained by Shambles Ltd, the age of the trespassers, and the nature of the premises. The courts have held that at least in respect of visitors of full capacity there is no need to warn of a danger where the danger is obvious, and the same body of law as applies to visitors applies to non-visitors. A fence and razor wire represent obvious dangers and no warning need be given.

Shambles Ltd may argue that under the 1984 Act, s. 1(5) they have discharged their duty by taking sufficient steps to discourage Fabio from taking the risk in the first place. They have erected a fence which is topped with razor wire. They may also suggest that in respect of Sven they warned of the risk, and the earlier discussion applies to this point.

Causation may also be raised. For example, in *Scott v Associated British Ports* (unreported 2000) it was found that the gap in the fence which allowed the trespassing youths access to a railway line was not causative of their injuries caused by 'surfing' on a train, because the evidence was that they would have scaled the fence in any event in order to carry out what was a fundamentally dangerous activity. Here it can be argued that Fabio was so intent on theft that he would not have been deterred even had the fence not been faulty.

Finally, it could be argued that Fabio and Sven are contributorily negligent, having failed to take reasonable precautions for their own safety and having been in part a cause of the harm they suffer: *Jones v Livox Quarries* [1952] 2 QB 608.

Question 2

Pleasureland Limited own and operate Thrill Towers an entertainment park. At the entrance to the park there is a prominent notice that 'Pleasureland Limited and Kidikicks Limited can accept no liability for any injury suffered'. One of the attractions, the Serpent, has been leased from Pleasureland Limited by Kidikicks Ltd; the lease provides for Kidikicks to maintain the ride. The Serpent is a notoriously frightening car ride which for part of its route travels underground. At the entrance to the Serpent ride there is a notice which states:

'All possible precautions are taken in the interests of safety. This tunnel for this ride has a low ceiling. People taller than 6 feet 3 inches are not permitted on this ride.'

Adam, aged 21, is 6 feet 4 inches tall but decides that this cannot matter and bends his knees as he passes under the height checking device provided by Kidikicks Ltd. During the ride, the Serpent dips sharply into an underground cavern and Adam, who is sitting high up in his seat, suffers a glancing blow to the head from a low light used in emergencies but which has come free from its support. Sitting behind Adam is Bronwen who is also struck by the light; she is

5 feet 3 inches tall. The light has recently been maintained by Sparky an independent contractor. Both are seriously injured.

Advise Adam and Bronwen as to the potential liability of Pleasureland and Kidikicks under the **Occupiers' Liability Acts**.

Commentary

This question is concerned with the liability of an occupier to a visitor. The first thing to notice is that the rubric asks the student to focus on the legislation and not common law negligence. The rubric identifies the **Occupiers' Liability Acts**, which is a hint that there may be a trespassing non-visitor to consider. The question demands a similar approach to other questions on occupiers' liability: identify the core elements of occupier, the visitor or non-visitor, the duties, and any defences. The use of cases is critical. Use the cases to make clear statements of principle supported by sufficient facts to draw out the application of the principles clearly.

Answer plan

- Identify who the occupier is.
- Consider the status of those entering the land.
- Consider if the scope of the occupier's duty applies only to the state of the premises.
- Identify the relevant duties.
- State how a warning of danger may affect liability.
- If there is a breach of duty does it cause the harm suffered?

Suggested answer

The duty under the **Occupiers' Liability Acts** is placed on the occupier. The Acts identify the occupier as anyone who would have been an occupier at common law. In *Wheat v Lacon Ltd* [1966] **AC 552** control of the premises featured in the identification of the occupier and there must be sufficient control over the premises to allow a person to be placed under a duty of care. In addition, in that case it was held that there could be joint occupiers but that the nature and content of the duty owed by each would be dependent upon the nature of their control. So, in that case the manager of the pub and his wife could be liable in respect, say, of the state of the furnishings, but the brewery that owned the pub could be liable for the state of the electrical system. In the problem much will depend on the arrangements in place between Kidikicks Ltd and Pleasureland. It seems likely that both will be treated as occupiers under the **Occupiers' Liability Act (OLA) 1957** on the basis that they have control over the state of the premises but any liability for the light would depend on who had responsibility for it, as in *Collier v Anglian Water* where the liability for the uneven surface of a promenade was placed on the water company which occupied it and had responsibility for its fabric rather than the local authority who lit it and kept it clean.

For the purposes of the 1957 Act, the common duty of care is owed to any person who would have been treated as an invitee or a licensee at common law (OLA 1957, s. 1(2)). On the assumption that Adam has paid to enter Thrill Towers, he will be a contractual visitor to whom the common duty of care is owed under which states that: 'An occupier of premises owes the same duty, the common duty of care, to all his visitors'. Moreover, Adam can choose whether to sue in tort or under his contract with Pleasureland Ltd, but in either case, the same common duty of care will be owed (OLA 1957, s. 5(1)). As regards Adam and Kidikicks the position is more complex. If Adam's deception vitiates the implied consent to enter the land then he will become a trespasser and as such will be at best a non-visitor to whom a duty may be owed under the 1984 Act. If the deception does not vitiate the consent then Adam will, like Bronwen, be a visitor to whom the duty under the 1957 Act is owed. In *Tomlinson v Congleton Borough Council* [2003] 3 All ER 1022 there was some debate between their Lordships as to whether or not the claimant was a trespasser when he ran into the water or only when he began to dive/swim. The majority agreed with the concession that he was a trespasser at the moment he ran into the water with a view to diving. In *Keown v Coventry Healthcare NHS Trust* [2006] EWCA Civ 39 the 11-year-old clambering up the underneath of a metal fire-escape was accepted by the Court of Appeal as the closest example in real life of the example of a trespasser given by Scrutton LJ in *The Carlgarth* [1927] P 93, 110: 'When you invite a person into your house to use the staircase, you do not invite him to slide down the banisters, you invite him to use the staircase in the ordinary way in which it is used.' The alternatives will be considered.

Does the danger arise from the state of the premises? Each Act demands that this should be fulfilled before a duty of care can arise. The wording suggests that there must be something in the nature of a defect. In *Tomlinson* the shallow water with variable depth and obscured by mud was not defective, it was typical of inland water, unlike *Rhind v Astbury Water Park* [2004] EWCA Civ 756 where there was a hard object buried in the silt. The light-fitting hanging down is clearly a defect in the state of the premises and gives rise to a danger.

Suppose that Bronwen and Adam are to be treated as visitors: the **1957 Act** will apply and the duty will be owed irrespective of whether they would have been invitees or licensee at common law (it is the *common* duty). Section 2(2) sets out the common duty of care as 'to take such care as in all the circumstances of the case is reasonable to see that the visitor is reasonably safe in using the premises for the purposes for which he is invited or permitted by the occupier to be there'. Reasonable care will take into account all the normal issues for deciding that point under negligence, such as the degree of risk and cost. In this case there are none of the social issues mentioned in *Tomlinson*. Kidikicks will point to the fact that they have discharged their duty of care by using an independent contractor to do the work within s. 2(4)(b). They will have to show that they had acted reasonably in giving the work to the independent contractor, that they had taken reasonable steps to satisfy themselves as to the competence of the contractor and that the work had been properly done. In this case little is revealed about the competence of Sparky but it is reasonable to obtain the services of an independent contractor for these purposes. Arguably the more complex the job the greater the need for supervision (as in *AMF v Magnet* where the complex structure being built demanded that there should be architect supervision of the contractors). Here perhaps a visual check would suffice. If s. 2 (4) has been satisfied then Kidikicks will have performed their duty and no liability on their part will arise. Any potential liability of Sparky would be considered under negligence principles.

In any event the fact that Adam has taken the liberty of travelling when he ought not to have, and that he knew that this was forbidden for a good reason (the low ceiling) he might be taken to have voluntarily consented to the risk within s. 2(5). But, here the risk arose from a defective light fitting and not the low ceiling so this will not apply.

Kidikicks Ltd may argue that they have discharged their duty under the Act by means of a warning notice prominently displayed at the entrance to the ride, though s. 2(4)(a) provides that a warning on its own is not sufficient to discharge the duty unless in all the circumstances of the case it is sufficient to enable the visitor to be reasonably safe. In *Roles v Nathan* [1963] 2 All ER 908, two industrial chimney sweeps had been warned by an engineer that they should not work on certain boiler flues if the fire in the boiler was lit. They ignored these instructions and were overcome by carbon monoxide fumes that were a danger to which they had been alerted. It was held by the Court of Appeal that the warning was sufficient to discharge the occupier's duty of care. Here the warning does not provide any guidance as to how the user of the ride could be safe and the warning is insufficient to discharge the duty (it might be otherwise if the warning had told passengers not to hold their arms extended above their heads and the harm had arisen from this action).

An alternative defence, contributory negligence, is available by virtue of s. 2(3) of the Act, which provides that circumstances relevant to the discharge of the duty of care 'include the degree of care, and want of care, which would ordinarily be looked for in such a visitor'. Thus, it may be that Adam, as an adult, will be treated as having failed to take reasonable care for his own safety and may be guilty of contributory negligence, so that any damages awarded may be reduced under the provisions of the Law Reform (Contributory Negligence) Act 1945.

The defence will operate to reduce his damages only if the injury was due to, or was made worse by, his being too tall for the ride.

Suppose that Adam is to be treated as a trespasser. He will be a non-visitor and thus outside the scope of the 1957 Act. The 1984 Act does not create an automatic duty on the part of the occupier towards non-visitors; the non-visitor must establish this. Under s. 1(3) in summary the conditions are that (i) the occupier knows or has reasonable grounds to believe that the danger exists (ii) the occupier knows or has reasonable grounds to believe that the non-visitor is or will come into the vicinity of the danger (iii) the risk is one against which in all the circumstances it is reasonable to offer the other some protection.

Arguably, in respect of a simple maintenance matter, the occupier ought to have been aware of this danger.

As regards the non-visitor and vicinity to the danger, in *Higgs v WH Foster* [2004] EWCA Civ 843 the trespassing police officer claimant fell into a bus company's inspection chamber at night when trying to reach a vantage point to investigate a possible crime in an adjoining property. He could not show that the company had reasonable grounds to believe that he might come into the vicinity of the danger (the pit). Ease of access to the site was not sufficient to establish this; and, simply prohibiting an activity will not be sufficient to show this, whether the prohibition is before the event or after the event, as occurred in *White v St Albans*. The more difficult question is whether the non-visitor should reasonably be offered some protection. Here the wider social comments in *Tomlinson* can be borne in mind: the need not to deter lawful enjoyment (by removing the sand beside the lake) and to allow self-determination and risk taking (by the youths jumping into and swimming in the river). Here neither seems to apply: there is no conscious risk taking or any deterrence to enjoyment by others. It is also possible to contrast a merely careless trespasser and a deliberate trespasser such as a burglar. The former may receive greater tolerance than the latter. Here the relatively minor risk-taking may be regarded as tolerable and some protection offered.

Finally, there is an exclusion notice. Although permitted by the 1957 Act exclusion of liability under the Act is not permitted under Unfair Contract Terms Act and the notice will be of no effect where business premises are concerned. However, the position as regards the 1984 Act is less clear. The Act itself is silent on the matter of exclusion or modification of the duty and the failure of Parliament to adopt the formula suggested by the Law Commission may suggest that exclusion is not permissible. If this is so then possibly this will place the non-visitor to whom a duty is owed (which is going to be very rare) in a better position than a visitor to business premises.

Question 3

The Grotbag Trust, a charitable organization, owns a 50-acre estate consisting of gardens and country walks, which are open to the public on the payment of a small charge to defray the expenses of the charity. Day-to-day management of the estate, including all aspects of care and maintenance of the garden, is entrusted to Dastardly Ltd, which charges the Grotbag Trust a management fee.

At the public entrance to the estate, there is a prominently displayed notice which states:

'Dastardly Ltd and the Grotbag Trust ask you to take care on these premises. Children must be accompanied and supervised by responsible adults. No responsibility can be accepted for injury or damage suffered while on these premises.'

Tadeusz and his wife Harriet take their child, Marta, aged six, for a day trip to the Grotbag estate. Tadeusz and Harriet are keen gardeners but Marta became bored and wandered off. She comes upon a bush bearing bright red berries. In front of the tree there is a notice which states that the berries are poisonous and should not be eaten. The notice carries a symbol of a skull and cross bones to indicate poison. There is also a small fence around the bush which Marta is able to step over. Marta eats some of the berries and is taken very ill.

Tadeusz is walking in the grounds when a tree-branch hanging over the path falls on to his head. The branch had been left carelessly suspended over the path by Rhoda Dendron, an independent tree surgeon employed by Dastardly.

Despite a sign which says 'No paddling', Harriet decides to cool off in the pond which she sees is murky. She uses a stick to test the depth of water but does so only in an area where there is, unknown to her, a planting ledge. Her testing suggests that the water is very shallow and therefore safe. As she steps from the planting ledge she falls into a deep hole and suffers serious injury.

Advise the Grotbag Trust Ltd and Dastardly Ltd as to their potential liability under the 1957 and 1984 Occupiers' Liability Acts.

Commentary

This question raises the narrow issue of occupiers' liability under the legislation and does not require an account of potential liability under other possible causes of action such as negligence. Use the terms 'visitors' and 'non-visitors', although since trespassers are the commonest category of non-visitor 'trespasser' may be used provided the point is made clear at the outset that this is for convenience. Again, avoid the temptation to use an overly simplistic shorthand version of each of the sections. Concentrate on encapsulating within your version the important aspects. Answers should contain reference to the recent cases which address broad issues of principle.

The question concerns the liability of an occupier of premises to both visitors and non-visitors. It differs from the previous question in that the issue of exclusion of liability is raised as well as the issue of the duty owed in the case of children rather than the experts in that problem. As regards the matter of exclusion, the question is a tort question and detailed analysis of when an organization becomes a business for the purposes of the **Unfair Contract Terms Act 1977** would be beyond the scope of the answer; simply identify the issue that turns upon this point and then move on.

Answer plan

- Identify who is an occupier and what duty may be owed.
- Identify who is a visitor and who a non-visitor.
- Consider what duty is owed to young children.
- Consider whether a warning notice will suffice.
- Identify the principle that applies to obvious dangers.
- State whether and how the duty be discharged by the use of an independent contractor.
- Deal with the structure and impact of the **Occupiers' Liability Act 1984.**
- Consider whether exclusions or restrictions on liability are permitted and in what circumstances the **Unfair Contract terms Act 1977** comes into play.

Suggested answer

The first step is to identify who may owe a duty of care. The person who owes the common duty of care to visitors under the Occupiers' Liability Act 1957, or who may owe the duty to non-visitors under the 1984 Act, is the occupier. The duties are based not on ownership but on occupation. The 1957 Act states that the 'occupier' is to be determined by reference to the common law, and the 1984 Act states that for its purposes an occupier is anyone who is an occupier for the purposes of the 1957 Act. In *Wheat v Lacon & Co* [1966] AC 552, construing the Occupiers' Liability Act 1957, s. 1(2)(a), occupation was held to relate to control and that to be an occupier the person must have sufficient degree of control to put them under a duty of care to visitors. Furthermore, it was held in *Wheat v Lacon & Co* that it is possible for there to be more than one occupier of premises. For example, in *Collier v Anglian Water* (1983) *The Times*, 26 March a local authority was occupier of a sea-wall and so too were the water company. But, it must be appreciated that the control exercised by each was different. Thus, the water company controlled the physical integrity of the sea-wall and were the responsible occupier when the uneven surface caused the plaintiff to trip. It would have been otherwise had she slipped on a banana skin left lying around in breach of duty by the local authority whose control extended to cleaning the surface. Here it is likely that each of Grotbag Trust and Dastardly Ltd will be occupiers and that the content of the duty each owes will be dependent upon the relative degree and the nature of the control. Since day-to-day management of the estate has been entrusted to Dastardly Ltd, this would seem to suggest that they have primary control of the premises and it could be that the Grotbag Trust has little relevant control.

Turning to the 1957 Act, s. 2(2) provides that the occupier owes a common duty of care to all visitors. This is a duty to take such care as in all the circumstances of the case is reasonable to see that the visitor is reasonably safe in using the premises for the purposes for which he is invited or permitted by the occupier to be there. The reference to common duty is an indication that the statute no longer regards the status of the entrant as licensee or invitee to be relevant to the content of the duty.

Taking Tadeusz first, he is a visitor and is owed the common duty of care. The nature of the control by Dastardly Ltd is the day-to-day maintenance of the gardens and their duty would seem to extend to this particular danger. On the other hand, Grotbag Trust would seem not to have any duty in respect of this particular aspect of the estate. The House of Lords in *Tomlinson v Congleton BC* [2003] 3 All ER 1022 emphasized that the particular risk has to be clearly identified. There the risk did not arise from the state of the premises or from anything done or omitted on the premises—there was nothing extraordinary about the lake it that case, all lakes have murky water of unpredictable depth. There is in the problem a risk of injury due to the state of the premises—the tree has been left in a dangerous state.

The issue is whether or not Grotbag Trust has discharged its duty of care towards Tadeusz. The 1957 Act, s. 2(4)(b) provides that an occupier is not to be treated as answerable for damage caused by any work of construction, maintenance or repair by an independent contractor if in the circumstances of the case, it was reasonable to entrust the work to an independent contractor and that such steps as are reasonable have been taken to ascertain that the contractor was competent and the work was properly done. In *Ferguson v Welsh* [1987] 3 All ER 777 it was held using a purposive approach to statutory interpretation that demolition fell within the scope of s. 2(4)(b). Would it be reasonable to suppose that a similar result would flow here? If it is, then Grotbag Trust would be able to discharge its duty of care by showing that it had reasonably entrusted the work to an independent contractor (and an occupier would generally be treated as acting reasonably in employing someone to do lopping etc.) and had taken reasonable care in the selection of the independent contractor. If the work done by the contractor is technical, which the occupier cannot be expected to check, it may be sufficient that the occupier has ascertained that the contractor is competent before employing him: *Haseldine v Daw & Sons Ltd* [1941] 2 KB 343, but in *AMF International Ltd v Magnet Bowling Ltd* [1968] 2 All ER 789, it was suggested that the more complex the project then the more complex had to be the supervision. It is suggested that Grotbag Trust has discharged, i.e. performed, its duty of care provided that it has perhaps reviewed the work done by the contractor. Tadeusz's remedy would then lie against Rhoda in negligence. If either of Dastardly or Grotbag Trust were to be found liable then the issue of the exclusion clause would become relevant, and this is dealt with later.

As to Marta, it is a moot point whether or not the risk arises from danger due to the state of the premises; there is certainly nothing defective about the bush, and the analysis of *Tomlinson v Congleton* would be equally applicable here, but it would be argued that siting the bush in this place and knowing that people including children will be allowed into close proximity will amount to a danger due to the state of the premises, as it did in *Glasgow Corporation v Taylor*, a pre-Act case on the common law duty.

Assuming that there is a danger due to the state of the premises then the fact that Marta is six is a relevant consideration since the 1957 Act, s. 2(3)(a) provides a non-exclusive explanation of the circumstances relating to the discharge of the duty of care. It provides that in deciding what is reasonable, an occupier must expect children to be less careful than adults. Although in the cases of premises generally where dangers may not be obvious this rule is sound, both the nature of the premises and the role and duty of parents or carers should also be considered relevant, e.g. as to oversight of children of very young age.

Because the nature of the premises is relevant to the content of the specific duty, there is an essential difference between the problem and the position in *Glasgow Corporation v Taylor* where a child ate poisonous berries and died. There, the location was a recreation park adjoining botanic gardens and all the parties expected children to go there unaccompanied and unsupervised. Here there is an expectation that young children would be supervised and the essence of the garden is viewing the plants and grounds and nothing else. The House of Lords emphasized in the *Glasgow Corporation* case that both the parents and the occupier had to act reasonably, in that case the parents had acted reasonably but the corporation had not because it had left in such a place a poisonous bush. The parental oversight of young children was specifically relied on by the court in *Philips v Rochester Corporation* [1955] 1 QB 540 (five-year-old child in the care of an older sibling and allowed by parents to cross open land forming part of a building site where the younger child fell into a trench). Since Marta's parents have allowed her to wander off on her own, it may be that they do not regard the estate to be a dangerous place, in which case, the occupiers may also be able to argue that the estate is not dangerous (*Simkiss v Rhondda BC* (1983) 81 LGR 640).

If it is held that the occupier has acted unreasonably then the issue of the warning becomes relevant. Under s. 2(4)(a) a warning may discharge the duty of care provided it would enable the visitor to be reasonably safe. Lord Denning in *Roles v Nathan* gave the example of a warning which indicated that a particular bridge was dangerous and that there was a safe alternative. Here the notice may not be sufficient to discharge the duty owed to a child visitor, since it is possible that a six-year-old child cannot appreciate the message or may take no notice of the warning. The warning would not be such as to enable her to be reasonably safe.

As regards Harriet, by disobeying the sign she has become a trespasser (as did the claimant in *Tomlinson v Congleton* when he ran in to the water prior to diving forwards, according to the majority in the House of Lords). Another example might be the claimant in *Keown v Coventry Healthcare NHS Trust* [2006] EWCA Civ 39 – he was an 11-year-old who climbed the underneath of a metal fire-escape. This was accepted by the Court of Appeal as the closest example in real life of the example of a trespasser given by Scrutton LJ in *The Carlgarth* [1927] P 93, 110: 'When you invite a person into your house to use the staircase, you do not invite him to slide down the banisters, you invite him to use the staircase in the ordinary way in which it is used.' Accordingly Harriet is a non-visitor and any duty of care would have to be discovered by reference to the Occupiers' Liability Act 1984. In contrast to the 1957 Act the existence of a duty of care is not automatic; s. 1(3) provides that a duty of care is owed to a non-visitor if the occupier is aware of the danger or has reasonable grounds to believe that it exists; and that he knows or has reasonable grounds to believe that the other person is in the vicinity of the danger or may come into that vicinity; and that the risk is one against which the occupier may reasonably be expected to offer some protection. The House of Lords in the *Tomlinson* case explored the criteria for the creation of a duty in great detail in speeches which emphasized the balance which has to be drawn between the behaviour of the claimant on the one hand and over onerous duties on the other. It came down in favour of not imposing onerous duties on occupiers where the harm was in reality brought on the claimant of full competency by their own high-spirited behaviour.

But the starting point in that case was the analysis of risk of injury by reason of a danger due to the state of the premises. It was held that the lake in that case was an ordinary lake without hidden dangers or obstacles. Accordingly, there was no danger due to the state of the premises such as would give rise to a duty of care. Here the position is broadly similar. The pond is murky and of uneven depth, but so are many ponds. Accordingly Harriet's case would fall at this very early hurdle.

Under s. 1(3)(b), even if there was a danger within the meaning of the Act then it would have to be shown that Dastardly Ltd were aware or had reasonable grounds to believe that it existed and that the other person would come into the vicinity of the danger. Finally, under s. 1(3)(c), it would have to be shown that the risk was one against which the occupier may reasonably be expected to offer the other some protection. The members of the House of Lords in the *Tomlinson* case pointed out that even if the trespassing swimmer in that case had been a visitor then no duty to warn of a danger would have been owed because the risks of diving in a lake were obvious (see similar cases such as the obvious danger arising from an algae-covered breakwater in *Staples v West Dorset* (1995) 93 LGR 536 or high cliffs in *Cotton v Derbyshire Dales DC* (1994) *The Times*, 20 June or the weed-infested lake in *Darby v National Trust*). If nothing more could be expected of an occupier in respect of a visitor then there was no reason why a trespasser should be placed in a better position.

Furthermore there had to be a balance drawn which, as in the case of common law negligence, took into account not only the likelihood that someone may be injured and the seriousness of the injury, but also the social value of the activity which gives rise to the risk and the cost of preventative measures. In *Tomlinson*, the social value was of major concern to the House of Lords who felt that it would be unfair to restrict the ordinary lakeside activities of visitors in order to protect trespassing divers. The balance in the problem may not be as clear cut since measures such as appropriate planting could be sympathetically carried out so as not to destroy the attraction of the pond to other visitors. But, Harriet would have great difficulty in maintaining that she should have been warned of the uneven bottom given the obviousness of the dangers in paddling in a pond.

Even if a duty is owed under s. 1(3), it has to be considered whether there is a breach of that duty. In this respect, s. 1(4) provides that the occupier must take such care as is reasonable in all the circumstances of the case although the approach in *Tomlinson* comes close to deciding the standard issue since the relevant failure has essentially been considered when asking the key question whether the risk was one in respect of which some protection ought to have been offered. This creates an objective standard which will require consideration of, *inter alia*, the magnitude of risk, the precautions which could have been taken to guard against the risk. It is likely that a similar conclusion would be reached as under s. 1(3)(c).

Finally as regards the exclusion notice, the position may vary as between visitors and non-visitors. The duty owed to visitors may be restricted, modified or excluded by agreement or otherwise, so far as this is permitted by law, s. 2(1) of the 1957 Act. The word 'or otherwise' will be sufficient to cover a general notice modifying the common duty of care, even though it does not form part of a contractual arrangement (*Ashdown v Samuel Williams & Sons Ltd* [1957] 1 QB 409). The notice will also be subject to the provisions of the **Unfair Contract Terms Act (UCTA) 1977**, provided the occupiers fall within the intended scope of that Act. It is clear that in order for the **1977 Act** to apply, the premises must be occupied in a business capacity (UCTA 1977, s. 1(3)). We are told that the Grotbag Trust makes a charge for entry, but that this is merely to defray its expenses as a charity. Simply by virtue of being a charity does not prevent an organization being a business, after all the National Trust, Eton College, and the RNLI are charities but would be regarded as businesses. If a purely charitable organization is not a business, the result is that the Trust will not be affected by the provisions of the **1977 Act**. In contrast, Dastardly Ltd charge a management fee, which might be taken to suggest that they are in business with a view to profit, in which case, the provisions of **UCTA 1977** will affect their ability to exclude or limit their liability to lawful visitors.

By virtue of **UCTA 1977**, s. 2(1), any attempt to exclude or limit liability for death or bodily injury caused by negligence is void. For these purposes, negligence is defined as including a breach of the common duty of care under

1957 Act (UCTA 1977, s. 1(1)(c)). Accordingly, Dastardly Ltd will not be able to exclude liability for the injury caused to Tadeusz (assuming that they are otherwise liable).

Even if Grotbag Trust does owe a relevant duty and is somehow in breach of it, on the assumption that it does not act in the course of a business, the provisions of the 1977 Act will have no application to its operations, and it would seem that the exclusion, insofar as it relates to its liability, will be operative as regards visitors.

On the other hand, there is nothing in the 1984 Act which sanctions (or prohibits) the use of exclusion notices. The Law Commission recommended exclusion but Parliament may or may not have deliberately rejected this. Arguments suggest that if the prohibition of trespassing will not prevent the creation of a duty in the first instance then how can an exclusion notice exclude the operation of any duty found? Further as a matter of policy, if the duty imposed by the 1984 Act is akin to the duty of common humanity created in *British Railways Board v Herrington* [1972] AC 877, this might suggest that it is a basic level of protection which cannot be excluded by way of a notice or a disclaimer of liability. Accordingly, if Harriet is a trespasser then the exclusion of liability will have no effect in relation to any duty which may be found, even if the finding of such a duty and subsequent breach is most unlikely.

Further reading

Law Commission Report No. 75, Cmnd 6428, 1976.

9

Product liability

Introduction

This chapter contains questions relating to liability for harm caused by defective products. The regime imposed by the **Consumer Protection Act 1987** is a form of strict liability the rationale for which has been extensively explored both in the standard legal journals and the cases. Students should be aware of this theoretical underpinning which helps explain the interpretation of the legislation. The form of strict liability adopted here may also be compared with that adopted by the common law as regards vicarious liability (see Chapter 7) and with the statutory liability for harm caused by animals (see Chapter 10).

If a person produces a defective product, the traditional common law response is that he will only be liable in damages if it can be proved by the claimant that there has been a failure to exercise reasonable care on the part of the manufacturer. This emerged most clearly in *Donoghue v Stevenson* and the cases arising under the fault-based principle in that case. However, the European Community required Member States to impose a form of strict liability based on consumer expectations of safety. Since the introduction of the **Consumer Protection Act 1987**, strict liability has emerged but, arguably, closer examination of the defences available under the Act and the definition of 'defect' suggest that there are still elements of fault-based liability present in the statutory regime.

The **1987 Act** did not displace the fault-based form of liability in negligence under the narrow principle emerging from *Donoghue v Stevenson*. It is therefore necessary to identify in any question which form of liability the answer is required to deal with: frequently it will be both. As in other areas, what matters is that students should reflect the principles underpinning the law and should do more than simply recite the facts and the result. The same may also be said of cases under the common law.

Question 1

Albert is a fruit and vegetable farmer who grows apples, some of which he processes into cider, others he supplies to local retailers. Jane purchases five bottles of Albert's cider and 10 pounds of Albert's apples from George, a local retailer who has since gone out of business. Jane eats one of the apples, but becomes ill due to the presence of insecticide traces on the skin.

The bottles of cider all bear the warning that it has a very high alcohol content and that no more than two litres should be consumed in any period of 24 hours. Albert is also aware that he has used a preservative in the cider which possesses hallucinogenic qualities.

Jane arrives home for her evening meal. After the meal, a curry, Jane opens a bottle of cider, but as she does so, a plastic plug flies off the bottle top and part of the contents of the bottle splash into the face of Susan, Jane's sister. Susan licks the cider and suffers from a delusion that she can walk on water. She then jumps into Jane's swimming pool and drowns. Jane consumes three litres of the cider as a means of coping with Susan's death. Subsequently she feels sick. It transpires that her sickness is due partly to a chemical reaction between the contents of the cider and traces of curry she had recently eaten and partly due to excessive alcohol consumption. An article in the little heard of *Journal of Apple Science* has recently identified the possibility of a chemical reaction between certain varieties of curry and strong cider.

Advise Albert of his potential liability.

Commentary

This question concerns the liability of a manufacturer of a product for the physical harm suffered by a consumer of his product and requires consideration of the different approach to defective products according to whether the action is based in the tort of negligence or under the strict liability regime created by the **Consumer Protection Act 1987**. The former focuses on the conduct of the manufacturer whereas the latter has as its central focus consumer expectations as to the safety of the end product.

Answer plan

- What is the narrow rule in **_Donoghue v Stevenson_**?
- How is fault established?
- Is the manufacturer the cause of the harm suffered?
- What is a defective product under the **Consumer Protection Act 1987**?
- What defences to liability are available?

Suggested answer

The 'narrow' rule in *Donoghue v Stevenson* [1932] AC 562 states that a manufacturer of products, which he sells in such a form as to show that he intends them to reach the ultimate consumer in the form in which they left him with no reasonable possibility of intermediate examination, and with the knowledge that the absence of reasonable care in the preparation or putting up of the product will result in an injury to the consumer's life or property, owes a duty to the consumer to take reasonable care.

Being a variety of negligence, the narrow rule creates a form of fault-based liability on the part of the manufacturer. Although the word manufacturer is used to describe the potential defendant, it is better to think in terms of a person who has put a product into circulation, so that anyone in the chain of distribution is capable of owing the duty of care. Accordingly a farmer who puts agricultural produce into circulation is capable of being a producer, provided fault on his part can be proved.

Fault on the part of a manufacturer may be established in a number of ways. First, there may be a breakdown in the production process whereby there is one or more 'rogue' products which are capable of causing harm to the consumer. For example, in *Grant v Australian Knitting Mills* [1936] AC 85, the manufacturer failed to wash clothing adequately after it had been bleached in a sulphur-based solution, with the result that the consumer contracted dermatitis. Had adequate precautions been taken, the excess sulphites would not have contaminated the clothing. By analogy, the failure by Albert to wash his apples so as to rid them of traces of insecticide before putting them into circulation may amount to a breach of his duty to take care, especially if he ought reasonably to have foreseen that the presence of traces of the insecticide would be harmful to a consumer of the apples. Moreover, the use of inadequate materials in the product or its packaging is also capable of constituting a breach of duty. Thus if a bung comes out of a bottle so that the contents injure the user (*Fisher v Harrods Ltd* [1966] 1 Lloyd's Rep 500), or if the packaging used is generally unsafe (*Hill v James Crowe (Cases) Ltd* [1978] 1 All ER 812), there is a potential breach of duty.

A further possible breach of duty arises where the manufacturer fails to give an adequate warning of a known risk. The question informs us that Albert has warned of the danger of over-consumption, but he has not warned of the possible hallucinogenic qualities of his cider. It is clear that a warning can be inadequate for what it does *not* say. Thus in *Vacwell Engineering Ltd v BDH Chemicals Ltd* [1971] QB 88 a warning that a chemical gave off noxious fumes was not sufficient when the warning failed to refer to a probable violent reaction if the chemical were to come into contact with water. It may follow from this that the failure to warn of the hallucinogenic effect of the preservative used by Albert constitutes a breach of duty, especially since this indirectly results in Susan's death.

There is also the possibility of a breach of duty where a range of products suffers from a design fault. The question indicates that the cider may chemically react with certain varieties of curry so as to cause illness. Since this possibility has only been referred to in an obscure scientific journal, this may not be a fact of which Albert can reasonably have been aware. It is important that in a fault-based enquiry the defendant is only judged by reference to information available to him at the time of the alleged breach of duty (*Roe v Minister of Health* [1954] QB 66).

The mere fact that there is a potential breach of duty does not settle the matter since it must also be shown that the breach of duty is the cause of the harm suffered by the claimant. In relation to Jane, it is important to consider the possibility of intermediate examination and of possible consumer misuse. If the manufacturer can reasonably expect another person to inspect or do something to the product before it reaches the ultimate consumer, this possibility of intermediate examination may exonerate the manufacturer on the basis that his fault is no longer the cause of the harm suffered. In *Grant v Australian Knitting Mills*, it was unsuccessfully argued that the consumer ought to have washed the underwear he had purchased. This shows that the mere opportunity for intermediate examination is not sufficient to point to a cause other than defective manufacture and that the manufacturer must reasonably expect someone else to take up the opportunity to examine the goods. If there is a reasonable expectation that the product would be tested before use and the test fails to reveal the defect, the tester is likely to be regarded as the cause of the harm suffered (*Perrett v Collins* [1998] 2 Lloyd's Rep 255). This reasonable expectation will arise where the manufacturer has issued an appropriately worded warning (*Kubach v Hollands* [1937] 3 All ER 907), but there appears to be no warning given by Albert which requires any sort of examination. However, there is a warning which pertains to consumer misuse. Albert has warned that no more than two litres of his cider should be consumed in a period of 24 hours, and Jane fails to heed this warning. If it transpires that her misuse of the product in the face of the warning is the cause of the illness she suffers, it seems reasonable to assume that Albert will not be liable (*Farr v Butters Bros Ltd* [1932] 2 KB 606).

The burden of proving the causal link between Albert's breach of duty and the harm suffered by Jane lies on Jane herself and upon Susan's estate in relation to Susan's death. Jane will have to prove that it is the chemical reaction rather than her own misuse of the cider which is the cause of the harm she has suffered. If she cannot satisfy the burden of proof on this matter, she will fail in her action (*Evans v Triplex Safety Glass Ltd* [1936] 1 All ER 283). In any case, even if she does prove this link, it has been observed already that Albert may not be in breach of his duty in respect of this possible chemical reaction.

A possible difficulty in the action by Susan's estate, is that while only a very small amount of the cider has resulted in the delusion that leads to Susan's death, Jane has consumed a considerably greater quantity of the same cider without suffering the same reaction. This may suggest that Susan is unusually prone to suffer from this type of delusion. However, in a negligence action, the 'egg-shell skull' rule indicates that where a claimant is unusually prone to a particular type of harm, the defendant must 'take his victim as he finds him' (*Smith v Leech Brain & Co Ltd* [1962] 2 QB 405). This principle has also been applied to an extreme neurotic who has sustained much greater damage than would have been suffered by an ordinary individual (*Brice v Brown* [1984] 1 All ER 997).

As an alternative to a negligence action, Jane personally and Susan's estate may have an action under **Part I of the Consumer Protection Act (CPA) 1987**. This purports to create a regime of strict liability in respect of defective products that cause physical harm to the person or to property (**CPA 1987, s. 2(1)**). As a producer of a processed product (the cider) Albert will be subject to the Act (**CPA 1987, s. 1(2)(a)**). Furthermore, as the grower of the apples, he will also be a producer due to an amendment to the EC Directive (**Directive 99/34EC** amending **Directive 85/374/EEC**) and the **CPA 1987** that includes primary agricultural produce within the regime applied by this legislation.

Section 3(1) of the Act provides that a product is defective if it is not as safe as persons generally are entitled to expect. In determining what persons generally are entitled to expect s. 3(2) requires the court to consider (a) the manner in which and the purposes for which the product has been marketed, (b) what might reasonably be expected to be done with the product, and (c) the time of supply. In *A v National Blood Authority* [2001] 3 All ER 289, the claimants had been infected with the Hepatitis C virus following a blood transfusion using blood supplied by the defendants. In this case, Burton J drew a distinction between standard and non-standard products, regarding the blood as the latter, since it was different from the norm that the producer intended for use by the public. In concluding that the blood was defective, Burton J chose not to accept the defendant's argument that the presence of the defect was unavoidable. This might suggest that natural products such as blood (and manufactured products) that contain an abnormal defect will always be regarded as non-standard and therefore defective. However in *Tesco Stores Ltd v Pollard* [2006] EWCA Civ 393 the defendants were not liable for the illness suffered by a 13-month-old child who had been able to open the 'child-proof' safety cap on a bottle of dishwasher powder and consume part of the contents. It was concluded that all the public could expect was that the cap would make it more difficult for a child to open the container, which purpose it did serve.

Here, the apple eaten by Jane is a natural product that is contaminated by traces of insecticide. As such it would appear to be a non-standard product that is abnormally dangerous and Albert probably intended such contamination to be eliminated before his apples were put into circulation. The defect is also avoidable, unlike that in *Tesco v Pollard* so it seems likely that Albert will be liable for Jane's illness.

Conversely, all of Albert's cider appears to have a high alcohol content and the presence of the hallucinogenic preservative also appears to have been intended by Albert. These facts seem to suggest that the cider is a standard product in relation to the harm suffered by both Jane and Susan. For these purposes, it is for the claimant to prove that there is a causal link between the defectiveness of the product and the harm he or she has suffered (*Foster v Biosil* (2001) 59 BMLR 178).

The bottles of cider would appear to raise different considerations, due to their intended target market. Being an alcoholic drink prepared for human consumption, persons generally would expect it to be consumed only by those over the age of 18. Although Jane's age is not stated, it would be reasonable to assume that she is an adult as she appears to own her own house. However, the question remains whether the cider put into circulation by Albert achieves the desired level of safety in the light of its alleged defects. The **CPA 1987, s. 3(2)(b)** allows the court to consider what can reasonably be expected to be done with the product. This would appear to raise the issue of consumer misuse in the light of the warning printed on the bottles of cider. A danger that is adequately warned against may cease to be a danger at all. In the present case, Jane has consumed three litres of the cider when the printed warning advises against consumption of more than two litres of the beverage in a 24-hour period. This might make it difficult for Jane to be able to establish the causal link between the alleged defect in the cider and the harm she has suffered. A court might be persuaded that Jane's failure to heed the warning is the cause of the harm she has suffered. Alternatively, it is also clear from **CPA 1987, s. 6(4)** that the defence of contributory negligence provided for in the **Law Reform (Contributory Negligence) Act 1945** will apply to an action in respect of a defective product, so that the claimant's damages may be reduced in accordance with his or her degree of blameworthiness.

The death of Susan raises different considerations. It may be reasonable to assume that the cider is a standard product since Albert is stated to be aware of the hallucinogenic qualities of the preservative he has used in the recipe for the cider. There is no warning about the danger this might give rise to and Susan has not deliberately consumed the cider with a view to experiencing its hallucinogenic effects. The issue to consider, in this context, will be whether persons generally would consider that cider possessing these qualities is as safe as can be expected. The cider appears to have been marketed as a product intended for human consumption and if such a small amount as a splash on the lips is capable of producing such extreme consequences as the delusion from which Susan suffers, this might suggest that the cider has fallen below the standard of safety that might generally be expected. However, Jane has also consumed a much larger quantity of cider than did Susan, without suffering the same consequences. This might suggest that there is something unusual about Susan that makes her more prone to suffer from delusions of the kind under consideration. It may be that the cider is safe to consume for the majority of consumers and that there is something very unusual about Susan. In this last event, a court might be able to conclude that the cider is not unsafe in the light of general expectations. Conversely, if the effect upon Susan is one that is likely to be repeated in other consumers, it would seem to follow that the cider is not as safe as persons generally are entitled to expect. In this case, perhaps the only means of rendering the product safe will be to have it withdrawn from the market altogether.

In relation to Jane, there is the further problem that the risk of chemical reaction between strong cider and curry is little known to the scientific world. While the 1987 Act purports to introduce a regime of strict liability, there is a possible defence under s. 4(1)(e) in relation to development risks. Section 4(1)(e) provides that it is a defence for the producer to show that the state of scientific and technological knowledge was not such that a producer of products of the same description as the product in question might be expected to have discovered if the defect had existed in his products while they were under his control. This rather complex wording might appear to differ in certain important respects from that used in the EC Product Liability Directive, which the 1987 Act was intended to implement, since the Directive appears to ask, rather more simply, what was the state of scientific and technical knowledge at the time the product was put into circulation. In particular it was thought by some that s. 4(1)(e) imported a test based on the subjective knowledge of the producer whereas the Product Liability Directive set an objective test of knowledge. However the European Court of Justice has ruled in *EC Commission v United Kingdom (Re The Product Liability Directive)* (Case C-300/951) [1997] 3 CMLR 923 that there is nothing wrong in the wording used in the 1987 Act and that in their opinion, it does not set a subjective standard. In *A v National Blood Authority* [2001] 3 All ER 289, Burton J considered the position under art. 7(e) of the Directive (CPA 1987, s. 4(1)(e)) to be that the state of scientific knowledge is the most advanced available to anyone, although this does require an inquiry into what is discoverable evidence. It was also asserted that art. 7 is not concerned with the conduct of the individual producer, but is concerned with the expected conduct of producers, generally, in the light of what was objectively discoverable. In determining what is objectively discoverable, Burton J considered that standard industry practice could be discounted. The relevant question, therefore, appears to be whether Albert has failed to take the necessary precautions to guard against the defectiveness of the cider by not considering the article published in the *Journal of Apple Science*. The question states that the article has only recently disclosed the link between strong cider and certain varieties of curry. If the article was published after the cider was put into circulation by Albert, this will raise an issue of defectiveness, since the CPA 1987, s. 3(2)(c) directs the court to consider the time when a product was put into circulation in determining whether it is defective. If the product was in circulation before the date on which this item of scientific knowledge became available there appears to be a presumption that the product is not defective, unless the claimant can prove otherwise: *Piper v JRI Manufacturing Ltd* [2007] EWCA Civ 1344.

If the relevant copy of the *Journal of Apple Science* was in existence before the cider was put into circulation the question is whether this is information Albert should have had regard to before marketing his cider. In *EC Commission v United Kingdom (Re The Product Liability Directive)*, Tessauro A-G gave the example of a piece of scientific evidence published in Chinese in a Manchurian scientific journal, compared with an article published in a major scientific publication widely available to the English-speaking world. While the latter would normally be objectively discoverable by a UK producer, the former might not. In the present case, it would be necessary to have regard to the obscurity of the relevant journal and whether other cider producers, generally, might have taken account of it, especially in the light of the fact that there is only a possibility of the identified chemical reaction and that the reaction only occurs with some, but not all, varieties of curry.

In *EC Commission v United Kingdom* the court did opine that in order for a producer to be able to take into account the relevant state of scientific and technical knowledge, that knowledge had to be accessible. It may be the case that since the only reference to the possible reaction is in an obscure journal, it may not be regarded as accessible knowledge. Conversely, the relevant journal specializes in apple science and this might be regarded as a publication of which an apple and cider producer ought to have been aware.

Question 2

Koffman Latrash plc manufacture a pharmaceutical product called 'Offenden' which is marketed as a cure for morning sickness suffered by pregnant women, subject to a warning that the drug should not be used by people who suffer from high blood pressure. Extensive trials have failed to reveal any other defect in the drug despite the fact that an article published in a New Zealand medical journal has established that the principal ingredient in 'Offenden' may be capable of causing severe foetal limb abnormalities in rats in one per cent of cases in which the drug is used.

Neelam, who knows herself to be pregnant, attends the surgery of Dr Vijay who recommends the use of 'Offenden'. Neelam has high blood pressure, a fact of which she is aware but which is not known to Dr Vijay since he failed to make appropriate enquiries.

Neelam suffers a heart attack in the course of giving birth to her son, Sanjay, but she survives. The heart attack is shown to have been caused by high blood pressure exacerbated by ingredients in 'Offenden'. Sanjay is born with shortened arms and severe sight defects. Two months after the birth of Sanjay, a major scientific journal establishes incontrovertibly that one of the ingredients in 'Offenden' is likely, in more than 50 per cent of cases of use, to cause sight defects in new-born children.

Advise Neelam and Sanjay.

Commentary

This question requires consideration of the liability of a pharmaceuticals manufacturer for injuries caused to the immediate consumer of a drug and the effect of such consumption on an unborn child.

Answer plan

- Is there a breach of duty to exercise reasonable care and how does the issue of a warning affect liability?
- Is the doctor in breach of a duty of care?
- Does the **Consumer Protection Act 1987** apply to the drug and if so, is it defective and what defences are available?
- Is the unborn child protected by the **Congenital Disabilities (Civil Liability) Act 1976**?

Suggested answer

Neelam is a consumer of the drug 'Offenden'. As such she is owed a duty of care by the manufacturer of the drug, Koffman Latrash plc, under the narrow rule in *Donoghue v Stevenson* [1932] AC 562. This states that a manufacturer of products which he sells in such a form as to show that he intends them to reach the ultimate consumer in the form in which they left him with no reasonable possibility of intermediate examination, and with the knowledge that the absence of reasonable care in the preparation or putting up of the product will result in an injury to the consumer's life or property, owes a duty to the consumer to take reasonable care. A major difficulty in this instance is that the drug 'Offenden' suffers from a design defect. In such cases, the burden of proof that rests on the claimant is very difficult, but not impossible, to discharge. (For a rare instance of success see *IBA v EMI Electronics & BICC Construction* (1980) 14 BLR 1.)

Koffman Latrash plc have warned that the drug should not be used by persons with high blood pressure. If a manufacturer is aware that his product may cause harm if used in a particular way or by particular people, the best way he can discharge the duty of care he owes is by giving a warning or by issuing detailed instructions as to use (*Kubach v Hollands* [1937] 3 All ER 907). Moreover, where a warning of this kind has been issued, the manufacturer may have a reasonable expectation that an intermediary will check to ensure that the instructions are complied with. For example, in *Holmes v Ashford* [1950] 2 All ER 76, the manufacturer of a hair dye warned that before it was used, the dye should be patch tested to ensure that it did not have any adverse effect on customers. A hairdresser failed to heed this warning and the claimant contracted dermatitis. Since the manufacturer had done all that was reasonable in the circumstances, he was not in breach of the duty of care he owed. Moreover, the hairdresser's failure to take note of the warning rendered him liable for his negligence (see also *Perrett v Collins* [1998] 2 Lloyd's Rep 255). So far as Neelam is concerned she is unlikely to succeed in an action against Koffman Latrash plc, since there is a specific warning against the use of 'Offenden' by patients with high blood pressure. However, she may have an action against Dr Vijay on the basis that, under the principle in *Bolam v Friern Hospital Management Committee* [1957] 2 All ER 118, he has failed to act in the way that reasonable medical practitioners, in making enquiries, would act, having regard to Neelam's blood pressure and the warning issued with the drug.

Sanjay may also want to bring an action for negligence. Despite some uncertainty, an unborn child does have a potential common law action (*Burton v Islington Health Authority* [1992] 3 All ER 833). However, for practical purposes, this only applies to children born before 22 July 1976, because from that date the provisions of the Congenital Disabilities (Civil Liability) Act (CD(CL)A) 1976 supplant the common law. Under s. 1(1) of that Act, if a child is born disabled as a result of an occurrence before its birth and a person other than the child's mother is answerable for those disabilities, then the child may sue for the wrongful damage. The occurrences to which the Act applies include those which affect the mother during pregnancy, so that the child is born with disabilities which would not otherwise have been present (CD(CL)A 1976, s. 1(2)(b)). The defendant is only answerable, however, if he is or would have been liable in tort to the parents had actionable damage been sustained (CD(CL)A 1976, s. 1(3)). The problem this creates is whether Neelam could have maintained an action against Koffman Latrash plc had she suffered any injury.

The facts of the problem indicate that the propensity of 'Offenden' for causing sight defects is only established after the drug is put into circulation. It is important that in a fault-based enquiry the defendant is only judged by reference to information available to him at the time of the alleged breach of duty (*Roe v Minister of Health* [1954] QB 66). This would seem to suggest that no action would have been available in this respect as negligence on the part of the producer cannot be established. On the other hand there is evidence to show that the drug has caused foetal abnormalities in one per cent of rats on which the drug has been tested. If this converts into a similar percentage risk in relation to human beings it may be evidence of negligence on the part of Koffman Latrash plc, but the information must have been reasonably available to the manufacturer and since the relevant research is contained in an obscure journal, it may not amount to a failure to exercise *reasonable* care not to have been aware of it.

As an alternative to a negligence action, both Neelam and Sanjay may seek to bring an action under the Consumer Protection Act (CPA) 1987. The CPA implements the EEC Product Liability Directive (Dir. 85/374/EEC) with a view to applying the same product liability regime throughout the EU. With this in mind, it has been held by the European Court of Justice that Member States may not implement or retain rules that are more stringent than those provided for in the Directive (*Commission v France*, Case C52/00; *Sanchez v Medicina Asturiana SA*, Case C183/00). Although the following analysis is based on the provisions of the CPA 1987, should there be any discrepancy between its provisions and those of the Directive, the wording of the latter will prevail (*A v National Blood Authority* [2001] 3 All ER 289).

Koffman Latrash plc are producers of the drug by virtue of CPA 1987, s. 1(2)(a). Drugs, being substances which are not otherwise excluded from the scope of the Act, are products (**CPA 1987, s. 45(1)**).

The central issue is whether or not the drug is defective within the meaning of CPA 1987, s. 3. The burden of proving that there is a causal link between the defectiveness of the product and the harm suffered by the claimant will rest on the claimant (*Foster v Biosil* (2001) 59 BMLR 178).

For the purposes of the Act, a product is defective if it is not as safe as persons generally are entitled to expect (**CPA 1987, s. 3(1)**). It should be noted that what persons, generally, expect by way of safety could, in some cases, amount to perfection. For the purposes of s. 3(1), the decision of Burton J in *A v National Blood Authority*, above, discounts from consideration factors such as the fault of the defendant and whether the defendant could have taken steps to make the product safer. Also regarded as irrelevant were the social utility and beneficial nature of the product, except to the extent that there may be cases in which the public is aware that a product has a potential for causing harm, but still tolerates the product because of the benefits it confers. For example, everyone knows a knife has a sharp blade, but a sharp knife would not be a defective product if marketed as a kitchen knife. On this analysis, an enquiry into the defectiveness of a product does not take into account all of the factors relevant in determining whether a defendant is at fault (see also *Abouzaid v Mothercare (UK) Ltd* [2000] All ER (D) 2436 at para. 37 *per* Chadwick LJ). Conversely, factors that Burton J in *A v National Blood Authority* did consider to be relevant were whether or not the harmful characteristic in the product caused the injury complained of and whether the product was a standard or non-standard product. A standard product is one that has been produced as intended by the producer, whereas a non-standard product is one that fails to reach the normal standard set by the producer. The drug 'Offenden' was produced as designed and, as such would be a standard product, but that, in turn, will require a consideration of the nature of the design defect from which the drug suffers. If the design defect causes the product to be unsafe, it may be that the producer will have to accept responsibility for that lack of safety, unless he is able to successfully plead one of the defences to liability considered below.

In deciding what persons generally are entitled to expect by way of safety, CPA 1987, s. 3(2) provides that regard may be had to the manner in which the product has been marketed, the purposes for which it has been marketed and any instructions or warnings as to use. Thus a product may be declared to be defective if it is aimed at child consumers, even if the product would not be harmful to an adult (*A v National Blood Authority* [2001] 3 All ER 289, para. 22). In this case, the drug 'Offenden' is promoted with pregnant women in mind as the target market, but it will also be a consideration that the drug is likely to be available only on prescription and under the supervision of a qualified medical practitioner. This will also be relevant in the light of CPA 1987, s. 3(2)(b) which allows the court to consider what can reasonably be expected to be done with the product. Assuming the producer can expect supervision by a medical practitioner, taken in conjunction with the warning that the drug should not be used by those suffering from high blood pressure, it would seem to follow that the drug may not be defective, insofar as it has resulted in Neelam suffering a heart attack. In relation to Neelam's heart attack, the warning issued by Koffman Latrash plc will also be relevant in determining whether the drug is defective, since a danger which is adequately warned against may cease to be a danger at all.

Finally, by virtue of s. 3(2)(c) the courts are guided to have regard to the time at which the product was put into circulation. So far as Neelam is concerned, such defects as there are in 'Offenden' existed at the time the product was put into circulation. However, the same appears not to be true of the defects that affect Sanjay. An 'obscure' article has been published in scientific literature to the effect that one of the ingredients in 'Offenden' may cause foetal limb abnormalities. There is also scientific evidence that establishes, incontrovertibly, that an ingredient of 'Offenden' is a substantial cause of sight defects in new-born children. However, the latter only comes to light two months after the drug is first put into circulation. On the basis that a court may have regard to the time at which a product was first circulated, it may follow that, so far as Sanjay's sight defects are concerned, the drug is not to be regarded as a defective product. In relation to the defect resulting in limb abnormalities, it will be necessary to consider whether Koffman Latrash plc can raise any of the defences to liability, considered below.

It can be seen from the interpretation of the concept of defectiveness in *A v National Blood Authority* that art. 6 of the Directive (CPA 1987, s. 3(1)) sets a very high standard. In that case, blood products were supplied to members of the public, but those products were infected with Hepatitis C. This was not a defect of which everybody could be taken to be aware (such as the sharpness of a kitchen knife). Furthermore, the public legitimately expected that blood products would be tested and precautions taken to ensure the safety of the blood. The problem facing the National Blood Authority was that, at the time, the necessary tests were impossible to carry out. Nevertheless, the blood was still regarded as a defective product because it failed to live up to public expectations of safety.

The one area where Koffman Latrash plc may be liable is in relation to the foetal abnormality which results in Sanjay's shortened arms. The question shows that the manufacturer may have been aware of the propensity of the drug for causing this variety of harm, due to the existence of obscure scientific evidence of the defectiveness of the drug at the time it was put into circulation. Although the 1987 Act is supposed to have introduced a regime of strict liability, it also provides a development risks defence in s. 4(1)(e). This provides that it is a defence for the producer to show that the state of scientific and technical knowledge was not such that a producer of products of the same description as the product in question might be expected to have discovered if the defect had existed in his products while they were under his control. The manner in which s. 4(1)(e) is worded might suggest that it does not provide for a purely objective test, but rather requires consideration of subjective elements such as the resources of the particular manufacturer in question. The rather complex wording of s. 4(1)(e) might appear to differ in certain important respects from that used in the EC Product Liability Directive, which the 1987 Act was intended to implement, since the Directive appears to ask, rather more simply, what was the state of scientific and technical knowledge at the time the product was put into circulation. In particular it was thought by some that s. 4(1)(e) imported a test based on the subjective knowledge of the producer whereas the Product Liability Directive set an objective test of knowledge. However the European Court of Justice has ruled in *EC Commission v United Kingdom (Re The Product Liability Directive)* (Case C-300/951) (1997) 3 CMLR 923 that there is nothing wrong in the wording used in the 1987 Act and that in their opinion, it does not set a subjective standard. Conversely, the European Court of Justice did opine that in order for a producer to be able to take into account the relevant state of scientific and technical knowledge, that knowledge had to be accessible. In *A v National Blood Authority* [2001] 3 All ER 289, Burton J considered the position under art. 7(e) of the Directive (CPA 1987, s. 4(1)(e)) to be that the state of scientific knowledge is the most advanced available to anyone, although this does require an inquiry into what is discoverable evidence. It was also asserted that art. 7 is not concerned with the conduct of the individual producer, but is concerned with the expected conduct of producers, generally, in the light of what was objectively discoverable. In determining what is objectively discoverable, Burton J considered that standard industry practice could be discounted. The relevant question, therefore, appears to be whether Koffman Latrash plc has failed to take the necessary precautions to guard against the defectiveness of their product by not considering the article published in the New Zealand medical journal. In *EC Commission v United Kingdom (Re The Product Liability Directive)*, Tessauro A-G gave the example of a piece of scientific evidence published in Chinese in a Manchurian scientific journal, compared with an article published in a major scientific publication widely available to the English-speaking world. While the latter would normally be objectively discoverable by a UK producer, the former might not. In the present case, it would be necessary to have regard to the obscurity of the relevant journal and whether other drug producers, generally, might have taken account of it, especially in the light of the fact that the article is less than conclusive on the matter of foetal limb abnormalities in human beings. Possibly, it might be a piece of evidence that, objectively, Koffman Latrash plc could have chosen not to take into account.

Further reading

Howells, G., et al., *Product Liability*, 2nd edn (London: Butterworths, 2007).

Newdick, C., 'The Future of the Development Risks Defence—The Role of Negligence in Product Liability Actions' (1987) 103 LQR 288.

Stoppa, A., 'The Concept of Defectiveness in the Consumer Protection Act 1987' (1992) *Legal Studies* 210.

10

Liability for animals

Introduction

Liability in respect of the harm caused by animals may be based upon a wide range of torts, such as negligence, trespass to the person or land, and nuisance. The common law also developed special rules in connection with animals and these were enacted with modifications by the **Animals Act 1971**. The **1971 Act** does rather more than simply provide for civil liability; it also contains measures relating to the power to detain straying animals and to shoot dogs worrying livestock. In this chapter we will look at the forms of strict liability under the **Animals Act 1971** for injury caused by animals. Candidates also should have close regard to the range of defences available under the **Animals Act 1971, s. 5**.

Under the Act, the particular form of strict liability depends on the species of animal concerned. The Act distinguishes between those animals which belong to a dangerous species, in respect of which a very strict liability regime prevails, and those animals which do not belong to a dangerous species, in respect of which a less strict version of liability is provided. The Act defines dangerous species in s. 6(2) and students should note carefully the criteria contained in that section.

The Act is complex and often obscure in meaning. This has two important consequences. First, it requires students to concentrate on the statutory language and to avoid the use of shorthand phrases (such as 'domesticated species' or 'wild animal') which are not used by the Act. Secondly, it requires students to demonstrate their understanding of the statutory interpretation employed by the courts. In other words, students must show that they know and understand the principles underpinning the cases and not just the facts. Students should also be careful not to leap to conclusions as to which form of liability applies to the species in a problem. Trends in farming mean that animals such as ostrich or llama may from time to time be encountered in England and Wales. A question featuring an ostrich would have to deal in the alternative with the forms of strict liability since it is surely unclear whether or not the species is 'commonly domesticated' in the British Islands, this being the first part of the statutory test for a dangerous species. A problem featuring a horse or a crocodile would not usually require such caution.

Question 1

Desmond, a farmer, takes his prize bull to market in a lorry. Instead of using the market lorry-park, Desmond parks outside a nearby china shop owned by Pushpa. While Desmond is leading the bull from the lorry to the market-place, it is startled by the sound of a fire-engine siren. It breaks away and runs into Pushpa's shop. It causes considerable damage to Pushpa's stock of china and glassware and completely destroys a hugely expensive Ming vase on loan, for exhibition purposes, from the Victoria & Albert Museum.

Consider the potential liability of Desmond under the Animals Act 1971.

How, if at all, would your answer differ if the damage had been caused by a camel which was being taken on a parade through the street to a local circus? If so, why?

Commentary

This question is designed to test the candidate's knowledge of the **Animals Act 1971** and the cases that have been decided under this. Typically, the question asks the student to consider two species to which different subsections of the Act apply, each of which has its own form of strict liability. Again, typically, the question demands a good understanding of the sections. You may or may not have access to the wording of the Act in an examination (but it will be different for assessed coursework) so you need to be clear in your understanding of the main features of the relevant sections. Furthermore, questions of this sort demand rigorous attention to structure: you must proceed in a logical and methodically organized fashion. Untypically, this problem asks you to deal with straying animals. Appropriate authorities must be considered carefully; cases in this area tend to be complex and the legal principles need to be stated with especial care.

Answer plan

- Identify the basis of liability for straying livestock.
- Identify the basis of liability for animals that belong to a non-dangerous species.
- Identify the basis of liability for animals that are members of a dangerous species.
- Consider the strictness or otherwise of the duty imposed upon the keeper of different kinds of animal.
- Consider if there is any contributory negligence.
- Comment on the relevance of defences at common law and under the **Animals Act 1971**.

Suggested answer

A bull would reasonably be recognisable as falling within a bovine species and would be within the meaning of cattle, and all types of cattle are 'livestock' within the meaning of the **Animals Act 1971, s. 11**. The expression 'livestock' covers most farmyard animals including horses, pigs, sheep, goats, and poultry as well as cattle.

The general rule under the **Animals Act 1971, s. 4** is that a person who has possession of livestock is responsible for any damage which it may cause to land or other property, but not for personal injuries. This liability does not depend on proof of negligence and is a statutory replacement of the old common law rules relating to 'cattle trespass'. Liability under s. 4 extends to all of the damage caused, not just to that which is reasonably foreseeable. Nevertheless, the defendant will be able to disclaim liability under s. 5(1) for any damage which was wholly due to the claimant's own fault and may also rely on the **Law Reform (Contributory Negligence) Act 1945** if the claimant was partly responsible for any of the damage caused. However, on the facts, there seems to be little to suggest that Pushpa is in any way to blame for the damage caused by Desmond's bull, except insofar as leaving a Ming vase exposed may amount to contributory negligence.

Desmond may argue that, under the **Animals Act 1971, s. 5(5)**, strict liability for the trespassing livestock does not extend to cases in which an animal strays from the highway on to adjoining land, if their presence on the highway constitutes a lawful use of the highway. This effectively replaced in statutory form the rule of the common law illustrated by *Tillett v Ward* (1822–23) 10 QBD 17. This rule was to the effect that a keeper of animals was not to be liable in the absence of negligence where the animal strayed from the highway onto adjacent land (in that case an ironmonger's shop) and caused damage. Those who have land beside the highway hold it subject to the risk of injury from inevitable risk. Here, it does seem reasonable to assume that the use of the highway in a market town for the passage of livestock may be regarded as a lawful use of that highway, so Desmond will only be liable if there is proof of negligence. In this regard, much will depend on expert evidence as to how bulls should be handled when being taken to market. Also, there may be some evidence of negligence in that Desmond has not used the lorry-park at the market, but has chosen to park in the street.

The Act defines dangerous species to which the form of strict liability in s. 2(1) applies. Animals which do not fall within that definition will automatically fall within the form of strict liability in s. 2(2). Turning first to the bull, the general provisions of s. 2(2) of the 1971 Act apply to cows and bulls because they belong to a species which is not a dangerous species: cows and bulls are commonly domesticated in the British Islands and so excluded from belonging to a 'dangerous species' under s. 6(2). To succeed under this section Pushpa would have to establish: first, that the damage was of a kind which the animal, unless restrained, was likely to cause or was likely to be severe (s. 2(2)(a)); secondly, that the likelihood of the damage or of its being severe was due to characteristics of the animal not normally found in such animals or not normally so found except at particular times or circumstances (s. 2(2)(b)); thirdly, that those characteristics were known to the keeper (s. 2(2)(c)). Section 2(2) differs from liability in s. 2(1) in so far as at some stage the focus is on the particular animal under consideration not the species as a whole. In other words, if a particular animal acts uncharacteristically for that species, e.g. by biting or kicking when the generality of the species does not, then liability may follow. The Act has been interpreted as establishing a rule of policy that the keeper of an animal will be liable even though the animal is doing only what is normal for that species under particular (i.e. abnormal) circumstances. This was held to be so by the House of Lords in *Mirvahedy v Henly* [2003] 2 All ER 401, although the decision was 3:2. In that case the particular horses when panicked ran headlong and without regard to danger in a way normal for all horses in that abnormal situation and fell within the second part of s. 2(2)(b) and liability followed. Here it might be argued (subject to expert evidence) that all startled bulls will have a propensity to run away and that they will blunder about causing damage, i.e. that there is the likelihood of damage found in that species in particular circumstances. Subject to the knowledge on the part of Desmond, the keeper, then liability under s. 2(2) will follow here.

On the other hand, a camel does not fall into the definition of livestock, and the rules in relation to straying from the highway do not apply. But, the camel will be regarded as a dangerous species under the Animals Act 1971, s. 6(2). This was held to be in *Tutin v Chipperfield Promotions* and precedent demands that this should be followed. The logic in that case was that camels, as a species, are not normally domesticated in the British Islands. Furthermore, although a fully grown camel is unlikely to cause severe damage unless it is restrained, due to its size and strength, any damage caused by a camel is likely to be severe. In *Behrens v Bertram Mills Circus Ltd* [1957] 2 QB 1, an elephant albeit of a placid sub-species, was held to be the pre-Act equivalent of a dangerous species largely due to its size and potential for causing damage. Accordingly, when, having been startled by a dog, it trampled a circus booth in which the plaintiff was standing, liability for the damage it caused was strict even though the animal was docile. In *Tutin v Chipperfield* the strict liability in s. 2(1) applied to harm caused by a camel whose typically uneven gait caused an amateur rider to be thrown (although in that case there was found to be a voluntary assumption of the risk).

If the damage in Pushpa's shop, was caused by a camel, the Animals Act 1971, s. 2(1) provides that the keeper of that animal will be liable for any damage caused. For the purposes of the 1971 Act, a keeper is defined in s. 6(3) and includes a person who owns or has the animal in his possession. Liability is not confined to damage to land and other property, but also extends to cover personal injury, including psychiatric damage. Moreover, liability is strict in that s. 2(1) does not require proof of negligence. For the purposes of s. 2(1), what matters is whether the species to which the animal belongs is dangerous, and that it has caused damage. Thus, it will be no defence to argue that this particular camel was friendly, not known to be dangerous, or unpredictable in its behaviour, or not fully grown, since the test in s. 6(2) relates to the species of which this animal is a member.

The key issues, therefore, will be those of causation and remoteness of loss. The Animals Act 1971 does not state whether any particular remoteness test applies to its provisions and, historically, liability for animals has set a very high standard, requiring the keeper to keep an animal (especially one belonging to a dangerous species) at his peril. More recently, developments in other areas of supposed strict tortious liability seem to suggest a shift towards a greater use of the reasonable foresight of harm test established in the *Wagon Mound (No. 1)* [1961] AC 388 (see *Cambridge Water Co Ltd v Eastern Counties Leather plc* [1994] 1 All ER 53 in relation to the rule in *Rylands v Fletcher*). The position at common law would seem to have been somewhat contradictory. Statements by Devlin J in *Behrens v Bertram Mills Circus Ltd*, to the effect that the keeper of an escaped but amiable tiger would remain liable for injury to a claimant who suffered a heart attack on witnessing the tiger sitting on his bed, would seem to suggest that liability was very strict. Conversely, in *Brook v Cook* (1961) 105 SJ 684, the keeper of a monkey was held not to be liable for the claimant's broken wrist when she took fright at the sight of a monkey and fell in her panic. Apparently, the reasoning behind this decision rested on the fact that the keeper would only be liable if his animal were to attack the victim. The position under the Act would seem to have been resolved in *Tutin v Mary Chipperfield Promotions Ltd* (1990) 130 NLJ 807, in which damage due to a fall from a camel (a dangerous species under the Act) was held to have been caused by the animal. The animal, like all camels, had an unwieldy gait and it was this that caused the plaintiff to fall off. The case itself was decided on common law negligence principles because although the plaintiff had consented to the risk under the Act she had not consented to the risk of the race being started in a careless fashion. It would seem, therefore, that the keeper of the camel will be liable for *any* damage it has caused.

Under the Law Reform (Contributory Negligence) Act 1945, the court has a power to reduce the claimant's damages in accordance with the claimant's share of the responsibility for the damage suffered. Under the 1945 Act, the defence will be available where the damage to the claimant, or of it being more severe than would otherwise have been the case, is reasonably foreseeable (*Jones v Livox Quarries Ltd* [1952] 2 QB 608). Moreover, the claimant's conduct must be, in some way, a cause of the harm suffered, although it does not have to be a cause of the accident that results in that harm (*Jones v Livox Quarries Ltd*). Desmond may contend that the damage to the Ming vase was caused by Pushpa's fault in leaving it in such an exposed position without regard to its value. Both arguments – voluntary assumption of risk under s. 5, and contributory negligence – seem doomed to fail, however, since the fact that an object happens to be more valuable than average is not to be equated with the extent of the damage being more severe. It seems clear from the facts that the damage would not have occurred but for the trespassing of Desmond's bull. The idea that it might in some way be the fault of a china shop owner that she failed to foresee and protect her stock from straying bulls would surely stretch the imagination too far. The law requires that 'people guard against reasonable probabilities, but they are not bound to guard against fantastic possibilities' (*Fardon v Harcourt-Rivington* [1932] All ER Rep 81, *per* Lord Dunedin).

Question 2

Indira, a professional trapeze artiste, is engaged to appear at Bronco Bill's Circus for an eight-week summer season. Indira's act includes a mid-flight trapeze exchange with Mickey, a monkey owned by Bronco Bill's Circus, but specially trained by Indira. During a rehearsal, Indira and Mickey attempt to exchange trapezes in mid-flight, but both fail to catch their target and fall into the safety net. Being frightened, Mickey bites Indira's big toe and runs out of the circus tent into a neighbouring garden owned by Tilly, an 80-year-old pensioner. As Tilly is hanging out her washing, Mickey, still being very frightened after his fall, screams at her and bares his teeth. Tilly suffers a heart attack.

Indira is making her way to the first-aid caravan when she encounters Humpy, the pregnant camel. Humpy is normally a very docile animal, but because of her delicate state, is apt to be aggressive. Humpy spits at Indira and kicks her in the stomach. Humpy then runs out of the circus and collides with Donald's car on the highway causing serious damage.

Indira enters what she believes to be the first-aid caravan, but which is, in fact, Bronco Bill's personal caravan. Bronco Bill's pet dog Gnasher (a cross between an Alsatian and a Bull Mastiff) immediately attacks Indira, believing its own territory to have been invaded by a stranger. Indira is seriously injured as a result of this attack and requires extensive hospital treatment.

Advise Indira, Tilly, and Donald as to their claims under the Animals Act 1971.

Commentary

The problem is structured to allow the student to reveal that the form of liability under the **1971 Act** is a curious form of strict liability. It is a good idea to establish clearly the initial classification of the animals since this will direct the answer to the relevant form of liability. An answer should do two things. It should refer to the leading authorities such as ***Mirvahedy v Henley*** and should state the terms of the Act as accurately as possible — avoid sloppy expressions. Typically the problem asks the student to deal with animals which fall within both forms of liability. Many animals will obviously belong to a dangerous species, e.g. elephants and crocodiles. Some will equally obviously belong to non-dangerous species, e.g. cows and horses. But there may be areas of doubt because it is unclear whether the characteristics satisfy the requirements of a dangerous species, e.g. as to the commonness of domestication. There are traps in the question. For example, the monkey is not described and it by no means follows that **s. 2(1)** will be applicable. It would be otherwise if the animal were an ape, such as a chimpanzee, which is well known to possess enormous strength. A small monkey may well not fall within the definition of a dangerous species and **s. 2(2)** would have to be mentioned and applied to it, although discussion of that could be blended with the analysis of **s. 2(2)** when considering the liability for Gnasher. It is generally a sound approach to deal with common issues together and a good answer will bring together the different animals to which a common regime attaches. Avoid too many references to the common law, these will serve only to confuse. If citing pre-Act cases then make this clear and state clearly how the point remains relevant. Finally, do not fall into the trap of developing factual arguments; courts have the advantage of hearing evidence; you do not. Show your knowledge and understanding of the law.

Answer plan

- Establish briefly the scheme of the Act.
- Consider which category each animal falls into.
- Explore which animals belong to a dangerous species, and describe and apply the form of strict liability relevant to that species.
- Identify the animals belonging to a non-dangerous species and describe and apply the relevant form of strict liability.
- Identify who is the keeper.
- Consider what defences apply.

Suggested answer

The **1971 Animals Act** creates a different regime of liability depending on whether or not a particular animal belongs to a dangerous or a non-dangerous species. The first is very strict and does not depend on knowledge of any dangerous characteristic and liability will apply even if the harm flows from a non-dangerous characteristic of that particular animal: the focus is the species. The second, is less strict and requires a comparison of the particular animal to the species, a link between the dangerous characteristic and the harm, and knowledge on the part of a keeper.

The first question to consider is whether a monkey and a camel belong to dangerous or a non-dangerous species. Section 6(2) provides that a dangerous species, first, is one which is not commonly domesticated in the British Islands and, secondly, that fully grown animals of the species concerned have characteristics that they are likely, unless restrained, to cause severe damage or that any damage they may cause is likely to be severe.

There are many different types of monkey, some are kept in captivity in zoos, and some as pets, but this probably will not be sufficient to amount to domestication, and certainly not to common domestication. In *Mirvahedy v Henly* [2003]

2 All ER 401 Lord Scott thought that 'domesticate' had a number of possible meanings but he preferred the view that in the context of s. 6 it meant 'to tame or bring under control'. So species of animals which are commonly tamed and brought under control in this country cannot belong to a 'dangerous species'. In *Tutin v Mary Chipperfield Promotions Ltd* (1990) 130 NLJ 807 it was suggested that domesticate meant to accustom to the usages of mankind and that the fact that camels occurred in zoos did not mean that they were commonly domesticated.

The additional elements of s. 6(2) must be applied. It must be shown either that adult animals of that species have characteristics such that they are likely unless restrained to cause severe damage (such as might well be the case with a tiger) or that any harm they could cause would be likely to be severe (as might well be because of the size and power of the animal, e.g. an elephant may be unlikely to cause severe damage but any damage it would cause would be likely to be severe). In asking these questions the particular animal has to be ignored. So, by way of example from the common law (which is not exactly the same as the Act), the elephant in *Behrens v Bertram Mills Circus Ltd* [1957] 1 All ER 583 was a gentle creature which, when startled by a dog, trampled on the plaintiff. It was held that elephants fell within the common law category of animals *ferae naturae* and that the strictest form of liability followed from this classification. Thus, the gentle nature of the particular camel is irrelevant.

Even though camels as a species were held under the common law (*McQuaker v Goddard* [1940] 1 KB 697) to be animals *ferae mansuetae* (because they were domesticated in certain parts of the world) the test under s. 6 is different and it was held in *Tutin v Mary Chipperfield Promotions Ltd* (1990) 130 NLJ 807 that camels are not commonly domesticated in the British Islands and that a fully grown camel generally has characteristics which make it likely that any damage they cause will be severe and, as a result, that a camel is now to be regarded as belonging to a dangerous species to which s. 2(1) applies.

On the other hand little is known about Mickey's species' characteristics (such as propensity to bite, or attack, or its size). Even though the species is most unlikely to be commonly domesticated in the British Islands we cannot say whether or not the species to which Mickey belongs has fully grown animals whose characteristics are such that it is likely, unless restrained, to cause severe damage or that any damage it would cause would be severe. Accordingly the liability of the keeper will be addressed in the alternative.

Liability under s. 2 of the Act is placed on the keeper. For these purposes, the **Animals Act 1971, s. 6(3)** states that a keeper is someone who (a) owns the animal, or (b) has it in his possession, or (c) is the head of a household in which a person under the age of 16 owns or possesses the animal. It is stated that Mickey is owned by Bronco Bill but is trained by Indira. Also, Mickey's escape occurs when he and Indira are engaged in a training session but it may not be sufficient for possession. What is important is that the list of keepers in s. 6(3) is stated in the alternative, so that it is possible that more than one person may be regarded as a keeper. This would seem to suggest that Tilly may choose between Bronco Bill and Indira as possible defendants, but the more likely of the two to be insured against injury caused by circus animals is Bronco Bill.

On the assumption that both Mickey and Humpy are animals which belong to a dangerous species then s. 2(1) applies; this provides that where any damage is caused by an animal which belongs to a dangerous species the keeper is liable for the damage unless one of the defences in the Act applies. Indira will be able to recover even though she too may be a keeper – in *Flack v Hudson* the Court of Appeal confirmed that the 1971 Act would allow one keeper of an animal to sue another keeper. Applying s. 2(1) Indira will also be able to recover in respect of the harm caused to her by Humpy. These are simple cases where there is a clear causal link.

The problem as regards Tilly is that she suffers the harm in a way which is unexpected and not necessarily connected with any dangerous characteristic of Mickey. The fact that liability under the 1971 Act is strict might suggest that the defendant will be liable regardless of the foreseeability of the harm suffered. However, in recent years, the courts have demonstrated a general unwillingness to impose strict liability and also to hold the defendant liable for remote losses (See, for example, *Cambridge Water Co v Eastern Counties Leather plc*, [1994] 2 WLR 53 applying the same remoteness test to actions under the rule in *Rylands v Fletcher* as applies to a nuisance action.) The position at common law seems to have been that the keeper of a dangerous animal was liable for all damage caused by it and the words used in s. 2(1) are simple and reflect a view of where the burden should be placed. This would seem to suggest that the position has not changed and that the keeper will be liable for any damage which is directly caused by the animal. By contrast the position is a little more complicated for the purposes of non-dangerous species, the keeper is only liable under s. 2(2) for damage which can be expected of that particular animal in the light of characteristics which it possesses and which are known to the keeper. The point seems to have been concluded in *Tutin v Mary Chipperfield Promotions Ltd.* It was held that a rider thrown off by the unwieldy gait of the camel suffered injury caused by the camel In other words it need not be the particular characteristic which makes the damage likely to be serious which need cause the actual harm suffered (not need the harm actually suffered be serious). This reflects the position at common law and in *Behrens v Bertram Mills Circus Ltd* [1957] 2 QB 1, Devlin J stated *obiter* that if a man woke up to find an escaped tiger in his bedroom and suffered a heart attack as a result, the keeper would be liable no matter how tame or docile the tiger might have been. On the view in *Tutin v Mary Chipperfield Promotions Ltd*, Tilly will be able to recover since Mickey caused her injury. (In that case, although the point was not before the court, it must have been the case that the harm would have been reasonably foreseeable.)

Applying this to the harm suffered by Donald, Donald may succeed in an action against Bronco Bill so long as a causal link can be forged between Humpy's escape and the damage to Donald's car. Incidentally, s. 8(1) removed the common law rule in *Searle v Wallbank* prohibiting an action in negligence in respect of animals straying on to the highway. Donald would be able to bring an action in negligence in respect of this straying (and arguably also under the rule in *Rylands v Fletcher*).

Dogs, as a species, are commonly domesticated in the British Islands and, as such, will not be regarded as belonging to a dangerous species. Instead, the liability of the keeper falls to be considered under s. 2(2) of the 1971 Act. What are the rules which apply to animals which do not belong to a dangerous species, i.e. Gnasher and, possibly, Mickey?

This very 'cumbrously worded' (according to Lord Denning MR in *Cummings v Granger*) provision states that a keeper of a non-dangerous animal will be liable if:

(a) the damage caused by the particular animal is of a kind which the animal, unless restrained, was likely to cause, or if caused by that animal, was likely to be severe; and

(b) the likelihood of the damage or it being severe was due to characteristics of the animal which are not normally found in members of its species, or are not normally so found except at particular times, or in particular circumstances; and

(c) those characteristics were known to the keeper, a member of his household under the age of 16 or anyone employed by the keeper who is in charge of the animal.

What is clear from this wording is that liability under s. 2(2) is not as strict as under s. 2(1) since the keeper will not be responsible for harm caused by a dangerous characteristic of which he was not aware. It is also important to emphasize that for the purposes of s. 2(2), the court is concerned with the characteristics of the particular animal (in this case the particular monkey and the particular cross between a Bull Mastiff and an Alsatian dog) rather than the characteristics displayed generally by the species to which the animal belongs.

In *Curtis v Betts* [1990] 1 All ER 769 a normally docile Bull Mastiff attacked the plaintiff as he approached it as it sat in the back of a Land Rover. It was held in *Curtis v Betts* that each separate part of the section has to be taken in turn. Thus s. 2(2)(a) requires the court to consider simply the likelihood of damage or the likelihood that such damage would be severe. In *Curtis v Betts* the judge had held that for s. 2(2)(a) any damage the particular dog might cause would be likely to be severe but that it was unlikely to cause harm at all. This finding was not challenged. The Court of Appeal concentrated on s. 2(2)(b) and the phrase 'the likelihood of the damage or of it being severe'. It took the view that the draftsman probably intended the phrase to mean 'the damage' and that the court should consider whether there is a causal link between the particular characteristic of the animal and the damage. The crucial 'particular characteristic' was that Bull Mastiffs are very territorial and will attack to defend their territory, and therefore the damage was caused by this characteristic. This sits uneasily with the judge's finding that the dog was unlikely to cause harm.

This confusing approach was not adopted by the Court of Appeal in *Clark v Bowlt* [2006] EWCA Civ 978, a horse moved unexpectedly into the path of a car. The judge had held that any damage caused was likely to be severe, and the Court of Appeal confirmed that this was so because the horse was large and heavy. But since this is common to all horses it could not be said to be an unusual characteristic and thus liability could not arise under the corresponding part of s. 2(2)(b). The Court of Appeal advocated a logical progression linking each of the relevant parts of (a) and (b). Although it did not refer to *Curtis v Betts*, this case relied on *Mirvahedy v Henly* and is thus to be preferred to *Curtis v Betts*. It also makes clear that s. 2(2)(a) may assume greater importance then previously.

The second part of (b) has proved equally controversial. The House of Lords in *Mirvahedy v Henley* has by a majority of 3:2 confirmed that s. 2(2)(b) of the 1971 Act applies to behaviour which although abnormal to the species for the most part, is nevertheless normal for that species in the particular (i.e. abnormal) circumstances which had occurred. It rejected the view preferred by the minority that normal behaviour in abnormal circumstances fell outside the scope of the Act. Applying this, Gnasher has attacked because of its territorial tendencies. This tendency may be regarded as a particular circumstance which is common to dogs of that breed. For example, it was regarded as a particular circumstance in *Cummings v Granger* that an Alsatian dog was being used as a guard dog and might therefore savage an intruder. Assuming Bronco Bill is using the dog to guard his private premises, this, taken with the territorial nature of Bull Mastiffs, should suffice to satisfy the requirements of s. 2(2)(b).

Given that Bull Mastiffs, generally, have these characteristics, this might be a fact known to Bronco Bill and if the animal has previously displayed territorial tendencies, this is damage for which he may be liable. The knowledge required by s. 2(2)(c) is actual knowledge. Generally, this will require the animal to have displayed characteristics in the past which show that it is likely to act in the way in which it did on the occasion under consideration. On the facts of the question, there is no evidence one way or the other.

Similarly, with regard to Mickey (if it does not belong to a dangerous species) it would have to be shown that he was likely unless restrained to cause that harm or that any harm he did cause would be likely to be severe. This would depend on facts of which we are unaware. It would then have to be shown that the damage was caused either by Mickey possessing abnormal characteristics for the species (such as a vicious tendency) or by characteristics normal for that species in particular circumstances, e.g. to bare its teeth and attack when scared (compare the behaviour of the terrified horses in *Mirvahedy v Henley* which fled in blind panic—a characteristic common to all horses in those circumstances). The causal factor has to relate to the specific characteristics. Finally the characteristic would have to be known to the keeper—something on which we have no information.

Apart from the question of initial liability under s. 2(2), it is possible that Indira may be met by one of a number of defences provided for in the **Animals Act 1971, s. 5**. Under s. 5(1), it is a defence for the keeper of an animal to show that the harm suffered by the claimant is due 'wholly to the fault of the person suffering it'. This would seem to involve the claimant in taking some conscious, risky decision such as entering a leopard's cage to pick up a dropped cigarette (*Sylvester v Chapman Ltd* (1939) 79 SJ 777). On the facts of the question, we are informed that Indira believed she was entering the first-aid caravan, and it may be that it cannot be regarded as entirely her fault that she inadvertently encounters the dog. Even if she was partly at fault this would not allow the defence to apply, in *Cummings v Granger* the Court of Appeal concluded that the bite to the plaintiff was not wholly her fault and that the defence under s. 5(1) did not apply.

Bronco Bill may argue that Indira voluntarily accepted the risk of the bite and the kick. Two things would suggest that this will not succeed. First, voluntary acceptance of the risk was applied in *Tutin v Mary Chipperfield Promotions Ltd*. There the claimant was well aware of the fact that camels ran awkwardly and she had seen other riders fall in similar fashion. She was taken to have accepted the risk. This was also applied in *Cummings v Granger* where the plaintiff entered the scrap yard knowing that there was a dog there which had a characteristic of attacking strangers. There is no suggestion here of any awareness of any characteristic which would make it likely that harm would be caused. Secondly, s. 6 (5) states that where a person is employed as a servant by the keeper and incurs a risk incidental to the employment then that person shall not be treated as accepting the risk voluntarily. This will depend on the status of Indira and what risks were incidental to the trapeze act or more generally in connection with her work.

In relation to the attack by the dog, it may be reasonable to assume that an employee is still 'employed' while seeking first aid following a work injury. However, the problem will be whether the risk of being bitten by a dog in a private caravan is a risk incidental to Indira's employment. In any event, the defence is one of voluntary assumption of risk, and it may be that because Indira inadvertently strays into the private caravan, she is taken not to have voluntarily accepted the risk.

While Indira will clearly have permission to be on circus premises, she may become a trespasser when she strays into Bronco Bill's private caravan. In these circumstances, s. 5(3) provides that a keeper will not be liable for harm caused to a trespasser where the animal is (a) not kept there for the protection of persons or property, and (b) it is not unreasonable to keep the animal where it is kept. The question does not specifically inform us that the dog was kept there as a guard dog. If it is not, the defence will not help Bronco Bill, but even if it is kept as a guard dog, its presence may be regarded as perfectly reasonable, as was the case in *Cummings v Granger*. If the keeping of the dog in the caravan is regarded as reasonable, the effect of this will be to provide Bronco Bill with a defence.

Further reading

Amirthalingam, K., 'Animal Liability: Equine, Canine and Asinine' (2003) 119 LQR 563.

Howarth, D., 'The House of Lords and the Animals Act: Closing the Stable Door' (2003) 62 CLJ 548.

North, P. M., *The Modern Law of Animals* (London: Butterworths, 1972).

Sharp, C., 'Normal Abnormality? Liability for Straying Horses under the Animals Act 1971' [2003] JPI 172.

11

Torts relating to land

Introduction

This chapter is concerned with the competing interests of landowners and other miscellaneous matters concerned with the land ownership. Public and private nuisance are both actionable as torts, although the former is also a crime. Public nuisance can take many forms but for present purposes we are concerned with interferences which affect a class of Her Majesty's subjects and generally these interferences must have a wide-ranging effect. Where there is a sufficiently widespread public nuisance then the local authority will have power to take steps to obtain an injunction, or those affected can bring an action in the name of the Attorney-General to obtain an injunction. Private nuisance is concerned with private property rights and is based on the unreasonableness of the defendant's interference with the claimant's use or enjoyment of land. The principal underlying theme is one of give and take. Landowners can expect to put up with some inconvenience from their neighbours, but not to an unreasonable extent. For the purposes of private nuisance it is not the actions of the defendant which matter (except, perhaps, where malice is a factor) but the activity or state of affairs which has been allowed to continue. While damages may be an appropriate remedy, nuisance may frequently attract the remedy of an injunction, since the nature of many nuisances is that that they are liable to continue.

The rule in *Rylands v Fletcher* (1868) **LR 3 HL 330** is ostensibly a rule of strict liability based on the notion of escape. However, as a rule of strict liability it has not survived well, because of the judicial hostility which seems to exist towards the imposition of liability in the absence of fault. In now appears that the rule in *Rylands v Fletcher* is little more than a special application of rule of nuisance in the context of an isolated escape, thus reducing any impact the rule may have had in terms of environmental protection. This is especially so in light of the defences to liability under the rule and the interpretation of the concept of non-natural user in *Cambridge Water Co v Eastern Counties Leather plc* [1994] 4 All ER 53.

The third of the 'land torts' is that of trespass to land which is concerned with deliberate invasions of the claimant's right to peacefully enjoy property in his possession. Frequently this action will be used to decide on matters such as boundary disputes but in other instances it may be used where nuisance is not made out. The questions which follow attempt to show how each of these land-related torts operate and how they can overlap.

Question 1

Atif buys a farmhouse and the surrounding farm buildings in Toddington. He plans to convert the house into a 50-bed private hospital, retaining an apartment for his private use. Planning permission to convert the land from agricultural use has been granted by Toddington District Council.

During the building works, Desmond, a neighbouring landowner, complains that dust produced by Bashitt Ltd, the building contractors employed by Atif to convert the farm buildings, has clogged up the engine of his, Desmond's, car. When the hospital opens, Desmond objects to the increased traffic to the premises and retaliates by frequently firing guns, day and night, on his own land. Desmond claims this is necessary in order to control the rabbit population and to frighten off birds.

Some weeks after Atif's private hospital received its first patients, Desmond let some of his outbuildings to John, who organizes a 'rave' on one night only. Many of the patients at the hospital are unable to sleep and one of the patients, Mary, suffers a broken arm when she falls down some stairs on her way to complain to Atif about the noise. Many of the patients ask to be transferred elsewhere, resulting in loss of income to Atif.

Electrical discharge from the generators installed by John to power the amplifiers for the rave causes interference with Atif's television reception. As a result Atif can not view an Open University transmission forming part of his part-time degree studies.

Advise Atif, Bashitt Ltd, Desmond, and John of their liability in tort and how, if at all, can Atif prevent raves from taking place in future.

Commentary

This question deals with the problem of disputes between neighbouring land owners and requires consideration of both public and private nuisance. It is important to bear in mind that the characteristics of the different forms of action, in terms of legal standing, type of damage covered and remedy sought, must be considered in relation to their suitability for each of the claimants.

Answer plan

- Is there a public nuisance and has special damage been suffered so that it is actionable in tort?
- Who has standing to sue for a private nuisance and who is a potential defendant?
- What criteria identify an unreasonable state of affairs?
- What is the most appropriate remedy, and are any defences available?

Suggested answer

A public nuisance is generally a crime, which is actionable as a tort on proof of special damage and is defined as an act or omission which materially affects the reasonable comfort and convenience of life of a class of Her Majesty's subjects (*Attorney-General v PYA Quarries Ltd* [1957] 2 QB 169). It is concerned with 'public rights', but those rights are not clearly defined, although interferences with public health appear to be covered. A class of people has to be affected, and although this usually refers to a neighbourhood, the 50 patients and Atif may well be a sufficiently large group. Private rights are irrelevant, thus there is no need for a claimant to have an interest in land in order to be able to sue for a public nuisance. This will be important to Mary, in particular.

For a person to succeed in public nuisance in tort, by way of a private action arising out of a public nuisance, it must be shown that the claimant has suffered special damage, i.e. damage over and above that suffered by others. What is unclear is whether the special damage must be a different kind to that suffered by others, or whether a difference in terms of extent will suffice. Here the inconvenience caused by the noise is suffered by everyone, but there are items of damage specific to particular individuals, for example, Mary's broken arm and the loss of income to Atif caused by the departure of patients. According to *Walsh v Ervin* [1952] VLR 361, the damage must be substantial, direct and not consequential, although it may include general damage. Although personal injury has previously been held to be recoverable in public nuisance (*Castle v St Augustines Links* (1922) 38 TLR 616), this is now much less certain since the House of Lords' decision in *Hunter v Canary Wharf Ltd* [1997] 2 All ER 426 which suggested that personal injury claims should no longer be considered within any form of nuisance but instead be brought under the 'now fully developed law of negligence'. In any event, given the circumstances in which Mary's arm was broken, the injury should arguably be regarded as consequential rather than direct damage. Financial loss such as loss of income is also recognized as special damage (*Benjamin v Storr* (1874) LR 9 CP 400). The dust produced by Atif's contractors may also give rise to public nuisance liability, since it causes damage to property (*Halsey v Esso Petroleum Co Ltd* [1961] 2 All ER 145; *Hunter v Canary Wharf*). However, in this last instance, there is no evidence that anyone other than Desmond has been affected so, in the absence of an adverse effect on a class of people, the dust may not constitute a public nuisance – a consideration of the effect on the neighbourhood would be needed.

A private nuisance is unreasonable interference with a person's use or enjoyment of land. In order to be able to sue for a private nuisance, the claimant must have a proprietary interest in the land affected, e.g. as owner, tenant, or having an exclusive right of occupation (*Malone v Laskey* [1907] 2 KB 141; *Hunter v Canary Wharf Ltd* [1997] 2 All ER 426). Atif and Desmond have no problems in this respect as they are both owners. But Mary, as a patient, is likely to be no more than a contractual visitor. In any case, all she complains of is personal injury and there is no English authority which recognizes this as a recoverable head of damage in private nuisance, since the tort is concerned exclusively with land interests (*Hunter v Canary Wharf Ltd*).

An action for private nuisance may be brought against anyone with a degree of responsibility for the nuisance (*Sedleigh-Denfield v O'Callaghan* [1940] AC 880), including the creator of the nuisance and the occupier of the land from which the nuisance emanates. Thus John and Bashitt Ltd (as creators) may be sued even though they have no interest in the land (*Southport Corp v Esso Petroleum Ltd* [1953] 3 WLR 773). The occupier can also be sued in respect of a nuisance committed by an independent contractor. Where the nuisance is an inevitable consequence of the work undertaken (e.g. dust from the building operation) the occupier cannot escape responsibility by passing the works to the contractor (*Matania v National Provincial Bank* [1936] 2 All ER 633). However, temporary building works will not generally give rise to an action in private nuisance unless they are carried out in an unreasonable manner. Generating sufficient dust to clog a car engine would tend to suggest a want of care on the part of the builders, which would suggest that Desmond may succeed in claiming damages for his car repairs. Furthermore, a landlord can be sued where he lets premises and in doing so authorizes an activity which amounts to a nuisance. This covers a local authority letting a piece of land which they knew was to be used for go-carting (*Tetley v Chitty* [1986] 1 All ER 663) so the same should apply to Desmond in letting for the purpose of holding a rave at which loud music is played, provided he is aware of the planned activity.

Private nuisance is based on the principle of give and take and the role of the court is to try and reach a balance between the competing interests of the neighbours (*Kennaway v Thompson* [1980] 3 All ER 329). The relevant factors in this process are whether there is a substantial interference with use or enjoyment of and whether the defendant can show that his use of the land is reasonable, although liability finally turns on whether the interference (rather than the acts which caused the interference) is reasonable or not. Nuisances may be seen to fall into three main categories: encroachments; physical damage (or 'sensible material harm'); and unreasonable interferences (or 'sensible material discomfort'), according to *St Helens Smelting Co v Tipping* (1865) 11 HL Cas 642, approved in *Hunter*. Of these three, the first two will almost always be automatically unreasonable, whereas the third is a question of degree and calls for a complex balancing process of a number of relevant factors.

So far as inconvenience nuisance, such as noise, is concerned, it is relevant to consider the locality within which the activity takes place. Thus it was said in *Sturges v Bridgman* (1879) 11 Ch D 852 that 'what is a nuisance in Belgrave Square would not necessary be so in Bermondsey'. In the question, the general locality is a rural area within which a noisy event such as a rave might not be regarded as falling within what is normally acceptable.

So far as Desmond's objection to the hospital is concerned, Atif might argue that he has planning permission for the changed use of the land, however, this will not afford him an outright defence (in the way that statutory authority would), though it may have the effect of altering the character of the neighbourhood so that what once would have been an intolerable interference may, over the passage of time, become an acceptable state of affairs in the locality affected. Thus in *Gillingham Borough Council v Medway (Chatham) Dock Co Ltd* [1992] 3 WLR 449, planning permission was granted to convert a naval dockyard into a commercial port with the result that there was a substantial increase in heavy traffic, especially at night. It was held that no nuisance was committed on the basis that the character of the locality had changed. However, this should not be taken to mean that the granting of planning permission will, in all cases, prevent action for nuisance. For example, in *Wheeler v JJ Saunders Ltd* [1995] 2 All ER 697, planning permission granted to a farmer to build two pig housing units on land next to the claimant's was not held to have changed the nature of the entire locality. It seems to be largely a question of scale, and the facts in the question offer no clear outcome—a change of use of a relatively small piece of property seems, on the face of it, unlikely to change a locality but one which brings with it a change in volume of traffic is rather more far-reaching.

One thing is clear, locality is irrelevant where material property damage is caused by the alleged nuisance (*St Helens Smelting Co v Tipping*), so Desmond's action for damage to his car should succeed.

A second important factor is the duration of the interference. Generally a 'one-off' event will not be sufficient to establish a nuisance since this is likely to be regarded as insufficiently substantial. What matters for private nuisance is the state of affairs created by the defendant. An isolated event may suffice but only if it arises from an underlying state of affairs (*Sedleigh-Denfield v O'Callaghan*; *Castle v St Augustines Links*). In this case, the rave may be difficult to establish as part of a wider state of affairs, unless there is some indication that a series of similar events will be arranged in future. There is also authority to suggest that a temporary nuisance carried on at night, thereby causing sleep loss is unreasonable (*de Keyser's Royal Hotel v Spicer Bros* (1914) 30 TLR 257) which may be sufficient to allow the rave to be regarded as an unreasonable interference.

While malice is not usually relevant to liability in tort, it may convert an otherwise reasonable act into one which is unreasonable. This covers deliberately making a noise with a view to annoying one's neighbour (*Christie v Davey* [1893] 1 Ch 316) or in a manner calculated to cause damage (*Hollywood Silver Fox Farm Ltd v Emmett* [1936] 2 KB 468). This may mean that Desmond, in deliberately firing guns all day and night has created an unreasonable state of affairs. Although the sound of gunshots may be expected in a rural area, the fact that Desmond's activity is intended to cause a nuisance may be enough to make it actionable.

So far as the interference with Atif's television reception is concerned, John will raise the argument that Atif's requirements are 'hypersensitive'. Although the notion of hypersensitivity has in recent cases been absorbed within the fundamental question whether the interference complained of is unreasonable (*Morris (Soundstar Studio) v Network Rail Infrastructure Ltd* [2004] All ER (D) 342 (Feb.)), it is based on the proposition that the defendant's interference would not affect a person of ordinary susceptibilities (*Robinson v Kilvert* (1889) 41 Ch D 88) and is not, therefore, an actionable nuisance. Although the use of television is not strictly hypersensitive, it was considered in *Bridlington Relay Ltd v Yorkshire Electricity Board* [1965] Ch 436 that the reception of TV pictures was not an ordinary use of property. A Canadian authority (*Nor-Video v Ontario Hydro* (1978) 84 DLR (3d) 221) suggests that widespread interference with television reception is actionable in private nuisance, but this line was rejected by the House of Lords in *Hunter v Canary Wharf Ltd*. The decision in that case was also underpinned by the finding that the reception of television signals was not a right protectable by law, so that the mere presence of a building, in the absence of some specific nuisance emanating from the defendant's land, did not disclose a cause of action. In the problem, the interference is caused not by the passive presence of a structure but electrical discharge from the generators on Desmond's land. This might be taken to suggest that an action for private nuisance cannot be ruled out. However, Lord Lloyd in *Hunter v Canary Wharf Ltd* was of the opinion that damages for nuisance must be measured by reference to the diminution of the value of the land, so any remedy would be based on the potential unwillingness of a purchaser to buy premises in which television (and perhaps other electrical equipment) could not be used.

Social utility, though not a defence, may be a relevant factor in assessing reasonableness in the sense that a person is expected to put up with some degree of interference resulting from activities which are necessary for trade, the enjoyment of property and for the benefit of the public at large (*St Helens Smelting Co v Tipping, Kennaway v Thompson*). Generally, the courts are more concerned with private rights than public interests when considering the primary question of whether there is a nuisance (*Bellew v Cement Co* [1978] IR 61) but the more useful the defendants activity, the less likely the court to grant an injunction, or at least to structure it in such a way as to maximize the rights enjoyed by both parties (*Kennaway v Thompson* [1981] QB 88).

Two remedies are available in the event of a private nuisance—damages and an injunction. A claimant such as Atif may well be seeking both: damages for past losses; and an injunction either to order a continuing nuisance to cease or to prevent a recurrence in the future. Damages being the legal remedy, they will be awarded as of right once the nuisance is made out, but injunctions are a discretionary remedy. Although, in most circumstances, an injunction will readily be granted there are certain circumstances in which a court may decide it is equitable to withhold an injunction. In general there are four guiding principles (*Shelfer v City of London Electric Lighting Co* [1895] 1 Ch 287). These are that damages will be awarded instead of an injunction if the injury to the claimant's legal right is (i) small; and (ii) can be estimated in money terms; and (iii) can be adequately compensated by a small money payment; and (iv) it would be oppressive to grant an injunction. It may be that the public interest is relevant to the granting of a temporary injunction, although the cases are divided on this issue. For example, the fact that heavy job losses might result from the closure of the factory has been ignored in granting a temporary injunction on a factory (*Bellew v Cement Co* [1978] IR 61). But in *Miller v Jackson* [1977] QB 966, an injunction was refused against a cricket club at least partially on the grounds that there was a public interest in preserving playing fields for recreation; another factor taken into account was the fact that the claimants were well aware of the proximity of the cricket ground before deciding to move into their house. In *Dennis v MOD* [2003] All ER (D), low-level training flights by military aircraft were held to be a nuisance but an injunction was withheld on the basis of public interest. None of this reasoning would seem to assist John.

Question 2

Cockroach plc produces chemicals. As part of their operation, they use a fume-suppression device which is extremely noisy. The device is widely regarded as efficient and reliable but, occasionally, noxious fumes are nonetheless discharged into the atmosphere. Numerous residents in the locality have complained of the noise and the fumes produced by Cockroach plc's operations. These residents allege it is impossible to sleep with the windows open and that they cannot now sunbathe in their back gardens.

Ellen, one of the local residents, complains that her highly sensitive African violets, grown in her greenhouse, have all died as a result of the pollution caused by Cockroach plc. Moreover, Tom, a lodger in Ellen's house, complains that the combined effect of the noise and the fumes has caused him to suffer from a respiratory illness and extreme fatigue brought on through loss of sleep so that he has become permanently incapable of work.

Advise Cockroach plc.

Commentary

The question is concerned primarily, with private nuisance, but it also raises the possibility of an action in public nuisance, negligence and under the rule in *Rylands v Fletcher*. Once again, the range of potential actions should be considered in light of characteristics that might limit their usefulness to a claimant, e.g. due to lack of legal standing or the nature of the damage suffered.

Answer plan

- Who can sue and who is the potential defendant in an action for private nuisance?
- What factors indicate whether a private nuisance constitutes an unreasonable state of affairs?
- For the purposes of a private nuisance what is the relevant standard of care?
- Is personal injury damage recoverable in a private nuisance action and, if not, is an action in public nuisance a viable alternative?
- What remedies are available?
- Does *Rylands v Fletcher* apply to intangible escapes?

Suggested answer

A private nuisance is defined as an unreasonable interference with a person's use or enjoyment of land. In order to be able to sue for a private nuisance, Ellen must have a proprietary interest in the land affected, e.g. as owner or tenant or a licensee with exclusive possession (*Malone v Laskey* [1907] 2 KB 141; *Hunter v Canary Wharf Ltd* [1997] 2 All ER 426). There is nothing in the question to suggest that Ellen lacks such an interest.

An action for private nuisance may be brought against anyone with a degree of responsibility for the nuisance, including the creator of the nuisance and, in certain circumstances, the occupier of the land from which the nuisance emanates (*Sedleigh-Denfield v O'Callaghan* [1940] AC 880). Since Cockroach plc is both the creator and the occupier, it appears to be the only possible defendant.

Private nuisance is based on the principle of give and take and the role of the court is to try and reach a balance between the competing interests of neighbours (*Kennaway v Thompson* [1980] 3 All ER 329). The relevant factors in this process are whether there is a substantial interference with use or enjoyment and whether the defendant can show that his use of the land is reasonable, although liability finally turns on whether the interference is reasonable or not, but it is not necessary to prove that the defendants acts are unreasonable. That is important in this context, since we are told that the fume-suppressing system is widely regarded as efficient and reliable.

Relevant in determining whether an interference is unreasonable is the issue of locality. In *St Helens Smelting Co v Tipping* (1865) 11 HL Cas 642, a distinction was drawn between property damage and sensible personal discomfort. Locality is relevant to the latter, but not the former. Thus since Ellen complains of damage to property (her African violets), the character of the neighbourhood in which she and the offending factory are situated will be irrelevant. In this instance the only relevant issue is the potential over-sensitivity of the claimant.

So far as the death of Ellen's plants is concerned, Cockroach plc will raise the argument that the African violets are 'hypersensitive'. Although the notion of hypersensitivity has in recent cases been absorbed within the fundamental question whether the interference complained of is unreasonable (*Morris (Soundstar Studio) v Network Rail Infrastructure Ltd* [2004] All ER (D) 342 (Feb.)), it is based on the proposition that the defendant's interference would not affect a person of ordinary susceptibilities (*Robinson v Kilvert* (1889) 41 Ch D 88) and is not, therefore, an actionable nuisance. So, if Ellen's violets are unusually sensitive and there is evidence that other plants would not be damaged in the same way, there is no nuisance. However, if Cockroach's activity would have interfered with ordinary land use in any event, the fact that the claimant is unusually sensitive will make no difference (*McKinnon Industries v Walker* (1951) 3 DLR 557). Plants which have to be grown in a greenhouse may appear to be sensitive, but many other plants require similar treatment. Moreover, if the extent of the pollution is such that other plant life also dies, the *McKinnon* approach seems to be the better one here. Evidence from other residents who have been affected by the fumes will assist Ellen's case.

A further issue is that of the duration of the alleged nuisance. What matters for private nuisance is that the defendant's activity must be capable of causing a continuing, unreasonable state of affairs. A dangerous underlying state of affairs which manifests itself in an isolated occurrence is still capable of being repeated in the future (*Castle v St Augustines Links* (1922) 38 TLR 615) and the fact that there has been only one escape will not prevent this from being a continuing state of affairs, which will satisfy the duration requirement (*Sedleigh-Denfield v O'Callaghan* [1940] AC 880).

On balance, particularly in the light of the observations on sensitivity, there is probably a nuisance, but consideration must be given to the standard of care required of Cockroach. A negligence action will probably be unsuccessful because Cockroach's act in using the fume-suppression system is not sufficiently unreasonable to constitute a breach of any duty of care the company may owe. But liability in nuisance differs. It was said in the *Wagon Mound (No. 1)* [1961] AC 388 that negligence in the narrow sense is not necessary in a nuisance action. But negligence in the wider sense of foresight of harm under the remoteness test is a requirement. Thus if it is foreseeable to Cockroach that Ellen might suffer damage through the emission of fumes, an action may lie (*Wagon Mound (No. 2)* [1967] 1 AC 617). On this basis, it is probably foreseeable that the fumes emitted from Cockroach's factory could cause damage of the kind actually suffered.

All the factors considered above will also apply to the other local residents referred to in the question in respect of an action based on private nuisance.

Tom is a lodger. This creates the immediate problem of standing to sue—the claimant must have an interest in the land affected, but it is necessary to consider what is a sufficient interest. In *Hunter v Canary Wharf Ltd* [1997] 2 All ER 426, it was held that since the tort of private nuisance is directed at protecting the claimant's enjoyment of his rights over land, the action must be confined to a person with a sufficient interest. Often described as a proprietary interest, this is readily understood in light of their Lordships' emphasis on the role of private nuisance in protecting the amenity value of the land. In other words, if the value of the land is diminished by the fact that it cannot be freely used and enjoyed due to the effects of the nuisance, the only persons affected *in law* are those with an interest in the value of the land. However, none of the forms of proprietary interest would seem to cover Tom in his capacity as a lodger, unless he has a right of exclusive occupation of part of Ellen's house, in which case he might have a sufficient interest, and his action will be similar to that of Ellen, except that he has suffered personal discomfort and personal injury.

On the discomfort issue, locality is a factor. Where there is an inconvenience nuisance (e.g. noise, smells, etc.), it is relevant to consider where the alleged nuisance takes place. Thus it was said in *Sturges v Bridgman* (1879) 11 Ch D 852 that 'what is a nuisance in Belgrave Square would not necessarily be so in Bermondsey'. The facts reveal that others in the area have had to close their windows, which establishes that the interference is widespread. If Tom lives in a quiet residential area, the fumes will probably be a nuisance, but if there are a number of other factories in the area, it may be that Tom has to put up with the inconvenience caused. However, even in an industrial area, if the extent of interference is great, it may still be a nuisance (*Rushmer v Polsue and Alfieri Ltd* [1907] AC 121). As for the noise, the courts have many times shown their willingness to regard loss of sleep as far from trivial (*Halsey v Esso Petroleum* [1961] 2 All ER 145; *Andreae v Selfridge*), which should further aid Tom's claim.

The other important issue concerning Tom is that of personal injury. Generally, private nuisance is concerned with damage to an interest in land. Respiratory ailments and fatigue do not immediately come into this category, and it has been said that only land interests are protected (*Read v Lyons* [1947] AC 156). Although there are also cases in which it had been held that a personal injury associated with damage to a land interest is actionable (*Hale v Jennings* [1938] 1 All ER 579), in *Hunter v Canary Wharf Ltd* the House of Lords affirmed the general rule established in *Read v Lyons*, namely that since private nuisance is a tort concerned with the amenity value of land there is no cause of action in nuisance for damages for personal injury. Personal injury is evidence that the land is affected, but the cause of action in this respect lies in the tort of negligence and fault must be proved. On the facts, it would seem that the duty of care may have been discharged by Cockroach's use of reputable equipment, which may prove fatal to Tom's claim.

There remains the possibility that Tom may have a claim in public nuisance. A public nuisance is a crime, which is actionable as a tort on proof of special damage and is defined as an act or omission which materially affects the reasonable comfort and convenience of life of a class of Her Majesty's subjects (*Attorney-General v PYA Quarries Ltd* [1957] 2 QB 169). It is concerned with 'public rights', but those rights are not clearly defined, although interferences with public health appear to be covered. A class of people has to be affected. The fact that other residents have complained suggests an effect on a class of people, but Tom, for damages, also has to prove special damage, i.e. damage over and above that suffered by others in the class (*Benjamin v Storr* (1874) LR 9 CP 400). What is less clear is whether the special damage must be different in kind from that suffered by others or whether a greater extent will suffice, though in *Halsey* the fact that the claimants lived closer to the noise and other nuisances emanating from an oil depot was held to be enough to distinguish them from the rest of the class. Here the inconvenience caused by the fumes is suffered by everyone, but there are items of damage specific to Tom, namely the respiratory illness and his consequent loss of earnings. According to *Walsh v Ervin* [1952] VLR 361, the damage must be substantial, direct and not consequential, although it may cover general damage. There remains the question whether Tom's respiratory illness and collapse from exhaustion, being forms of personal injury, may be compensated under public nuisance. While such damage has, in the past, been recoverable (*Castle v St Augustines Links*) more recently the House of Lords in *Hunter v Canary Wharf Ltd* observed that the now fully developed law of negligence available to claimants in modern times should mark an end to personal injury claims brought under any form of nuisance. If correct, this returns Tom to the position set out above.

Assuming a nuisance is established, which is more likely in Ellen's case than in Tom's, the appropriate remedy must be considered. The options are damages and/or an injunction, but an injunction would shut down a factory placing employees out of work. In general there are four guiding principles (*Shelfer v City of London Electric Lighting Co* [1895] 1 Ch 287). These are that damages will be awarded instead of an injunction if the injury to the claimant's legal rights is: (i) small; and (ii) can be estimated in money terms; and (iii) can be adequately compensated by a small money payment; and (iv) it would be oppressive to grant an injunction.

It may be that the public interest is relevant to the grant of an injunction, although the cases are divided on this issue. For example, the fact that heavy job losses might result from the closure of a factory has been ignored in granting a temporary injunction on a factory (*Bellew v Cement Co* [1948] IR 61). But in *Miller v Jackson* [1977] QB 966, an injunction was refused against a cricket club on the ground that there was a public interest in preserving playing fields for recreation. The fairness and utility arguments may prevent an injunction from being granted provided the interference is not excessive.

There may be the possibility of an action under the rule in *Rylands v Fletcher* (1868) LR 3 HL 330, but generally this requires the accumulation of something tangible which is likely to do mischief if it escapes. Fumes and smells do not normally satisfy this requirement, which means that a *Rylands* action may not be applicable.

Question 3

Chromoshine Ltd, a cleaning firm, stores large quantities of a toxic industrial cleaning chemical on its land on an industrial estate close to a residential housing estate. Evidence shows that a group of badly behaved teenagers has been seen in the area on various occasions over the past two months. Mysteriously, a barrel of the toxic fluid is overturned and ruptures with the following results.

Mary, a catering assistant who works in Chromoshine's canteen, steps in the spilled fluid. Her legs are badly burned and her shoes are seriously damaged.

A quantity of the fluid seeps into an underground water supply used by the South Downs Water Company with the result that the latter must find an alternative source of supply in order to meet its statutory obligations to water consumers in the area.

The fluid flows into the street outside Chromoshine Ltd's premises. Traffic in the street sprays the fluid on to Alice's front garden rendering it in need of decontamination. The smell of the fluid causes Alice physical illness and she also has to vacate her house for two weeks while remedial action is taken.

Consider the liability of Chromoshine Ltd under the rule in *Rylands v Fletcher*.

Commentary

The tort which emerged from the decision of Blackburn J and the House of Lords in *Rylands v Fletcher* is heavily circumscribed by rules laid down not only in those decisions but in many authorities of the Privy Council and the House of Lords, most recently in *Transco plc v Stockport MBC*. This question calls for a detailed knowledge and application of those principles. It also allows for some comment upon the continued utility of the rule in *Rylands v Fletcher*, which was heavily analysed in the *Transco* case. The question asks you to address only the rule in *Rylands v Fletcher* and it would be unnecessary and inappropriate to stray into the law relating to private nuisance generally or to dwell on the potential for applying other torts such as negligence or breach of statutory duty.

Answer plan

- Identify whether or not the substance is within the rule, i.e. was it brought on to the land and is it likely to do mischief?
- Consider whether there has been an escape: *Read v Lyons*; *Transco plc v Stockport MBC*.
- Discuss whether or not the defendant company was engaged in a 'non-natural use' of its land: *Rickards v Lothian*; *Read v Lyons*; *Cambridge Water Co v Eastern Counties Leather plc*?
- Is the harm suffered an actionable loss for the purpose of *Rylands v Fletcher*; *Read v Lyons*; *Transco plc v Stockport MBC*?
- Suppose there has been the unforeseeable act of a third party causing the escape: *Rickards v Lothian*?
- What are the relevant rules on remoteness of damage under the rule in *Rylands v Fletcher*; *Cambridge Water Co v Eastern Counties Leather plc*?

Suggested answer

The rule in *Rylands v Fletcher* (1868) LR 3 HL 330 requires that a defendant, in the course of the non-natural user of their land, must bring on to that land, or keep or collect there something which, if it escapes, is likely to do mischief. In jurisprudential terms, the tort is one of strict, but not absolute, liability. This means that where an escape occurs and causes relevant harm, the defendant is *prima facie* liable for that harm, but they may nevertheless successfully defend an action if they are able to raise one of several recognized defences.

For the purposes of analysis it is best to discuss and apply each of the strict criteria for applying the rule in turn.

First, there has to be an accumulation by the defendant for the defendant's own benefit of something likely to cause harm if it escapes. The stringency of this requirement was emphasized by Lord Bingham in the *Transco* case, and it is tolerably clear that there has to be something exceptional and recognized subjectively the defendant or objectively as creating an exceptionally high degree of risk. The importing into the site of water for domestic purposes, albeit in bulk in a large diameter pipe, did not meet that criterion. A large number of things have been held to fall within this aspect of the rule, from water (*Rylands* itself) to gypsies (*Attorney-General v Corke* [1933] Ch 89) to a flag pole (*Schiffman v Order of St John* [1936] 1 KB 557) although the correctness of the latter two may be doubted following the decision in *Transco plc v Stockport MBC* [2004] 1 All ER 589, see later. The core element appears to be accumulation rather than the operation of nature. Here there is a deliberate accumulation and if the product is known or ought to be known to carry a risk of exceptional harm, i.e. likely to do 'mischief' if it escaped, then liability may flow.

Secondly, because of the apparent limitation placed on the operation of the rule by Lord Cairns, the accumulation must be as part of a non-natural use of land. This point has proved to be the most crucial of the control mechanisms available to the courts in extending or reducing the scope of the rule. As interpreted, this phrase has been taken to refer not to a contrast between artificial and natural but as to the ordinariness or otherwise of the use. This may well be to deviate too far from Blackburn J's formulation which included in his examples what were perfectly ordinary uses of land. *Rickards v Lothian* [1913] AC 263 is the leading case on the point and Lord Moulton made it clear that it was not every ordinary use of the land which would attract the operation of the rule but it must be some special use bringing increased danger. In that case the supply to the land of ordinary domestic water in small bore pipes was held to be not within the rule. Lord Bingham in *Transco plc v Stockport MBC* tried to keep distinct the elements of increased risk and ordinary/extraordinary use but the other members of the House of Lords rolled up the questions together. Lord Bingham thought that 'ordinary user' is preferable to 'natural user', and that the rule applied only where the defendant's use is shown to be extraordinary and unusual. In that case the use of a large bore pipe to take domestic water to a tower block was an ordinary user of its land. On the other hand, Lord Goff in the House of Lords in *Cambridge Water Co v Eastern Counties Leather plc* [1994] 1 All ER 53 made it clear that the storage of substantial quantities of chemicals on industrial premises was almost a classic case of non-natural use and that it could not be thought objectionable to impose strict liability for escape. Several cases including the *Transco* case and the *Cambridge Water* case have rejected the idea in *Read v Lyons* [1947] AC 156 that the manufacture of munitions in wartime could be a 'natural' or ordinary use of land. Applying these principles it would seem likely that a court would be entitled to hold that the storage of the chemicals by Chromoshine was a non-natural use of land. This would be so even though it was an industrial area, as was the land in the *Cambridge Water* case, and even though it provided employment in the area.

Thirdly, there has to be an escape. It is apparent from the House of Lords in *Read v Lyons* that a necessary pre-condition of the tort is that there must be an 'escape from a place where the defendant has occupation of, or control over, to land which is outside his occupation or control'. On this basis, it seems clear that Mary could not frame an action in *Rylands*, since, at the material time, she was still on the premises of Chromshine Ltd, as was the plaintiff in *Read v Lyons* who was injured by exploding munitions whilst still on the defendant's premises. This requirement has been reaffirmed by the decision in the *Transco plc* case where one of the members of the House of Lords felt that there had been no escape of water from land under the control of the defendant on to other land. The reason for this aspect of the rule is closely connected to the next point: that the object of the tort is to protect interests in land.

Fourthly, the relevant type of harm must be suffered. Since *Rylands* involved damage caused to a neighbour's land the question might be asked whether damage to chattels and personal injury are protected by the tort. These points have been mooted in the past but the current trend in cases such as the *Transco* case and the *Cambridge Water* case would be towards equating *Rylands v Fletcher* liability with nuisance liability and concluding that it is a tort concerned with protecting the interest which someone has in their land. In other words damages to chattels and personal injury harm would be outwith the scope of the rule. The *Transco* case contains the most recent comment on this point and although it is strictly *obiter* it nonetheless represents a clear indication that such damages will not be recoverable. Lord Bingham in that case drew support from *Cambridge Water* and *Hunter v Canary Wharf* [1997] 2 All ER 426. Thus, Mary will be unable to recover for this additional reason, nor will Alice be able to recover personal injury damages although she will be able to recover for the diminution in value of her property and the loss of use of the land. This calculation will involve assessing the cost of reinstatement of the property and the cost of alternative accommodation.

Fifthly, recovery of damages is dependent upon reasonable foreseeability of the type of harm. The *Cambridge Water* case decided that the test for the remoteness of damage in *Rylands* is the same as that in negligence: *The Wagon Mound (No. 1)* [1961] AC 388 test of reasonable foresight of the kind of harm suffered. In the *Cambridge Water* case the impact of the escaping chemicals on the water supply of the plaintiff was unforeseeable in the light of scientific knowledge and there was no recovery for this unforeseeable harm. Despite rather ambiguous language of Lord Goff in that case, it is the harm which has to be foreseeable and not the escape. With this in mind, it is arguable that the type of loss that Alice suffered would be regarded as not too remote a consequence of the spillage of some of the toxic fluid into a street down which motor traffic passes. The position of the South Downs Water Company will have to depend on the scientific evidence available. In the *Cambridge Water* case the type of chemical spilled was thought to evaporate into the atmosphere and that it could not be absorbed into the ground and thence to the water bearing rocks. If this type of contamination is foreseeable then Chromoshine will be liable for the diminution in the value of the land which will reflect the consequential economic loss.

As regards the defences that may be open to Chromshine Ltd the only defence that might be available is 'act of a stranger'. According to this defence, a defendant may avoid liability where the escape is attributable to the act of a third party over whom the defendant had no control unless the claimant can go on to show that the act which caused the escape was an act of the kind which the owner could reasonably have contemplated and guarded against. The facts do not illuminate the point beyond saying that the spillage occurred mysteriously, yet it is probably not unreasonable to suppose an element of human instrumentality, in which case the defence may well be able to be invoked. In *Rickards v Lothian*, property was damaged by water. The overflow of the water was caused by an unknown third party blocking the waste pipe in a sink. It was held that this provided a defence akin to the defence of 'act of God' or sudden overwhelming force such as an attack by enemies of the State.

Question 4

'A strong case can be made for the view that the rule in *Rylands v Fletcher* is but an application or instance of liability in nuisance.'

(Salmond, Heuston, and Buckley, *Law of Torts*)

Discuss the interrelationship between the two torts in the light of this statement.

Commentary

The so-called rule in *Rylands v Fletcher* has provoked a considerable debate both as to its relationship with private nuisance and its continued usefulness. Discursive essay style questions will often focus on this controversial formulation of liability. Equally possible are discursive questions on the relationship between private nuisance and negligence, since in some instances, private nuisance may involve an evaluation of duty relationships and there have been considered academic calls for the revision of private nuisance to fall in with negligence in these instances.

In particular this question requires discussion of the House of Lords' decisions in *Cambridge Water Co Ltd v Eastern Counties Leather plc* in which Lord Goff subjected the interrelationship between these two torts to detailed examination, and to a lesser extent to the House of Lords' decision in *Transco plc v Stockport MBC*. The answer also requires consideration of the principles underlying the imposition of liability in nuisance and under the rule in *Rylands v Fletcher* with emphasis being placed upon both common and distinguishing features. Reference will also be made to the decision of the House of Lords in *Hunter v Canary Wharf Ltd*, which addressed a number of important issues about the scope of the tort of nuisance. It may also be worthwhile making the point that it is very difficult to find modern reported cases where the Rule in *Rylands v Fletcher* has been the foundation for deciding a case in favour of the claimant other than in the context of damage by escape of fire.

Answer plan

- Identify the rule.
- Identify the similarities to private nuisance.
- Identify any distinctions.

- Deal shortly with the key elements of the rule.
- Demonstrate a good working knowledge of *Cambridge Water Co Ltd v Eastern Counties Leather plc*.
- Demonstrate a good working knowledge of *Transco plc v Stockport MBC*.

Suggested answer

Liability under the rule in *Rylands v Fletcher* (1866) LR 1 Exch 265 is imposed on a defendant where in the course of non-natural use of his land he accumulates upon it for his own purposes anything likely to do mischief if it escapes and which does escape and cause damage. Briefly, the facts of the case were that the defendants had employed independent contractors to construct a reservoir on their land in order to supply water to the defendant's factory. Due to the contractors negligently failing to discover and block a disused mine shaft, water from the reservoir burst through the shafts and flooded the plaintiff's mine. The defendants were held personally liable despite the absence of fault on their part. The existing law did not appear to provide redress in this situation. There was no trespass as the flooding was not direct and immediate. Neither was it certain that there could in law be a nuisance for an isolated escape which caused damage. Finally, on generally accepted principles there was no vicarious liability for the acts or omissions of the independent contractor amounting to negligence. Nonetheless, the defendant was found liable on the basis outlined, although the final version of liability was muddied by inadvertent differences between the formulation of Lord Cairns LC in the House of Lords and Blackburn J at first instance.

There are numerous instances where the overlap between this rule and the tort of nuisance is apparent. Liability in the tort of nuisance arises where there has been an unreasonable interference with the claimant's proprietary interest in land. In *Read v Lyons* [1947] AC 156, Lord Simonds pointed to Blackburn J's original formulation of the rule as recognizing that in most cases the law of nuisance and the rule in *Rylands v Fletcher* may be 'invoked indifferently.' Also, in nuisance the principle of reasonable user in nuisance means that a defendant acting reasonably (in the nuisance sense) will not be liable for harm to his neighbour's enjoyment of his land. This is closely allied to the principle of natural use found in the rule in *Rylands v Fletcher* although in *Transco plc v Stockport MBC* [2004] 1 All ER 589 Lord Bingham considered that the principle would be better described as ordinary rather than natural, applying the Privy Council analysis in *Rickards v Lothian*. Lord Bingham also restated the proposition that Blackburn J had regarded the facts of *Rylands v Fletcher* itself as being a simple case of nuisance and that in *Ross v Fedden*, itself a case on domestic water supply, he had rejected any notion to the contrary. To this extent the rule in *Rylands v Fletcher* was regarded by the House of Lords as no more than an application of well-known principles to an isolated and non-persistent interference.

However, there are marked distinctions between the torts. *Rylands v Fletcher* is founded upon the non-natural accumulation of something by the defendant on his land which is likely to do damage if it escapes. By definition this excludes things naturally on the defendant's land. Thus, an occupier is not liable for damage caused by ordinary trees on his land given that growing a tree is a natural use of soil (*Noble v Harrison* [1926] 2 KB 332). On the other hand, in *Crowhurst v Amersham Burial Board* (1878) 4 Ex D 5, a yew tree on the defendant's land projected over land belonging to the plaintiff on which cattle grazed. The leaves of yew trees are poisonous, and the plaintiff's horse died after eating some of them. The defendants were held liable under the rule in *Rylands v Fletcher* on the basis that it was not a natural use of land to plant on it a poisonous tree. In contrast, liability in nuisance may arise from acts of nature occurring on land. Thus, in *Goldman v Hargrave* [1967] AC 645 the Privy Council held that an occupier of land was under a duty to take reasonable steps to abate a fire started by lightning striking a tree on his land which had spread to his neighbour's property. This was followed by the Court of Appeal in *Leakey v National Trust for Places of Historic Interest or Natural Beauty* [1980] QB 485 where the defendants, who owned a hill which it was feared would slip on to the plaintiff's land due to natural weathering, were held liable in nuisance. In *Rylands v Fletcher* the water had been brought on to the land by the defendants. Where water is naturally on the land, the defendant will not be liable if it escapes. Thus, in *Smith v Kendrick* (1849) 137 ER 205 rain water had formed a subterranean lake surrounded by a coal seam. When the coal was mined the water escaped and flooded the plaintiff's mine. It was held that the defendant was not liable given that the adjoining mine owners each had a 'natural' right to work their respective mines in the manner best suited to them, even though the natural consequence of their work could be prejudicial to the other.

A further distinction is that nuisance covers damage caused by intangible escapes such as noise and so in *Rushmer v Polsue and Alfieri Ltd* [1906] 1 Ch 234, the plaintiff successfully brought an action in respect of noise at night caused by printing presses, even though he lived in the printing area of London. *Rylands v Fletcher* is confined to the accumulation of a tangible object on land which is likely to cause damage, either upon its own escape or upon its giving off fumes, electricity or gas which escape.

A potential distinction that can be drawn between the rule in *Rylands v Fletcher* and the tort of nuisance relates to 'standing to sue'. With respect to the former, it was stated by Lawton J in *British Celanese v A. H. Hunt* [1969] 1 WLR 959 that once an escape is established, anyone who suffers damage as a consequence may claim irrespective of whether or not they are occupiers of adjoining land. As we have seen, nuisance is premised upon protecting proprietary interests in land and is therefore narrower in its scope of protected interests. Since the claimant must satisfy the requirement of having either a possessory interest or some other proprietary interest in order to bring an action in nuisance, members of his family who lack this interest will be precluded from suing even though they have suffered personal injuries as a result of the defendant's activity, as in *Malone v Laskey* [1907] 2 KB 144. The correctness of the decision in *Malone* was confirmed by the House of Lords in *Hunter v Canary Wharf* [1997] 2 WLR 684, in which it was held by a majority of their Lordships that an action in nuisance can only be brought by a person in 'exclusive possession' of the affected land, or by an owner without exclusive possession. Whether the approach in *British Celanese v A. H. Hunt* will survive the decision in *Hunter v Canary Wharf* may well be doubted, especially in the light of the *dicta* in the *Transco* case which clearly align nuisance and *Rylands v Fletcher*.

It has been said that neither the rule in *Rylands v Fletcher* nor the tort of nuisance requires proof of fault on the part of the defendant. Yet it is apparent, particularly in more recent decisions culminating in *Cambridge Water Co Ltd v Eastern Counties Leather plc* [1994] 2 WLR 53, that the judges are steadily eroding non-fault based liability. In his speech in *Read v Lyons* Lord Porter alluded to the concepts of 'justice' and 'reasonableness' when reviewing the judicial process for determining whether liability under the rule should be imposed. He pointed to the fact that judges have regard to all the surrounding circumstances including the time, place and practice of mankind so that what might be regarded as non-natural may vary according to the circumstances. In *Mason v Levy Auto Parts of England Ltd* [1947] 2 QB 530, MacKenna J in equating 'non-natural' user with unreasonable risk recognized the similarities inherent in this approach with those considerations applicable in negligence. Moreover, the concept of 'unreasonableness' is central to the tort of nuisance, and fault is a concomitant of unreasonableness. Further, the importance of fault-based liability in nuisance was recognized by Lord Reid in *Wagon Mound (No. 2)* (1966) 1 AC 617 when he stated that 'fault of some kind is almost always necessary and fault involves foreseeability'.

Finally, the law of private nuisance does not extend to include recovery of damages for personal injury (*Malone v Laskey, Hunter v Canary Wharf*); despite conflicting decisions of the point it seems likely that personal injury damages will not be recoverable under *Rylands v Fletcher*; it too is a tort concerned with land. This is stated clearly, but *obiter*, by Lord Bingham in the *Transco* case.

The decisions of the House of Lords in *Cambridge Water Co v Eastern Counties Leather plc* and *Transco* have clarified the confusion which has marked the development of the tort. In the former the defendant operated a tanning business and had used large quantities of chemical. Much of this chemical had been spilt and contrary to scientific understanding, had seeped into the ground, however its effects at that time were considered to be innocuous. The plaintiffs' purchased a well located over a mile away from the defendant's factory. At the time of purchase the plaintiffs had had the water tested and it was found to be perfectly fit for consumption. Subsequently, an EEC Directive in 1985 governing water purity standards was passed and it became illegal to supply water from this source due to chemical contamination. The defendants successfully appealed to the House of Lords where, following the restrictive approach adopted in *Read v Lyons* with respect to the imposition of strict liability, it was held that strict liability under the rule in *Rylands v Fletcher* only arose if the defendant knew or ought reasonably to have foreseen that the escape would cause damage. Liability under the rule is strict in the sense that the defendant could be held liable for an escape resulting from the non-natural use of land notwithstanding that he had exercised all due care to prevent the escape occurring. But, given that the defendants could not have reasonably foreseen that the seepage of the chemical through the factory floor would cause the pollution to the plaintiffs' borehole, they were not liable under the rule in *Rylands v Fletcher*.

The gist of Lord Goff's extensive treatment of this point was that *Rylands v Fletcher* and private nuisance derived from the same core and that since the authoritative cases on private nuisance led inevitably to the conclusion that reasonable foreseeability of damage was an essential element of private nuisance so too must it be an essential element of recovery under the rule in *Rylands v Fletcher*.

The judicial trend noted above which has heralded the erosion of non-fault based liability was further reinforced by the trial judge and by the House of Lords in *Cambridge Water*. The first instance judge and Lord Goff shared the view that the imposition of strict liability in respect of high-risk operations should be left to Parliament. It was stated that statute would be the appropriate means of ensuring that precise criteria were laid down governing the incidence and breadth of such liability.

The House of Lords in the *Transco* case refused either to follow the trend set in other jurisdictions and jettison the rule entirely or to extend it. Lord Bingham stated clearly that 'The rule in *Rylands v Fletcher* is a sub-species of nuisance.' This approach is a clear way of reaffirming the place of *Rylands v Fletcher* within private nuisance. It is consistent with the rejection of other attempts to allow it to break free of its nuisance straitjacket, for example, in *Read v Lyons* where the House of Lords refused to endorse the attempts to use *Rylands v Fletcher* to create a species of strict liability for dangerous activities or dangerous things.

Question 5

Paresh owns a farm in the country and a disused plot of land in central London. The farm is situated near to an airfield used by a gliding club. Some of the gliders have occasionally landed in the fields of surrounding farms, damaging the crops, but the gliding club has always paid compensation to the farmers in such circumstances. The plot of land in central London is adjacent to a building site owned by Bipin and on which he is building a new office block. The jib of a tall crane constantly oversails into the airspace above Paresh's plot. Bipin has offered to buy the plot of land from Paresh, but he has always asked for more than they are prepared to pay.

Paresh is now seeking to obtain an injunction against the gliding club, preventing them from flying over his farm, and against the developers of the building site, preventing them from intruding into the airspace above his land with their crane, even though it will be very difficult for them to redevelop their land without doing this.

Advise Paresh.

Commentary

This question is concerned primarily with the tort of trespass to land (and in particular airspace). Trespass to land is an ancient and relatively straightforward tort and its characteristics may be simply stated at the outset. The problem really raises the issue of invasion of land in the possession of the claimant. Nuisance may or may not involve an invasion. Here the facts to prompt anything other than a cursory analysis of nuisance are very sparse and care should be taken not to invent or speculate on such matters; keep that aspect of the discussion to a bare minimum. In most cases what the claimant wants is an injunction preventing the activity. In nuisance there is greater flexibility over the terms of the injunction (consider the detailed injunction in *Kennaway v Thompson)* whilst in trespass to deny an injunction may well result in depriving the claimant of their property rights. This question does ask for a description and application of the rules which apply to the discretionary remedy of an injunction. There is also some scope for comment on the statutory immunity for aircraft although a detailed statutory knowledge would not normally be required.

Answer plan

- Identify the core elements of trespass to land.
- Consider how far the interest in land extends.
- Discuss the principles that govern the award of an injunction.

Suggested answer

Trespass to land involves direct and intentional invasions of land in the possession of another, although the intention relates to the voluntariness of the invasion rather than knowledge that the land belongs to someone else or in the mistaken belief that the land is the trespasser's. Like all trespasses, trespass to land is actionable *per se*, i.e. it is complete without proof of actual harm. This makes it very useful in the resolution of boundary conflicts or as a mechanism for asserting rights, e.g. to exclude people from land. It may also be used to raise issues of constitutional importance, such as entry by executive officers, see, for example, *Entick v Carrington*. Although at one early stage in the development of the law it was said that the land of the claimant extends to the earth below and the heavens below (*usque ad coelum, usque ad inferos*) this rather out dated concept (described as 'fanciful' by one judge) no longer represents a statement of the law, if it ever did. Conflicting *dicta* as to whether or not there might be invasion of the airspace above a claimant's land were resolved in 1957 in *Kelsen v Imperial Tobacco Company* [1957] 2 QB 334 where an overhanging advertising sign was held to be capable of amounting to a trespass and that the plaintiff need not rely on nuisance. The court then had to decide whether or not to grant an injunction ordering it to be removed. So, on the authority of this case it can be safely said that Paresh has an interest in the airspace above his land which can be protected against invasion by structures adjoining or nearby his land. But the invasion was at a relatively low height in *Kelsen* and was by a fixture and not an aeroplane.

In *Bernstein v Skyviews & General Ltd* [1978] QB 479, it was held there would be no trespass by an over-flying aeroplane unless the aeroplane flies so low that it penetrates the airspace at a height which is within the 'normal user of the land'. As an aspect of ownership any occupier is entitled to bring within their control the airspace above their land (subject to normal regulatory procedures or covenants), but above the height at which such control is possible there are no greater rights in the landowner than anyone else. Griffiths J in *Bernstein* concluded that there had to be a balance drawn between the rights of the owner and those of the general public to take advantage of scientific developments in travel. Therefore an owner has rights in the land extending only to such height as is necessary for the ordinary use and enjoyment of the land. In that case there was no trespass and subject to questions as to the height of the gliders it would seem reasonably clear that there is no trespass into Paresh's airspace.

Note that Griffith J used language carefully and he did not require there to be an actual interference with the use of enjoyment of land. A distinction is drawn between trespasses and nuisance. Where there is actual interference with the use and enjoyment of the land, e.g. by noise then a nuisance by over-flying aircraft may be made out, even where there is a pressing military need: *Dennis v Ministry of Defence* [2003] Env LR 34. There is nothing here to suggest that the activities of the club amount to a nuisance.

The question arises whether the intrusion of the jib of Bipin's crane into the air-space above Paresh's plot amounts to a trespass to that airspace. There is no suggestion that there is an interference with the use and enjoyment of the land, e.g. by noise or danger of items dropping so it will not be a nuisance on that basis. But there is an encroachment and that will be a nuisance if damage ensues, which it does not here. If a nuisance or trespass is threatened then an injunction may lie and the claimant does not have to wait for actual damage.

In *Anchor Brewhouse Developments Ltd v Berkley House Ltd* [1978] 2 EGLR 173, the defendant company had sought to argue that their cranes over hung the plaintiff's land but that this was not a trespass because of the public interest in developing a major site in London and the inordinate cost to them of re-siting them and building a building with a smaller 'footprint'. It was held that the decision in *Bernstein v Skyviews* had not altered the law and that where there was an invasion by a structure adjoining the land of the plaintiff then there would be a trespass. The defendant was taking into possession, no matter how briefly, air space which the plaintiff was entitled to reduce into actual possession. There was no scope for balancing interests in the way adopted in *Bernstein v Skyviews*. Accordingly, the invasion by Bipin's crane will amount to a trespass.

The defences in trespass are matters such as necessity and consent and none of these seem to be applicable to this problem. Over-flying and possible noise nuisance may be subject to immunity under the Civil Aviation Act 1982, ss. 76 and 77. This immunity extends to both trespass to air space and to nuisance, but it only arises if the club was complying with an air navigation order made under s. 60. There is no such immunity against claims arising from damage caused by an aircraft falling from the air, or by people or things falling from aircraft on to land below, even where negligence cannot be proved (Civil Aviation Act 1982, s. 76(2)). Any such claim would equate to a claim for trespass to land, although it is a statutory cause of action in its own right.

Suppose that there is a trespass in the instance of the crane jibs. What remedy is available in the absence of any actual damage. Paresh seems to be using his land in London as a 'ransom site', i.e. a strip of land which frustrates development on neighbouring land unless it is bought for whatever price the owner cares to name. There is no remedy against this at common law, since generally in the exercise of rights of ownership a person may make whatever lawful use of their own land they choose (*Bradford Corporation v Pickles* [1895] AC 587). The only statutory remedies are those which relate to the compulsory purchase of land by a local authority and those procedures made available to private landowners by the Access to Neighbouring Land Act 1992. The developers in this case do not possess any powers of compulsory purchase and the Access to Neighbouring Land Act 1992 is confined to cases in which access is necessary for the purpose of the preservation of neighbouring or adjacent land. The Act does not apply to works for the alteration, adjustment, improvement or demolition of any buildings or other land unless those operations are incidental to works of 'preservation'. In any event, even if the developers are entitled to rely on the 1992 Act, they cannot go ahead with any entry onto the neighbouring or adjacent land without first obtaining a court order. Since Bipin is building something completely new they cannot take advantage of the legislation.

Normally an injunction will granted as a matter of course but not as a matter of right and subject to the normal equitable rules such as the behaviour of the claimant, e.g. they must not have encouraged the defendant to believe that the work was permitted, nor must they have delayed. The suspension of the operation of the injunction in *Woolerton & Wilson v Costain* [1970] 1 WLR 411 in which an injunction to restrain a developer from trespassing with a crane was effectively denied to a plaintiff who had adopted a wholly unreasonable attitude towards consenting to the proposed aerial invasion was disapproved of in later cases, including *Anchor Brewhouse*. This case confirmed that the plaintiff was entitled to an injunction as a matter of course if the trespass was going to be repeated. It does not seem to matter that the plaintiff might be acting as a 'dog in a manger' (*per* Scott J in *Anchor Brewhouse*).

But it would be open to Bipin to argue that damages would suffice. By virtue of statute, equitable damages in lieu of an injunction may be granted and the general principles governing the grant of damages were set out in *Shelfer v City of London Electric Lighting Company* [1895] 1 Ch 287. These were that the injury to the plaintiff's rights is small; the injury can be estimated in financial terms; the injury can be adequately compensated in money terms; it would be oppressive to the defendant to grant an injunction. The grant of damages in such a case is intended to compensate for future invasions and represents a judicial removal of the claimant's bargaining tool.

The grant of an injunction is discretionary within these general principles and there is ample scope for the judges to give differing weight to factors. Certainly there is nothing in principle to prevent the court granting an injunction to prevent the continued over-sailing of the crane jib.

Further reading

Bagshaw, R., 'Rylands Confirmed' (2004) 120 LQR 388.

Buckley, R. A., *The Law of Nuisance* (London: Butterworths,1996).

Gearty, C., 'The Place of Nuisance in the Modern Law of Torts' (1989) 48 CLJ 214.

Ingman, T., 'Continuing Trespass and Breach of Covenant: Injunction or Damages' [1995] Conv 141.

Lee, M., 'What is Private Nuisance?' (2003) 119 LQR 298.

McNall, C., 'Holding Back the Tide of Negligence, Rylands Resurgent' [2004] Conv 240.

Morgan, J., 'Nuisance and the Unruly Tenant' (2001) 60 CLJ 382.

Murphy, J., 'The Merits of Rylands v Fletcher' (2004) 24 OJLS 643.

Nolan, D., 'The Distinctiveness of Rylands v Fletcher' (2005) 121 LQR 421.

Newark, F. H., 'The Boundaries of Nuisance' (1949) 65 LQR 480.

Wightman, J., 'Nuisance—The Environmental Tort' (1998) 61 MLR 870.

12

Liability for statements not made negligently

Introduction

This chapter is principally concerned with the torts of defamation. The tort allows a person to clear his name where a statement has been made by the defendant which attacks the claimant's reputation.

Defamation requires a publication of a statement which tends to subject the claimant to ridicule or contempt or tends to lower the claimant in the minds of right-thinking members of the public. For the most part, it is a tort which does not require proof of damage unless the statement is made in a merely transitory form. The core elements of the tort have remained much the same over the years: the statement must be defamatory, it must refer to the claimant, and it must be published. Most emphasis in recent years has been on the development of the defences and in particular the defence of qualified privilege that has received extensive consideration and expansion by the higher courts.

Defamation does not attract legal aid, with the result that a person who wishes to protect his reputation but who cannot afford to fund a defamation action may choose to sue for malicious falsehood. However, this tort is not primarily concerned with protecting reputation, but it may sometimes be used to clear the claimant's name. The ingredients of malicious falsehood differ in a number of respects from the elements of defamation. In the first place, malicious falsehood protects a person's economic interests, and does require proof of economic damage. Secondly, the defendant's statement must be false, whereas a defamatory statement may be literally true, but may contain some actionable innuendo. For the purposes of malicious falsehood, there must be an intention to disparage, whereas there can be an entirely innocent defamation.

Question 1

Fatima is a student of the Du Maurier College of Melodrama. She believes that she is being sexually harassed by Omar, one of the lecturers at the college. She writes a letter, addressed to all the governors and lecturers at the college, which includes the statement: 'Omar sexually harasses female students'.

Fatima takes the letter to the public library, in order to make 200 copies of it. By mistake, she leaves the original letter in the photocopier, where it is found by Nosey, who reads the letter and posts it, anonymously, to Omar's wife.

Fatima sends copies of her letter to every governor and lecturer at the college, using the internal post. Each letter is in a brown envelope, addressed to the recipient and marked 'confidential'. Two days later, one of these letters is found pinned to a notice board in the students' common room. Omar denies the allegation of sexual harassment.

Advise Omar as to his cause of action, if any, in defamation. You should ignore any issues of vicarious liability.

Commentary

Very often problem questions on defamation require a broad treatment both of the substantive law required to establish what defamation involves and the available defences. Although you should identify the tests for when a statement may be defamatory in law, do not go overboard on demonstrating when a statement is defamatory unless the question demands it. For example, in this problem it will be necessary to establish that the statement is defamatory but the answer should seek to address this bearing in mind that the real thrust is to establish the range of possible publications. Although the answer should reflect on why most of the defences do not apply do not take too long to do this; move as quickly as possible to look at the issue of qualified privilege raised by the problem. Unless the problem demands it, it is rarely necessary to speculate at length on the issue of the appropriate remedy.

Answer plan

- State briefly the three core elements of the tort of defamation.
- Identify when a statement will in law be defamatory of the claimant.
- Consider whether there has been a publication to a third party.
- Identify the issue of remoteness of harm.
- State briefly what defences are available and what are not.
- Consider by reference to relevant cases whether the defence of qualified privilege is available.

Suggested answer

Omar will have to establish the three core elements of defamation, these are the same whether the statement is written (libel) or oral (slander). He will have to show that words used were defamatory, that the statement referred to him and that it was published to a third party. The judge will first determine whether the words are capable as a matter of law of bearing a defamatory meaning. Once the judge has concluded that the words are defamatory in law then it is for the jury to determine whether the words are defamatory in fact. There is no single test for when words are defamatory but one commonly accepted test is to ask whether the words in question would 'lower the claimant in the estimation of right thinking members of society': *Sim v Stretch* [1936] 2 All ER 1237. This is not always useful; for example in *Berkoff v Burchill* [1996] 4 All ER 1008 the plaintiff succeeded on the basis that he had been held out to ridicule by a newspaper review that described him as hideously ugly. The whole context should be looked at to see whether the statement can be said to be defamatory and the claimant cannot select parts of the whole to demonstrate the libel if there are other parts which rectify any impression created. For example, in *Charleston v News Group Newspapers* [1995] 2 All ER 313 the text of an article provided the 'antidote' to the 'bane' created by an otherwise defamatory headline and photograph. However it should be noted that by virtue of the **Defamation Act 1996, s. 7** either the plaintiff or defendant may apply for an order to determine, before trial, whether the words are capable of bearing a defamatory meaning. It is suggested that given Omar's profession, the statement that he sexually harasses female students is defamatory. It is in written form, and therefore an action will lie for libel which is actionable *per se*, i.e. without proof of actual harm.

The statement is clearly about Omar but the requirement of publication is not straightforward in the present case.

Each publication is a new libel and will be a major factor for the jury to take into account when assessing the amount of any damages to be awarded. Will the law regard each publication as having been made by Fatima? The library authorities will not be liable despite the discovery of the letter on their photocopier because they have not published the libel. Although the defamatory material has been published by Fatima to the governors and lecturers at the college who received copies of the letter in the internal post, she may seek to introduce a defence, see later.

More problems arise where the publications to Nosey, to the students, and to Omar's wife occur.

Omar will wish to argue that the letter has been published to Nosey because a publication may occur even if the maker of a statement negligently allows a third party to read it. For example, in *Theaker v Richardson* [1962] 1 WLR 151, the writer of a letter was held to have published it to the addressee's spouse because he had sent it in a business envelope and did not make it clear that the contents were intended for the addressee only. In *Weld-Blundell v Stephens* [1920] AC 956, the plaintiff wrote a letter to his accountants about the financial affairs of a particular company. A member of the firm of accountants negligently left the letter at the offices of that company where it was seen by the manager who noted that it made defamatory remarks about two individuals. These individuals successfully sued the plaintiff for defamation. The plaintiff then successfully sued the firm of accountants for breach of contract in failing to take reasonable care of the letter. The negligent leaving of a letter in a public place is, therefore, an example of a publication of that letter to any member of the public who reads it.

Omar may also allege that the college is responsible for the publication of the letter on the students' notice board (whether or not Fatima shares responsibility for that incident). It is not clear how a copy of Fatima's letter appeared on the students' notice board but Omar will allege that the college is responsible for the continuation of this state of affairs because the college authorities should have removed the copy of the letter from the notice board and that, by failing to do so, they adopted the defamatory statement and published it to the users of the common room. To remove the letter would involve no expense, and no damage to the structure of the building. Where an anonymous defamatory notice appeared in a club-house and the managers failed to remove it they were held liable: *Byrne v Deane* [1937] 1 KB 818. Omar must show, however, that the college authorities had a reasonable opportunity to discover the letter and to remove it from the notice board.

Who should be responsible for the publication to Omar's wife? It may be noted in passing that, although there is no 'publication' of a statement between a husband and wife when they communicate with each other, the law does not take the same approach when the communication is made by a third person to one partner about his or her spouse (*Wenman v Ash* (1853) 13 Ch 836). Although to make a statement to the person defamed does not amount to a publication of a defamatory statement, a publication can occur if the statement is made to the spouse of the claimant. Nosey has published the letter to Omar's wife, but will Fatima be liable for this unauthorized publication?

In *Cutler v McPhail* [1962] 2 QB 292, it was held that the author of a defamatory letter sent to a newspaper was also responsible for its subsequent publication by that newspaper. In *Slipper v BBC* [1991] 1 QB 283, it was held that the makers of a defamatory television programme should have foreseen that it would be reviewed in a national newspaper, thereby spreading the allegations to a wider audience. The Court of Appeal, however, took the view that the actions of an unauthorized person could break the chain of causation, thereby releasing the original maker of the statement from any responsibility for its further publication. This argument may not apply, however, to a person who has negligently left a document in a public place. In *MacManus v Beckham* [2002] 4 All ER 497 the issue was slightly different. The defendant volubly attracted public attention during an argument in a shop and her defamatory comments were headline news. It was held that she should be liable for the extent of the loss caused by the press publication, i.e. as a question of remoteness of harm. Liability for damage resulting from a further publication by a third party, should be decided on the basis whether it was just that the defendant should be held responsible for that damage. There the defendant must herself have been aware that the matter would be reported and a reasonable person would have realized that it would. Normally an unforeseen publication will break the chain of causation.

Several defences may be available to the various defendants. The defence of justification may be available but it would be for the defendant to prove the 'sting' of the defamatory statement. For example in *Alexander v North Eastern Railway Company* (1865) 34 LJQB 152, the defendant was able to show that the plaintiff had been convicted of an offence and sent to prison and had served two weeks. The jury was entitled to regard the original statement (that he had served three weeks) as having been justified. In *Wakley v Cooke & Healey* (1849) 4 Exch 511, the statement that the plaintiff journalist was a libellous journalist was taken to mean that he made a habit of writing libels and not that he had done so once (which was true)—the defendant could therefore not justify the statement. Demonstrating that Fatima was harassed may very well not prove the 'sting' of the allegations.

Secondly, it would be unlikely that there would be available the defence of fair comment. This requires that there should be a comment on a matter of public importance where the underlying basis of fact is shown to be true. We are told only that there are allegations of fact and the problem does not reveal comment.

The governors and the lecturers of the college are the intended recipients of Fatima's letter. Fatima may invoke the defence of qualified privilege. In this defence the law recognizes that it is in the public interest to protect some communications provided that there is no malice. Usually this defence arises when A makes a statement to B, because she has a duty to make it to him, or because she (A) has a legitimate interest to protect in bringing it to his attention. B should also have a corresponding duty or interest. In the absence of such reciprocity there will be no privilege. Fatima has an interest to protect in complaining about Omar to the proper authorities within the college, and the college authorities have a reciprocal duty or interest to receive it. More recently the courts have taken the view that where there is a pre-existing relationship then there is no need to establish the exact nature of the duty-interest involved: *Kearns v General Council of the Bar* [2003] 2 All ER 534.

In this particular problem, the question arises whether Fatima has circulated her allegations too widely. In *Adam v Ward* [1917] AC 309 it was suggested that a publication to the public at large could be protected by the defence of qualified privilege if it related to a matter of the widest public importance. However, this is a rare situation which has recently been the subject of analysis by the House of Lords in *Reynolds v Times Newspapers* [1999] 4 All ER 609 in the context of a newspaper article attacking a leading Irish politician. The facts were very far removed from this problem and involved a newspaper, the privilege was also highly constrained in that case because the report normally will have to reflect both sides and show that the claimant has been asked for their side of the story, i.e. achieving a standard of responsible journalism.

The general rule is that the defence of privilege will be lost if the defendant exceeds the privilege by communicating the allegations to persons who have no legitimate interest in hearing them. Thus in *Chapman v Lord Ellesmere* [1932] 2 KB 431, it was held that the publication of a disciplinary decision of the Jockey Club was privileged when it appeared in *The Racing Calendar*, but not privileged when it appeared in *The Times* newspaper. Likewise in *De Buse v McCarthy* [1942] 1 All ER 19, a town clerk sent out a notice convening a meeting of the council to consider a committee report about the loss of petrol from one of its depots. The report was attached to the notice which was posted in public libraries. The plaintiffs sued in defamation. The defendants claimed qualified privilege on the ground that there was a common interest between the council and the ratepayers. The court held that since the report was only a preliminary stage of the investigation there was no common interest and the report had been circulated too widely to receive the protection of qualified privilege. The defence was examined in *Kearns v General Council of the Bar* [2003] 2 All ER 534. Here the Bar Council, which has responsibility for the professional conduct of barristers, had circulated to all barristers incorrect and defamatory material about a firm of solicitors. This was retracted two days later but the claimants sued. The Court of Appeal held that the communication was between parties in an established relationship which required the flow of free and frank communications and that qualified privilege applied.

Any communication between a student and the governors of the college ought to entitle the student to rely on the defence of qualified privilege if it relates to the conduct of a member of staff. There is a clear incidence of the duty—interest relationship identified in *Adam v Ward*. The fact that the governing body might be a large number of people does not matter. In *Horrocks v Lowe* [1975] AC 135, the House of Lords held that qualified privilege extended to a complaint made against a town councillor published to all the other councillors. The vital question is whether Fatima had any right to circulate her allegations amongst the academic staff, most of whom would not have had any powers of management over Omar. If the articles of government of the college show that all the lecturers have the right to participate in the running of the college the net of qualified privilege will reach further. It will not be enough for Fatima to show that the allegations would be of some interest to the academic staff, in the sense of being newsworthy for their own sake.

Even if it were apparent who had sent the letter to Omar's wife it has been suggested in some cases that there may be a qualified privilege in communications to one spouse about the activities of another. In *Watt v Longsdon* [1929] All ER Rep 292 this question arose. The court refused to set down broad guidelines on this matter but found on the facts that there had been no privileged communication to the wife about the husband's alleged unpaid bills and alleged extra-marital affair.

The defence of qualified privilege will be defeated by malice. If Omar can show that Fatima was motivated by malice, she will not be able to invoke the defence, no matter to whom the allegations were sent (*Horrocks v Lowe*). But there is no evidence of the ill-will or spite which would suggest malice required by this case.

Finally, the Defamation Act 1996, ss. 8–10 introduced significant reforms into the conduct of defamation proceedings but the jury continues to play a very important role. The so-called 'fast-track' procedure enables the court, in the absence of a jury, to dispose summarily of a case if it appears that the action has 'no realistic prospect of success'. Conversely, the procedure enables the court to provide 'summary relief' in a case if it appears that there is no defence and the claim has 'a realistic prospect of success'. By s. 9(1)(c) of the Act, summary relief is restricted to actions which can be adequately compensated by an award not exceeding £10,000. Perhaps Omar might be tempted to opt for a jury trial given that by the nature of his vocation, he would hope for an award in excess of that figure and juries are notoriously generous in assessing damages for libel. Until s. 8 of the Courts and Legal Services Act 1990, the Court of Appeal lacked the power to reduce jury awards unless they were completely 'divorced from reality' but that power is now available generally: see, for example, *Kiam v MGN Ltd* [2002] 2 All ER 219.

Question 2

Sanjay, the Member of Parliament for Wessex North, is in the process of introducing a private members Bill in Parliament authorizing the redesignation of agricultural lands in his constituency for industrial development. This would allow Wover Cars Ltd to build a manufacturing plant in the area. During the Parliamentary debate, the MP for a neighbouring constituency, Peter Piper, who belongs to the Wessex Alliance Party, emerged as the Bill's most vociferous opponent.

On hearing of the debate, Nick Whippet the chairman and chief executive of Wover, wrote to Sanjay stating: 'Wover Cars' principal opponent in the House is a hypocrite like the party he belongs to whose opposition to the scheme has more to do with the fact that he has recently purchased several farms in Wessex North which he stands to lose than with his apparent concern for the preservation of the countryside.'

Sanjay confronts Piper with the allegations during a Parliamentary debate and accuses him of abusing his position by failing to disclose his personal interests. The *Wessex Daily Globe* is interested in this matter and publishes a detailed report of the debate. Sanjay has also written to the *Wessex Daily Globe* stating that 'Peter Piper MP is a liar whose only interest is to protect his own property at the expense of bringing employment into the region.' Using this information which it does not check with Peter Piper, the newspaper prints an editorial criticizing Peter Piper in similar terms. In fact Peter Piper does not own property in the Wessex North constituency.
Consider the law of defamation as it applies to the potential liability of the parties.

Commentary

This question requires consideration of the core requirements to establish what amounts to defamation together with the defences, whether common law or within the **Defamation Act 1952** or the **Defamation Act 1996**. The distinction between libel and slander can also be introduced. The answer should try to balance the amount of material devoted to each of these topics given that there is no obvious focus on any single issue relating to demonstrating the substance of a defamatory statement. On the other hand the particular defence emphasized is privilege (absolute and qualified), but it should be mentioned why the other defences do not apply. Qualified privilege in this problem does extend to the *Reynolds* defence and it raises the question whether or not the newspaper has achieved the standard of responsible journalism.

Answer plan

- Distinctions between libel and slander.
- Explain the meaning of defamation.
- Identify and explain the core elements of defamation.
- **Defamation Act 1952; Defamation Act 1996**.
- Publication.
- State the available defences and consider in particular absolute and qualified privilege.
- Explain and consider the application of the *Reynolds* privilege.
- Refer briefly to the **Defamation Act 1952** and the **Defamation Act 1996**.
- Important cases include *Reynolds v Times Newspapers*; *Loutchansky v Times Newspapers* (No. 2).

Suggested answer

Peter Piper may be able to bring an action in the tort of defamation against Nick Whippet, Sanjay, and the *Wessex Daily Globe*. A defamatory statement will usually be spoken or written but it may take another form of representation such as a photograph. The statement may be conveyed in any medium, and in the past has included a wax effigy and a gravestone. But it is the nature of the particular medium which determines whether Peter Piper's action lies in slander or libel, the two forms of defamation.

As a broad rule, if the defamatory statement is conveyed in a permanent form it is libel, whereas if it is in a temporary form, it is slander. There are statutory classifications of such matters as television and radio broadcasts. The distinction between the two varieties stemmed from the early jurisdictional claims between state and religious courts. But now the distinction between the two forms of action is important because libel is actionable *per se* (without proof of damage) whilst slander is actionable only upon proof of actual damage. This requirement in slander is subject to certain exceptions, the most important of which for the purposes of Peter Piper's action is an imputation of unfitness or incompetence. The Defamation Act 1952, s. 2 provides that where the words are calculated to disparage the plaintiff in any office, profession, calling, trade, or business carried on by him there is no need to prove special damage, 'whether or not the words are spoken of the plaintiff in the way of his office, profession, calling, trade or business'. It is therefore not necessary for Peter Piper to prove defamation in the context of his office provided the words are likely to injure him within it. It should be noted that on grounds of public interest in freedom of expression, the courts will not allow free speech to be fettered by permitting organs of government, whether local or central, to sue for libel (*Derbyshire CC v Times Newspapers* [1993] AC 534: a local authority; *Goldsmith v Bhoyrul* [1997] 4 All ER 268: a political party). However, individuals within such organizations (such as officers or councillors, MPs, and party candidates) may bring proceedings for defamation in their personal capacity if identified.

Having identified whether the particular statements can be categorized as slander or libel, it is necessary for Peter Piper to prove the three elements of the tort of defamation: that the particular words used were defamatory; that they referred to him; and that they were published to a third party by the defendant.

Nick Whippet's letter is in permanent and written form and so the action against him will lie in libel. Peter Piper will have to prove that the words are capable of bearing a defamatory meaning. Although there is no single test for this, a classic definition of defamation was suggested by Parke B in *Parmiter v Coupland* (1840) 6 M & W 105, in which he said that a defamatory publication is one which 'is calculated to injure the reputation of another by exposing him to hatred, contempt or ridicule'. This formula has been criticized as being too narrow since a plaintiff's reputation can be damaged without him or her being necessarily exposed to hatred, ridicule or contempt (see, for example, *Tournier v National Provincial Union Bank of England Ltd* [1924] 1 KB 461, Scrutton LJ). A wider test for determining whether the defendant's words are capable of being defamatory was formulated by Lord Atkin in *Sim v Stretch* [1936] 2 All ER 1237. His Lordship said that the requisite question is: 'Would the words tend to lower the plaintiff in the estimation of right-thinking members of society generally?' Thus, there is no requirement that the defamatory statement should impute moral turpitude (*Youssoupoff v Metro-Goldwyn-Mayer Pictures Ltd* (1934) 50 TLR 581 where the victim of a rape or seduction could not be said to have been guilty of moral laxity). In *Berkoff v Burchill* [1996] 4 All ER 1008 (a case involving exposing the plaintiff to ridicule), Neill LJ cited with approval the approach adopted in *Cropp v Tilney* (1693) 3 Salk 225, in which the plaintiff complained of a publication which he said had resulted in his failing to be elected as a Member of Parliament. The defendant had alleged that the plaintiff was beaten by his wife. Holt CJ said that scandalous matter is not necessary to establish a libel but rather it is sufficient if the defendant induces in others an ill opinion of the plaintiff.

If the judge considers that the words are capable of bearing a defamatory meaning they are put to the jury as 'right thinking members of society' to determine whether or not the words are in fact defamatory. By virtue of the Defamation Act 1996, s. 7 either party may apply for an order to determine before trial whether the words are actually capable of bearing a defamatory meaning. The description of Peter Piper as a 'hypocrite' by Nick Whippet in his letter to Sanjay would appear to be libellous within the broader approach adopted by Holt CJ and subsequently by Lord Atkin. The words will be given their ordinary meaning and evidence will not be given to elaborate on that meaning. The jury will have to find the specific meaning of the words in the context of the case where words may have different meanings.

Although the words do not expressly refer to Peter Piper this will not bar his action since he can introduce extrinsic evidence to show that he was the person referred to in the letter as happened in *Morgan v Odhams Press Ltd* [1971] 1 WLR 1239 where the claimant was unnamed. Sanjay's special knowledge would be relevant here. The test was said in the *Morgan* case to be the impression that would be conveyed to an ordinary sensible man having knowledge of the circumstances.

The third element of the tort is publication which has been defined as the communication of defamatory words to a third party, i.e. to some person other than the plaintiff. It is evident that Nick Whippet has in fact published the statement to Sanjay (a third party).

If on the face of things the letter is a defamatory statement then what defences are available?

The defence of justification is not available to Nick Whippet. He has to prove the 'sting' of the defamatory statement. For example in *Alexander v North Eastern Railway Company* (1865) 34 LJQB 152, the defendant was able to show that the plaintiff had been convicted of an offence and sent to prison and had served two weeks. The jury was entitled to regard the original statement (that he had served the three weeks) as having been justified. In *Wakley v Cooke & Healey* (1849) 4 Exch 511, the statement that the plaintiff journalist was a libellous journalist was taken to mean that he made a habit of libels and not that he had done so once (which was true)—the defendant could therefore not justify the statement. Given that Peter Piper does not own the farm land claimed, and therefore has no vested interest in opposing the scheme, there is no truth in the defamatory statement that he is a hypocrite seeking to protect his property.

Similarly, fair comment is not available to him as a defence since there must be a comment and this must be a comment about facts that are true. By way of comparison in *London Artists Ltd v Littler* [1969] 2 All ER 193, the defendant was unable to show that there was any factual basis for his suggestion that there was a conspiracy to keep his show out of theatres and the defence of fair comment on such a conspiracy failed.

The law recognizes that there may be situations where inaccurate information may be passed on and where the public interest in maintaining the free flow of information (even inaccurate information) outweighs the interest in the reputation of the claimant wronged by such a statement provided that there is no malice behind the statement. Such occasions are said to be protected by qualified privilege. Qualified privilege may well be available provided Nick is able to demonstrate that he has an interest in bringing the matter to the attention of the MP and that Sanjay has a corresponding duty to receive the information, or that there is a common interest and a reciprocal duty. There must be a reasonable belief in the truth of what is said although the actual truth need not be established. A plea of qualified privilege may be defeated by demonstrating that there is no privileged occasion, or that there was malice on the part of the defendant. An example of an occasion being protected by qualified privilege may be seen in *Watt v Longsdon* [1930] 1 KB 130 where correspondence between a director of a company and the chairman of the company concerning the behaviour of one of its overseas managers was protected. The director was under a moral or business duty to inform his chairman of the behaviour and that there was a corresponding interest in receiving the information. Here, communicating with an MP with a view to raising matters in debate would seem to be protected by qualified privilege even though the statement was factually inaccurate.

As to the proceedings in debate, the allegation made by Sanjay that Peter Piper abused his position is *prima facie*, slanderous in that it disparaged him in the conduct of his office. Further, on the basis of the **Defamation Act 1952, s. 2**, special damage need not be proved. However, the statement was made during a Parliamentary debate and it enjoys absolute privilege both at Common Law (*Ex parte Wason* (1869) LR 4 QB 573) as reiterated in the **Bill of Rights 1688, art. 9**, and under statute: the **Defamation Act 1996, s. 13(4)**, so that no action will lie in respect of it (although by s. **13 of the 1996 Act** this privilege can be waived; this is unlikely on the given facts). The categories of absolute privilege are quite narrowly drawn and reflect the policy of the law that in rare instances the free flow of information in the general public interest is such as to allow even maliciously motivated statements to be protected.

Normally Parliamentary privilege will be used by MPs against litigants to stifle civil actions as in the *Church of Scientology of California v Johnson-Smith* [1972] 1 QB 522 where the plaintiffs sued the defendant MP for a libel alleged to have been made on a television programme. The defence was fair comment. The plaintiffs pleaded malice which would negate this defence. To establish malice they wanted to use extracts from *Hansard* but it was held that this evidence could not be used because of Parliamentary privilege. **Section 13** was passed in the light of several prominent actions by MPs against newspapers in order to permit MPs to waive privilege and allow their own actions to proceed relying on extracts from *Hansard*.

Neither will an action lie against *Hansard* when Sanjay's words are published, since any statement in a paper published by the authority of Parliament is privileged by the **Parliamentary Papers Act 1840**, passed after an extensive tussle between the courts and Parliament.

At common law and under statute there is qualified privilege in newspaper or other reports of proceedings in Parliament providing that the reports are fair and accurate, i.e. that there should be a reasonably balanced report without embellishment or embroidery by the newspaper, although a humorous pen picture will be unlikely to be regarded as unfair. Proof of malice would remove the privilege.

Sanjay's letter to the *Wessex Daily Globe* is libellous in that it would tend to lower Piper in the estimation of right-thinking members of society. It has clearly been published to a third party, the newspaper and, as with Whippet, since the statement is based on the false assertion that Peter Piper is motivated by protecting his property interests, the defences of justification and fair comment are not available to him. Qualified privilege would depend upon the existence of a duty — interest relationship. Relationships which fall within this defence are narrowly confined and would not normally extend to publication to a newspaper. For example, in *Beach v Freeson* [1972] 1 QB 14 an MP wrote to the Law Society and the Lord Chancellor and his letter repeated defamatory statements made to him by a constituent about a solicitor. It was held that he had a duty to make the statement and that the recipients were under a duty to receive these.

Saying that there is a rumour as to a particular fact is taken by the courts to be an assertion that the rumour is true. Similarly, the newspaper will be liable for libel even if it has expressly stated in the editorial that it is merely reproducing what the editors have been told by Sanjay. It has often been said in the cases that it is no defence to say that the writer is simply repeating what was said. Simply repeating a rumour will be a publication of the statement within the rumour, as was confirmed by the House of Lords in *Lewis v Daily Telegraph* [1963] 2 All ER 151; each publication is a fresh publication. Accordingly, the writer of the editorial, the newspaper proprietor, and its printers will each be held liable for its publication. One possible defence here might be for the newspaper to try to bring itself within the wide view of qualified privilege upheld by the House of Lords in *Reynolds v Times Newspapers* [1999] 4 All ER 609. There it was held that in exceptional circumstances there might be a duty to disseminate information to the general public in a newspaper and a corresponding interest in receiving it. The Court of Appeal in *Loutchansky v Times Newspapers Ltd (No. 2)* [2002] 1 All ER 652 held that in deciding whether there had been a duty to publish defamatory words to the world at large the standard to be applied was that of responsible journalism. Lord Nicholls in *Reynolds* had indicated a list of factors which should be taken into account in deciding this, and he included such matters as the seriousness of the allegation, the extent to which the subject-matter is a matter of public concern and the steps taken to verify the information and the urgency of the matter, whether comment was sought from the claimant, whether the article contained the gist of the claimant's side of the story. The principles were confirmed in *Jameel v Wall Street Journal* [2006] UKHL 44 and applied in *Seaga v Harper* [2008] UKPC 9 by the Privy Council, which said that the criteria identified by Lord Nicholls were not individual hurdles to be overcome. They had to be applied practically and pragmatically to reflect the real world of journalism. In the latter case the failure to check sources when there was plenty of time available put the speaker in breach of the standard of responsible journalism. Applying these factors it would be unlikely that there would be a qualified privilege in the article; see the example of *Galloway v Telegraph Group Ltd* [2006] EWCA Civ 17 where the newspaper embellished their account and went beyond the standard of responsible journalism. Merely reporting allegations that are made by someone may not be defamatory repetition where the newspaper makes it clear that they are not adopting the statements as true; this is 'reportage'. But, going beyond the allegations and adopting them as true or embellishing them (as occurred in *Galloway*) will render the newspaper liable, as was the case in *Charman v Orion Publishing* [2007] EWCA Civ 972 where the publishers of a book were liable where the book went beyond the reporting of allegations and investigated the background to the statements in a piece of undercover investigative journalism.

The newspaper may make an 'offer of amends' to Peter Piper by offering to publish an apology or correction and pay him damages even before the writ is served (Defamation Act 1996, ss. 2–4). If Peter Piper accepts such an offer the issue must be settled by an agreement between him and the newspaper. The court will only intervene, if necessary, to adjudicate as to the amount of compensation or on the nature of the apology or correction. Acceptance of an offer will operate to terminate the defamation proceedings.

The Defamation Act 1996, ss. 8–10 introduced significant reforms into the conduct of defamation proceedings. The so-called 'fast-track' procedure enables the court, in the absence of a jury, to dispose summarily of a case if it appears that the action has 'no realistic prospect of success.' Conversely, the procedure enables the court to provide 'summary relief' in a case if it appears that there is no defence and the claim has 'a realistic prospect of success'. By s. 9(1)(c) of the

Act, summary relief is restricted to actions which can be adequately compensated by an award not exceeding £10,000. It is suggested that Peter Piper may wish to opt for a jury trial given that by the nature of his vocation, he would hope for an award in excess of that figure. Juries are notoriously generous in assessing damages for libel and until **s. 8** of the **Courts and Legal Services Act** the Court of Appeal lacked the power to reduce jury awards unless they were completely 'divorced from reality' but that power is now available generally, see for example *Kiam v MGN Ltd* [2002] 2 All ER 219. On the other hand, there have been significant and newsworthy examples of politicians being hugely embarrassed in their own libel actions.

Question 3

During a local radio phone-in programme Bill Birch, the leader of the majority party on the Council for the city of Bilchester, announces that he intends to push through his plans to deregulate gambling in the city and its suburbs. He explains that he wishes to see Bilchester become a second Las Vegas.

Mary Priggish, a well-known member of the 'Moral Crusade Party', telephones the programme and is put on the air. She states that: 'Birch is an immoral clown who wants to see law and order disintegrate in our city. If he were to marry he might give up his hedonistic lifestyle and start pushing for family virtues.'

In fact Bill Birch is married to Primrose Hill, a charity worker who is also a governor of the local primary school. Shortly after the broadcast, Bill's wife is told that the chairman of the school governors wishes her to resign. He feels that it is inappropriate for someone who is cohabiting outside of wedlock to hold such a position.

William Birch is a professional clown who is unmarried and who is often employed at children's parties. Some friends have said that they thought the comments referred to him.

Advise Bill Birch, Primrose Hill and William Birch.

Commentary

This question requires consideration of the three elements of the tort of defamation but with particular emphasis on the meaning of defamatory and reference to the claimant where the words are capable of applying to more than one person. Typically the question demands that you identify these core elements with considerable care and by reference to a good selection of relevant cases. The available defences must also be considered.

Answer plan

- **Section 166** of the **Broadcasting Act 1990**.
- Innuendo.
- The defence of unintentional defamation (**Defamation Act 1952, s. 4**; and **Defamation Act 1996, ss. 2–4**).
- The defence of fair comment.
- The defence of qualified privilege.
- Reference to the claimant.

Suggested answer

Bill Birch and Primrose and William Birch (the clown) may have an action in defamation against Mary Priggish and the radio company. Section 166 of the Broadcasting Act 1990 provides that the publication of any words during the course of a broadcast programme, on television or radio, shall be treated as publication in permanent form. Their action will therefore lie in libel which is actionable *per se* (without proof of actual damage), and thus the request for Primrose to resign from the school governors is not material to her claim (other than as to damages). Accordingly, it is necessary for each of them to prove the constituent elements of the tort, namely that the statement was defamatory, that it referred to them and that it was published to a third party by the defendants.

Bill Birch has two possible claims. First, that the statement that he is an 'immoral clown' is capable of being defamatory since it would tend to lower him in the estimation of right-thinking members of society (*Sim v Stretch* [1936] 2 All ER 1237, *per* Lord Atkin), or the words could expose him to 'hatred, contempt or ridicule' (*Parmiter v Coupland* (1840) 6 M & W 105, *per* Parke B). A good illustration of words exposing someone to ridicule is to be found in *Berkoff v Burchill* [1996] All ER 1008 where describing a well-known actor and director in terms which suggested he was hideously ugly were held to be defamatory as exposing him to ridicule. But, as *Norman v Future Publishing* [1999] EMLR 325 shows, the entirety of the article has to be looked at and not just a few selected passages; in that case the article was generally highly complimentary and the words could not bear a defamatory meaning.

Whether or not the statement is capable of bearing a particular meaning is a question for the judge to determine. The judge will therefore lay down the limits of the range of possible defamatory meanings of which, in law, the words are capable, it is then for the jury to decide if the actual meaning of the statement falls within that permissible range. It is submitted that an imputation of immorality is capable of being defamatory within the tests laid down by Parke B and Lord Atkin, particularly in light of the nature of Bill Birch's public office. Recourse to the Defamation Act, s. 2 (slander affecting official, professional, or business reputation) is not necessary given that Bill Birch's action lies in the tort of libel. Secondly, although the suggestion that he is unmarried is not *prima facie* defamatory, it must be considered against the fact that he is married to Primrose. It is immaterial if the people who know that he lives with Primrose conclude that they are unmarried but nevertheless do not think any less of him, since the test for determining whether the statement is defamatory is dependant upon its effect on 'right-thinking members of society'. Although the courts do not permit actions for defamation brought by organs of local and central government since there is a public interest in free speech on matters relating to government (*Derbyshire CC v Times Newspapers Ltd* [1993] AC 534), proceedings by individuals such as councillors, MPs and candidates are nonetheless allowed (*Goldsmith v Bhoyrul* [1997] 4 All ER 268).

Bill Birch will need to introduce extrinsic evidence to establish the meaning of this true innuendo, i.e. words not defamatory on their face but rendered defamatory by virtue of knowledge or understanding of facts known to others. Thus, in *Tolley v Fry* [1931] AC 333 the assertion that a person might have been paid to lend their name and image to an advertisement would not usually be defamatory but it was in the instance of the plaintiff who was a famous golfer bound by his amateur code to refrain from receiving payment in respect of his sporting activities. A true innuendo is to be distinguished from a false innuendo which is simply the attribution of meaning to explain the understanding or meaning of a particular word. The decision of the Court of Appeal in *Cassidy v Daily Mirror Newspapers Ltd* [1929] 2 KB 331, is clearly pertinent to his claim. The defendant newspaper published a picture of Mr Cassidy, also known as Michael Corrigan, and a woman. The caption stated that it was 'Mr M Corrigan, the race horse owner, and Miss X, whose engagement has been announced.' Mrs Cassidy sued for libel claiming that the caption and photograph were capable of meaning that her husband was a single man, and that therefore she was living in immoral cohabitation with him. Several of her female acquaintances gave evidence that they had assumed from the article that Mrs Cassidy was unmarried and had no legal right to bear that name. It was held that in the light of the extrinsic evidence that Mr Cassidy was in fact married, the publication was defamatory. It was immaterial that the defendant was unaware of the extrinsic facts, provided that the paper had been read by those who did and who knew that it applied to the claimant. The same reasoning will apply in Bill's case.

With respect to the action by Primrose, the suggestion that Bill is unmarried carries the imputation that she is living with him outside of wedlock and the decision in *Cassidy v Daily Mirror Newspapers Ltd*, is similarly apposite. The fact that she is not referred to does not bar her claim given that ordinary sensible people, proved to have special knowledge of the facts, might reasonably believe that the statement referred to her. In *Morgan v Odhams Press Ltd* [1971] 2 All ER 1156, the House of Lords held that there was no requirement that the words themselves should expressly refer to the claimant provided extrinsic evidence could be adduced to show that she was referred to. Thus the key factor is the inference which an 'ordinary sensible' listener would draw from the statement.

When making her statement on the phone-in Mary knew that it would be broadcast contemporaneously and is therefore liable for its publication (*Adams v Kelly* (1824) Ry & M 157). Similarly, the radio company as the 'publisher' of the statement is also liable (*M'Pherson v Daniels* (1829) 10 B & C 263). Further, the programme's production staff may also be found liable on the basis that they disseminated the defamatory statement. The defendants may raise the defence of unintentional defamation provided by the **Defamation Act 1996, s. 1**, in relation to the innuendo. However the defence is available only if a person innocently publishes words alleged to be defamatory *and* has exercised all reasonable care in relation to the publication. As a public figure it would not have been difficult to ascertain Bill's marital status, and therefore reasonable care had not been taken to avoid defaming him and, by implication, Primrose. In the absence of reasonable care, it is immaterial that the defendants were unaware of the external facts which turned a presumptively innocent statement into one which is defamatory (*Newstead v London Express Newspaper Ltd* [1940] 1 KB 377). The defence of unintentional defamation, originally in **s. 4** of the **Defamation Act 1952**, may now become more widely used due to the procedural reforms contained in **ss. 2–4** of the **Defamation Act 1996** as a result of which a defendant may make a written 'offer to make amends' to the claimant to publish an apology and a correction and pay damages even before an action is commenced. The offer may be in relation to the defamatory statement generally or to a specific defamatory meaning within the statement, in which case it is called a 'qualified offer'. If Bill Birch and Primrose accept the offer then the matter is settled by agreement and the court will only intervene, if necessary, to adjudicate on the amount of compensation or on the nature of the apology and/or correction to be published by the radio broadcasting company. Their acceptance of the offer will terminate any proceedings against the company. If, however, they do not accept the offer of amends it can be withdrawn by the company and either a new offer may be made in its place, or the original may be left to stand and may be used as a defence.

As regards the defence of fair comment on a matter of public interest, the law recognizes that one aspect of freedom of speech is to allow robust criticism in public matters. The notion of what is a matter of public interest has been generously applied by the courts so as to promote freedom of speech and it would extend to the suitability for office of politicians and their policies. But, it has to be shown that the statement is a matter of comment on a matter of fact and not an assertion of fact. It may be difficult to distinguish a statement of fact from a comment but there has to be an underlying stratum of fact about which a comment may be made. There was such a stratum of fact in *Kemsley v Foot* [1952] AC 345 (the standard of reporting of a newspaper group and the type of story covered) but not in *London Artists v Littler* [1969] 2 QB 375 where the assertion that there was a conspiracy to oust an impresario from a theatre was not comment about a fact since there was no stratum of facts amounting to such a conspiracy. The allegations about Bill Birch may amount to comment but there is an incorrect statement of facts and the defence will not be available.

In addition the defence can be defeated by a plea of malice, i.e. motivated by ill-will or spite. Malice outweighs the suggestion that the comment was fair, i.e. a statement that an honest person could make even if incorrect. According to the Court of Appeal in *Telnikoff v Matusevitch* [1992] 2 AC 343, generally, once the defendant has shown that the opinion is one that a reasonable man could hold he does not have to go on to prove that he actually held it. It is for the claimant to show that the statement is unfair and that the opinion was motivated by malice, one aspect of which may be that it was not an opinion genuinely held. In the case of newspapers or other broadcasters reporting the statements of others (and where they will not usually be able to show such genuine belief) then this approach protects the newspaper from liability unless malice is shown in some other way.

Given the breadth of the assertions and the general context in which they are made it is unlikely that the broadcast will satisfy the requirements laid down by the House of Lords in *Reynolds v Times Newspapers* [1999] 4 All ER 609 for the defence of qualified privilege. In this context, where the broadcast is very wide and by the press, the test is one of responsible journalism. This involves giving the claimant an opportunity to comment upon the allegations and the urgency of the matter. These conditions are not the requirements of a statute and must be applied sympathetically according to the House of Lords in *Jameel v Wall Street Journal* and by the Privy Council in *Seaga v Harper*.

Finally, as regards William Birch (the clown), the question is whether or not the statement can be said to refer to him. It is not a requirement that the speaker should intend the words to refer to the claimant and there is an element of strict liability: if they are taken by reasonable person to refer to him then in law they do refer to him. This derives from *Newstead v London Express Newspapers* where the text of a newspaper story was capable of referring to the claimant and therefore did so refer. The story referred to a Harold Newstead, 30-year-old man from Camberwell. This description fitted the claimant who was entitled to sue in respect of the defamatory statement that he was a convicted bigamist, even though it was true of another person intended by the newspaper to be the subject of the story. Similarly in *Hulton v Jones* a story referring to a fictitious Artemus Jones, churchwarden of Peckham, was held to refer to Artemus Jones, a barrister from Manchester (there being evidence that friends had believed the account to be about him). Subject to the other elements of the tort being made out as described above then there is no reason why William Birch cannot sue, although, subject to any offer of amends, a jury might well award a relatively low level of damages, as it did in the Newstead case (but not in *Hulton v Jones*).

Further reading

Barendt, E., 'Libel and Freedom of Speech in English Law' [1993] PL 449.

Gatley, J. C. C., *Gatley on Libel and Slander*, 11th edn (London: Sweet & Maxwell, 2008).

Loveland, I., '*Reynolds v Times Newspapers* in the House of Lords' [2000] PL 351.

Trindade, F. A., 'Defamatory Statements and Political Discussion' (2000) 116 LQR 185.

Williams, K., 'Defaming Politicians: The not so Common Law' (2003) 63 MLR 748.

13

Interference with chattels and business interests

Introduction

One purpose served by the law of torts is to protect members of society against harm to the person, but it also protects property rights and, to a much lesser extent, a person's legitimate business interests.

The first of the questions that follow is primarily concerned with the tort of conversion which requires consideration of the claimant's right to possession of goods. Both conversion and the tort of trespass to goods require proof of an intention, on the part of the defendant, to interfere. Moreover, since these are intentional torts, the remedies available to the claimant differ from torts which require a lesser state of mind.

The other two questions consider the economic torts of intentional infliction of harm by unlawful means, conspiracy and inducement to breach of contract. While these provide some protection against intentional interference with economic interests, they also illustrate a strain in the law in that they compete with the right of another to make a living. A balance has to be struck between legitimate business competition or hard bargaining and unacceptable interference with the interests of another. In some way, the law has to attempt the difficult task of identifying those unlawful acts which interfere with the trade or business of another without unduly restricting the right of others to engage in free competition. As the development of the tort of conspiracy and inducement to breach of contract illustrate, this is not easy.

(1) Trespass to goods and conversion

Question 1

Paresh, a keen golfer, while looking for a lost golf ball, finds a heavy gold chain round the neck of a skeleton at the bottom of a lake on the Victoria Park golf course, a site owned and run by Graspshire County Council. The clasp on the chain is imperfect with the result that Paresh asks Harold, a jeweller, to carry out repairs. Harold sells the chain to Atika for £500, claiming that it belongs to a friend of his who has given him authority to obtain the best possible price. Paresh lends the skeleton to Patrick, a friend who is a medical student, for the period of his degree studies. The skeleton is deliberately damaged by Vijay, Patrick's flat-mate during a party. Atika then gives the chain to her boyfriend, Albert, as a birthday present. Albert, a dealer in jewellery, has now displayed the repaired chain in his shop window at a price of £1,500.

Advise the parties whether there is any action for conversion.

Commentary

This question requires consideration of the proper scope of the tort of conversion and the defences available to a person alleged to have converted chattels in respect of which another person has a higher claim. Other relevant factors include the problem posed where a person does some act which has the effect of increasing the value of goods that are later claimed to have been converted.

Answer plan

- Define conversion.
- Is a finder of goods someone who has standing to sue—see *Parker v British Airways Board*?
- What effect does the existence of a bailment relationship have on the liability of the bailee?
- What effect does the common law defence *jus tertii* have in the light of the **Torts (Interference with Goods) Act 1977, s. 8**?
- What remedies are available in respect of the tort of conversion in the light of the **Torts (Interference with Goods) Act 1977, s. 3**?
- What are the rights of an improver under the **Torts (Interference with Goods) Act 1977, s. 6**?

Suggested answer

Conversion is the intentional dealing with goods which is seriously inconsistent with the possession, or right to immediate possession, of another person (Murphy, *Street on Torts*, 12th edn (Oxford: Oxford University Press, 2007). Conversion is confined to interference with personal chattels, with the result that there is not a tort of conversion of a chose in action such as a contractual right (see *OBG Ltd v Allan* [2007] UKHL 21, [2007] 2 WLR 920). However, Lord Nicholls and Baroness Hale (dissenting) were willing to extend the tort to cover intangible property. Trespass to goods involves a direct interference with goods in the possession of the claimant, whether the interference is intentional or careless.

There is an initial question whether the chain and the skeleton are goods that may be converted. The chain should cause little difficulty in this respect as it is a moveable chattel that may be owned and possessed. The skeleton, however, may be different. It has been held that while there can be no property in a corpse (*Dobson v North Tyneside Health Authority* [1996] 4 All ER 474 and *A and others v Leeds Teaching Hospital NHS Trust* [2004] EWHC 644) it may be possible to obtain property in a preserved specimen (*R v Kelly* [1999] QB 621). However, this is a skeleton found at the bottom of a lake in a public area with a chain around its neck. This may suggest that it is the remains of a decomposed body of a victim of crime or an accident. In this case it would be difficult to describe it as a preserved specimen. On balance, the skeleton may not be an item of personal property that can be converted.

If the skeleton is capable of possession, it is technically in the possession of both Paresh and Patrick, since Paresh is a bailee and Patrick has actual possession. However, Paresh and Patrick cannot both sue, and whichever of the two elects to sue Vijay first will have to account to the other possible claimant in respect of his interest (*Nicholls v Bastard* (1835) 2 Cr M & R 659; *O'Sullivan v Williams* [1992] 3 All ER 385).

If Vijay is to be liable, he must have committed an act of conversion. For these purposes, merely damaging the goods will not be enough (*Fouldes v Willoughby* (1841) 8 M & W 540). However, if Vijay's act of damaging the skeleton is so serious as to amount to destruction of the goods, it may amount to an act of conversion, if done intentionally.

Since Paresh has found the chain at the bottom of a lake on a golf course owned by someone else, it has to be established from the outset that he has a right to possession of the chain which is capable of protection by the torts of conversion or trespass. It appears that there is truth in the common assertion 'finders, keepers' since the fact of simple possession is sufficient to create an interest in the goods. In *Parker v British Airways Board* [1982] QB 1004, it was held that the finder of a chattel acquires rights over it if the true owner is unknown, the chattel appears to be abandoned or lost and he takes the chattel into his care or possession. In such a case, the finder acquires a right to the goods which is valid against everyone except the true owner, or a person who asserts a prior right to the goods which subsisted at the time the finder took possession. Similarly, if a customer finds banknotes on the floor of a shop, the customer will have a better claim to the notes than the shopkeeper, since until informed of their presence by the customer, the shopkeeper is unaware that they are there (*Bridges v Hawkesworth* (1851) 21 LJQB 75).

In *Amory v Delamirie* (1722) 1 Stra 505, a boy found a ring containing a jewel and handed it to a goldsmith for valuation. When the goldsmith declined to return the jewel, now removed from its setting, it was held that the boy was entitled to succeed in an action for conversion. The facts of the problem suggest that the chain has been found below the surface of the water but on the bed of the lake. This may suggest that Graspshire County Council has a superior interest. For example, a prehistoric boat embedded in soil, six feet below the surface, was held to belong to the landowner rather than the finder on the basis that the landowner owns not just the surface of the land but also everything which lies beneath the surface down to the centre of the earth (*Elwes v Briggs Gas Co* (1886) 33 Ch D 562). Similarly, in *Waverley Borough Council v Fletcher* [1995] 4 All ER 756 the defendant, using a metal detector, found a medieval gold brooch some nine inches below the surface of a public park owned by the claimant authority. The authority subsequently claimed a declaration that the brooch was their property, but the defendant relied on the defence of 'finders, keepers'. Although the trial judge found in favour of the defendant on the basis that the owner of a public park impliedly licensed members of the public to go to the park to engage in rec- reational activity, the Court of Appeal found in favour of the claimant authority on the basis that they had a superior right to the brooch than did the finder of it. While recreational activity was impliedly permitted, the license was considered not to extend to the right to dig up the ground, which could be regarded as a variety of trespass. However, the problem in the present case is that Paresh has not had to dig in order to find the chain, but on the other hand the surface of the water may be regarded as the top of the County Council's land, in which case the chain may be regarded as equivalent to being buried.

In *South Staffordshire Water Co v Sharman* [1896] 2 QB 44, an employee was instructed by a landowner to clean out the bottom of a pool. At the bottom of the pool, two gold rings were discovered. The Divisional court concluded that the rings were found 'in' the land rather than simply 'on' it. Accordingly, the land- owner had the better claim to possession. Unfortunately, in the course of giving judgment, Lord Russell seems to have said that whether a chattel is found in or on land, the chattel will still belong to the landowner if he has a manifest intention to exercise control, which might be taken to undermine the position adopted in cases like *Parker v British Airways Board*.

Conversely, the finder has a better interest in the goods if they are merely on the land rather than being attached to it, provided the owner has not shown an inten- tion to exercise control over the land and things upon it. Thus in *Parker v British*

Airways Board there was no evidence to show that the defendants had any intention to exercise control over a bracelet found by the claimant on the floor of the departure lounge at an airport. In contrast in *London Corporation v Appleyard* [1963] 2 All ER 834, the discovery of banknotes in a box in a wall safe showed that the owner of the land did have an intention to exercise control over the property. In the present case, there appears to be little evidence of an intention to control the chain on the part of Graspshire County Council, which may be taken to suggest that Paresh has a greater interest.

However, there still remains the problem that if the chain, like the rings in *South Staffordshire Water Co v Sharman*, is taken to have been found in the land, then the County Council may have the stronger claim. After finding the chain, Paresh hands it to Harold for repair. As a repairer, Harold is a bailee who has a lien over goods entrusted to him for the purposes of repair, but only in respect of his right to payment for the work he has done. However, if the bailee wrongly parts with possession, he loses his lien. By selling the chain to Atika, Harold loses his lien. Moreover, his act also amounts to conversion, thereby entitling the owner to sue him (*Mulliner v Florence* (1878) 3 QBD 484).

At common law many conversion actions succeeded even where the defendant could show that a third party had a better title than the claimant, because the defendant was not allowed to plead *jus tertii*. However, following the enactment of the Torts (Interference with Goods) Act 1977, s. 8(1), the common law rules on *jus tertii* were abolished so that the better title of a third party at the date of the alleged conversion (*De Franco v Metropolitan Police Commissioner* (1987), *The Times,* 8 May) may be pleaded as a defence to conversion. It follows that if Graspshire County Council have a better title to the chain, an action in conversion against Harold, Atika or Albert is likely to fail.

For a person to be liable for an act of conversion, there must be an intentional act which results in an interference with the claimant's goods (*Ashby v Tolhurst* [1937] 2 KB 242). However, if the defendant intends to deal with the goods in such a way as to interfere with the claimant's right of control, it does not matter that he is unaware that he has challenged the true owner's right to property or possession (*Caxton Publishing Ltd v Sutherland Publishing Ltd* [1939] AC 178). It follows that there is no defence of mistake or good faith (*Hollins v Fowler* (1875) LR 7 HL 757 and see also *Kuwait Airways Corp v Iraqi Airways Co (Nos 4 and 5)* [2002] AC 883). Clearly, Harold intends to deal in the chain in a manner which is inconsistent with Paresh's right of possession. Since Harold is only given possession for the purposes of repair rather than sale, it is unlikely that there will be a sale with the consent of the owner for the purposes of the Factors Act 1889, ss. 1(1) and 2(1) (*Pearson v Rose & Young* [1951] 1 KB 275). Moreover, Atika has also acted intentionally by delivering the chain to Albert and the fact that she is unaware that she has challenged Paresh's right to possession is irrelevant.

Albert presents a slightly different problem since he has merely invited offers for the purchase of the chain. As such he has not sold the chain nor is there any agreement to sell, with the result that there is no transfer of possession and, therefore, no conversion (*Lancashire Wagon Co v Fitzhugh* (1861) 6 H & N 502). However, Albert may have 'used' the chain as his own. For example, it has been held that merely wearing a pearl is an act of conversion (*Petre v Hemeage* (1701) 12 Mod Rep 519). Purporting to sell an article may be similarly treated with the result that Albert may have converted the chain as well.

The remedies for conversion are such that the claimant is entitled to compensation to the extent of the value of the goods converted. This will normally be the market value of the converted goods at the date of conversion: *Uzinterimpex JSC v Standard Bank plc* [2007] EWHC 1151, [2007] 2 Lloyds Rep 187. In this case, if Albert's price for the chain represents its market value, that amount will be £1,500. However, the relevant date for assessment of damages is the date of conversion (*BBMB Finance Ltd v Eda Holdings Ltd* [1991] 2 All ER 129). In *Kuwait Airways Corp v Iraqi Airways Co (Nos 4 and 5)* [2002] AC 883, Lord Nicholls drew a distinction between a person who converts in good faith and one who converts deliberately. The former would be liable for consequential losses only to the extent that those losses were reasonably foreseeable, whereas the latter will be liable for damage flowing 'directly and naturally' from the tort.

By repairing the chain, Harold may have increased its value. Generally, it is not open to the claimant to recover that enhanced value (*Caxton Publishing Ltd v Sutherland Publishing Ltd*). If the act of conversion occurs after the improvement, as in Harold's case, the Torts (Interference with Goods) Act 1977, s. 6(1) applies. This provides that if the defendant has improved the goods in the mistaken belief that he has a good title, an allowance can be made. Under s. 6(2) a similar allowance may also be made in favour of subsequent purchasers provided they act in good faith. It seems unlikely that Harold will be able to argue that he honestly believed he had a good title, but Atika may be able to show that she did purchase in good faith, having been told that Harold was selling the chain on behalf of a friend. Albert is unlikely to be able to use s. 6 in his favour, since it only applies to a subsequent purchaser, and as Atika gave him the chain as a present, he is a volunteer.

(2) Conspiracy

Question 2

'Although no branch of the law of torts has a higher proportion of decisions of the House of Lords . . . the scope of the tort is as obscure as its history.'

(Salmond, Heuston and Buckley, *The Law of Torts*)

How far is this an accurate reflection on the tort of conspiracy?

Commentary

One of the difficulties associated with the torts concerned with interference with contract or trade, is that the courts have to seek to achieve a balance between conduct that oversteps the bounds of what is acceptable and the right of a person to pursue his trade or livelihood. While a person has a right to pursue his own business, he must not do so if his conduct impinges on the rights of other traders to do the same. Broadly speaking the torts of intentional infliction of harm by unlawful means, conspiracy and inducement to breach of contract are all connected by the common thread that they apply in circumstances in which the conduct of the defendant has wrongly interfered with the right of another to carry on his lawful business.

This question requires a critical examination of the scope of the tort of conspiracy, including where it came from and the present range of unlawful acts capable of falling within the definition of the tort.

Answer plan

- Define the tort.
- Show its links with the criminal law.
- Differentiate between the tort of intentional infliction of harm by unlawful means, conspiracy to injure and unlawful means conspiracy.

Suggested answer

Conspiracy amounts to the commission of a tort when two or more persons agree to commit an act which would be lawful if committed by one person acting alone. In order for there to be an actionable conspiracy, there must be an intention to cause damage and actual damage must result from the acts of the conspirators. Conspiracy takes one of two forms: 'simple' conspiracy, namely a conspiracy to injure another in his trade and conspiracy to carry out an unlawful act such as the commission of a crime or a tort. There have been those who argued that 'unlawful means' conspiracy was a redundant concept, but the House of Lords in *Customs & Excise Commissioners v Total Network SL* [2008] UKHL 19, [2008] 2 All ER 413 has confirmed that this tort is not a variety of accessory liability and remains a valuable tool in dealing with groups of people working in combination to harm another.

In addition to the two named varieties of conspiracy, the courts have also developed a 'genus' tort of using unlawful means to cause loss to another. See *OBG Ltd v Allan* [2007] UKHL 21, [2008] 1 AC 1 which appears to be easier to establish than conspiracy *per se*, since there is a much broader definition of unlawful means.

In *Allen v Flood* [1898] AC 1, it was held that motive alone does not turn that which is lawful into something that is unlawful. 'Simple' conspiracy must be viewed as an exception to the rule, since the motive of injuring a person in their trade is the central feature of this form of conspiracy.

Moreover, why the deeds of two people acting in combination should be actionable when the actions of a multinational corporation, as a single juristic person, are not, has attracted criticism. Indeed, for this very reason, doubts have been expressed by the House of Lords as to the rationale of the tort of conspiracy, although on each occasion, the existence of the tort has been confirmed (see *Lonrho Ltd v Shell Petroleum Co* [1982] AC 173; *Lonrho plc v Fayed* [1992] 1 AC 448).

Essentially, the tort consists of an agreement between two people to do an act that is, in itself, perfectly lawful, if it is done with the intention to cause harm to the claimant and the act was done for no good reason. For these purposes there must be an agreement; thus if an employer orders his employees to do an act that will injure the claimant, there will be no conspiracy as there has been no agreement (*Crofter Hand Woven Harris Tweed Co v Veitch* [1942] AC 435, 468 *per* Lord Wright).

If the act is done for a good reason, no tort is committed. Thus if the court concludes that the agreement between two people was done to further their business interests, there will be no lawful means conspiracy even if this results in the exclusion of the claimant from a lucrative business market (*Mogul Steamship Co v McGregor, Gow & Co* [1892] AC 25). Likewise, an agreement between two trade union officials will not be a conspiracy, provided there is evidence that the agreement they have reached is intended to further the legitimate interests of the union or its members (*Crofter Hand Woven Harris Tweed Co v Veitch* [1942] AC 435).

In contrast, if the agreement between the defendants is intended to punish the claimant for acting in a particular way or for holding a particular opinion, it is unlikely that this will be regarded as a good reason for making the agreement. Thus in *Quinn v Leathem* [1901] AC 495 the claimant employed workers who did not belong to the trade union of which the defendants were officials. The defendants maliciously threatened to compel the claimant's most important customer not to deal with the claimant unless he dismissed the non-union employees. The combined actions of the defendants were held to be an actionable conspiracy since there was actual damage in the form of lost custom.

Following *Quinn v Leathem* it was thought that malice was an ingredient of the tort, but it is clear since *Crofter Hand-Woven Harris Tweed Co Ltd v Veitch* [1942] AC 435 that spite or malevolence is not a necessary requirement, although it may actually be present in some cases. The decision in *Crofter* made it necessary to consider the predominant purpose of the defendants' actions, which should be to injure the claimant (*Metall und Rohstoff AG v Donaldson, Lufkin & Jenrette* [1990] 1 QB 391), although the emphasis should be on intention rather than motive (*Lonrho plc v Fayed* [1992] 1 AC 448). In *Crofter* the defendant's (a trade union) predominant purpose in placing an embargo on the importation of woollen yarn to the Isle of Lewis was the protection of the interests of its members, but in *Quinn v Leathem* there was a desire to punish the claimant.

A conspiracy to injure occurs where there is a wilful act which is intended to and does cause damage to the claimant in the course of his trade or business. For these purposes, there is still a conspiracy if the defendants know all the facts and intend to cause damage even if they are unaware of the illegality of their actions (*Pritchard v Briggs* [1980] Ch 388). It is important to emphasize that the gist of the action is actual pecuniary loss. Accordingly, it has been held that injury to reputation, including injury to business reputation in the form of damage to good-will, is not a recoverable head of damage in an action for conspiracy (*Lonrho plc v Fayed* (No. 5) [1994] 1 All ER 188). Such losses are the proper province of the tort of defamation in which justification may be pleaded by the defendant.

The burden of proving absence of justification for the defendant's actions may lie on the claimant if the analogy between conspiracy as a crime and as a tort is maintained. However, in modern civil law it may be better to require the defendant to justify his actions, especially since the basis of the tort is that the defendant has intentionally caused the damage complained of. What is clear, however, is that the defendant who proves that his principal aim was to further his legitimate trade interests will succeed.

The second kind of actionable conspiracy, namely unlawful means conspiracy, requires a combination between two or more people to engage in criminal conduct at common law or by statute, whether or not that conduct also gave rise to an independently actionable civil wrong, with the result that the claimant suffers damage (*Customs & Excise Commissioners v Total Network SL* [2008] UKHL 19, [2008] 2 WLR 711).

For these purposes, 'unlawful means' includes conduct that goes beyond something that would be independently actionable as a civil wrong, but the opinions in *Total Network SL* are unclear on how much broader the definition should be. The unlawful means must be employed in order to intentionally inflict harm on the claimant. Thus in *Total Network SL* the defendants engaged in a practice known as a 'carousel fraud' which involved Company A, a UK business, importing goods from the defendants, registered to pay VAT in Spain. This transaction is VAT exempt under European Union rules, so company A would not have to pay any VAT to the Customs & Excise Commissioners. Company A sold the goods to Company B, another UK business, charging VAT in the price. Company B then immediately exported the goods back to the defendants. In turn, Company B could recover from the Customs & Excise Commissioners the VAT they had paid to Company A as input tax. However, through this practice the Customs & Excise Commissioners had been deprived of a balancing payment which ought to have been due to them from Company A.

Although there was no independent tort committed by the defendants, their actions did amount to the common law crime of cheating the public revenue, so the companies concerned in this fraud had, by unlawful means, combined to intentionally inflict harm on the claimants by depriving them of the taxation revenues due to them.

It does not follow from this that all agreements to commit a crime will amount to unlawful means conspiracy as there are indications in the opinions of Lords Walker, Mance and Neuberger that special significance was attached to the fact that the crime in *Total Network SL* related to protecting the revenue. It may be the case that the tort will only apply where the criminal offence has been created in order to protect the claimant's interests.

For the purposes of this tort, proof of a predominant intention to injure the claimant is not an essential element (*Lonrho plc v Fayed* [1992] 1 AC 448). In *Lonrho Ltd v Shell Petroleum Ltd* (No. 2) [1982] AC 173, the defendants intentionally agreed to import oil into Southern Rhodesia from South Africa, in breach of a statutory prohibition. By acting in this way, the defendants substantially increased their profits at the expense of the claimants. On these facts, it was held that there was no intention to injure the claimants since there was no tort unless the defendants acted for the purpose not of protecting their own interests but of injuring the interests of the claimants. However, since *Lonrho plc v Fayed* [1992] 1 AC 448, the fact that a reason or even the predominant reason for acting unlawfully is the furtherance of one's own interests is not to be regarded as a defence.

The 'genus tort' of using unlawful means to cause loss to another, confusingly, requires the unlawful means employed by the defendants to amount to an independently actionable tort or, at least, something that would have been actionable as a tort had damage been caused (*OBG Ltd v Allan* [2008] 1 AC 1). For the purposes of this tort, 'unlawful means' may include an action amounting to a tort, a breach of contract and a crime.

So far as acts amounting to a tort are concerned, if the defendant intentionally causes the claimant to suffer loss by committing a tort in relation to X, so that X finds his freedom to deal with the claimant is interfered with, the defendant will have committed the genus tort. The same result will also obtain even where the defendant's acts do not cause X to suffer any kind of actionable loss (*OBG Ltd v Allan* [2008] 1 AC 1 at [49]–[50], *per* Lord Hoffmann; *Lonrho v Fayed* [1990] 2 QB 479).

Where the defendant breaches his contract with a third party in order to cause harm to the claimant, initially it might be difficult to regard the defendant's conduct as 'unlawful means' as, ordinarily there would be no order for compulsory performance. Despite this, it has been held that a threat to break a contract can amount to an unlawful threat and is little different from a threat to commit a tort (*Rookes v Barnard* [1964] AC 1129; *OBG Ltd v Allan* [2008] 1 AC 1 at [48] *per* Lord Hoffmann).

Where the conduct of the defendant amounts to both a crime and a tort at the same time, there should be no difficulty in treating this as 'unlawful means', but there is more difficulty where the crime is, for example, created by statute and regulatory in nature. In OBG Ltd v Allan the House of Lords was divided on this issue but, in the event, a majority accepted Lord Hoffmann's view that a crime should only count as unlawful means if it was actionable in tort at the instance of the third party.

In order for the tort to be committed, the defendant's act must interfere with the freedom of a third party to deal with the claimant. According to Lord Hoffmann in OBG this will be the case where the defendant's act makes it impossible to perform a contract, he threatens the third party if he performs a contract, or misleads the third party so that he acts otherwise than had he not been misled.

Finally, the genus tort requires, on the part of the defendant, an intention to cause loss to the claimant. This requires a distinction to be drawn between something that is part of the defendant's means and what is merely a consequence of using those means. If it transpires that the defendant intended to cause the loss suffered by the claimant, it will make no difference if the defendant would have preferred that the loss did not result. For example, in *Rookes v Barnard* [1964] AC 1129 the defendant would have preferred the claimant to resign from his position rather than be sacked, but as the defendant's actions were intended to produce the end result, they had committed the tort.

In *OBG* both Lord Hoffmann and Lord Nicholls opined that an outcome will be intended if the defendant knows that it is the 'other side of the same coin' as the loss complained of. Thus in *Douglas v Hello!* (No. 3) [2008] 1 AC 1 the claimants (the owners of *OK!* magazine) had exclusive rights to publish photographs of a celebrity wedding and the defendants were the publishers of a magazine (*Hello!*) that managed to procure and publish illicit photographs of the same wedding taken by a member of the paparazzi. The defendants argued that they did not intend to reduce the sales of *OK!*, but that they merely wished to protect the market position of *Hello!*. However, in the House of Lords, the two positions were regarded as opposite sides of the same coin, so that the defendants could be said to have intended the loss suffered.

There may also be cases in which the defendant intends one kind of loss, but actually causes a different type. In *OBG* Lord Hoffmann stated on more than one occasion that what the tort requires is an intention to cause loss, not the particular type of loss suffered by the claimant.

(3) Inducement to breach of contract

Question 3

'While the tort of inducement to breach of contract may have started its life in the form of an action for enticing the services of the employee of another, it is better now to regard the tort as one concerned with contractual relations of any kind.'
  Discuss.

Commentary

This question is concerned with the scope of the tort of inducement to breach of contract and how its use has spread beyond interference with employment relations into other areas. It is a tort, the existence of which has been criticized on the ground that if there is a breach of contract, the claimant will have an action against the contract breaker in respect of his breach; so why should the claimant also have a 'windfall' action against the defendant for inducing that breach of contract in the first place?

Answer plan

- The origins of the tort in the field of employment contracts.
- Consideration of the elements of the tort including the meaning of inducement.
- The necessary state of mind required on the part of the defendant.
- Defences to liability.
- A critical evalualtion of the purposes served by the tort.

Suggested answer

If the defendant intentionally and without lawful justification induces or procures a person to breach a contract he has made with the claimant, the latter may recover damages in respect of the inducement, provided he, the claimant, has suffered actionable damage. For these purposes, it is not necessary that any unlawful means were used in achieving the breach of contract, indicating that the tort does not fit within the 'genus' tort of unlawful interference with trade. 'Inducement' should not be taken to include cases in which the defendant makes it impossible for the third party to perform the contract as in such cases, the third party may have good reason not to perform and, therefore, not be in breach of contract (*OBG Ltd v Allan* [2008] 1 AC 1).

The origins of the tort lie in actions flowing from the inducement of an employee to leave the services of his employer. In *Lumley v Gye* (1853) 2 E & B 216, it was held that for the defendant to be liable, he must maliciously induce a person to break a fixed-term contract for the provision of exclusive personal services consisting of either a single act or a course of dealing. However, since that time, it has become apparent that other contractual relations may fall within the scope of the tort.

The key elements of the tort are that, first, there is a contract between the claimant and the third party (T); secondly, that the defendant induced T to breach that contract; thirdly, that the defendant had the necessary state of mind and, fourthly, that the defendant had no justification for the way in which he acted.

In order to have the required state of mind, the defendant must know that he is inducing a breach of contract (*OBG Ltd v Allan* [2008] 1 AC 1 [39] *per* Lord Hoffmann). Thus if the defendant genuinely believes that what he has procured will not amount to a breach of contract, even if he is mistaken, there will be no tort. In *Mainstream Properties Ltd v Young* [2008] 1 AC 1 two employees of the claimant incorrectly told the defendant that they were in a position to buy a plot of development land. However, if the employees went ahead with this arrangement it would amount to a breach of the employees' contracts with the claimant. The question arose whether the defendant knew that he was procuring a breach of contract if he went ahead. The House of Lords held that although the two employees would be liable for their breaches of contract, it could not be said that the defendant had the required knowledge to commit the tort of inducement to breach of contract. What was important was that he genuinely believed that the two employees of the claimant were entitled to go ahead with the proposed venture (see also *Meretz Investments NV v ACP Ltd* [2007] EWCA Civ 1303). In contrast, if the defendant has suspicions that acting in a particular way may induce a breach of contract, but he deliberately does nothing to confirm or deny those suspicions, he will be taken to be aware that his actions may induce a breach of contract. As Lord Hoffmann observes in *OBG* there is a difference between honest belief that stems from gross negligence and a conscious decision not to confirm a suspicion (*OBG Ltd v Allan* [2008] 1 AC 1 [40]–[41]).

In addition to the required knowledge of inducement, the defendant must also intend to induce the breach. Accordingly, if the breach of contract was merely a consequence of the defendant's actions, not being something he was seeking to achieve, he will not have committed the tort.

Following the decision in *OBG Ltd v Allan* it is now a requirement of this tort that there is an actionable breach of contract, as the House of Lords regarded the tort of inducement to breach of contract as a form of secondary liability ([2008] 1 AC 1 at [44] *per* Lord Hoffmann). This in turn will require the third party also to be liable for breach of contract. This, accordingly, requires a distinction to be drawn between actions that do amount to a breach of contract and those that do not.

It follows that if the defendant persuades the third party to lawfully terminate a contract with the claimant, no tort will be committed. This is consistent with the earlier decision in *Allen v Flood* [1898] AC 1 in which it was held that no tort was committed where the defendant persuaded the third party not to enter into a contract with the claimant in the first place. As there was no contract to breach, the defendant could not have committed the tort.

Similar reasoning will also apply where the defendant persuades the third party to rescind a voidable contract. This tends to confirm the correctness of pre-*OBG* case law that assumes no tort is committed where a person exercises such a right (see *Greig v Insole* [1978] 1 WLR 302; *Smith v Morrison* [1974] 1 WLR 659).

The final element of the tort is that the defendant should have no justification for acting in the way he did. It should be emphasized that the focus here is upon the defendant's action, not whether the third party had any justification for doing as he did. There may be circumstances in which the defendant is legally justified in acting in the way in which he did. For example in *Edwin Hill v First National* [1989] 1 WLR 225 the defendant had lent money to a property developer to assist in the purchase of Wellington House. Subsequently, it became apparent that the developer was having difficulty repaying the loan. The defendant could have forced the sale of Wellington House, but chose to continue to finance the development provided the developer broke his contract with the firm of architects he had engaged. It was held that as the defendants had a superior right to force the sale of the property, it could be said that the defendants had acted reasonably in seeking to protect its right to repayment of the money lent to the developer.

In some instances, the defendant may be able to argue that he was morally justified in inducing a breach of contract, although the circumstances in which this is likely to be a defence are probably very limited. Thus it has been held that merely having good motives is not the same as moral justification (see *South Wales Miners' Federation v Glamorgan Coal Co Ltd* [1905] AC 239 at 252 *per* Lord James). However, if an employer is paying such low wages to his employees that they are being forced into immorality and prostitution, a defendant may claim moral justification in seeking to persuade those employees to breach their contract (*Brimelow v Casson* [1924] 1 Ch 302).

There are criticisms of the existence of this tort as it appears to provide the claimant with an additional 'windfall' action against the defendant when he already has an action for breach of contract against the contract breaker. However, there may be some justification for the existence of the action where it is unlikely that the contract breaker will be able to pay for the losses occasioned by the breach of contract. Moreover, in some of the trades union cases, such as *South Wales Miners' Federation v Glamorgan Coal Co Ltd* [1905] AC 239 the employers probably would not have wanted to sue their workforce the day it returned to work following a strike, but the trade union made an alternative and perhaps more palatable defendant.

The existence of the tort can also be criticized on the ground that it promotes economic inefficiency by providing an additional incentive not to break a contract. In some instances a breach of contract may be economically efficient where it is known that if the contract is broken, another potential contracting party may produce a more efficient end product than the broken contract actually envisaged.

Further reading

Arden, Dame M., 'Economic Torts in the Twenty-first Century' (2006) 40 The Law Teacher 1.

Bagshaw, R., 'Can the Economic Torts be Unified?' (1998) 18 OJLS 729.

Carty, H., 'Intentional Violation of Economic Interests: The Limits of Common Law Liability' (1988) 104 LQR 250.

McBride, N., and Bagshaw, R., *Tort Law*, 3rd edn (Harlow: Pearson/Longman, 2008), chs 16, 17, 20–22.

14

General defences

Introduction

This chapter is concerned with the general defences available to a defendant who is faced with an action in tort. While a number of torts carry with them a range of specific defences, there are defences which apply across the whole range of tortious liability. In particular, this chapter considers the application of the defences of contributory negligence, *volenti non fit injuria* (otherwise known as the defence of consent or, in the context of negligence, voluntary assumption of risk) and the defence of illegality encapsulated in the latin maxim *ex turpi causa non oritur actio* (a man cannot benefit from his own misdeeds). This last defence is most closely linked to public policy.

The first of the questions that follow considers the limitations placed on the scope of the defence of contributory negligence by the definition of fault in **s. 4 of the Law Reform (Contributory Negligence) Act 1945**. In particular, it examines the extent to which contributory negligence can be used as a defence in an action for breach of contract in the light of the development of the notion of concurrent contractual and tortious liability, and whether there is any form of tortious liability in respect of which the defence is not available.

Question 2 considers the confused state of the defence of *volenti non fit injuria* and considers what are its true requirements and whether the defence serves any useful purpose in the light of the other available defences which may adequately explain the claimant's lack of complete success.

The last of the questions in this chapter continues on similar lines and is a problem question which illustrates the extent of overlap between the defences of contributory negligence, *volenti* and public policy.

Question 1

How far is the application of the Law Reform (Contributory Negligence) Act 1945 s. 1(1) affected by the definition of the term 'fault' in s. 4 of the same Act?

Commentary

This question requires a consideration of the meaning of fault as used in the **Law Reform (Contributory Negligence) Act 1945 s. 4.** Since the term fault is applied both to defendant and claimant it is necessary to consider (a) what forms of conduct on the part of a defendant might trigger the potential applicability of the Act; and (b) whether the defence applies simply to careless conduct on the part of the claimant, or whether a deliberate act will similarly lead to a reduction in damages.

Answer plan

Does the defence apply to:

- A breach of contract.
- An intentional tort.
- A strict liability tort.

Additional consideration must be given to the availability of the defence of contributory negligence before the **1945 Act** was passed, since the effect of the language of **s. 4** is that regard must be had to two questions. The first of these is whether the defendant has acted in a manner that renders him personally responsible for the harm suffered by the claimant and the second is whether the partial blameworthiness of the claimant would have provided the defendant with a defence to liability at common law.

Suggested answer

The defence of contributory negligence applies where a person 'suffers damage partly as a result of his own fault and partly as a result of the fault of [the defendant]. In such a case, the claimant's damages 'shall be reduced to the extent that the court thinks is just and equitable, having regard to the claimant's share in the responsibility for the damage' (Law Reform (Contributory Negligence) Act 1945, s. 1(1)). For these purposes, fault is defined in s. 4 of the Act as 'negligence, breach of statutory duty or other act or omission which gives rise to a liability in tort or would, apart from this Act, give rise to the defence of contributory negligence'.

The word 'fault' in s. 4 is used in two contexts. First, the words negligence, breach of statutory duty or other act or omission that gives rise to a liability in tort refer to the fault of the defendant. Second, the fault of the claimant falls within the closing words of s. 4, which raise the question whether contributory negligence was an available defence at common law prior to the passing of the 1945 Act (see *Reeves v Metropolitan Police Commissioner* [2000] 1 AC 360, 382 *per* Lord Hope; *Standard Chartered Bank v Pakistan Shipping Corp* [2002] 3 WLR 1547, 1551 *per* Lord Hoffmann). In this context, the fault of the claimant is not restricted to instances of carelessness on his part and can comprise his deliberate actions. Thus in *Reeves v Metropolitan Police Commissioner* [2000] 1 AC 360, the estate of a sane police prisoner who knowingly and deliberately committed suicide while in custody lost 50 per cent of the damages that would, otherwise, have been awarded. However, it should be appreciated that the purpose of the 1945 Act is to relieve claimants whose actions would previously have failed due to the all or nothing nature of the common law defence. It was not intended to provide defendants with a windfall defence by reducing the liability of defendants in cases where damages would have been awarded prior to 1945 (*Standard Chartered Bank v Pakistan Shipping Corp* [2002] 3 WLR 1547, 1551–2 *per* Lord Hoffmann).

The principal issues associated with the definition of fault in s. 4 **of the** 1945 Act are threefold. First, is a breach of contract on the part of the defendant fault within the meaning of s. 4? Secondly, do all torts attract the defence, and thirdly, is the defence available under the 1945 Act where its availability was doubtful at common law?

The issue of contributory negligence as a defence in an action for breach of contract has been subjected to a wide-ranging review by the Law Commission (Law Comm No. 219, 1993) in which it was recommended that contributory negligence should be a defence in all actions for breach of contract, except those involving the breach of a strict contractual duty, such as a breach of the implied terms in the Sale of Goods Act 1979 relating to the quality and fitness of goods. But this is certainly not the present law.

The present state of the law is affected by the nature of the defendant's breach. It has been observed that there are three different types of breach of contract on the part of a defendant which may attract different responses to the availability of the defence of contributory negligence (*Forsikringsaktieselskapet Vesta v Butcher* [1986] 2 All ER 488, Hobhouse J). First, the defendant may be in breach of a strict contractual duty such as the implied statutory obligation in a sale of goods contract which requires the goods to be of satisfactory quality. In this case, it is clear that there is no fault on the part of the seller with the result that the defence of contributory negligence is not available (*Quinn v Burch Bros (Builders) Ltd* [1966] 2 QB 370; *Barclays Bank plc v Fairclough Building Ltd* [1995] 1 All ER 289).

The second type of breach of contract is one in which the loss is of a type not recoverable in the ordinary law of tort. This would include varieties of economic loss in respect of which no tortious duty of care is owed. If the wording of s. 4 is interpreted so that the word negligence is not qualified by the words 'which gives rise to liability in tort', a breach of such a contractual duty of care might be regarded as negligence in the wider sense (*De Meza & Stuart v Apple, Van Staten, Stena & Stone* [1974] 1 Lloyd's Rep 508). Conversely, the manner in which a contractual term is broken has been said to be immaterial (*Quinn v Burch Bros* (**above**)) with the result that the phrase 'other act or omission' should be taken to refer to potential tortious liability only (*AB Marintrans v Comet Shipping Co Ltd* [1985] 3 All ER 442).

The third relevant variety of contractual breach is one where liability sounds concurrently in contract and tort. Examples include contracts for the supply of services in which there is an implied term requiring the exercise of reasonable care and skill, and contracts entered into by an occupier of land who owes the common duty of care under the **Occupiers' Liability Act 1957**. In such cases, it is accepted, possibly controversially, that the defence of contributory negligence is available if there is fault on the part of both the claimant and the defendant (*Sayers v Harlow UDC* [1958] 1 WLR 623).

Even if it is the case that the fault of the defendant comprised in a breach of contract may, in some circumstances, give rise to the defence of contributory negligence, the definition of the claimant's fault may serve to deny the availability of the defence. The wording of s. 4 of the 1945 Act refers to an act or omission which would, apart from the Act, give rise to the defence of contributory negligence. This may mean that the claimant's conduct must be such as would have given rise to the defence at common law. If this is so, there is authority which suggests that the defence was not available in such circumstances (*Forsikringsaktieselskapet Vesta v Butcher* [1988] 2 All ER 43). An alternative view is that if the defendant is concurrently liable in tort and contract and the defence of contributory negligence would have been available at common law had the action been framed in tort, then the defence should be available if the claimant sues for a breach of contractual duty.

Where the action is framed solely in tort, the definition of fault in s. 4 may still give rise to problems since the claimant's conduct must be such that the defence would have been available apart from the Act. If this means that the defence must have been available at common law, it follows that the defence is inapplicable where the tort committed by the defendant is that of deceit, as deceit requires the defendant to have intentionally misled the claimant (*Redgrave v Hurd* (1881) 20 ChD 1; *Standard Chartered Bank v Pakistan National Shipping Corp* (No. 4) [2002] 3 WLR 1547). The policy justification for this rule is that the defendant should not be allowed to plead that the claimant's negligence reduces his liability in damages for what was a deliberate act of inducement (*Standard Chartered Bank v Pakistan National Shipping Corp (No. 4)* [2002] 3 WLR 1547 at 1553 *per* Lord Hoffmann). Moreover, in cases of deceit, the defendant has intended the claimant to rely on his statement, in which case it is not open to the defendant to argue that the claimant should have avoided his loss by taking more care not to be duped by the defendant (*Alliance & Leicester Building Society v Edgestop Ltd* [1994] 2 All ER 38; approved in *Standard Chartered Bank v Pakistan National Shipping Corp (No. 4)* [2002] 3 WLR 1547). The same reasoning should also mean that the defence is not available in respect of the torts of conspiracy and inducement to breach of contract.

Historically, the defence of contributory negligence did not apply to the tort of trespass to the person. However, in *Barnes v Nayer* (1986) *The Times*, 19 December it was said that there was no logical reason why the defence should not apply to cases of battery (see also *Watson v Chief Constable of the Royal Ulster Constabulary* (1987) 8 NIJB 34).

The question whether or not the defence of contributory negligence is available where the defendant is in breach of a duty of care arising out of the rule in *Hedley Byrne v Heller* raises difficult issues. It might be argued that, since under the rule in *Hedley Byrne* the claimant should have reasonably relied on the defendant's advice, the defence will be unnecessary since if the claimant has acted unreasonably in relying on the advice, the necessary ingredients of the tort will not be in place (see *Gran Gelato Ltd v Richcliff (Group) Ltd* [1992] 2 WLR 867; *JEB Fasteners Ltd v Marks, Bloom & Co* [1981] 3 All ER 289). Moreover, if the defendant has told the claimant that he should do X, it seems nonsensical that his damages should be reduced if he acts in accordance with that advice. In contrast, it was suggested in *Gran Gelato* that the defence might be relevant to an action under the Misrepresentation Act 1967, s. 2(1).

A second possibility is that the extent of the claimant's loss is exacerbated by his contributory negligence. In these circumstances, the defence of contributory negligence is applicable, but it must operate within the restriction on damages principle to be found in *South Australia Asset Management Corp v York Montague Ltd* [1997] AC 191 (SAAMCO principle) which drew a distinction between negligent advice and negligent supply of information. If advice is given in order to achieve a particular objective or to avoid particular harm then the claimant will be able to sue, but if information is supplied without that objective or that harm being the focus, the claimant will not be able to sue. The principle complicates matters in contributory negligence cases under the rule in *Hedley Byrne* as it may be necessary to determine what is the starting point for assessment before deducting an amount representing the claimant's contributory fault.

In *Platform Home Loans v Oyston Shipways Ltd* [2000] 2 AC 190 the claimants lent £1 million to H in the belief, induced by the defendants, that property put up as security was worth £1.5 million. H subsequently defaulted when the property was only worth £400,000 due to a slump in the property market, resulting in loss to the claimant of £600,000. Additionally the claimants were considered to be 20 per cent to blame for their loss as they had not checked whether H was a credit risk and that the £1 million loan was excessive. Under the SAAMCO principle the claimant was restricted to damages of £500,000 (being the sum of the overvaluation). This presents the problem of determining whether the claimant is entitled to recover £600,000 minus 20 per cent (£480,000) or £500,000 (the SAAMCO limit) minus 20 per cent (£400,000). The Court of Appeal had preferred the latter approach, but the House of Lords opted for the former, treating the SAAMCO principle as placing a cap on the damages payable.

In *Standard Chartered Bank v Pakistan National Shipping Corp (No. 4)* [2002] 3 WLR 1547, Lord Hoffmann held that while the defence of contributory negligence is not an available defence in an action for fraudulent misrepresentation, it was an open question whether it might be a defence where there was a non-fraudulent misrepresentation coupled with some negligent causative conduct on the part of the claimant (ibid. at 1553).

It is clear that the defence did not and does not apply where the defendant commits the tort of conversion or intentional trespass to goods (Torts (Interference with Goods) Act 1977, s. 11). Where negligence is an element in the tort committed by the defendant, the defence would have been available at common law. On this basis, the defence applies where the defendant commits a breach of statutory duty or the tort of nuisance.

Question 2

The confused state of the defence *volenti non fit injuria* is 'partly due to a considerable overlap with other conceptual techniques employed to limit or reduce a defendant's liability'.

(Jones, *Textbook on Torts*)

Discuss.

Commentary

This question requires an explanation of the main ingredients in the defence of *volenti non fit injuria,* and a consideration of its relationship with the other available defences and with duty of care.

Answer plan

- Voluntary choice.
- Agreement to accept the legal risk of harm.
- Knowledge of the existence, nature, and extent of the risk of harm.

Suggested answer

Roughly translated, *volenti non fit injuria* means, 'to one who is willing, no harm is done'. As such, it is a defence based on consent and where it operates, it serves to displace the duty which would otherwise be owed by the defendant. The principal ingredients of the defence are that the claimant must have made a voluntary choice amounting to something approaching an agreement to accept the legal risk of harm with full knowledge of the nature and extent of that risk.

The requirement of voluntary choice means that the claimant must be in a position to make a free choice and must be aware of the circumstances relevant to the exercise of that choice (*Bowater v Rowley Regis Corporation* [1944] KB 476). It follows from this that an employee is not *volens* to the risk of injury at work merely because he is aware of a dangerous practice (*Smith v Baker* [1891] AC 325) since there may be other reasons why he continues to work, such as economic compulsion. Moreover, as a matter of policy the courts may recognize that certain people such as rescuers act in a manner which exposes them to a risk of injury because of the dictates of some social or moral duty rather than because they have voluntarily assumed the risk of injury (*Haynes v Harwood* [1935] 1 KB 146). This approach may be seen both as a recognition of the reality of the situation, within which free will gives way to moral compulsion, and of the public interest in encouraging such altruism rather than deterring it by withdrawing the protection of the law.

Another situation in which voluntariness falls into question relates to suicides. The defence has been defeated in a number of so-called 'custody cases', in which a negligent failure on the part of the defendant has created an opportunity for suicide (*Kirkham v CC Greater Manchester Police* [1990] 3 All ER 246; *Reeves v Metropolitan Police Commissioner* [2000] 1 AC 360) both on grounds, in most cases, of impaired autonomy, and also on the policy ground that a duty to guard against potential suicide should not be negated by the act itself.

Similarly, in cases of suicide consequent on negligently caused physical injury (*Pigney v Pointers Transport Services Ltd* [1957] 2 All ER 807; *Corr v IBC Vehicles Ltd* [2008] 2 All ER 943) the courts have recognized that an impairment of autonomy may be such as to defeat *volenti*, even though the deceased had been able, in many ways, to function fairly normally.

It is said that the defence of *volenti* requires some degree of agreement. If the notion of agreement is taken in its contractual sense, a person can be said to agree to the presence of certain terms in a contract only if he has been made aware of those terms before the contract is made and agreement is reached. If one were to substitute the notion of legal risk of harm for 'the terms of the contract' this would seem to suggest that in order to be *volens* the claimant must be aware of the risk of harm and consent to run that risk before it arises. The analogy of contract works well in relation to the intentional torts, where consent on the part of the claimant may be express (as in the case, for example, of medical treatment) or implied from their conduct (as in the case of participants in contact sports). In other words, in contract or the intentional torts it would be clear to an observer precisely what had been consented to whereas it is in the very nature of negligence that the boundaries of the risk are uncertain. Given the very precise connotations of the word 'consent', it is therefore generally more appropriate in negligence to describe the defence in terms of 'voluntary assumption of risk'.

Despite the terminology, however, any defence which deprives the claimant of a remedy is a serious matter and the defendant is required to prove that the claimant's conduct amounts to a clear demonstration of their intention to waive any legal rights that may arise from the harm that is risked—in effect a kind of estoppel. This is often described in terms of an agreement, as for example in *Wooldridge v Sumner* [1963] 2 QB 43 in which it was said that *volenti* should not be available in the absence of express consent to the legal risk of harm (see also *Nettleship*, below). By contrast, there are cases in which it has been held that the defence is available in cases where the claimant merely encounters an existing danger (*Titchener v British Railways Board* [1983] 3 All ER 770). This trend is also borne out in a number of statutory provisions which allow a defence in the event of conscious acceptance of an existing risk of harm (Occupiers' Liability Act 1957, s. 2(5); Unfair Contract Terms Act 1977, s. 2(3)), but these may be better viewed as varieties of 'statutory *volenti*', and not necessarily reflecting the proper view of the common law defence.

If a claimant is to be met by the defence of *volenti* he must be aware of the nature and extent of the risk of harm, although this knowledge alone will be insufficient to establish the defence. Thus in *Nettleship v Weston* [1971] 2 QB 691, it was held that mere knowledge that a driver is inexperienced is not sufficient to raise the defence. In that case, Lord Denning said that, 'Knowledge of the risk of injury is not enough. Nor is a willingness to take the risk of injury. Nothing will suffice short of an agreement to waive any claim for negligence.' On the facts of that case, the claimant's enquiry about insurance cover was evidence of his knowledge (and, perhaps, acceptance) of risk, but equally of his intention to seek compensation should the risk materialize.

In reality, the word 'agreement', in its usual sense, is rarely applicable in negligence cases but may be inferred from the claimant's conduct, most often manifesting itself by their willing participation in some kind of risky joint venture (*ICI Ltd v Shatwell* [1965] AC 656). In *Dann v Hamilton* [1939] 1 KB 509, knowingly (and willingly) travelling in a car whose driver was intoxicated was not held to be sufficient for the defence of *volenti* as the range of possible outcomes was too wide for the claimant to be taken to have accepted all of them. Asquith J said that *volenti* should operate only in respect of a risk so glaringly obvious as 'intermeddling with an unexploded bomb'. By contrast, the claimant in *Morris v Murray* [1990]

3 All ER 801 was a passenger in a plane (a rather more glaringly obvious risk), and had actively participated in the venture, having spent the afternoon drinking with the pilot and assisted him in preparing the plane for take-off and so on.

One difficulty created by the defence of *volenti* is that it sometimes appears to have been applied in circumstances in which some other limiting device might have been more appropriate. This may well have been due, at least in the older (pre-Act) cases, to the fact that common law contributory negligence was a complete defence, so that little was to be gained by arguing the defences in the alternative. It must be appreciated that *volenti* is a defence which displaces the primary duty and that before it can be invoked, an actionable tort must have been committed. Thus, if a reduced standard of care is expected of the defendant, there may be no actionable tort and to use the language of *volenti* is misleading and unnecessary. A photographer at a show-jumping event who takes photographs from within the jumping arena is not truly *volens* to the risk of harm when he is struck by a horse, because it can hardly be said that he has consented to the risk that he might be injured (*Wooldridge v Sumner*). Instead, it is probably better to say that the event organizers owe a lesser duty of care to such people so that the standard of care is more easily satisfied.

This reduced standard of care reasoning also works in other contexts. Thus one explanation for the application of the defence *ex turpi causa non oritur actio* is that it is difficult or impossible to ascertain what standard of care is required of the defendant in the light of the claimant's own illegal or immoral conduct. In *Pitts v Hunt* [1990] 3 All ER 344, the claimant failed in an action for damages against the deceased's estate where he had encouraged the deceased in driving a motor cycle in a dangerous fashion. Although it could have been argued that the claimant had consented to the injuries he suffered (by his willing participation in a risky joint enterprise), the defence was specifically rendered ineffective by the Road Traffic Act 1972, s. 148(3) (now s. 149(3) of the 1988 Act) and an alternative argument was needed if his claim was to fail. The interpretation favoured by Balcombe LJ was that the claimant's involvement in the series of events which led up to the accident was such that it was impossible to say what level of care was required of the deceased, in which case one could not say that a duty was owed in such circumstances.

The defence of *volenti*, if it succeeds, is a complete defence and absolves the defendant from all liability. The possibility of a more equitable compromise is offered by the Law Reform (Contributory Negligence) Act 1945, which replaces the common law approach which viewed contributory negligence as a complete defence and instead confers on the courts a discretion to reduce damages to take into account the partial responsibility of the claimant in failing to take reasonable care for their own safety. A good example of this approach in operation is in relation to the willing passengers of drunken drivers, where it seems that the normal judicial response will be to treat the claimant as merely contributorily negligent

(*Owens v Brimmell* [1977] QB 859—20 per cent reduction; see also *Donelan v Donelan and General Accident Fire & Life Insurance* [1993] PIQR P205—75 per cent reduction). It is suggested that the latter approach is legally correct since if *volenti* is properly understood, the claimant must assent to the legal risk that the defendant's actions will cause him harm but that he waives his right to sue for damages and that only in extreme cases such as *Morris v Murray* [1990] 3 All ER 801 should the claimant be denied damages altogether. Moreover, where the denial of liability is considered necessary, in most cases it is surely public policy that justifies the failure of the claimant's action, rather than the fact that the claimant has assented to the risk of injury since case law seems to indicate a general unwillingness on the part of the courts to see a negligent defendant's liability altogether extinguished.

Question 3

Vanya and Tomas, two students, having completed their final examinations, decide to spend a night out at the Mucky Duck, a public house. Vanya meets Tomas at the Mucky Duck. At the end of the evening, Tomas offers Vanya a lift home at a time when both of them are extremely drunk. Tomas drives his car down the middle of the road, occasionally swerving to frighten other road users. Vanya enthusiastically encourages Tomas in this venture.

Tomas drives through a red traffic light at speed and collides with a car driven by Gary. Gary who is not wearing a seatbelt is crushed behind the steering wheel of his car. Vanya is also seriously injured in the collision.

When taken to hospital, Gary refuses a blood transfusion on religious grounds. Because of this refusal and the seriousness of his injuries, Gary's arm has to be amputated.

Advise Tomas of his potential liability in tort.

Commentary

This question concerns liability for negligently caused personal injury, the issues of causation and contributory negligence and the availability of the general defences in an action for negligence.

Answer plan

- Whether and on what conditions the defence of *volenti non fit injuria* applies.
- Whether intoxicated driver cases are generally better dealt with under rules on contributory negligence.

- What principles apply to the issues of foresight of harm, causation and apportionment under the **Law Reform (Contributory Negligence) Act 1945**.

- The scope and application of the so-called illegality defence, *ex turpi causa non oritur actio*.

Suggested answer

There is no doubt that, as a road user, Tomas, in normal circumstances, would owe a duty of care to Vanya, since any person who uses the road owes a duty of care to other road users. Moreover, the manner in which Tomas drives also suggests that he has failed to exercise reasonable care since he has not reached the standard ordinarily expected of a reasonably competent driver (*Nettleship v Weston* [1971] 2 QB 691). However, Vanya's own involvement in the events of the evening may allow Tomas to plead one of a number of possible defences which may serve to reduce or negative his potential liability.

Tomas might argue that the defence of *volenti non fit injuria* applies. This defence requires a tort to have been committed, and where it operates, it serves to displace any duty which otherwise would have existed. What seems to be required is that the claimant should have assented to the legal risk of injury created by the defendant's negligence. Some cases go so far as to say that the claimant should have expressly or impliedly agree to waive any claim against the defendant before any risk had arisen (*Nettleship v Weston*). Conversely, other cases take the view that it is sufficient that the claimant encounters a known and existing danger created by the defendant (*Titchener v British Railways Board* [1983] 3 All ER 770). In a case such as the present, it may be difficult to find an express agreement to run the legal risk since at the time the lift is offered to Vanya, she is extremely drunk and may not be in a state to be able to give a valid consent. However, there are instances in which the courts have been prepared to find an implied agreement from the parties' conduct that the defendant will not be liable for future negligent conduct which results in injury to the claimant. Most frequently, this type of case has involved some sort of joint enterprise in which the defendant and claimant operated as equal partners. In *Dann v Hamilton*, for example, knowledge and apparent acceptance of the range of risks inherent in travelling with a drunk driver in a car was held to be insufficient to support a defence of *volenti*, though Asquith J said that similar circumstances might suffice provided the risk was so glaringly obvious as to be the equivalent of 'intermeddling with an unexploded bomb'. That test was met in *Morris v Murray* [1990] 3 All ER 801, in which the vehicle employed in the drunken escapade was an aircraft and the claimant had participated fully in the events leading to the crash.

A further difficulty is that the claimant must have subjective knowledge of both the existence of the risk and its nature and extent (*Smith v Austins Lifts Ltd*

[1959] 1 WLR 100). This might suggest that a passenger who is intoxicated does not have the necessary knowledge. In *Morris v Murray* the claimant was drunk, but not so drunk that he did not realize what he was doing, so that the defence applied. It was accepted by the Court of Appeal that the question was whether the claimant was so drunk as not to realize what he was doing, which produces the paradox that a person may be better off if he is extremely drunk rather than just a little! Although this may be so, in *Insurance Commissioner v Joyce* (1948) 77 CLR 39, an Australian case cited with approval in *Owens v Brimmell* [1977] QB 859, Latham LJ neatly side-stepped the paradox, at least in relation to contributory negligence by noting that a mildly intoxicated passenger was partially at fault for travelling with a drunk driver, while a very intoxicated passenger was at fault for rendering himself incapable of making a sensible decision.

The question states that Vanya and Tomas are both extremely drunk, which might mean that Vanya is unable to give the necessary assent required for the purposes of the defence of *volenti*. In any event, Vanya is injured in a road traffic accident and, in this regard, the **Road Traffic Act 1988, s. 149** prevents reliance on the defence of *volenti* where the compulsory insurance provisions of that Act apply. Here Tomas is driving on a public highway so he is subject to the requirement of compulsory third party insurance and so there can be no reliance on the defence of volenti (*Pitts v Hunt* [1990] 3 All ER 344).

Intoxicated driver cases are generally better dealt with under rules on contributory negligence (*Owens v Brimmell*). If Vanya accepts a lift from a person who is incapable of driving safely, she appears not to have acted as a reasonably prudent person would.

In order to establish contributory negligence, Tomas must prove that Vanya has not taken reasonable care for her own safety. In this respect, there are two principal issues. First, it must be asked whether harm to the claimant was reasonably foreseeable. The test is objective so that even if Vanya is so drunk as to be incapable of making a rational judgment, this will not matter for the purposes of this defence (*Owens v Brimmell*).

While the claimant's conduct does not have to be the cause of the accident, it must be causally relevant to the harm suffered. It will be sufficient if the claimant places herself in a dangerous position which increases the chance that harm within the foreseeable range will be caused (*Jones v Livox Quarries Ltd* [1952] 2 QB 608).

Where the defence applies, the court must apportion damages to such extent as it thinks just and equitable, having regard to the claimant's share in the responsibility for the damage (**Law Reform (Contributory Negligence) Act 1945, s. 1(1)**). The key factors here are those of damage, causation, and blameworthiness. The language used by the **1945 Act** is said to be mandatory in that there must be an apportionment, which means that the court cannot hold the claimant wholly responsible for the damage (*Pitts v Hunt*).

However, there are instances in which the claimant's degree of blameworthiness is great, in which case a large percentage reduction may be justified. For example, in *Donelan v Donelan and General Accident Fire & Life Insurance Co Ltd* [1993] PIQR P205 a 75 per cent reduction was considered appropriate where the defendant drove the car at the claimant's insistence when the claimant knew that the defendant was inexperienced and drunk. Similarly, in *Barrett v Ministry of Defence* [1995] 3 All ER 87, the defendants were held liable for failing to take proper care of the deceased once he was highly intoxicated (though not for allowing him to become so in the first place) but damages were reduced by two-thirds under the Act, to take account of his own fault.

If the court wishes to bar Vanya's claim altogether, the most likely way of doing this is through an application of the 'illegality' defence, *ex turpi causa non oritur actio* ('bad people get less'—Weir, *Casebook on Tort*, 9th edn (London: Sweet & Maxwell, 2000). In negligence cases, the basis on which the defence works is that the claimant's 'illegal' involvement is such that the court may choose not to recognize the existence of a duty of care. For example, in *Ashton v Turner* [1981] QB 137, no duty of care was owed by the driver of a get-away car to his partner in crime. An alternative way of approaching the problem in negligence cases is to say that the claimant's action will fail where the illegal nature of the venture in which the parties are engaged is such that the court feels unable to set an appropriate standard of care (*Pitts v Hunt* [1990] 3 All ER 344). Thus in *Pitts*, the claimant was a pillion passenger on a motorcycle driven by the defendant, who was drunk. The vehicle was driven recklessly, but the claimant had encouraged him to drive in that fashion. The Court of Appeal held that the claimant's injuries arose directly out of the illegal venture and were not merely incidental. Accordingly, at least on one analysis, it was impossible to set an appropriate standard of care to be expected of the defendant. A majority in the Court of Appeal has recently followed a similar approach in *Vellino v Chief Constable of Greater Manchester* [2002] 3 All ER 78, in which the claimant was injured by jumping out of a high window in order to escape police custody. Alternatively, since it is not all illegal acts that trigger *ex turpi causa*, the court has to balance the adverse consequences of granting relief against the adverse consequences of refusing relief, which inevitably involves a value judgment as between the parties (*Tinsley v Milligan* [1992] Ch 310, *per* Nicholls LJ) and as to the degree of moral turpitude, or wickedness, that would be sufficient to affront the public conscience to such a degree as to deprive a claimant of the protection of the law.

On either test, it is arguable that Vanya's claim in respect of her injuries might be rejected on the basis of the illegality defence, following *Pitts v Hunt*.

Tomas clearly owes Gary a duty of care and his driving is such that there is probably a breach of that duty, but problems may arise in relation to an award of damages. First, in relation to the injuries suffered in the traffic accident, it should be noted that Gary is not wearing a seatbelt. This is a well-established example of contributory negligence since it involves a failure by Gary to take reasonable care for his own safety (*Froom v Butcher* [1976] QB 286). Moreover, the failure to wear the seatbelt is very likely to materially increase the risk of injury should there be a traffic accident, in which case it will be regarded as causally relevant to the harm suffered by the claimant (*Froom v Butcher*), except in circumstances where the nature of the accident, e.g. where a vehicle is crushed by a falling object, makes the role of a seatbelt irrelevant.

In determining how damages should be apportioned, the Court of Appeal has sought to lay down guidelines, since seatbelt cases are likely to be fairly common. In *Froom v Butcher*, it was held that if wearing a seatbelt would have prevented altogether the damage suffered, an appropriate reduction in damages would be 25 per cent. If the injury would have been less severe, the reduction should be 15 per cent, but if the injury would have been the same whether a belt was worn or not, there should be no reduction at all. The fact that this case was decided before the wearing of seatbelts was made compulsory will not matter, since the defence is based on a failure by the claimant to take proper care for his own safety and not simply a failure to abide by the law (*Capps v Miller* [1989] 2 All ER 333).

Gary is crushed behind the steering wheel. Whether he was wearing a seatbelt or not, this is a kind of injury likely to be suffered by the driver of a car hit, at speed, by another vehicle. This would seem to suggest a maximum reduction in damages of 15 per cent, but if it is shown that the extent of injury would have been the same whether a seatbelt was worn or not, then Gary's damages should not be reduced at all.

When Gary is taken to hospital, he refuses a blood transfusion, with the result that his arm has to be amputated. It must be decided whether the cause of the amputation is the seriousness of Gary's injuries resulting from the traffic accident or whether Gary's refusal to have a blood transfusion is a *novus actus interveniens*, such as to break the chain of causation between Tomas's negligence and the loss of Gary's arm.

An unlawful or unreasonable act of the claimant is capable of breaking the chain of causation (*McKew v Holland Hannen & Cubitts (Scotland) Ltd* [1969] 3 All ER 1621), but only in circumstances in which it would be fair to say that his act was such as to absolve the negligent defendant. Here, the emphasis is on whether the claimant has acted reasonably in the circumstances. It is less important to consider whether the claimant's act is foreseeable or not. In *Wieland v Cyril Lord Carpets Ltd* [1969] 3 All ER 1006, it was said to be foreseeable that an injury caused by the defendant's negligence may affect the claimant's ability to cope with the vicissitudes of life and thereby lead to (and be the legal cause of) another injury.

The difficulty which arises in this case is that Gary's refusal is based on religious grounds. This will face the court with the daunting prospect of deciding whether it is reasonable for a person to hold a particular belief! The likely approach in these circumstances is that Tomas will have to take Gary as he finds him and that Gary's refusal will not break the chain of causation. A similar approach has been taken in the criminal law, where a person has been found guilty of murder where his victim refused a blood transfusion on religious grounds (*R v Blaue* [1975] 3 All ER 446). The tort law equivalent of this approach is the 'egg-shell skull rule' under which unusual or unforeseeably extensive injury is not regarded as too remote where it results from some peculiarity of the claimant himself (*Smith v Leech Brain & Co* [1962] 2 QB 405), though a slightly different approach might be adopted by analogy with the case *Emeh v Kensington & Chelsea & Westminster AHA* [1985] QB 1012, in which the court rejected an argument that a woman's failure to terminate an unwanted pregnancy after the defendant's negligent treatment was a *novus actus*. Although partly underpinned by policy relating to the sanctity of life, this is a good example nonetheless of the courts' general unwillingness to disregard genuinely held moral or religious beliefs.

Further reading

Fulbrook, J., 'Alcohol and third parties – "dram shop liability" and beyond' [2007] JPIL 220.

Hudson, A. W., 'Contributory Negligence as a Defence to Battery' (1984) 4 *Legal Studies* 332.

Law Commission No. 219, *Contributory Negligence as a Defence to an Action for Breach of Contract* (1993).

O'Sullivan, J., 'Employer's Liability for Injured Employee's Suicide' (2008) 67(2), CLJ 241.

Spowart-Taylor, A., 'Contributory Negligence–A Defence to Breach of Contract' (1986) 49 MLR 102.

15

Remedies and limitation of actions

Introduction

This final chapter considers perhaps the most important issue as far as a tort claimant is concerned, namely what remedy is available in the event of a tort on the part of the defendant. The two major remedies in tort law are an award of damages and the grant of the equitable remedy of injunction. This chapter concentrates on the issue of damages, but questions concerning the rules which apply to injunctions can be found in Chapter 11 (Torts Relating to Land), where the injunction plays an important role in providing a remedy for continuing torts such as private nuisance.

As far as the remedy of damages is concerned, it is important to consider not just the issues raised in this chapter but also related issues such as the rules on causation and remoteness in negligence actions.

The three principal types of damage for which a remedy may be available include personal injury (which includes death and psychiatric harm), property damage and, in rare circumstances, economic loss. The primary purpose behind an award of damages is to compensate the claimant for the loss or damage actually suffered and not, generally, to punish or deter the defendant from his wrongdoing. The principle which lies behind an award of tort damages is, so far as money can do this, to return the claimant to the position he was in before the defendant's wrong was committed.

In personal injury actions, it is sometimes difficult to achieve this result, particularly where harm such as pain and suffering is concerned, since these heads of loss are difficult to quantify in monetary terms.

In property damage cases there is sometimes a problem in identifying the appropriate basis for assessment of damages. For example, it might be appropriate to give the cost of repair, whereas in other cases the fairer measure of damages may be based on the diminution in value of the damaged property.

As far as the issue of limitation of actions is concerned, Parliament has seen fit to impose a time limit on bringing an action. As a general rule, the claimant must issue his writ within six years of the date on which damage is caused. However, the matter of limitation of actions has been the subject of review by the Law Commission, *Limitation of Actions* (Law Com. No. 270, July 2001). If their proposals are the subject of legislation, the likely result will be a shortened limitation period of three years, based on the knowledge or constructive knowledge of the claimant that he has suffered actionable harm.

If implemented, the Law Commission proposals will remove the present difficulty that a claimant can suffer damage without being aware of it until many years later. In personal injury cases, this problem can be met through the exercise of judicial discretion to allow a claim to be commenced out of time. However, the same is not true in property damage cases, in which case the claimant may be time barred before he realizes that he has a cause of action.

Question 1

Hector has been warned by his doctor that he must not drive. Since his wife has been taken seriously ill, he decides to rush her to hospital by car rather than wait for an ambulance. Tamara, Hector's daughter has recently telephoned the police to inform them that Hector sometimes drives a car despite the fact that he has been advised not to, but the police have done nothing about this. On the way to the hospital, Hector collapses at the wheel, and the car swerves off the road. Dougal, who is painting a second-floor window, is injured when he jumps from his ladder in an attempt to get out of the way of the car. The car comes to a halt after demolishing part of a shop owned by Zebedee. Twenty minutes later while the police are attempting to remove the car, part of a wall collapses on Florence and Ermintrude, two spectators. Ermintrude, who has recently been divorced from her husband, Dylan, is crushed to death in the space of three minutes and Florence is so badly injured that she suffers from depression and commits suicide three months later. Florence's live-in lover, Brian, is distraught at the death of his partner. Ermintrude's ex-husband, Dylan seeks to recover damages in respect of Ermintrude's death, including damages for the pain and suffering endured by her before she died.

Advise Dougal, Zebedee, Brian, and Dylan.

Commentary

This question concerns the duty of care owed by a road user to other road users and the question whether there has been a breach of that duty. In relation to the remedy of damages, consideration has to be given to the effect of death on an award and how this affects dependants of the deceased and those representing the deceased's estate. In relation to pre-death injuries it is also necessary to consider the form of an award of damages for pain and suffering.

Answer plan

- Is there a breach of duty?
- How relevant is the dilemma which Dougal faces?
- Do the actions of the police amount to a *novus actus interveniens*?
- Who is a dependant and what damages may be recovered in respect of such dependency?
- How do dependency damages differ from 'survival' damages?
- Is suicide a *novus actus interveniens*?

Suggested answer

It is well established that all road users owe a duty of care to other road users (***Nettleship v Weston*** [1970] 2 QB 691). It follows that there is a potential duty to Dougal and Zebedee in respect of the harm both suffer. That harm is respectively, personal injury suffered by Dougal and property damage suffered by Zebedee, both of which appear to be foreseeable consequences of a road traffic accident.

Whether Hector is in breach of the duty of care he owes to Dougal and Zebedee requires consideration of the magnitude of risk, the seriousness of the harm suffered, the utility of the defendant's conduct and any precautions which might have been taken to guard against the risk. Since Hector has been warned by his doctor that he should not drive, it seems to follow that there is a substantial risk that he may be the cause of an accident in the event of his collapse while driving. The position would have been different had Hector been unaware of the medical condition that makes it unsafe for him to drive (see ***Mansfield v Weetabix Ltd*** [1998] 1 WLR 1263), but that is not the case. However, regard should be had to the reason why he chooses this course of action, namely to ensure that his wife gets to hospital as early as possible in the light of her illness. In ***Watt v Hertfordshire County Council*** [1954] 1 WLR 853 (see also *S (a child) v Keyse* [2001] EWCA Civ 715; [2001] All ER (D) 236 (May)) the defendants required the claimant, a fire-fighter employed by them, to take up a potentially dangerous position so that life-saving equipment could be transported to the scene of a road traffic accident which threatened the life of another person. It was held that the utility of the defendants' conduct in seeking to save human life was justified and that the risk of harm to the claimant was acceptable in the circumstances. Nevertheless, regard must still be had to the risk created, especially to other road users. Thus it can still be a breach of duty for the driver of an ambulance to ignore a red traffic light (see ***Griffin v Mersey Regional Ambulance*** [1998] PIQR P34). Hector has taken a risk by driving a car when advised not to do so, but he has done so in order to avert the risk of more serious harm to this wife. Conversely, the alternatives available to Hector also have to be considered. He could have waited for an ambulance to arrive or he could have ordered a taxi. Whether these alternatives are feasible depends on the seriousness of the risk to his wife's life, but it is generally accepted that the defendant must take only reasonable precautions to guard against the risk, not all possible precautions (*Latimer v AEC Ltd* [1953] AC 643).

In relation to Dougal, regard must be had to the 'dilemma principle' since he has taken the possibly foolish action of jumping from a ladder in the belief that he is about to be struck by an oncoming vehicle. In *Jones v Boyce* (1816) 1 Stark 493, the claimant jumped from a moving coach in the belief that it was about to overturn. In fact, the coach did not overturn, but the defendant was still fully liable for the harm suffered on the basis that his negligence had placed the claimant in a dilemma and that the claimant had acted reasonably in the circumstances. Applied to Dougal, if he reasonably believes that Hector's car is about to strike the ladder on which he is standing, it may be reasonable for him to jump, even though this may result in injury.

Whether Hector or the police are liable for the death of Ermintrude and the injuries to Florence will depend on whether the actions of the police amount to a *novus actus interveniens*. While there may be circumstances in which it has been held that for reasons of public policy the police should not be subject to a duty to take care in relation to the conduct of a criminal investigation (*Hill v Chief Constable of West Yorkshire* [1988] 2 All ER 238, it does not follow that the police cannot be liable for their negligence in the course of ordinary operations. Thus the police may be liable for harm caused by the negligent use of a CS gas canister (*Rigby v Chief Constable of Northamptonshire* [1985] 2 All ER 985) or where a traffic accident was caused by the negligence of a supervising police officer (*Knightley v Johns* [1982] 1 All ER 861).

Similarly, the immunity suggested by some cases may be displaced for reasons of public policy, such as the proper protection of the public. Thus in *Swinney v Chief Constable of Northumbria Police* [1996] 3 All ER 449, the claimant supplied the police with confidential information about a group of known violent criminals, who obtained the information by breaking into a police vehicle. As a result of this, the claimant was subjected to violence and consequently suffered psychiatric harm. Because of the special relationship which existed between the claimant and the police, which set him apart from the general public, a duty of care was owed. The facts indicate that the police failed to take action after Tamara informed them that Hector was still driving his car. However, the principle in *Swinney* appears to be one which is personal to the informant, and since Tamara is not injured because of the failure of the police to take action, it is unlikely that the principle established in *Hill*, that a duty is not owed to the general public, will be displaced.

Although it is Hector's negligent driving that has caused the car to collide with the wall of Zebedee's shop, it may be that the manner in which the police conduct themselves amounts to a break in the chain of causation. Generally, if a third party is faced with a dilemma created by the defendant's negligence, a reasonable response by a third party will not break the chain of causation. This is so even where there has been time for reflection before the third party acts (*The Oropesa* [1943] P 32). Where the act of the third party is negligent, it is possible that it may amount to a *novus actus interveniens*, especially if it is characterized as a reckless act (*Wright v Lodge* [1993] 4 All ER 299), although no clear answer can be given. In *Knightley v Johns* [1982] 1 All ER 851, it was held that it should be asked whether the whole sequence of events is a natural or probable consequence of the defendant's negligence and whether it was more than just foreseeable as a mere possibility. In order to decide the question, it might sometimes be helpful to consider whether the third party's positive act is deliberate or whether he is guilty of no more than an omission or an innocent mistake or miscalculation. Thus in *Knightley* the defendant had caused a traffic accident at the exit to a tunnel. A supervising police officer did not immediately close the tunnel, as he should have done. The claimant was ordered to ride against the flow of traffic in order to close the tunnel and was struck by an oncoming vehicle. It was held that the defendant who caused the first accident was not liable for the injuries caused to the claimant since the collision with the driver coming in the opposite direction (the third defendant) was too remote a consequence of the first defendant's negligence, especially in the light of the numerous errors made by the supervising police officer (the second defendant). Accordingly the second and third defendants were liable.

In the case of the accident caused by Hector, there does not appear to be any evidence of a negligent act on the part of the police, and the initial damage to the wall has resulted from Hector's driving. This might seem to suggest that the actions of the police do not amount to a *novus actus interveniens* and that Hector will also be responsible for the death of Ermintrude and the injuries to Florence.

There are likely to be two actions for damages, one will be brought by Florence's lover, Brian, and another is likely to be brought by Dylan, Ermintrude's former husband. Both Dylan and Brian may have an action for dependency damages under the provisions of the **Fatal Accidents Act 1976**, despite the fact that Dylan is no longer married to Ermintrude. This is because the list of dependants set out in the **Fatal Accidents Act 1976, s. 1** includes spouses and former spouses, including those who have remarried (*Shepherd v Post Office* (1995), *The Times*, 15 June). Brian, as a cohabitee, will also be regarded as a dependant if he has lived with Florence for at least two years, although it is possible for a person to live in more than one household at the same time (*Pounder v London Underground Ltd* [1995] PIQR P217).

This is a new action which arises where death is caused by a wrongful act or default which is such as would have entitled the person injured to maintain an action and recover damages in respect of it. The person who would have been liable, had death not ensued, will be liable to an action for damages, notwithstanding the death of the person injured (**Fatal Accidents Act 1976, s. 1(1)**). The relatives covered by the action include spouses and persons who have lived with the deceased as husband or wife for a period of two years prior to the date of death (**Fatal Accidents Act 1976, s. 1(2)**), although persons falling into the latter category will be unable to recover set bereavement damages of £10,000, (amount increased by the Damages for Bereavement (Variation of Sum) (England & Wales) Order 2002, SI 2002/644) in the same way as a spouse may (s. 1A(2)). The action for dependency damages is brought by the executor or administrator of the deceased's estate on behalf of the dependant, or by the dependant if no action has been commenced within six months of the death. The action may only be brought if the deceased could have sued in his own right had he only been injured. The idea of damages under the Fatal Accidents Act 1976 is to give the dependant sufficient to represent the loss of a breadwinner. Accordingly, assessment of damages will start with a quantification of the wages the deceased was earning, subject to a deduction in respect of the deceased's own living expenses. This will produce a figure representing the deceased's earning capacity which is then subjected to a multiplier running from the date of death and representing the probable length of the deceased's earning period. The award is sub-divided into two parts covering respectively, the period from death to the date of trial, and from the date of trial on into the future (see *Cookson v Knowles* [1979] AC 556). In order to be considered for dependency damages, the dependant must prove financial loss in consequence of the death, and in the case of Ermintrude, this will include the value of any domestic services she might have provided as a wife.

Brian and Dylan may also have a 'survival' action under the Law Reform (Miscellaneous) Provisions Act 1934 if they represent the estate of the deceased person. This is not a new action in favour of the survivor, but represents the pecuniary and non-pecuniary loss suffered by the deceased in consequence of the defendant's tortious act and is therefore dependent on whether the deceased could have maintained an action against the defendant had he survived. In order to bring an action under the 1934 Act, it is necessary that both Brian and Dylan represent the estate of the deceased, which will depend on the terms of the will of the deceased or relevant rules on intestacy. It may be that as an ex-husband, Dylan is not included in Ermintrude's estate, but this is not clear from the language of the question.

In respect of actions for damages for pain and suffering, it appears that if the period between the defendant's initial tort and the subsequent death is so short as to be regarded as part of the death itself, no award in respect of pain and suffering may be made (*Hicks v Chief Constable of South Yorkshire Police* [1992] 2 All ER 65). This may suggest that the period of three minutes between the collapse of the wall whilst the police are attempting to remove Hector's car from Zebedee's shop and Ermintrude's death is too short to allow an award of damages for pain and suffering.

Assuming Brian represents Florence's estate, it will have to be shown that had Florence lived she could have maintained an action against Hector. A difficulty in this regard is that, in a state of depression, she commits suicide three months after the date of the accident caused by Hector's negligence. It must be decided if Florence's suicide amounts to a break in the chain of causation, for if this is the case, Florence will have no claim against Hector, which will, in turn, prevent Brian from maintaining an action under the 1934 Act. There is authority in the decision in *Pigney v Pointer's Transport Services Ltd* [1957] 1 WLR 1121 which suggests that insane suicide does not amount to a *novus actus interveniens* so that an action under the 1934 Act by a surviving spouse will not be prejudiced. However, this was a case based on a test of remoteness of damage which rendered the defendant liable for all direct loss flowing from his negligence. Moreover, at the time, suicide was a criminal offence, which would have entitled an insurer to refuse to pay out under the terms of a life assurance policy. Since that time, the House of Lords has signalled that public policy should not be a relevant factor in determining whether the estate of a person who has committed suicide should be denied a remedy (see *Reeves v Commissioner of Police for the Metropolis* [2000] 1 AC 360). Instead the appropriate test to apply is whether the suicide was caused by the breach of duty using the 'but for' test. In *Reeves*, however, the defendants were under a duty to prevent the deceased from committing suicide, as he was in police custody. Here Florence's state of depression is traceable to the injuries she has suffered in the accident caused by Hector's careless driving.

In *Corr v IBC Vehicles Ltd* [2008] UKHL 13, [2008] 2 WLR 499 it was held that it was unnecessary for the claimant to show that it was reasonably foreseeable that the defendants' negligence would result in her husband committing suicide. Instead all that was required was that she should show that if her husband suffered an injury at work those injuries might lead to depression. As the depression suffered by the claimant's husband was a logical consequence of the defendants' negligence, there was no break in the chain of causation. The House of Lords appear not to have addressed the question whether the act of suicide was too remote a consequence of the defendants' negligence, but through their silence they appear to have decided that the act of taking ones life was not too remote a consequence.

In the case of Florence's death, it will be necessary to determine whether sight of the accident caused by Hector's negligence is what has brought on the depressive state. If this is the case, the suicide will not be a *novus actus interveniens* and the death will not be regarded as damage that is too remote.

In *Reeves* the claimant's damages were reduced by 50 per cent for contributory negligence so as to take account of the fact that the deceased had committed suicide while of sound mind. Surprisingly in *Corr* Lords Bingham and Walker thought that no such deduction should be made, despite what had been decided in *Reeves*, since, on the facts, Mr Corr was not really to blame for his own death. However, a majority of the House of Lords did agree that, in principle, it would be right to reduce damages payable to the next of kin under the Fatal Accidents Act 1976 where the person committing suicide bears some responsibility for his own death.

Accordingly, the chain of causation emanating from Hector's breach of duty may not have been broken, thereby leaving Brian in a position to be able to maintain an action for damages, but those damages might be reduced to take into account the fact of suicide.

Question 2

Donald, aged 35, is badly injured in a road traffic accident caused by the admitted negligence of Charles. Donald's car, valued at £10,000, is written off. The extent of his injuries is such that prior to the date of trial Donald incurs private medical expenses of £12,500, but has also spent a number of weeks in a NHS Trust hospital at public expense, with the result that the household costs incurred by Rebecca, Donald's wife, are less than usual for part of the time, but greater than usual once Donald returns home for convalescence. During the period of hospitalization and medical treatment, Donald is unable to work as a research chemist at a salary of £25,000 per annum.

The extent of Donald's injuries is such that for the future he will be unable to continue in his employment for a further three years after trial and will be unable to continue his pastime as an amateur cricketer. Moreover, there is a distinct prospect that his injuries may worsen in years to come, although this is by no means certain. Donald took out a personal accident insurance plan a number of years ago, which will pay substantial benefits following the accident. Moreover, Donald has also received social security benefits and will continue to do so after the date of trial.

Advise Donald.

Commentary

This question is concerned mainly with personal injury damages and the different heads of damage under which an award may be made. A distinction must be drawn between pre-trial expenditure and future loss. Account must also be taken of any deductions which should be made from an award of damages so as to ensure that the claimant is not over-compensated. There is also a minor issue in relation to damages for harm to property.

Answer plan

- What pre-trial expenditure is recoverable and what off-sets must be made?
- How is loss of future earnings to be quantified?
- Instead of a lump sum award, is there the possibility of an award of provisional damages?
- What deductions from the award are to be made in respect of social security and insurance payments?
- How are damages for pain and suffering and loss of amenity to be assessed?
- Is the appropriate basis for damages in respect of the car the cost of repair or the diminished value of the vehicle?

Suggested answer

The question states that Charles admits negligence, therefore there is no need to consider whether a duty of care is owed or whether there is a breach of duty on Charles's part.

In an action for damages for personal injury, there are two distinct heads of damage. The first is expenditure incurred as a result of the tort of the defendant and the second is loss of earnings.

So far as pre-trial expenditure is concerned, any expenditure actually and reasonably incurred is recoverable against the defendant. This will include medical expenses such as the £12,500 private medical expenditure incurred by Donald, but there is a necessary deduction to be made in respect of any savings made through maintenance at public expense in a NHS Trust hospital. Any savings made must be offset against any loss of income (**Administration of Justice Act 1982, s. 5**). Moreover, the household expenditure incurred by Rebecca is reduced compared with what is the norm. Thus it will be appropriate to make a deduction in respect of expenditure which would have been incurred in maintaining Donald (*Harris v Empress Motors Ltd* [1984] 1 WLR 212). However, it is also the case that after Donald returns home for convalescence, household expenses increase, in which case, this increase may be taken into account. At one stage it was thought that the existence of a mere moral obligation to maintain the injured person was not sufficient to establish a pecuniary claim, but this is no longer the case (*Hunt v Severs* [1994] 2 All ER 385). Thus if Rebecca has to give up work in order to tend to Donald, an award may be made in respect of this expense, but Donald will hold such an amount in trust for Rebecca as a provider of the services.

Donald suffers loss of earnings as a result of his hospitalization. It is well established that a claimant may recover the amount he would have earned between the date of the tort and the date of trial, subject to deductions in respect of taxation liabilities (*British Transport Commission v Gourley* [1956] AC 185).

Donald is entitled to damages which take into account his future pecuniary loss, which for the most part will consist of his lost future income. The way in which this is identified is by calculating the claimant's net annual loss which is then multiplied by a figure which, as far as possible and if properly invested, will produce an overall amount equivalent to the lost income. This can be a substantial amount if the claimant, like Donald, is well-educated and has very good job prospects (see *Dixon v John Were Ltd* [2004] EWHC 2273). Furthermore, if Donald is handicapped in the labour market, an award can be made even though it may be a speculative process (see *Doyle v Wallace* [1998] PIQR P146). Taking account of investment is an important factor since the court must have regard for the fact that the damages are paid in the form of a lump sum. Accordingly the multiplier used will not equate exactly with the number of lost working years. The fact that Donald's injuries may worsen in years to come may affect his earning capacity in the future. This is a factor which may be considered when assessing damages if it is likely to serve as a handicap in the job-market (*Moeliker v A. Reyrolle & Co* [1977] 1 WLR 132). However, the rule seems to be confined to complete loss of job prospects, whereas Donald will be unable to work for three years, but may be able to work thereafter. Nonetheless a person who is out of work for three years may find it difficult to find replacement employment after that period.

A well-established problem with the lump sum system of paying damages is that it is not easy to deal with future uncertainties. It is now possible under the **Senior Courts Act 1982, s. 32A** for the court to award provisional damages, so that the claimant may return at a later stage to recover an additional payment if the circumstances warrant this. For the court to be able to make such an award, there must be a chance that at some definite or indefinite time in the future, the injured person will develop some serious disease or suffer some serious deterioration. It has been held that his means more than just some fanciful chance and must be capable of measurement (*Willson v Ministry of Defence* [1991] 1 All ER 638). The availability of this option is now a factor the courts will take into account in determining whether they should refuse to order a lump-sum payment, particularly if the degree of likely deterioration might result in death (*Molinari v Ministry of Defence* [1994] PIQR Q33).

The fact that there is no certainty that Donald's injuries will worsen may be an indication that the court will feel unable to make an award of provisional damages under s. 32A. Moreover, it is clear that continuing deterioration, such as the onset of osteo-arthritis after injuries consisting of broken limbs, will not fall within the ambit of s. 32A (*Willson v Ministry of Defence*).

When an award of damages is made in respect of pecuniary loss, the court must take account of any relevant offsets, so that the award does not over-compensate the claimant. As with liability to taxation, the court will also have to have regard to sources of financial support other than the award of damages itself. The question states that Donald has received and will continue to receive social security benefits and that he is due to receive a payment under a personal accident insurance plan. The policy moneys under the personal accident insurance plan will not be deducted from the award of damages (*Bradburn v Great Western Railway* (1874) LR 10 Ex 1), since the claimant has paid for the benefit and it would discourage people from making such provision were there to be a deduction from any subsequent award of damages.

The rule on social security benefits is different since tort damages and these state benefits are designed to compensate the same losses. Not to deduct such payments would involve over-compensation. The **Social Security (Recovery of Benefits) Act 1997** now provides that when assessing damages the amount of any relevant benefit paid or likely to be paid to or for the claimant is to be disregarded. Relevant benefits include attendance allowance, disablement benefit or pension, family credit, income support, incapacity benefit, mobility allowance, reduced earnings allowance, retirement allowance, severe disablement allowance, statutory sick pay, disability living allowance, disability working allowance, and unemployment benefit. The compensator is not permitted to pay any compensation until the Department of Social Security has issued a certificate detailing the total amount of benefit. Once this has been issued, the amount certified must be deducted in respect of a period of five years following the date of the accident and is payable to the Secretary of State. The deduction is made from the whole of the award which includes any element in respect of non-pecuniary loss. This remains the case even though social security benefits do not compensate for non-pecuniary losses such as pain and suffering.

In addition to pecuniary losses, an award of damages may also cover less easily quantifiable losses such as pain and suffering and loss of amenity. Provided it can be assumed that the claimant has endured pain, an award of damages for pain and suffering may be made. The one instance in which such an award is unlikely is where the claimant is and will remain permanently unconscious (*H. West & Son Ltd v Shephard* [1964] AC 326). Here there is nothing to suggest that Donald is comatose, in which case the award of damages may include an element in respect of pain and suffering. Donald is unable to continue his pastime as an amateur cricketer. This is a factor which may be reflected in any award of damages. Thus if the claimant loses the joy of life and cannot ride a bicycle or kick a football, he is entitled to damages representing his loss of enjoyment of life (*Heaps v Perrite Ltd* [1937] 2 All ER 60). It is important that Donald has played cricket before the date of the accident, since it is not open to a previously healthy person who has not engaged in a particular pastime to say that he has been prevented from pursuing that activity.

Finally, Donald's car is damaged in the accident caused by Charles's negligence. The question states that it has been written off and that it is valued at £10,000. Where a vehicle has been written off, it is considered uneconomic to repair it and the court is likely to treat this as a case of constructive total loss (*Darbishire v Warran* [1963] 1 WLR 1067). In the circumstances there is said to be no difference between the cost of repair and the reduction in market value of the damaged chattel. It follows that an award of damages will represent the replacement value of the damaged article, in Donald's case, £10,000.

Question 3

Tom through his admitted negligent driving damages a vintage Bentley car owned by Algernon. The car is so badly damaged that in normal circumstances it would be written off by an insurance company, but Algernon is so attached to it that he wants to have it repaired. Algernon has a badly paid job and has maintenance commitments to the children of his first marriage.

As a result of his financial position he cannot immediately afford to arrange for the necessary repairs, with the result that he waits for six months before doing anything. In the meantime Algernon takes advantage of a credit hire arrangement in order to be able to obtain a replacement vehicle while the Bentley is off the road. For this arrangement Algernon is not required to make any payment 'up-front', but the credit hire company will present an account when Algernon's tort action against Tom is concluded. The charge for this credit facility and the replacement car is the equivalent of paying £50 per day for a hire car, when the normal daily charge for an equivalent hire car would be £33.

Subsequently Algernon discovers that the specialist in Bentley cars who is to carry out the necessary work has raised the cost of the work by £1,250 to a total charge of £4,500. This amount is £500 more than a general car repairer would charge for the same work.

A further consequence of the collision between the two vehicles is that Tom's own car, after Tom was thrown from his vehicle, collided with a propane gas tank, causing an explosion which damages a derelict factory owned by Richmann Properties Ltd. Richmann had intended to clear this site for the purposes of future development.

Advise Tom of his potential liability in damages.

Commentary

This question concerns the rules on an award of damages for property damage. A car is badly damaged in circumstances in which it would be normal to see an award of damages based on market depreciation, but there is also the possibility of damages based on the cost of repair. Other factors such as consequential expenses, the impecuniosity of the claimant and rules on mitigation of damage must be considered. There is also a problem of damage to real property and the basis on which damages should be awarded.

Answer plan

- The difference between repair costs and diminution in value in respect of damage to chattels.
- The effect of Algernon's impecuniosity including its relationship with the rule on mitigation of damage, in the light of the fact that Algernon has elected to replace his car in a manner that involves increased expense.
- Whether the real property damage should be compensated on the basis of repair costs or diminution in value.

Suggested answer

Since the question informs us that Tom has admitted to driving negligently, there is no need to consider the issues of duty of care and breach of duty. Accordingly, the principal question concerns Tom's liability in damages for the harm suffered by Algernon and Richmann Properties Ltd.

The question states that Algernon's car is so badly damaged that in normal circumstances it would be written off by an insurance company. This is otherwise described as a constructive total loss (*Darbishire v Warran* [1963] 1 WLR 1067) and the award of damages will be based on the replacement value of the vehicle. Thus in *Darbishire v Warran* the cost of repairing the claimant's car, including hire charges, was £192, but the car itself had a replacement value of only £85. It was held that the claimant should not have sought to repair the vehicle but should have purchased a replacement. The basis of the decision is that the claimant had not taken reasonable steps to mitigate his loss. Exceptionally, the claimant may be allowed the cost of repair where the damaged property is effectively unique. For example, in *O'Grady v Westminster Scaffolding Ltd* [1962] 2 Lloyd's Rep 238, the claimant had carefully looked after and maintained a car, a replacement for which would have been very difficult to purchase on the market. In the light of the claimant's close attachment to the vehicle and the difficulty in finding a replacement, the court was prepared to award the cost of repairing the vehicle even though this was substantially in excess of its market value. It would appear that Algernon's position is very similar to that in *O'Grady* and that the cost of repair might be the appropriate measure of damages.

Consequential losses suffered as a result of the damage inflicted by the defendant may also be recovered. Thus the cost of hiring a substitute until replacement or repair is effected (*Darbishire v Warran*) and any profits which would have been earned by the chattel had it been capable of use may be recovered (*The Argentino* (1888) 13 PD 191). Here Algernon has incurred no immediate cost in hiring a replacement, but in accordance with the terms of the credit hire agreement, he will be presented with an account in due course. The problem this presents is that the hire charges are considerably inflated compared with the normal cost of hiring a car. However, Algernon may argue that he has been forced into doing this because of his impecuniosity, as he may not be in a position to pay the 'up-front' cost of hiring a car on a daily basis.

The rule established in *Liesbosch (Owners) v Edison (Owners)* [1933] AC 449 was that losses resulting from the impecuniosity of a claimant are too remote to be recovered. This principle was heavily criticized as inconsistent with the rule that the defendant has to take the claimant as he finds him. In the context of motorists who enter into credit hire arrangements, the House of Lords has had occasion to consider the status of the *Liesbosch* principle twice in *Dimond v Lovell* [2002] 1 AC 384 and *Lagden v O'Connor* [2003] 3 WLR 1571.

In *Dimond v Lovell* the claimant had been involved in a motor vehicle accident caused by the defendant's negligence. Her insurance policy made provision for a replacement vehicle while the damaged car was off the road, but the replacement was effected by means of a credit hire arrangement, which would have covered the cost of hire and the cost of providing credit over the interim period between the date of the accident and the date on which settlement was reached with the defendant and his insurers. The claimant was not short of available resources and could have paid for the cost of hiring a replacement car on the daily hire 'spot market', but the credit hire arrangement involved no cost to the claimant and the (substantially inflated) credit and hire charges were to be claimed as part of the damages sought from the defendant. The House of Lords held that the requirement that a claimant should mitigate her loss meant that damages in respect of the hire of a replacement car should be restricted to the normal daily hire rate and that the inflated costs (i.e. interest and administration charges) of the credit hire agreement should not be recoverable.

The problem in Algernon's case is that he is badly paid and has maintenance commitments towards the children of his first marriage. As a result of this, he may not have the resources immediately to hand to be able to pay the standard daily hire rate for a replacement car, while his own vehicle is off the road. In *Lagden v O'Connor* a similar, but not identical position prevailed. The unemployed claimant's Ford Granada was damaged by the defendant's negligent driving and he was unable to pay the cost of hiring a replacement vehicle. However, he was able to hire a Ford Mondeo using the services of a credit hire company, with the result that he did not have to make any initial outlay. A replacement car was a convenience, but not an absolute necessity for the claimant. A majority of the House of Lords departed from the principle established in the *Liesbosch* that additional costs, resulting from the impecuniosity of the claimant, should be disregarded as being too remote. The principal reason for this was that the *Liesbosch* rule was incompatible with the rule that a defendant should take the claimant as he finds him. Accordingly, provided the extra cost incurred by the claimant was not unforeseeable, the impecuniosity of the claimant was a factor that a court could consider in determining what damages should be awarded against a defendant and his insurer. A further reason given for departing from the *Liesbosch* was that it was decided before the establishment, by *The Wagon Mound* [1961] AC 388, of the reasonable foresight test for remoteness of damage in negligence cases, with the result that the decision in the *Liesbosch* was almost certainly influenced by the then prevailing directness of damage test applied in *re Polemis & Furness Withy & Co Ltd* [1921] 3 KB 560. Accordingly, whatever might be said of the correctness or otherwise of the decision in the *Liesbosch*, at that time, the law had moved on, and it was time for the House of Lords to recognize reality in *Lagden v O'Connor*.

In *Lagden*, the majority concluded that, given the claimant's lack of means, they were not constrained by the decision in *Dimond v Lovell*. It was reasonably foreseeable that the claimant would require a replacement car. Since he was not in a position to make any initial outlay on hiring a replacement on the daily hire spot market, it was foreseeable that he might take advantage of a credit hire arrangement, even though this would increase the claim for damages against the defendant.

The decision in *Lagden v O'Connor* is not without its difficulties, as was recognized by the majority. It will necessitate drawing a distinction between those who are impecunious and those who are not. Lord Nicholls (one of the majority) admitted that 'lack of financial means is, almost always, a question of priorities' ([2003] 3 WLR 1571, 1575). Lord Scott delivered a powerful dissenting judgment on this issue, preferring to follow the reasoning employed in **Dimond v Lovell**, so that the claimant would be confined to the standard daily charge for a hire car. Lord Scott observed that *Lagden* was not an instance in which the car was used for any particular business purpose, with the result that it was difficult for him to be able to discern any compensable loss suffered by the claimant through not having a car available to him. He could use public transport as an alternative. Lord Scott expressed the view that one of the main functions of the law of obligations is to construct a set of yardsticks for determining when legal injury has been suffered ([2003] 3 WLR 1571, 1597) and that the test of impecuniosity was overcomplicated and too impracticable to be of service (ibid.).

In the hypothetical example, Algernon has a job, albeit not well paid and has binding financial commitments towards the maintenance of his children, but he has also chosen to continue to own a vintage Bentley car, that in normal circumstances might be written off by an insurer. He might choose to sell his accident-damaged car to another Bentley enthusiast with the means to pay for its restoration, in which case he might achieve more than just the scrap value for a car of that kind. There may also be other reasons for his lack of means, albeit not mentioned in the facts of the problem. Does he smoke cigarettes and drink alcohol? As Lord Nicholls observed in *Lagden*, lack of financial means is a question of priorities. It is arguable that Algernon may have made an unreasonable choice in the circumstances and may be confined to the measure of damages applicable in *Dimond v Lovell* and the *Liesbosch*, namely, the market cost of a replacement vehicle, rather than the actual cost.

The *Liesbosch* principle only applies to the impecuniosity of the claimant. However, if there are other reasons for the increased cost, they may be relevant. Thus in *Martindale v Duncan* [1973] 2 All ER 355, a taxi driver whose cab had been damaged due to the negligence of the claimant chose to wait until he had obtained authorization from his insurers before he had his vehicle repaired. While the vehicle was off the road, the claimant suffered loss of business profit. This loss was held to be recoverable despite the fact that the claimant's reason for waiting was that he could not afford to have the repairs carried out himself. However, since there was another reason for the delay, namely that the claimant was awaiting the decision of his insurers, the *Liesbosch* principle was held not to apply. Similarly in *Perry v Sidney Phillips & Son* [1982] 1 WLR 1297, the claimant was able to recover damages for anxiety and inconvenience even though this anxiety arose principally from the claimant's inability to pay for the cost of repairs to the property concerned. Both of these cases are distinguishable from *Liesbosch* since in *Martindale* something other that the claimant's impecuniosity could be said to be the cause of the loss and in *Perry* the loss suffered by the claimant could not be described as a business loss, in which case the rule that the defendant must take the claimant as he finds him can be applied.

The *Liesbosch* principle was also distinguished in *Dodd Properties Ltd v Canterbury City Council* [1980] 1 WLR 433, where the cost of repairing a damaged building had risen sharply due to the effect of inflation. The claimants had not had the property repaired immediately, partly because they claimed their resources would have been stretched and partly because they were awaiting the outcome of the trial before effecting the repairs. It was held that the increased cost was recoverable since the claimants' impecuniosity was only one reason for the delay, and secondly that the case should be approached on the basis of mitigation principles rather than rules on remoteness of damage. On this latter basis, the claimant cannot reasonably be required to do something he cannot afford to do in order to reduce his losses. However, this approach can be criticized on the ground that the rules on mitigation apply to steps taken to reduce losses for which damages are going to be awarded in the future. If the case is dealt with as one concerned with remoteness of damage, the defendant ought not to be held responsible for losses which result from an unreasonable failure by the claimant to act in his own best interests.

Apart from Algernon's impecuniosity, the question also indicates that Algernon has waited for some time before arranging to have his vehicle repaired, during which time the cost of repair has risen. Given the age and value of the car, it would appear perfectly reasonable to employ the services of a specialist in Bentley cars, despite the fact that they are more expensive than general car repairers. It would be reasonable to assume that the extra cost may be taken to represent the specialization in this type of vehicle. On the matter of the delay itself, it may be that the reason can be traced to the defendant and his insurer in seeking to delay the commencement of proceedings or taking their time in the process of agreeing a settlement. In this case the delay may be regarded as something brought about by the defendant rather than the claimant. In *Alcoa Minerals of Jamaica Inc v Broderick* [2000] 3 WLR 23, the Privy Council sought to distinguish the *Liesbosch* in circumstances in which proceedings in respect of the cost ($211,140) of repairing a damaged roof were commenced in 1990. By 1994 the cost of repairing the same roof had escalated to $938,400. The claimant was still permitted to amend his claim, despite the fact that a reason why the roof had not been repaired was because the claimant could not afford to do so. The *Liesbosch* was distinguished on the basis that in that case the damage to the dredger and the cost of hire of the alternative were regarded as separate heads of damage. In *Alcoa*, there was only one head of damage, namely the cost of repairing the roof.

Applying all of this to Algernon, the principal issue appears to be whether or not he has acted reasonably in delaying the process of repairing the vehicle and in obtaining a hire car in the way he has done.

Algernon is a private individual, who appear to be treated differently from businesses. In such a case, it may well be foreseeable that such a person might not immediately be able to rectify the damage caused by the defendant's negligence. Assuming the delay in effecting repairs is reasonable, the cost incurred by Algernon in hiring a replacement will be recoverable and this may even include the additional charges incurred through taking out a credit hire agreement, depending upon whether Algernon is taken to have no practical choice other than to acquire the car in this way due to his financial plight. Moreover, the additional cost in employing the services of a specialist in Bentley cars does not seem out of the way, given the value of the vehicle.

The damage to the property owned by Richmann Properties Ltd also requires consideration. The basic principle which applies to harm to real property is that of *restitutio in integrum*, namely that the claimant should be put into the position he was in before the property was damaged. There are two ways in which this may be done. The first is to assess damages on the basis of the diminution in the capital value of the property and the second is to give the cost of effecting repairs. Generally, which is the appropriate measure will depend on the claimant's intended use of the property. For example, if the property is used by the claimant for the purpose of occupation or for the purposes of running a business, the appropriate measure will be the cost of repair, since it will be difficult for the claimant to sell the damaged property and purchase a replacement. This remains the case even where the cost of repairing the property is in excess of the depreciation in value and even where the effect of the repair is to give the claimant a better and more up-to-date set of premises (*Harbutt's Plasticine Ltd v Wayne Tank & Pump Co Ltd* [1970] 1 QB 447). Conversely, if the property has been acquired as an investment, it seems that the appropriate measure of damages is to be based on the diminution in value of the property (*CR Taylor Ltd v Hepworths Ltd* [1977] 1 WLR 659). This appears to be the more appropriate measure in the case of Richmann Properties as the question states that the land is intended for future development.

Question 4

Pankaj, a surveyor, was asked by the Mid-Counties Building Society to carry out a valuation of a residential property which Nikita was interested in purchasing using funds supplied under the terms of a mortgage offered by Mid-Counties. The property concerned was constructed two years earlier by Jerrybuild Ltd on behalf of South East Houses Ltd, but has been used by the latter since that time as a show house.

Since the valuation requested by Mid-Counties did not attract a substantial fee, Pankaj took only 15 minutes to look round the house, did not report any significant defect and valued the property at £165,000. In fact there was a serious defect in the foundations which resulted in minor cracking in an internal supporting wall between the garage and the main body of the house. Subsequent evidence shows that attempts have been made by Jerrybuild Ltd to disguise the defect in the hope that it will not be fully discoverable for many years.

Nikita bought the house for £163,000, after seeing a copy of the valuation report given to him by the Mid-Counties Building Society. Five years after purchase the first signs of external cracking to the defective supporting wall begin to appear. Nikita takes no action until two years later when the external cracks have become more prominent. After receiving the expert advice of a structural engineer, Nikita consults his solicitor and legal action is commenced seven years after the date of purchase and almost three years after the first external cracks began to appear in the supporting wall. Nikita claims that the foundation defects are such that he could sell the house for no more than £100,000, and only then to a professional builder and that in order to rectify the defects fully, if he is to remain in the house, the cost will be £75,000. Due to the fact that the value of the house is so diminished, the Mid-Counties Building Society has asked for additional security which Nikita says he cannot provide.

Advise Nikita.

Commentary

This question is concerned with the duty of care owed by a surveyor to a person he knows will rely on his advice, the duty of a builder to an occupier of the house he has built and the measure of damages applicable where economic loss has been suffered. The issue of limitation of actions is also relevant.

Answer plan

- In what circumstances does a surveyor owe a duty of care to a person he realizes will rely on his valuation of a property?
- What duty is owed by a builder to a person who subsequently acquires a house he has built?
- When is damage caused for the purposes of the accrual of a cause of action in tort and how does the common law rule differ from the position under the **Defective Premises Act 1972**?
- What is the effect of an attempt to conceal a defect for the purposes of rules on limitation of actions?

Suggested answer

The first issue to consider is the nature of any duty of care owed by Pankaj to Nikita. It is now established by the House of Lords in *Smith v Eric S. Bush (a firm)* [1990] 1 AC 831 that a surveyor who fails to exercise reasonable care in the course of conducting a building society valuation owes a duty of care to a person he realizes is likely to rely on that valuation. The general requirement of foresight of harm, proximity of relationship, and justice are all satisfied where a person at the lower end of the housing market buys a house in reliance on a building society valuation. As was explained in *Smith v Bush*, at the lower end of the housing market it is now the norm for purchasers not to a commission a private, contractual survey of a house before purchase and the majority of buyers rely on the building society survey which they, in fact, pay for themselves through a payment to the building society. For this reason, surveyors who carry out such a survey should realize that their report is likely to be heavily relied upon. The valuation is for the amount of £165,000. In *Smith v Bush* the duty of care was considered to be owed, partly because the overall value of the property was comparatively small and that purchasers at the lower end of the housing market might decide not to commission their own structural survey of that type of property. Nikita appears not to have commissioned a separate survey, but the valuation placed on the house is £165,000, which might lead a court to conclude that he ought to have commissioned his own survey. Nevertheless the principle in *Smith v Bush* was applied to a property worth over £100,000 in *Beaumont v Humberts* [1990] 49 EG 46, a very substantial price for a house in the 1980s.

The valuation requested by the building society is not substantially remunerated, but it is clear from *Smith v Bush* that this is not a reason for cutting corners. Where a property is in reasonably good order, there is no need to take too long over the process of valuation. On the other hand, if a defect is reasonably discoverable, it is clear that the surveyor is required to spend some time investigating it and if he does not do so with the result that the purchaser buys a house he might not have purchased had the true facts been known, there is a potential action for damages for negligence.

The risk which Pankaj fails to report is one which had resulted in minor cracking in an internal wall. If this is considered sufficiently suspicious for a professional surveyor to suspect more serious future damage, it is a matter which might justify further investigation. Moreover, simply reporting that there are no defects at all might be evidence of negligence on Pankaj's part. If there is a breach of duty on Pankaj's part, it must be decided what damages Nikita is entitled to and whether he has brought his action in time. Where a person has bought a house for more than it is worth, in reliance on a surveyor's report, the general rule is that an award of damages should put the claimant in the position he would have been in before the report was negligently prepared (*Watts v Morrow* [1991] 4 All ER 937). This, it seems is represented by the depreciation in value of the property and not the cost of repair and this remains so even if the occupier decides to remain in occupation (*Watts v Morrow*). The difference between the £163,000 paid for the house by Nikita and the £100,000 it is now worth is only £63,000, compared with the estimated £75,000 it will cost to effect repairs. However, the figure which is not provided in the question is the current market value of the property. What is clear from *Watts v Morrow* is that the cost of repair is not the appropriate measure of damages to apply.

Where property has been negligently over-valued as a result of which a lender of money has advanced more than the value of the building, it is possible that the lender may suffer loss. On the facts, the borrower (Nikita) has not yet defaulted, but this may become a possibility. In *South Australia Asset Management Corp v York Montague Ltd* [1996] 3 All ER 365 (see also *Andrews v Barnett Waddington (a firm)* [2006] EWCA Civ 93) the House of Lords held that a valuer would not be liable for any part of the loss suffered by a lender as a result of a fall in the general value of the property market, but would remain responsible for such loss as was attributable to the act of over-valuation. The so-called 'SAAMCO' principle seems to be that if the valuer owes a duty of care in respect of information given to the recipient and as a result, the recipient has suffered some loss or failed to obtain an expected benefit then the valuer will not be liable for that loss or failure to obtain the benefit unless he was asked to provide the information so as to avoid that loss or obtain the expected benefit. In contrast, if the defendant has undertaken to advise about the transaction, rather than merely provide information, he may be liable for the full loss (see *Aneco Reinsurance v Johnson & Higgins* [2002] 1 Lloyd's Rep 157). However this is not the case on the present facts with the result that the lender, as yet, has suffered no loss, but it is possible that they may do so in time.

As to the issue of limitation of actions, the general rule is that in an action for negligence, the limitation period runs for six years from the date on which damage is caused (**Limitation Act 1980, s. 2**). In negligent advice cases, the date of damage is said to be the date on which the claimant relies on the advice given by the surveyor (*Secretary of State for the Environment v Essex, Goodman & Suggitt* [1986] 1 WLR 1432). However, an alternative view in negligent valuation cases is that no loss can be established until the inaccuracy of the valuation can be demonstrated, which will be at a later stage. Despite this it was held by the House of Lords in *Nykredit Mortgage Bank v Edwards Erdman Group (No. 2)* [1997] 1 WLR 1627 that the purchaser's cause of action accrues at the time of purchase, so that time will begin to run against Nikita when he contracts to buy the house.

The problem states that the action is not commenced until eight years after the date of purchase, which would seem to suggest that the normal six-year rule has not been complied with and Nikita is therefore out of time. Alternatively, if the damage suffered by Nikita is not reasonably discoverable before the date on which the cause of action accrued (**Limitation Act 1980, s. 14A(1)**), namely the date on which damage is caused, an alternative limitation period may run for three years from the date on which the claimant acquired the relevant knowledge required for the purposes of bringing an action for negligence (**Limitation Act 1980, s. 14(5)**). The question states that the first signs of external cracking appear five years after purchase and that the action is commenced within three years of this date. Since economic loss in the form of diminution in the value of a building is actionable against a negligent surveyor, it would seem to follow that if the loss suffered by Nikita is classified as latent damage, he may have brought his action in time. Nikita may have an alternative action against Jerrybuild Ltd. At common law, the builder only very exceptionally owes a tortious duty of care to the purchaser of defective premises if the nature of the complaint is that the property is not worth the amount paid for it, that is, where the purchaser has suffered economic loss (*D & F Estates Ltd v Church Commissioners for England* [1988] 2 All ER 992; *Murphy v Brentwood District Council* [1990] 2 All ER 908). The exceptional cases referred to above are that a duty of care may be owed in respect of economic loss, in the form of diminution in property value, where there is a uniquely close relationship of proximity and where there has been reasonable reliance on negligently prepared advice. However, neither of these seems to apply in these circumstances.

Jerrybuild Ltd may be liable under the Defective Premises Act 1972, s. 1 which provides that a person taking on work for or in connection with the provision of a dwelling owes a duty to see that the work is done in a workmanlike or professional manner, and with proper materials, so that as regards that work the dwelling will be fit for habitation when completed. The duty also applies not just to carrying out building work badly, but also to a failure to carry out remedial work (*Andrews v Schooling* [1991] 3 All ER 723). Moreover, the duty is owed to the person who orders the work and to any person who subsequently acquires an interest in the dwelling. Accordingly, even though the work may have been carried out for the benefit of South East Houses Ltd, the duty is also owed to Nikita as a subsequent purchaser. The main problems with the provisions of the Defective Premises Act 1972, s. 1 is that they do not apply to a dwelling covered by an approved scheme which provides the owner with a remedy. This means that a dwelling covered by the National House Building Council insurance scheme does not fall within the scope of the Act. Since the NHBC scheme covers the majority of newly built houses, the 1972 Act may not apply broadly. However, if it is assumed that the NHBC scheme does not apply to Nikita's house, a duty will be owed under the 1972 Act.

Unfortunately, a further drawback with the 1972 Act is that the limitation period under it is particularly strict. The limitation period runs for six years from the date on which the building was completed (Defective Premises Act 1972, s. 1(5)). This contrasts with the normal limitation period in negligence actions which runs for six years from the date on which damage was caused. The date on which damage is caused is often many years after the date on which a building is completed. Moreover, had this been an action for negligence rather than one under the Defective Premises Act 1972, the fact that Jerrybuild Ltd had deliberately attempted to conceal the defect would have meant that the limitation period did not begin to run until the claimant did or could with reasonable diligence have discovered the concealment (Limitation Act 1980, s. 32(1)(b)). For these purposes, deliberate concealment requires a deliberate act that the concealer intends to cover up a breach of duty of which he is aware (*Cave v Robinson Jarvis & Rolf* [2002] 2 All ER 641, HL). However, s. 32 only applies to limitation periods prescribed by the 1980 Act and the special limitation period in defective premises cases is not one prescribed by the 1980 Act. Accordingly, it has to be decided if Nikita has commenced his action within six years of the date on which the building was completed. The facts of the problem show that the house was constructed two years before the survey was carried out by Pankaj. The first signs of damage appear five years after Nikita purchased the property but Nikita does not take action for a further two years after that. This suggests that Nikita will issue his writ nine years after the date on which building was completed, in which case he is out of time.

Further reading

Law Commission No. 270, *Limitation of Actions* (July 2001).

Law Commission No. 257, *Damages for Personal Injury: Non-pecuniary Loss* (1999).

Rogers, W. V. H., *Winfield & Jolowicz on Tort*, 17th edn (London: Sweet & Maxwell, 2006), ch. 22.

Stapleton, J., 'The Gist of Negligence' (1997) 113 LQR 1.

Index